STUDIES IN IMPERIALISM

General editors: Andrew S. Thompson and Alan Lester
Founding editor: John M. MacKenzie

When the 'Studies in Imperialism' series was founded by Professor John M. MacKenzie more than thirty years ago, emphasis was laid upon the conviction that 'imperialism as a cultural phenomenon had as significant an effect on the dominant as on the subordinate societies'. With well over a hundred titles now published, this remains the prime concern of the series. Cross-disciplinary work has indeed appeared covering the full spectrum of cultural phenomena, as well as examining aspects of gender and sex, frontiers and law, science and the environment, language and literature, migration and patriotic societies, and much else. Moreover, the series has always wished to present comparative work on European and American imperialism, and particularly welcomes the submission of books in these areas. The fascination with imperialism, in all its aspects, shows no sign of abating, and this series will continue to lead the way in encouraging the widest possible range of studies in the field. 'Studies in Imperialism' is fully organic in its development, always seeking to be at the cutting edge, responding to the latest interests of scholars and the needs of this ever-expanding area of scholarship.

Monarchies and decolonisation in Asia

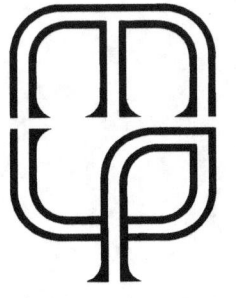

Manchester University Press

SELECTED TITLES AVAILABLE IN THE SERIES

WRITING IMPERIAL HISTORIES
ed. Andrew S. Thompson

GENDERED TRANSACTIONS
Indrani Sen

EXHIBITING THE EMPIRE
ed. John M. MacKenzie and John McAleer

BANISHED POTENTATES
Robert Aldrich

MISTRESS OF EVERYTHING
ed. Sarah Carter and Maria Nugent

BRITAIN AND THE FORMATION OF THE GULF STATES
Shohei Sato

CULTURES OF DECOLONISATION
ed. Ruth Craggs and Claire Wintle

HONG KONG AND BRITISH CULTURE, 1945–97
Mark Hampton

Monarchies and decolonisation in Asia

Robert Aldrich and Cindy McCreery

MANCHESTER
UNIVERSITY PRESS

Copyright © Manchester University Press 2020

While copyright in the volume as a whole is vested in Manchester University Press, copyright in individual chapters belongs to their respective authors, and no chapter may be reproduced wholly or in part without the express permission in writing of both author and publisher.

Published by MANCHESTER UNIVERSITY PRESS
OXFORD ROAD, MANCHESTER M13 9PL

www.manchesteruniversitypress.co.uk

British Library Cataloguing-in-Publication Data
A catalogue record for this book is available from the British Library

ISBN 978 1 5261 4269 6 hardback
ISBN 978 1 5261 7173 3 paperback

First published 2020
Paperback published 2023

The publisher has no responsibility for the persistence or accuracy of URLs for any external or third-party internet websites referred to in this book, and does not guarantee that any content on such websites is, or will remain, accurate or appropriate.

Typeset by Servis Filmsetting Ltd, Stockport, Cheshire

CONTENTS

List of figures—vii
Notes on contributors—x
Acknowledgements—xiii

1 Monarchies, decolonisation and post-colonial Asia   1
   Robert Aldrich and Cindy McCreery

2 All the king's men: regal ministers of eclipsed empires in India   22
   Priya Naik

3 Decolonised rulers: rajas, maharajas and others in post-colonial India   44
   Jim Masselos

4 The Himalayan kingdoms, British colonialism and indigenous monarchs after the end of empire   60
   Robert Aldrich

5 Conflict and betrayal: negotiations at the end of British rule in the Shan States of Burma (Myanmar)   80
   Susan Conway

6 Malaysia's multi-monarchy: surviving colonisation and decolonisation   95
   Anthony Milner

7 Celebrating the 'world's most ideal state': Sarawak and the Brooke dynasty's centenary of 1941   112
   Donna Brunero

8 Refashioning the monarchy in Brunei: Sultan Omar Ali and the quest for royal absolutism   134
   Naimah S. Talib

9 Colonial monarchy and decolonisation in the French Empire: Bao Dai, Norodom Sihanouk and Mohammed V   152
   Christopher Goscha

10 Loyalism and anti-communism in the making of the modern monarchy in post-colonial Laos   175
   Ryan Wolfson-Ford

CONTENTS

11 Indonesia: sultans and the state 192
Jean Gelman Taylor

12 Defending the Sultanate's territory: Yogyakarta during the Indonesian decolonisation, 1942–50 208
Bayu Dardias Kurniadi

13 The uses of monarchy in late-colonial Hong Kong, 1967–97 225
Mark Hampton

14 From absolute monarch to 'symbol emperor': decolonisation and the Japanese emperor after 1945 243
Elise K. Tipton

15 Dramatising Siamese independence: Thai post-colonial perspectives on kingship 260
Irene Stengs

Index—283

FIGURES

1.1 Members of the Indian Conference of Princes with the Viceroy, 1917. Photograph, Wikimedia Commons. — 6
1.2 One rupee Indian coin with George VI as King-Emperor, 1947. Collection of Arun Kumar Singh. Photograph, Wikimedia Commons. — 10
2.1 Seating plan of the Chamber of Princes, February 1928. Courtesy of National Archives of India, New Delhi. — 33
2.2 Detail of 1911 map of New Delhi, showing areas designated for maharajas and dewans. Courtesy of National Archives of India, New Delhi. — 35
3.1 Painted plaster of Paris figurine of a maharaja produced by Air India as a gift for passengers, c. 1970s–1980s. From the collection of Jim Masselos. — 54
3.2 Printed set of Air India playing cards featuring a maharaja, c. 1970s–1980s. From the collection of Jim Masselos. — 54
4.1 Ugyen Wangchuck in 1905 after his investiture with the Order of the Indian Empire. Photograph by John Claude White, British Library. Wikimedia Commons. — 62
4.2 General Sir Claude Auchinleck receives the Order of the Star of Nepal from King Tribhuvan, 1945. Photograph, Inter-Services Public Relations Directorate. Wikimedia Commons. — 70
4.3 Chogyal (King) Palden of Sikkim and Gyalmo (Queen Consort) Hope Cooke, with their daughter watch birthday celebrations, 1971. Photograph by Alice S. Kandell, Library of Congress Prints and Photographs Division Washington D.C. Wikimedia Commons. — 72
5.1 Shan sawbwas (princes) at the Delhi Darbar, 1903. Photograph by Underwood & Underwood, British Library. Wikimedia Commons. — 85
6.1 Signature of the Federation of Malaya Agreement by the Sultan of Perak, at King's House, Kuala Lumpur, 1948. Colonial Office Photographic Collection, CO 1069/504, The National Archives UK. Wikimedia Commons. — 106
7.1 'Sarawak's hundred years of rule under the White Rajahs', *Illustrated London News*, 4 October 1941, p. 22. © *Illustrated London News*/Mary Evans. — 122

LIST OF FIGURES

8.1 Sultan Omar Ali Saifuddin. Photograph, Historic Collection/Alamy Stock Photo. 139
9.1 Former Emperor Bao Dai of Vietnam at the Elysée Palace, Paris, 1948. Photograph OFF/AFP/Getty Images. Creative Commons. 155
9.2 King Sihanouk of Cambodia, c. 1949. Photograph, Studios Harcourt, Paris. Creative Commons. 158
10.1 King Savang and Queen Khamphoui in internal exile after the overthrow of the Lao monarchy. Unknown photographer, reproduced in Joanna C. Scott, *Indochina's Refugees: Oral Histories from Laos, Cambodia and Vietnam* (Jefferson, NC: McFarland & Co., 1989). 189
11.1 Paku Buwono X of Surakarta in Royal Netherlands Indies Army uniform, c. 1903. Photograph, Tropenmusem, Amsterdam, TMnmr-10001903, Wikimedia Commons. 193
11.2 President Joko Widodo receives eighty-eight rajas and sultans from across the archipelago at the presidential palace in Bogor, 4 January 2018. Photograph, Press Bureau Presidential Palace, Jakarta, Indonesia. 205
12.1 Sultan Hamengku Buwono IX of Yogyakarta. Public Domain. 210
13.1 The Queen pauses to talk to some of the thousands of people who greeted her at a Kowloon housing estate, May 1975. (Hong Kong Yearbook 1976). Courtesy of the Information Services Department, Hong Kong Special Administrative Region. 235
14.1 Emperor Hirohito visiting General Douglas MacArthur, 27 September 1945. Courtesy of The MacArthur Memorial Archives, Norfolk, Virginia, USA. 248
15.1 This famous, undated engraving by Jean-Baptiste Nolin depicts the audience of the French ambassador with King Narai on 18 October 1685. National Library of France, Paris. Wikimedia Commons. 264
15.2 Panel of the King Naresuan the Great Monument in Ayutthaya, depicting King Naresuan's declaration of independence. Photograph by Irene Stengs. 268
15.3 Panel of King Naresuan the Great Monument in Ayutthaya depicting the cockfight between the roosters of Prince Naresuan and the Burmese crown prince. Photograph by Irene Stengs. 271
15.4 Roosters offered by worshippers of King Naresuan at the King Naresuan the Great Monument in Ayutthaya. Photograph by Irene Stengs. 272

LIST OF FIGURES

15.5 Statue of King Naresuan mounted on a war elephant in Suphanburi province on Royal Thai Army Day 1991; this was reputedly the location where the king fought his victorious battle against the Burmese crown prince on 25 January 1592. Photograph courtesy of Sjon Hauser. 273

15.6 Image of Queen Suriyothai from the film *The Legend of Queen Suriyothai's Sacrifice* as reproduced on a can of Singha beer. Photograph by Irene Stengs. 276

Every effort has been made to obtain permission to reproduce copyright material, and the editors will be pleased to be informed of any errors and omissions for correction in future editions.

NOTES ON CONTRIBUTORS

Robert Aldrich is Professor of European History at the University of Sydney and the author of *Banished Potentates: Dethroning and Exiling Indigenous Monarchs under British and French Colonial Rule, 1815–1955* (2018). He is also the co-editor, with Cindy McCreery, of *Crowns and Colonies: European Monarchies and Overseas Empires* (2016) and *Royals on Tour: Politics, Pageantry and Colonialism* (2018).

Donna Brunero is Senior Lecturer in the Department of History at the National University of Singapore. She is the author of *Britain's Imperial Cornerstone in China: The Chinese Maritime Customs Service, 1854–1949* (2006). With Brian P. Farrell, she edited *Empire in Asia: A New Global History*, Vol. 2: *The Long Nineteenth Century* (2018), and, with Stephanie Villalta Puig, *Life in Treaty Port China and Japan* (2018). Her research explores the intersections between maritime and British imperial history in Asia in the nineteenth and twentieth centuries.

Susan Conway is Professor of Shan Studies at Shan State Buddhist University, Taunggyi and Research Associate at the Institute of Development Studies, Sussex University and the School of Oriental and African Studies, London University. She is author *The Shan: Culture, Art and Crafts* (2006) and other writings on Southeastern art, particularly textiles.

Christopher Goscha is Professor of International History at the Université du Québec à Montréal. He teaches international relations, world history and the Vietnam Wars. He is the author of *Vietnam: A New History* (2016), among other works. He is completing a book on the history of the First Indochina War, 1945–54.

Mark Hampton is Associate Professor of History at Lingnan University, Hong Kong. His books include *Visions of the Press in Britain, 1850–1950* (2004), *Hong Kong and British Culture, 1945–97* (2016), *Anglo-American Media Interactions* (2007, co-edited with Joel H. Wiener) and *The Cultural Construction of the British World* (2016, co-edited with Barry Crosbie).

NOTES ON CONTRIBUTORS

Bayu Dardias Kurniadi is a lecturer at the Department of Politics and Government, Gadjah Mada University Indonesia, and a PhD candidate at the Australian National University. His PhD thesis focuses on the politics of aristocracy in contemporary Indonesia.

Jim Masselos is Honorary Reader in History at the University of Sydney. He is the author of *Towards Nationalism* (1974), *Indian Nationalism* (1991) and *The City in Action: Bombay Struggles for Power* (2007). He has co-authored *Beato's Delhi* (2000) and *Dancing to the Flute: Dance and Music in Indian Art* (1997), and has edited numerous works on South Asia.

Cindy McCreery is Senior Lecturer in History at the University of Sydney. Her books include *The Satirical Gaze: Prints of Women in Late Eighteenth-Century England* (2004) and two other volumes (co-edited with Robert Aldrich) in the 'Studies in Imperialism' series: *Crowns and Colonies: European Monarchies and Overseas Empires* (2016) and *Royals on Tour: Politics, Pageantry and Colonialism* (2018). She is currently completing a monograph on the global voyages of Prince Alfred on HMS *Galatea*, 1867–71.

Anthony Milner is Professorial Fellow, University of Melbourne; Visiting Professor, University of Malaya; and Emeritus Professor, Australian National University. His writings on Malay history include *The Invention of Politics in Colonial Malaya* (1995) and *The Malays* (2008).

Priya Naik teaches political science in Zakir Husain Delhi College, University of Delhi. Her work is primarily on the Indian princely states, sovereignty and international relations. She has published in the *Third World Quarterly* and *South Asian Survey*, and is presently writing a book on the dewans of the princely states.

Irene Stengs is Professor by Special Appointment in the Anthropology of Ritual and Popular Culture at the Vrije University of Amsterdam and Senior Researcher at the Meertens Institute (Royal Netherlands Academy of Arts and Sciences, Amsterdam). In her research she focuses on popular religiosity, material culture, commemorative ritual and processes of heritage formation. She is the author of *Worshipping the Great Moderniser: King Chulalongkorn, Patron Saint of the Thai Middle Class* (2009).

NOTES ON CONTRIBUTORS

Naimah S. Talib is an Adjunct Senior Fellow in the Department of Political Science and International Relations at the University of Canterbury, New Zealand. Her current research focuses on Islamisation, the politics of Islam and Brunei's political development.

Jean Gelman Taylor is Honorary Associate Professor of History at the University of New South Wales, Sydney. Her publications include *The Social World of Batavia: European and Eurasian in Colonial Indonesia* (2009) and *Indonesia: People and Histories* (2003).

Elise K. Tipton is Honorary Associate Professor of Japanese Studies at the University of Sydney. She is the author of *Modern Japan: A Social and Political History* (2016). She also contributed the chapter entitled 'Royal symbolism: Crown Prince Hirohito's tour to Europe in 1921' to Robert Aldrich and Cindy McCreery (eds), *Royals on Tour: Politics, Pageantry and Colonialism* (2018).

Ryan Wolfson-Ford is a lecturer in Asian history at Arizona State University in the United States. His PhD thesis explores questions of ideology and agency regarding the Royal Lao Government as Laos became a key battlefield in the global Cold War.

ACKNOWLEDGEMENTS

We would like to extend our very warm thanks to Dr Briony Neilson for her active involvement with this volume – and our previous two edited collections in the 'Studies in Imperialism' series – and for her invaluable assistance with the preparation of the manuscript. We would also like to thank Dr Trevor Matthews for compiling the index for this volume, as he has for the previous ones.

We gratefully acknowledge financial assistance from the School of Philosophical and Historical Inquiry at the University of Sydney for the holding of a conference at which preliminary versions of several of these chapters were presented.

The chapters in this volume have been peer reviewed.

CHAPTER ONE

Monarchies, decolonisation and post-colonial Asia

Robert Aldrich and Cindy McCreery

Monarchies and Decolonisation in Asia is the third volume we have edited for Manchester University Press's 'Studies in Imperialism' series around the previously understudied theme of monarchy – the institution of the crown, the activities of individual sovereigns and other members of royal families, and the culture of royalty – in colonial contexts. The chapters in *Crowns and Colonies* revealed some of the ways European and non-European monarchies came into contact around the world in the colonial age, particularly at the time that imperial powers were conquering territory and consolidating their holdings from the 1700s onwards.[1] The contributions to *Royals on Tour* used the lens of visits to Europe by non-European royals, and to Asia, Africa and other parts of the world by touring European royals, as a way of viewing the complementary dynamics of politics and royal ceremonial in European expansion and in the reactions to it, especially in the late nineteenth and early twentieth centuries.[2] The present volume moves forward chronologically to the period of decolonisation in the mid- and late twentieth centuries to explore the ways in which both European and Asian countries remoulded themselves in the lead-up to and after the independence of the former colonies.

Historians' attention has long been drawn to the subject of kingship in Asia, ancient and modern. Comparatively little consideration, however, has been given directly to the question of the place of monarchs in the period covering late colonialism, decolonisation, and the foundation and development of independent successor states. Among other specific works about monarchies in the 'endgame of empire', Ian Copland's authoritative monograph provides an analysis of how the maharajas navigated through the last decades of British rule and the transition to independent India, and Yaqoob Khan Bangash has provided an account of the hereditary rulers and the independence of Pakistan.[3] Milton Osborne's classic biography of King Sihanouk offers a portrait of a king whose reign spanned the colonial and post-colonial history of Cambodia, and Geoffrey C. Gunn has examined in detail Sihanouk's role in bringing about Cambodia's independence from France.[4] Herbert P. Bix's biography of Emperor Hirohito shows how the Japanese sovereign faced the loss of a war, an overseas empire and his political powers, as well as American post-war occupation of Japan.[5] Kobkua Suwannathat-Pian has explained how the sultans of the Malay states successfully managed the transition from colonial rule to independence and beyond, and John Monfries has profiled the late Sultan of Yogyakarta, a rare Indonesian hereditary ruler whose throne survived republican independence.[6] Bruce Lockhart has chronicled the decline of the Vietnamese monarchy (which did not long survive the Second World War) and also offered comparative perspectives on the Vietnamese, Cambodian and Lao monarchies.[7] Grant Evans has brought together a valuable compendium of documents on the Lao royal family, from their rise under the French to their fall under the post-independence Communists.[8] Roger Kershaw's *Monarchy in South-East Asia* remains an essential volume of reference.[9] Many other important historical studies of the dynamics of decolonisation in Asia exist, of course, in English and in other languages. It is our hope that the chapters in this volume will make a further significant contribution to the literature on monarchy and decolonisation.

Social scientists have provided much insight into the theory and practice of monarchy. 'Kingship is one of the most enduring forms of human governance', as the anthropologists David Graeber and Marshall Sahlins remark, adding that 'it is attested during virtually all eras on all continents, and for most of human history the tendency was for it to become more common, not less'. They also point out that 'kings appear remarkably difficult to get rid of', and that 'even when kings are deposed, the legal and political framework of monarchy tends to live on', for example, with the notion that sovereignty has been 'displaced onto an entity called "the people"'. Moreover, 'when kings are gone – even when they are deposed by popular uprisings – they are likely to linger in ghostly form, precisely as such a unifying principle'. These affirmations, in this case from specialists examining case studies from such places as the Sudan, Mexico, the Congo and Madagascar, underline the importance and benefit of historical study of monarchies in the modern world, and, in particular, in relation to colonialism and decolonisation.[10]

Social scientists have also provided their own perspectives on Asian monarchies, as shown in studies by Benedict Anderson, Clifford Geertz, Stanley Tambiah and Nicholas Dirks.[11] Their research on 'imagined communities', the 'theatre state', 'galactic polities' and the impact of colonialism have contributed to an understanding of the theory and practice of monarchy in Asia, and challenged assumptions about monarchy based on Western history. From ancient times onwards, hereditary rule was common throughout Asia, though the forms of governance varied widely over time and place. Different religious and philosophical systems – Buddhism, Hinduism, Confucianism, Islam and others – determined the ideology and practice of rulership, as did local geographical, economic and social conditions, military actions, the expansion and contraction of polities, the personalities and rivalries of individual rulers, and the dynamics of family relations and succession to thrones. Some dynasties reigned over diminutive territories and small populations, while others held suzerainty over vast empires and remained in power for hundreds of years or even millennia. China, for instance, long maintained an imperial system in which the emperor was the 'Son of Heaven', whose performance of various rites was necessary to secure the well-being of his subjects. The centralised bureaucracy was composed of a corps of mandarins recruited on the basis of competitive examinations. The emperor treated peripheral or neighbouring rulers as the heads of feudatory states to whom power was delegated in return for tribute.[12] More common in Southeast Asia was a 'galactic' notion of kingship, where the ability to mobilise populations rather than demarcation of territory determined the ruler's status; territories overlapped and rulers sometimes paid tribute to several more powerful neighbouring sovereigns.[13] In Japan, the emperor claimed descent from the sun-goddess; Hindu rulers in India were incarnations of Shiva; in the Buddhist world, a ruler was semi-divine; and Islamic sultans were also guardians of the faith. New rulers and dynasties supplanted old ones, and foreign invasion could lead to regime change, as occurred with the Manchu invasion of Ming China. Even without such cataclysmic events, succession to thrones often encompassed intense and sometimes violent struggles between multiple would-be heirs.

From their earliest encounters with Asia, Europeans were awed by the power, mystery and often wealth of the great 'potentates' in the East, creating a long-lived fantasy about Oriental autocracy and luxuriance. However, their understanding of the principles and practices of governance in Asia remained limited. In the early modern period, Asian rulers held the upper hand over European merchants, missionaries and emissaries who pleaded for trading privileges, concessions of land, missionary access and other benefits. With the establishment of footholds in the name of European monarchs from the early 1500s, Western and Christian notions of kingship arrived in Asia and were imposed on places over which European conquerors, led by the Portuguese, and chartered companies, such as the English and

Dutch East India Companies, gained control.[14] European possessions, however, remained largely coastal enclaves, ruled with acquiescence from local maharajas, sultans and other indigenous figures (though the British holdings in India, augmented by warfare, grew ever larger).

By the 1800s, however, the balance of power had greatly changed, with rapacious expansion and the establishment of far more extensive colonial holdings under the formal aegis of European governments, as seen with the British annexation of Punjab and Awadh in the 1840s and 1850s.[15] The proclamation of British paramountcy over the Indian subcontinent in 1858, after the Great Uprising of the previous year, and the proclamation of Queen Victoria as Empress of India two decades later, underscored the new British imperialist *and* monarchical presence in the region. Meanwhile, through military campaigns in the late 1850s, the French under Emperor Napoleon III had established, in southern Vietnam, a foothold in Southeast Asia, while holding on to and seeking to develop the small French possessions in India. By the late 1800s, a scramble for Asia saw enlargement of the French colonial empire (though now under a republican government in Paris) throughout Vietnam, Cambodia and Laos while Britain moved further into Burma and the Malay states. The Dutch consolidated their holdings in the East Indies, placing thousands of islands under the rule of the Dutch sovereign, and waging war in Sumatra and Bali at the turn of the century to reinforce their *imperium*. The Japanese took over Taiwan in 1895 and Korea in 1905 in the name of their emperor. The Spanish monarchs retained control of the Philippines, over which they had long reigned, until defeat by the Americans in 1898. The Portuguese king continued to reign over that country's residual Asian holdings in Macao, East Timor, Goa and other Indian enclaves; the Portuguese monarchy was abolished after a revolution in 1910, but Lisbon kept its portfolio of overseas outposts. Western incursions into China, from the Anglo-Chinese War (the First 'Opium War' of 1840) onwards, weakened but did not topple the Chinese imperial monarchy, and led to British takeover of Hong Kong and the later establishment of foreign 'concessions', mostly on the Chinese coast. The sovereigns of Austria-Hungary, Britain, Russia, Italy and Japan thus gained small tracts of land, with trading privileges and legal rights of extraterritoriality, on the edge of the 'Middle Kingdom',[16] whose own imperial dynasty was overthrown by internal forces in 1911.

Asian monarchies experienced diverse fates through encounters with outside powers and cultures. It should be remembered that pre-colonial Asian polities were never stagnant and unchanging, and even after colonial incursions, many local rulers engaged of their own volition in programmes of modernisation – for example, with codification of laws, building of new infrastructure, promotion of education and other reformist initiatives. The transformation of Japan under the instigation of the restored Meiji emperor, and of Siam under King Chulalongkorn in the late 1800s and early 1900s count among the most significant and best-known examples.[17] Certain 'feudatory' monarchs and dynasties under 'paramount' colonial rule were also able to continue to pursue modernisation during and after colonisation, as is demonstrated notably by the Indian princely state of Mysore.[18] Indeed, as research on indigenous Asian dynasties progresses, the dynamism of many sovereigns, administrations and states is being revealed.[19]

Siam (later renamed Thailand) was the only state in Southeast Asia to remain independent. The Japanese overthrew the monarchy in Korea in 1910, five years after establishing a protectorate over the peninsula.[20] The British had abolished monarchies in Ceylon (in 1815) and Burma (in 1885), and in such Indian realms as the Sikh empire (in 1849) and Awadh (in 1856). However, they left on the throne traditional rulers of what became known as the 'princely states' in India – more than six hundred states of vastly disparate size and population covering about two-fifths of the subcontinent – and the sultanates of the Malay Peninsula. The Dutch retained sultans and rajas in the East Indies as 'regents', and the French left pre-colonial dynasties in place in their Southeast Asian 'protectorates' of Cambodia, Laos, Annam and Tonkin. However, the European conquerors substantially curtailed the powers of such 'potentates', especially in international relations and defence, and on occasion dethroned rulers considered resistant to colonial overlordship or simply charged with incompetence or impropriety.[21] Even when paying deference to traditional rulers and attempting to use them to win support among 'native' populations, colonial authorities worked to undermine their positions. Yet the colonisers also sought to select and groom heirs to local thrones – through education, travel and emoluments – who would be open to Western influence and willing to accommodate colonial overrule (Figure 1.1).[22]

Colonialists' hopes of 'pacifying' colonies were never realised. Throughout the colonial period, authorities faced both major and minor rebellions, sometimes inspired by demands for the restoration of pre-colonial dynasties, institutions and traditions, and the occasional prince could successfully defy Europeans dispossessing him of his power and assets.[23] Extant or abolished monarchies could serve as rallying points for anti-colonial sentiment. Royals themselves could be implicated in such uprisings, as occurred when rebels named the ageing Bahadur Shah Zafar, the final Mughal ruler, as 'Emperor of India' in the 'Mutiny' of 1857, or when Vietnamese emperors were involved in rebellions in 1885 and 1916. These three rulers paid a high

Figure 1.1 Members of the Indian Conference of Princes with the Viceroy, 1917

price for colonial resistance – the 'last Mughal' and the two Vietnamese emperors were all sent into exile.[24] Pretenders to abolished thrones, though occasionally with only dubious (or no) royal lineage, could also try to rouse rebellion, as occurred in Ceylon in the early 1800s and Burma in the 1930s.[25] A few royal dissidents ran the risk of criticising the colonial system openly, and sometimes suffered the consequences, as occurred when Prince Yukanthor, a son of King Norodom of Cambodia, damned French rule over his country during a visit to Europe in 1900; his allegations created scandal and he afterwards lived in exile. The British forced the abdication of one Indian ruler, the Maharaja of Nabha, as late as the 1920s because of his sympathy with an anti-colonialist Sikh group.[26] A later case of a nationalist royal from Southeast Asia is Prince Phetsarath of Laos, who headed the Lao Issara movement in the 1940s. Some ethnic and regional communities also searched for a messianic king to affirm their cultural identity and to contest colonial rule.[27]

Nevertheless, most Asian royals who were not deposed accommodated the Europeans, and thus incurred suspicion among nationalists (especially republicans and radicals). In the move to independence, many lost their traditional positions. The Vietnamese emperor abdicated his throne in 1945 in the face of Ho Chi Minh taking control in northern Vietnam. The Indian princes reluctantly – and under duress from the British and the Congress Party – signed agreements of accession to the new states of India and Pakistan in 1947, accords which substantially reduced their rights and powers. When the Nizam of Hyderabad stalled, retribution duly followed – the military forces of the new Indian state invaded his realm.[28] In Indonesia, royals suffered first under Japanese occupation and then after independence. The Japanese occupiers, who promoted the proclamation of the independence of Indonesia, massacred the royal family of Pontianak, and then the independent government arrested several surviving members of that family and the royal family of Ternate in the 1950s; other sultans' families also suffered violence. Only a very few sultans, notably the sultan of Yogyakarta, who had supported the republican nationalists, managed fully to retain a formal position after independence.[29]

In addition to the Yogyakarta dynasty, however, some of the other national or sub-national Asian dynasties weathered decolonisation. Indeed, in Malaysia, nine hereditary sultans and rajas still retain their role as head of individual states, and one among them is elected to serve a five-year term as Yang di-Pertuan Agong, the head of state (usually called its 'king'). In Brunei, the sultan remains absolute ruler of his small but wealthy territory. Emperor Hirohito and the Japanese monarchy survived defeat in the Second World War, American occupation and the loss of overseas empire. Other dynasties fared less well. The Shan princes of Burma – who, unlike the Burmese king, had not been overthrown with British colonisation – outlived independence, though like the Indian princes they had to accept the incorporation of their states into the independent Union of Burma; with a military coup in 1962, the princes lost their positions and many also lost their property and even lives.[30] The Indian princes kept their titles and privileges (and privy purses) until 1971, when they were abolished under Prime Minister Indira Gandhi, yet many of the princes successfully found new public roles for themselves as public servants, politicians and entrepreneurs.[31] The Lao monarchy was disestablished after a Communist takeover in 1975, and senior members of the royal family were sent into remote internal detention, where they perished in the poor conditions.[32]

The great survivor of colonial-era rulers was King Sihanouk of Cambodia, one of the most fascinating figures in modern Southeast Asian history, as Milton Osborne's work has shown. Crowned king of the 'protectorate' by French authorities in 1941, the young Sihanouk looked initially to be a loyal vassal of the colonisers, but in the next decade, he transformed into the leader of the nationalists and negotiated independence with the French. Sihanouk reigned on until 1955, when he abdicated (in favour of his father) in order to enter politics. In his colourful later career, Sihanouk was at various times prime minister, non-royal head of state, and president and puppet of the bloodthirsty Khmer Rouge, in addition to the lengthy periods he spent in exile. He was restored to his throne in 1993 and ruled until abdicating, this time in favour of his son, the current sovereign, King Sihamoni, in 2004. During his more than sixty years on and off the throne, Sihanouk also managed to undertake a major urban development programme in Phnom Penh, direct a long list of films (in which he occasionally acted), become an international celebrity and embody the aspirations and tragedies of Khmer history.[33]

In Asia today, monarchs reign, though with greatly varying real powers, in Bhutan, Brunei, Cambodia, Japan, Malaysia and Thailand.[34] In 2019, the enthronement with great pomp and pageantry of the newly elected Malaysian Yang di-Pertuan Agong, Al-Sultan Abdullah (the sultan of Pahang), Emperor Naruhito in Japan and King Maha Vajiralongkorn in Thailand demonstrated the continuing potency of the monarchy in these countries, while it also pointed up issues around such questions as royal succession and the contemporary role of the monarchy. The photogenic ceremonies and newly installed monarchs also attracted international attention, broadcasts emphasising to global viewers the local traditions and rites of the Asian monarchies. The rituals also displayed ways in which the monarchies had drawn on Western, colonial-era traditions of royal performance with crowns, honour guards, decorations and clothing – during the three days of festivities of the Thai coronation, the king appeared in Western military and civilian dress, traditional silken Thai clothing, and hybrid apparel. At his accession, the Japanese emperor wore an English-style morning suit (with the empress in a long gown) while at his coronation, he donned medieval Japanese vestments associated with Shinto rites.

Monarchy remains a key component of national life in the Asian countries where it survives through both the powers of the sovereign and royal 'spectacle'. Even where it has disappeared, however, monarchy has left deep imprints and living legacies. Royal figures of the past, and their dynasties, exercise great influence within their countries but also on diasporic populations; for example, in the veneration of the memory of the Punjabi Maharaja Dalip Singh among Sikhs in Britain and elsewhere.[35] Republican and radical regimes, and their supporters, have proved deft at revitalising and manipulating royal legacies (especially of ancient dynasties) to their own advantage. At the ceremony in which the British colony of Ceylon marked its independence in 1948, the throne and crown of the King of Kandy – whose dynasty was abolished after the end of British conquest of the island in 1815 – were exhibited on the dais; references and emblems from that dynasty remain prominent today, especially among Sinhalese Sri Lankans.[36] The military government of Myanmar included traditional motifs and statues of ancient Burmese kings as prominent features of the new capital of Nyapidaw (built 2002–12), and also undertook a rather soulless restoration of the old royal palace in Mandalay, which had been largely destroyed during the Second World War.[37] In Laos, the Communist head of state assumes the role previously taken by the country's king in religious observances of veneration of the Phra Bang, the country's Buddhist palladium.[38] The orthodox narrative of Vietnam's history lauds the three 'patriotic' emperors dethroned by French colonialists, and the state has turned the old royal palace in Hue (which suffered substantial damage during the Indochinese and American wars) into a tourist attraction.[39] Royal sites, collections in museums and other mementos of monarchy attract tourists to places as different as the grand palaces of India's maharajas (some of which are now luxury hotels) and the more modest remains of the presence of the Brooke dynasty, the 'White Rajahs' of Sarawak, including a new exhibition on the dynasty at the museum in Kuching.[40] Meanwhile, in Europe, such sites as the Durbar Room in Queen Victoria's Osborne House (on the Isle of Wight) and Empress Eugénie's Musée Chinois in the palace of Fontainebleau testify to royals' contested links with overseas campaigns and colonies.

Royal trajectories in Asia

The chapters in this volume illustrate the disparate trajectories of royal dynasties in Asia in the late colonial period, during decolonisation and in the decades since. For historians of modern empires, one of the most dramatic developments is the disappearance of colonial monarchies in Asia: the sudden and at times shocking end of British, Dutch and Japanese imperialist rule. Japan's surrender to the Allies in August 1945 brought to an end dominion over its old colonies of Taiwan and Korea, the puppet state of Manchukuo established in 1934 (with the former Qing emperor of China, Puyi, as sovereign), and the many Southeast Asian territories occupied during the Second World War. Military forces tried to restore Dutch rule to the East Indies for four years after the declaration of Indonesian independence by Suharto in August 1945, but in 1949, the Dutch monarch and government had to accept the loss of the vast East Indian territory, ruled, in some parts, since the 1600s. The British 'quit' India on 15 August 1947, the 'stroke of midnight' that brought independence to India and Pakistan – a dramatic moment not only for those old possessions but also for the British and their monarchy; no longer were the British king and queen 'Emperor and Empress of India' (Figure 1.2). There followed independence for Ceylon and Burma in 1948, and Malaysia (including Sarawak,

Figure 1.2 One rupee Indian coin with George VI as King-Emperor, 1947

which the British acquired from the 'White Rajahs' in 1946) in 1963, though the British held on to Brunei until 1984 and Hong Kong until 1997. After the independence of the South Asian colonies, however, the British monarch remained head of state in India for three years, in Pakistan for eight years, and in Ceylon for twenty-four years. The British monarchy even then did not entirely disappear in Asia, as seven Asian countries remain members of the Commonwealth of Nations, over which Queen Elizabeth II presides as head.[41]

With decolonisation, the British and Dutch monarchs were no longer 'Asian' sovereigns, and the Japanese imperial ruler was now one without an overseas empire, and with a comparatively nominal position in his own country. All three monarchies had to refashion themselves (and their downsized nations) for a post-imperial age. At the same time, they faced considerable political, economic, social and cultural challenges at home – in particular, moves away from the old conventions of deference and authority that monarchs once enjoyed and that had underpinned hierarchical societies. New currents of democratic thought and behaviour threatened, and even mocked, ancient traditions and hallowed institutions. Similar challenges faced the dynasties and conservative orders in independent Asian states, and indeed those currents ultimately overwhelmed some of the royal houses.

Central to all of the developments discussed in the following chapters is the disappearance of the colonial monarchies (and the republican regime of France) as institutions in Asia. The Second World War marked a turning point in the history of colonial rule over Asia, but also for indigenous and foreign monarchies within Asia.

MONARCHIES, DECOLONISATION AND POST-COLONIAL ASIA

One manifest case is presented in Donna Brunero's chapter on Sarawak, where the Brooke dynasty celebrated the centenary of its rule in 1941 and proclaimed a new constitution only months before Japanese military occupation of the state. The Brooke royals returned very briefly at the end of the war before ceding their 'realm' (in return for certain benefits) to the British – simultaneously the end of one monarchy in Asia and the assumption of power (though only for a decade) by another royal house. Japanese occupation of the Dutch East Indies also provided the context for the nationalist movement formally to declare Indonesian independence only two days after the Japanese surrender on 15 August 1945. However, as Jean Gelman Taylor shows in her wide-ranging chapter, sultans and rajas had long been central figures in the political and cultural life of three hundred-odd polities wielded together by the Dutch as the Netherlands East Indies. Many retained key roles under the colonial system, both in performing traditional rites and duties, and serving as 'protected' vassals who, Europeans hoped, would buttress the colonial overrule. There had been much discussion about the future institutions of a unified and independent Indonesia, and the role that sultans and rajas would or would not play. Bayu Dardias Kurniadi's chapter points to the key position in the mid-1940s occupied by the Sultan of Yogyakarta, almost alone among his peers, as promoter of nationalism and independence, and as a figure almost uniquely able (at the time and since) to secure his position as sultan and hold senior ministerial and gubernatorial appointments in the republican state.

'Princely' India encompassed over six hundred states – from ones as large as some European countries to others barely bigger than small towns – over which reigned hereditary sovereigns bearing a diversity of titles. Most threw their weight behind the British paramount rulers and reaped benefits from their accommodation. As in Indonesia, their position on independence, and their fate in an independent India and Pakistan, was a subject of intense debate and manoeuvring. Jim Masselos, in this volume, charts the ways in which the maharajas and other princes navigated through the changes wrought by decolonisation, showing how many found ways to adapt to the new political and social order after 1947 (and even after the abolition of their privileges twenty-four years later). Standing side by side with the princes in colonial India were their advisers and the public servants of their states, and Priya Naik's chapter analyses the dewans, the chief ministers of the princes. The dewans were primarily other Indians (though sometimes Britons) – men who served in states of which they were generally not native but where they were recruited for their positions – and were the senior administrators and counsellors of the maharajas and other princes. Naik suggests that, unlike the princes, the former dewans found it particularly difficult to adapt to post-independence political situations in which their employment was no longer wanted, and where they were left without pensions, and without the inherited wealth of many of the royals. This provides a reminder of the need to consider the effects of decolonisation on the extended communities of officials, retainers and servants in royal courts, as well as families connected with the royal houses, a subject that awaits further research.

The varied situations in French Indochina – Vietnam, Cambodia and Laos – are examined in two chapters. Christopher Goscha demonstrates how the last Vietnamese emperor, Bao Dai, head of a dynasty much weakened but kept on the throne by the French colonisers, proved unable in 1945 either to assume leadership of the nationalist Communist and republican movements, or alternatively to legitimise the restoration of French rule over his 'protected' state. By contrast, King Sihanouk, as mentioned, crafted a place for himself in the 1940s and immediate post-war years as architect of Cambodian independence and moderniser of his country. In Laos, as explained in Ryan Wolfson-Ford's chapter, the French essentially promoted the hereditary ruler of Luang Prabang to become the king of the unified nation in 1945, setting in place a dynasty that lasted until 1975. Wolfson-Ford details ways in which the Lao kings (like their Cambodian counterparts) used administrative reform, cordial relations with the old colonial power, efforts to galvanise public support (for instance, among youths in the Scout movement) and personal charisma to bolster a fledging dynasty. Ultimately, however, the Lao throne would topple following a Communist coup – by which time, Sihanouk was also off the throne (though he would later return), and the Vietnamese Bao Dai had long been ensconced in exile in Paris.

Varied monarchical itineraries are also explored in Robert Aldrich's chapter on the Himalayas. By warfare, coercion and negotiation, the British had established privileged relations with the dynasties of Bhutan, Nepal and Sikkim, as well as trying to bring Tibet, with its dynasty of reincarnated Dalai Lamas, into the British sphere of influence. The British provided an imprimatur to the formation of a unified kingdom of Bhutan, left Nepal and its king on the outskirts of their Asian empire, and more or less incorporated Sikkim into the princely states of India. After the British left South Asia, the monarchy of Bhutan endured and gradually spearheaded modernisation and opening to the wider world. Sikkim succumbed to Indian annexation in 1975, its final ruler dying in exile. Nepal's throne was brought down by a Maoist revolution in 2008. Another case of princes surviving independence only to perish in later years is that of the thirty-odd Shan princes (sawbwa) in eastern Burma, the focus of Susan Conway's chapter. Returning loyalty to the British for recognition of their positions after the colonial takeover of the country in the nineteenth century, the Shan princes, like the Indians, hoped to safeguard their rights after independence as a reward for joining the new state. However, the post-independence lifespan of the Shan dynasties was shortened by military authorities who had no use for rival centres of power or ancestral traditions of ethnic groups deemed different from the majority of the people of a newly named Myanmar.

Mark Hampton's chapter looks at the last phase of the British monarchy's sovereign presence in Asia, where the queen reigned in Hong Kong down to 1997. 'Decolonisation', in the case of Hong Kong, however, involved not independence but cession of the colony to the People's Republic of China, itself the heir to the old empire of the Qing dynasty. The lowering of the British flag in Hong Kong – with the Prince of Wales representing Queen Elizabeth II – and the final winding down of Portuguese rule in Macau two years afterwards brought to an end five hundred years of European colonial presence in Asia – and also five hundred years of European monarchical rule over Asian dominions, even if France and Portugal (and the United States, which had ousted the Spanish monarchy in the Philippines) were republics by the time they relinquished their colonies.

Four of the chapters in *Monarchies and Decolonisation in Asia* examine surviving monarchies. These include Thailand, which was never colonised by Europeans; the strength and popularity of the monarchy there was indeed credited for the Siamese success in repulsing colonialism though the country did lose territory to both the British and the French. Irene Stengs points out that the Chakri dynasty made a transition from absolutist to constitutional rule in 1932 and has also surmounted coups and considerable political strife since that time. She also shows how memories of monarchies past form key components of collective Thai memory today, and how memory and national narrative have been revitalised in monuments, television series and other ways. Japan also escaped colonial takeover, and indeed acquired a large overseas empire of its own. Elise K. Tipton demonstrates how the end of the Second World War changed the emperor from head of state, commander-in-chief of the Japanese military and a godly figure in Japanese tradition into a 'symbol' emperor, and she assesses how Emperors Hirohito and Akihito struggled to define the new role – a challenge to be faced by the new Emperor Naruhito as well. If the emperor of Japan has no political power, though exercising much influence as 'symbol' and through personal actions, the case of Brunei lies at the other end of the spectrum of royal rule. Brunei's current sultan is an absolute head of state and government (and holds several ministerial portfolios), his power little tempered by assemblies, public dissent or reform. Naimah S. Talib analyses how the old sultanate of Brunei survived as a British protectorate until the 1980s, and how the ruler actually reclaimed many powers even in the face of strong British attempts to democratise the small state. Anthony Milner examines another surviving monarchy, or rather a set of monarchies, in contemporary Malaysia. He shows the enormous intertwined power of monarchy and custom (*adat*) in Malay culture, and argues that many sultans intelligently and effectively negotiated with the British overlords to retain their position under colonialism and in the newly independent state. In addition to these monarchs, there is also the example of Bhutan, and Aldrich's chapter suggests how the dynasty has reformed the previously isolated kingdom from the 'top down'. Goscha's chapter, though not focusing on the most recent years in the history of Cambodia, is also a reminder of the survival of that monarchy and the passing on of the throne from Sihanouk to Sihamoni, though real power in Phnom Penh is tightly held by the long-serving prime minister and his government.

The history of monarchies in Asia in the 'endgame' of empire, to use Ian Copland's phase, and in the years since independence offers a complex narrative. It features generally reluctant European withdrawal from colonies (and forced Japanese surrender), in some cases the loss of thrones for Asian dynasts, and in others the consolidation of indigenous royal power. These developments in Asia find parallels in the decolonisation of other regions, as Goscha's study intimates with its comparison of the Vietnamese and Cambodian cases with that of Morocco, which gained independence from the French in 1956 under a sultan who, like Sihanouk but unlike Bao Dai, assumed leadership in the nationalist movement. Decolonisation produced diverse effects for the monarchies in North Africa, just as in Asia. Morocco's strong monarchy is another survivor, while that of nearby Tunisia disappeared soon after independence (also in 1956), Egypt's King Farouk had been toppled by a military coup in 1952, and Libya's King Idris was overthrown by Colonel Muammar Gaddafi in 1969.

Elsewhere in the Islamic world, Iraq had been administered by Britain under a League of Nations mandate immediately after the dissolution of the Ottoman Empire as a consequence of the First World War. The British set King Faisal I on the throne of an independent Iraq in 1921 (after Faisal had an ephemeral reign as king of Syria), but his successor Faisal II lost his throne and was executed following a coup in 1958. The Qajar dynasty of Persia (Iran) for long had managed to keep the imperialists at bay, but after the Second World War, the alignment of the Pahlavi dynasty (which had usurped the throne in the 1920s) with the West proved its downfall; the end of the monarchy followed an Islamist revolution in 1979. Jordan, Saudi Arabia and the Gulf states, by contrast, represent one of the largest concentrations of monarchies – often absolutist ones – in today's world.[42] The regions of North Africa and the Middle East thus provide comparative case studies of the differing encounters experienced by indigenous dynasties and the West.

The many dynasties of sub-Saharan Africa fell under European colonial rule, though some, such as the Asante and Zulu royal houses, kept official positions and episodically continued to exercise considerable influence on their subjects under the Europeans. Few monarchs, however, emerged as kings over newly independent nation-states after decolonisation – republicanism trumped royalism in African decolonisation. However, there are exceptions. Haile Selassie, the emperor of Ethiopia, had been dethroned by the Italians in 1936; he returned to the throne after the Second World War, only to be ousted again by revolutionaries in 1974. The king of Buganda, driven into exile by the British, returned to his homeland in 1955 and became Uganda's head of state on its independence but he, too, fell (and again went into exile) in the aftermath of a coup in 1966. Only the kings of the small states of Lesotho and Swaziland, enclaves within South Africa, reign on. However, other traditional kings – including the heir to the Zulu throne in South Africa, whose position (like that of several other hereditary chiefs) is recognised in the post-apartheid constitution – continue to play a prominent public role in several African countries, and indeed recent years have seen a 'return of the kings' to public life in sub-Saharan Africa.[43] The place of living or late dynasties in national narratives, collective memories and contemporary politics in Oceania exhibits parallels.[44] Given the successful challenges of republicanism (and more radical forms of governance) over the last century, monarchy has proved a surprisingly long-lived and even resilient institution.[45]

New perspectives on Asian monarchies and decolonisation

Taken together, the chapters in this collection offer new theoretical perspectives on the history of monarchy and decolonisation in Asia, ones that may perhaps be applicable in some measure to areas outside of Asia. They place indigenous and colonial monarchies squarely near the centre in the process of decolonisation, showing that monarchs held crucial positions in regime transitions that also involved ideological debate about the form of government – monarchical, republican or other – in former colonies emerging as independent states. Adopting a republican government in many cases meant not only casting off a European monarchy or the Japanese one (or the republican heirs of monarchical colonialism in the American, French and Portuguese cases) but also rejecting the re-establishment of an indigenous, pre-colonial monarchy. Finding a new king, often from a ruling family in another country, and founding a new dynasty – which had been the practice in such newly independent European countries as Greece, Belgium, Norway and Serbia in the nineteenth and early twentieth centuries – seldom appeared as a desirable option.

Independence nevertheless required the willing or coerced acquiescence of local and colonial monarchs, and the cession of some or all of their sovereign rights, to new states. Accord was sometimes given with great reluctance, after sustained resistance or with acceptance of the unavoidable. Thus, Hirohito kept his throne when he bowed to the inevitable in accepting surrender to the Allies in 1945. He realised that this meant the dismantlement of the Japanese overseas empire and the radical diminution of the role and powers of the emperor at home (as well as a period of American 'colonial' occupation of Japan following the war), but it assured the survival of one of the world's oldest dynasties and perhaps helped safeguard the very independence of Japan. George VI, victor rather than vanquished in the Second World War, nevertheless also had to bow to the inevitable by formally agreeing to the independence of Britain's South Asian possessions and the loss of his imperial title. The consolation was that the British monarch would at least remain Head of State in India, Pakistan and Ceylon and sovereign over Malaysia, Brunei and Hong Kong – though just for a time, as it turned out. The Commonwealth of Nations, with Queen Elizabeth II as its head, preserved in the most tokenistic fashion the presence of the old 'king-emperor' in latter-day states (and indeed has been criticised for doing so). The Dutch monarch was forced to recognise the independence of Indonesia after four years of military and political struggle, with support from the crown, to re-establish control of the Netherlands over the East Indies (and two decades later with objections to a sham referendum on West Papua). Among the indigenous monarchs, many of the Indian princes only unwillingly agreed to the integration of their states into India in 1947, and did so with a caveat and, they hoped, guarantee about the preservation of their rights. The Shan princes did the same in Burma the following year. In Laos, the regional dynasty of Champasak had to relinquish its rights to the ruler of Luang Prabang, who had become king of a unified state, in return for residual privileges. Bao Dai in 1945, in the face of the Ho Chi Minh's position in northern Vietnam, abdicated his throne, nominally served without his title under the French again from 1949, and then had no choice but to acknowledge the manipulated referendum that deprived him of the position of nominal head of state in southern Vietnam in 1955. Nation- and state-building in modern Asia, as well as in other places and times, thus involved the extension or withdrawal of dynastic rights in the face of pressures from rival sources of authority and new forms of governance. Many European and Asian rulers proved as powerless as King Canute in turning back the tide of decolonisation.

Monarchies survived in Asia, in general, this book argues, when the transition to independence was a negotiated one: the continued reign of the British sovereign (for a time) in South Asian states, the success of King Sihanouk and King Sisavang Vong in working out a 'deal' for the independence of Cambodia and Laos, the transition from British to local monarchical rule in Malaysia and Brunei. When decolonisation involved protracted violence, notably in Vietnam and Indonesia, monarchs did not survive (the sultan of Yogyakarta an exception). The chapters presented here also suggest that when more militantly nationalist or radical political movements emerged in Asian countries, surviving thrones stood in the direct line of fire. Heightened national sentiment in Pakistan and India led to the declaration of republics in those countries in the 1950s, and a further shift ended the privileged position of the Indian princes in 1971. Indian annexation of Sikkim, which also occurred under Indira Gandhi's nationalist government, ended the rule of that country's maharaja in 1975. A military *coup d'état* resulted in the extinction of the Shan dynasties in 1962, and the election of a leftist government in Ceylon opened the way for more radical change in the newly named Democratic Socialist Republic of Sri Lanka in 1972. A Communist coup in Laos ended the dynasty there three years later, and a Maoist movement brought to an end the monarchy in Nepal in 2008. Cambodia, as ever, presented a complex scenario during particularly turbulent and tragic decades.

Monarchies that remained in place in Asia (with the exception of Brunei) are constitutional rather than absolutist, though a full parliamentary system was only established in Bhutan in 2008. In Japan, the emperor is a 'symbol' of the nation and its unity – not, technically, even the Head of State with such prerogatives as assenting to legislation – while in Malaysia, the Yang di-Pertuan Agong is essentially *primus inter pares* among the hereditary sultans. In Cambodia, autocratic prime ministerial government has reduced the throne to little more than a facade. In most countries, constitutions, universal suffrage and regular elections – despite corruption, irregularities in the elections, censorship and crackdowns on dissidents – provide a level of popular participation in politics and public life that hardly existed in either colonial or pre-colonial times. And, despite *lèse-majesté* restrictions, monarchy is subject to closer scrutiny than in the past.

A final conclusion to be drawn from this volume centres on the legacy of monarchy, as seen in the way that contemporary governments call upon the ancient and more recent dynasties to buttress their own legitimacy and popularity. Monarchy remains a potent principle, most evident, of course, in those countries where kings still reign, yet republican and other leaders have taken on the mantle of monarchs as military commanders in chief, arbiters of justice, executors of legislation, patrons of the arts, 'founts of honour' for honorary orders and decorations, symbols of the nation, and figures presiding at celebrations and commemorations.[46] Ancient or later dynasties have provided powerful examples of heroism in battle, wisdom in codifying law, piety in protecting religion, and paternalistic concern for subjects – as well as strategies for attacks on real or perceived enemies outside and within – that could be invoked, activated and instrumentalised by their republican, socialist or authoritarian successors. Royal sites could be repurposed as national 'heritage' or made profitable as tourist attractions, and royal ceremonials (or re-enactments of 'traditional' rites) used to focus attention on particular ethnic or national cultures with pomp, exoticism and nostalgia. Individual leaders and dynastic families have fashioned themselves in the guise of old sovereigns.[47] The 'courts' of the non-monarchical state, replete with soldiers, courtiers and servants, have often mimicked those of royal courts. Monarchs are legion in the pantheon of Asian rulers, and their legacy is long lasting. In the *longue durée* of encounters between Asians and Europeans, crowns, the principle of hereditary rule, and individual monarchs – both Asian and European – have occupied leading positions.

Notes

1. Robert Aldrich and Cindy McCreery (eds), *Crowns and Colonies: European Monarchies and Overseas Empires* (Manchester: Manchester University Press, 2016).
2. Robert Aldrich and Cindy McCreery (eds), *Royals on Tour: Politics, Pageantry and Colonialism* (Manchester: Manchester University Press, 2018).
3. Ian Copland, *The Princes of India in the Endgame of Empire, 1917–1947* (Cambridge: Cambridge University Press, 1997); Yaqoob Khan Bangash, *A Princely Affair: The Accession and Integration of the Princely States of Pakistan, 1947–1955* (New York: Oxford University Press, 2015).
4. Milton Osborne, *Sihanouk: Prince of Light, Prince of Darkness* (Honolulu: University of Hawai'i Press, 1994); Geoffrey C. Gunn, *Monarchical Manipulation in Cambodia: France, Japan, and the Sihanouk Crusade for Independence* (Copenhagen: NIAS Press, 2018).
5. Herbert P. Bix, *Hirohito and the Making of Modern Japan* (New York: Harper, 2000).
6. Kobkua Suwannathat-Pian, *Palace, Political Party and Power: A Story of the Socio-Political Development of Malay Kingship* (Singapore: NUS Press, 2011); John Monfries, *A Prince in a Republic: The Life of Sultan Hamengku Buwono IX of Yogyakarta* (Singapore: Institute of Southeast Asian Studies, 2015).

MONARCHIES, DECOLONISATION AND POST-COLONIAL ASIA

7   Bruce McFarland Lockhart, *The End of the Vietnamese Monarchy* (New Haven, CT: Yale Center for International and Area Studies, 1993), and 'Monarchy and decolonization in Indochina', in Marc Frey, Ronald W. Pruessen and Tan Tai Yong (eds), *The Transformation of Southeast Asia: International Perspectives on Decolonization* (New York: Routledge, 2015), pp. 52–71.
8   Grant Evans (ed.), *The Last Century of Lao Royalty: A Documentary History* (Chiang Mai: Silkworm Books, 2009).
9   Roger Kershaw, *Monarchy in South-East Asia: The Faces of Tradition in Transition* (London: Routledge, 2001).
10 David Graeber and Marshall Sahlins, *On Kings* (Chicago: Hau Books, 2017), pp. 1–2, 12.
11 Benedict Anderson, *Imagined Communities: Reflections on the Origin and Spread of Nationalism* (London: Verso, revised version, 2006); Clifford Geertz, *Negara: The Theatre State in Nineteenth Century Bali* (Princeton: Princeton University Press, 1980); Stanley Tambiah, 'The galactic polity in Southeast Asia', *HAU: Journal of Ethnographic Theory*, 3:3 (2013), 503–34 (first published in 1973); and Nicholas Dirks, *The Hollow Crown: Ethnohistory of an Indian Kingdom* (Cambridge: Cambridge University Press, 1988). A number of prominent historians of Asian monarchy are referenced in the various chapters of the current volume.
12 See, for example, David C. Kang, *East Asia before the West: Five Centuries of Trade and Tribute* (New York: Columbia University Press, 2010); and Peter Zarrow, *After Empire: The Conceptual Transformation of the Chinese State, 1885–1924* (Stanford: Stanford University Press, 2012).
13 Tambiah, 'The galactic polity in Southeast Asia'.
14 Sanjay Subrahmanyan, *Courtly Encounters: Translating Courtliness and Violence in Early Modern Eurasia* (Cambridge, MA: Harvard University Press, 2012).
15 Michael Alexander and Sushila Anand, *Queen Victoria's Maharajah: Duleep Singh 1838–93* (London: Smithmark, 1979); Rosie Llewellyn-Jones, *The Last King in India: Wajid 'Ali Shah* (London: Hurst, 2014).
16 Robert Nield, *China's Foreign Places: The Foreign Presence in China in the Treaty Port Era, 1840–1943* (Hong Kong: Hong Kong University Press, 2015).
17 Donald Keene, *Emperor of Japan; Meiji and His World, 1852–1912* (New York: Columbia University Press, 2002); and Maurizio Peleggi, *Lords of Things: The Fashioning of the Siamese Monarchy's Modern Image* (Honolulu: University of Hawai'i Press, 2007).
18 Janaki Nair, *Mysore Modern: Rethinking the Region under Princely Rule* (Minneapolis: University of Minnesota Press, 2011).
19 Priya Naik, 'The case of the "other India" and Indian IR Scholarship', *Third World Quarterly*, 35:8 (2014), 1496–1508.
20 Hoo Nam Seelmann, *Lautloses Weinen: Der Untergang des koreanischen Königshauses* (Würzburg: Königshausen & Neumann, 2011).
21 Robert Aldrich, *Banished Potentates: Dethroning and Exiling Indigenous Monarchs under British and French Colonial Rule, 1815–1955* (Manchester: Manchester University Press, 2018); Gananath Obeyesekere, *The Doomed King: A Requiem for Sri Vikrama Rajasinha* (Colombo: Snailfish, 2017); Peter Carey, *Destiny: The Life of Prince Diponegoro of Yogyakata, 1785–1855* (Bern: Peter Lang, 2014); Ronit Ricci (ed.), *Exile in Colonial Asia: Kings, Convicts, Commemoration* (Honolulu: University of Hawai'i Press, 2016).
22 Colin Newbury, *Patrons, Clients, and Empire: Chieftaincy and Over-rule in Asia, Africa, and the Pacific* (Oxford: Oxford University Press, 2003). See also David Cannadine, *Ornamentalism: How the British Saw Their Empire* (London: Allen Lane, 2001).
23 See Moin Mir, *The Prince Who Beat the Empire: How an Indian Ruler Took on the Might of the East India Company* (Stroud: Amberley, 2018), on the eighteenth-century Bengali ruler Meer Jafar Ali Khan.
24 William Dalrymple, *The Last Mughal: The Fall of a Dynasty, Delhi, 1857* (London: Bloomsbury, 2006); Nguyen Thé Anh, *Monarchie et fait colonial au*

Viet-Nam (1875–1925): Le crépuscule d'un ordre traditionnel (Paris: L'Harmattan, 1992).

25 Kumari Jayawardena, *Perpetual Ferment: Popular Revolts in Sri Lanka in the 18th and 19th Centuries* (Colombo: Social Scientists' Association, 2010); Maitrii Aung-Thwin, *The Return of the Galon King: History, Law, and Rebellion in Colonial Burma* (Singapore: NUS Press, 2011).

26 Pierre L. Lamant, *L'Affaire Yukanthor: autopsie d'un scandale colonial* (Paris: Société française d'histoire d'Outre-Mer, 1989); Søren Ivarsson and Christopher E. Goscha, 'Prince Phetsarath (1890–1959): nationalism and royalty in the making of modern Laos', *Journal of Southeast Asian Studies*, 38:1 (2007), 55–81; J. S. Grewal and Indu Banga, *A Political Biography of Maharaja Ripudaman Singh of Nabha: Paramountcy, Patriotism, and the Panth* (Oxford: Oxford University Press, 2018). On a dissident Thai royal, Prince Prisdang, see Tamara Loos, *Bones Around my Neck: The Life and Exile of a Prince Provocateur* (Ithaca, NY: Cornell University Press, 2016).

27 See, for example, Mai Na M. Lee, *Dreams of the Hmong Kingdom: The Quest for Legitimation in French Indochina, 1850–1960* (Madison: University of Wisconsin Press, 2015); and Mikael Gravers, 'Waiting for a righteous ruler: the Karen royal imaginary in Thailand and Burma', *Journal of Southeast Asian Studies*, 43:2 (2012), 340–63.

28 Copland, *The Princes of India*, and Bangash, *A Princely Affair*.

29 Monfries, *A Prince in a Republic*.

30 For the memoir of one prince's widow, see Inge Sargent, *Twilight over Burma: My Life as a Shan Princess* (Honolulu: University of Hawai'i Press, 1994).

31 See, for example, Marzia Balzani, *Modern Indian Kingship: Tradition, Legitimacy and Power in Rajasthan* (Oxford: James Currey, 2003).

32 Christopher Kremmer, *Bamboo Palace: Discovering the Lost Dynasty of Laos* (London: HarperCollins, 2003); Mangkra Souvannaphouma, *Laos: autopsie d'une monarchie assassinée* (Paris: L'Harmattan, 2010).

33 Osborne, *Sihanouk*, and 'An Epilogue for Norodom Sihanouk', in *Pol Pot Solved the Leprosy Problem: Remembering Colonial and Post-Colonial Worlds, 1956–1981* (Redland Bay, QLD: Connor Court Publishing, 2018), pp. 275–87.

34 On contemporary monarchies in Asia, see Kershaw, *Monarchy in South-East Asia*; Michael Vatikiotis, *Blood and Silk: Power and Conflict in Modern Southeast Asia* (London: Weidenfeld and Nicolson, 2017), ch. 3, 'Divine kings and dark princes', pp. 55–82; and Gerry van Klinken, ch. 7, 'Return of the sultans: the communitarian turn in Indonesian politics', in Jamie S. Davidson and David Henley (eds), *The Revival of Tradition in Indonesian Politics: The Deployment of Adat from Colonialism to Indigenism* (London: Routledge, 2007), pp. 149–69.

35 Tony Ballantyne, *Between Colonialism and Diaspora: Sikh Cultural Formations in an Imperial World* (Durham, NC: Duke University Press, 2006), ch. 3, 'Maharajah Dalip Singh, memory, and the negotiations of Sikh identity', pp. 86–120.

36 Robert Aldrich, 'The return of the throne: the repatriation of the Kandyan regalia to Ceylon', in Aldrich and McCreery, *Crowns and Colonies*, pp. 139–62.

37 Guy Lubeigt, *Nay Pyi Taw, une résidence royale pour l'armée birmane* (Paris: Les Indes savantes, 2012).

38 John Clifford Holt, *Theravada Traditions: Buddhist Ritual Cultures in Contemporary Southeast Asia and Sri Lanka* (Honolulu: University of Hawai'i Press, 2017), ch. 1, 'Phra Bang: venerating the Buddha image in Lao religious culture', pp. 11–66.

39 Vu Hong Lien, *Royal Hue: Heritage of the Nguyen Dynasty of Vietnam* (Bangkok: River Books, 2015).

40 Ploysi Porananond and Victor T. King, *Tourism and Monarchy in Southeast Asia* (Newcastle upon Tyne: Cambridge Scholars Publishing, 2016).

41 Philip Murphy, *Monarchy and the End of Empire: The House of Windsor, the British Government, and the Postwar Commonwealth* (Oxford: Oxford University Press, 2013), and *The Empire's New Clothes: The Myth of the Commonwealth*

(London: C. Hurst, 2018). On the transitions from monarchy to republic, see Harshan Kumarasingham, *A Political Legacy of the British Empire: Power and the Parliamentary System in Post-colonial India and Sri Lanka* (London: I. B. Tauris, 2012).

42 Sean L. Yom and F. Gregory Gause III, 'Resilient royals: how Arab monarchies hang on', *Journal of Democracy*, 23:4 (2012), 74–88; Mohamed Daadaoui, *Moroccan Monarchy and the Islamist Challenge* (London: Palgrave Macmillan, 2011); Tariq Moraiwed Tell, *The Social and Economic Origins of Monarchy in Jordan* (London: Palgrave Macmillan, 2013); Christopher M. Davidson, *After the Sheikhs: The Coming Collapse of the Gulf Monarchies* (New York: Oxford University Press, 2013).

43 See, for example, Claude-Hélène Perrot and François-Xavier Fauvelle-Aymar (eds), *Le Retour des rois: les autorités traditionnelles et l'état en Afrique contemporaine* (Paris: Karthala, 2003); John L. Comaroff and Jean Comaroff, *The Politics of Custom: Chiefship, Capital, and the State in Contemporary Africa* (Chicago: University of Chicago Press, 2018); Kwasi Ampene and Nana Kwadwo Nyantakyi III, *Engaging Modernity: Asante in the Twenty-First Century* (Ann Arbor: Michigan Publishing, 2016); Susan Cook and Rebecca Hardin, 'Performing royalty in contemporary Africa', *Cultural Anthropology*, 28:2 (2013), 227–51; Adedayo Emmanuel Afe and Ibitayo Oluwasola Adubuola, 'The travails of kingship institution in Yorubaland: a case study of Isinkan in Akureland', *Nebula*, 6:4 (2009), 114–32; Dwayne Woods, 'Monarchical rule in Swaziland: Power is absolute but patronage is (for) relative(s)', *Journal of Asian and African Studies*, 52:4 (2017), 496–513.

44 On the South Pacific, see, for example, Stephanie Lawson, *Tradition versus democracy in the South Pacific: Fiji, Tonga and Western Samoa* (Cambridge: Cambridge University Press, 1996), especially ch. 3, 'The monarchy versus tradition in the Kingdom of Tonga', pp. 79–116; and Fanny Wonu Veys, 'Materialising the king: the royal funeral of King Taufa'ahau Tupou IV of Tonga', *The Australian Journal of Anthropology*, 20 (2009), 131–49.

45 Jack Corbett, Wouter Veenendall and Lhawang Ugyel, 'Why monarchy persists in small states: the cases of Tonga, Bhutan and Liechtenstein', *Democratization*, 24:4 (2017), 689–706; Ludger Kühnhardt, 'The resilience of Arab monarchy', *Policy Review*, June–July 2012, 57–67.

46 Robert Aldrich and Cindy McCreery, 'European royals and their colonial realms: honors and decorations', in Christina Jordan and Imke Polland (eds), *Realms of Royalty: New Directions in Researching Contemporary European Monarchies* (Bielefeld: Transcript, forthcoming, 7–32).

47 New 'dynasties' have also emerged: three generations of Kims as rulers of North Korea, the Nehru-Gandhi family in India, the Banadaraike family in Sri Lanka, the election to the presidency of Indonesia and the Philippines of the children of former rulers, and so on.

CHAPTER TWO

All the king's men: regal ministers of eclipsed empires in India
Priya Naik

The British never ruled over the entire Indian subcontinent. All maps truthfully showed the areas 'directly ruled' under British India as pink and the ones ruled 'indirectly' as yellow, that is, the princely states.[1] There were nearly six hundred princely states not ruled directly by the British; their exact number was never quite certain, with the British themselves adding at least one with the creation of Benaras as late as 1911. These varied from Hyderabad, almost as large as France, to Alwar, not more than 3,198 square miles. Not until the Delhi Darbar of 1911 were the states sorted according to size and scale, the largest and most powerful – Baroda, Gwalior, Hyderabad, Kashmir and Mysore – being given 21-gun salutes, trickling down to the 9-gun salute states of Panna and Dewas. While the states were granted internal autonomy under paramountcy (1858–1947), technological developments such as aviation, roads, telegraphs and railways nibbled away at these boundaries between the Indian princely states and British India, so much so that motorcars belonging to each state had to bear the state's name on a red number plate.[2] This was a time of artificial stillness. During this period not a single state was annexed, as had earlier been the case, under the principle of the 'doctrine of lapse' (by which the British allowed themselves to take over an Indian state if there was no successor – or one considered acceptable to them – to a reigning dynasty).

During the Paramountcy, the Indian princes for the first time formed a corporate body in 1921, the Chamber of Princes, which lobbied for self-preservation of the states, negotiated with the British for their collective future, and came close to achieving what Winston Churchill imagined to be 'India, Pakistan and Princestan'.[3] Although they almost crossed the line into independent India, the disparity in power between these hundreds of states, as well as regionalism and the sheer inability to modernise, got the better of them. Their political rival, the Indian

National Congress, pronounced their death even while they were alive and thriving, with Jawaharlal Nehru declaring, 'I am no believer in kings and princes'. While quite a few had undertaken the task of building obvious markers of modernity such as hospitals, schools and roads, at the core, they remained feudal and undemocratic. Shail Mayaram, for instance, argues that these pre-colonial and traditional structures could not be modern in any genuine way.[4] In recent years, however, scholars have begun questioning the accepted inevitability of their fatality in modern India.[5]

On 15 August 1947, the British Parliament passed the Indian Independence Act, bringing to an end the British Indian Empire. In that year, the princely states had the choice of acceding to either India or Pakistan. A few of these states, Junagadh, Hyderabad and Kashmir, held out from acceding to India. The Nawab of Palanpur wrote to Sardar Vallabhai Patel, a member of the Governor General's Executive Council in the Interim Government, and later Deputy Prime Minister in free India, stating: 'I heard of Junagadh's folly [in resisting accession] when I was in Europe. If the Ruler of Junagadh had a dewan [minister] of the right type, I am sure the things would have not taken this turn. Junagadh has always been a slave of his Dewans. No minister could have given more idiotic and foolish counsel than Sir Shah Nawaz Bhutto.'[6] Two years later, a panicky Nawab of Junagadh, having fled to Pakistan and attempting to sort out the mess he had landed in, wrote to Sardar Patel, too. He explained, 'Allow me to return, I am even willing to appoint a dewan like Mirza.'[7] The reference was to Sir Mirza Ismail, an elegant and efficient minister with the distinction of serving the modern state of princely Mysore for nearly two decades.

While much has been written about the 'men who ruled India', or the Indian Civil Service (ICS), we know little of the civil administration of the Indian princely states under 'indirect' rule.[8] British India was governed directly by the India Office, Whitehall, London via His Majesty's Secretary of State, usually a cabinet minister of the British government, in conjunction with the Government of British India based in Calcutta, later New Delhi. The princely states, however, were ruled indirectly via the Foreign Department, created in 1843, within the Government of British India. Indian princely states were seen as 'internal' foreign states, whereas Afghanistan and Aden were seen as 'external' foreign states. The branch which dealt with the Indian princes changed names intermittently in its history of more than a century and had various names, such as 'Internal Branch' and 'Political Branch', between 1923 and 1937.[9] Its supervision of non-military employment, such as the dewans in the princely states, remained a constant. It was overseen by the Viceroy, a title given to the Governor

General of India as the representative of Britain's royal family. The Foreign Department's Secretary 'advised' the Viceroy on the princely states and, in 1913, as the scope of work mounted, the position of Political Secretary was created to provide specialist political advice.[10]

The Paramountcy brought the princes and the British into a new bureaucratic relationship, which was rather complicated. While the Viceroy was the acme of British administration, 'Residents' were appointed to the 21-gun salute states such as Hyderabad, Kashmir, Baroda and Mysore, and reported directly to the Viceroy. Conglomerates of princely states, such as that of the Rajputana and Punjab states, were often placed 'under' a single 'Agent', and those overseeing several states were known as Agents to the Governor General (AGGs). Robin Jeffrey has defined a typology of the modes of interaction among maharajas, diwans and residents, based on his research in Travancore. At times, a 'dominant Resident' controlled the dewan and the ruler was reduced to redundancy; at other times, rule was 'balanced', which meant that the British allowed anglicised rulers and ministers to have their way. Or rule was 'laissez-faire', according to which rulers and ministers were left largely alone, provided that the state remained free of blatant disturbances or misrule. Finally, rule might involve an 'imposed minister', where an anglicised, trustworthy 'native' from outside the state, or sometimes a European, was established as minister.[11]

The Viceroy, in turn, often took tours of princely states, culminating in a grand 'darbar', a matter of prestige for the princes who often vied for the Viceroy's attention. Given the number of states, a Viceroy's visit to an individual state – involving considerable, if tedious, ceremonial fanfare, with almost always a hunt thrown in – was a matter of great honour.[12] States were keen to show off their able administration, and for this much depended on the dewan, who remains a shadowy figure in the history of Indian monarchies, but was manifestly a man of some importance in the Indian princely states.[13] The Political Branch maintained a ledger of men keen to be employed as dewans, and influenced which man went where. Since the position was one of great privilege, appointments were sought and granted to both Indians and Europeans. It was the princes as employers, however, who had the last word.

The dewans

The term *dewan* is Persian in origin, like the word *darbar*, and means 'administration'. The term *dewankhana* refers to the place where the administrator conducted the daily duties of running a kingdom. While the *darbar* was the court – the grand, curated and visible part of the kingdom – the dewankhana was much like the modern bureau where the actual running of routine affairs was conducted. The term has percolated down to modern India, where the term *dewani* means matters which are revenue related, which indicates that the dewan as the head of the administration had multiple roles, including overseeing the crucial revenue collection. In the early 1920s, with the growing recognition that democracies rather than autocracies are more attuned to popular will, many Indian princes sought to change the nomenclature of Dewan to a more British title. In 1922, Maharaja Tukoji of Indore, for instance, changed the position in his state from Dewan to Prime Minister.[14] Conversely, the ruler of Alwar, keen to demonstrate his Hindu identity, designated his Prime Minister 'Sumantra', after a minister of the same name in the ancient Indian epic of *Ramayana*.[15]

The British crown clearly disapproved of the use of 'Prime Minister' in the princely states, noting that the 'the term PM is misappropriated and is historically associated with Western institutions'. The matter was finally laid to rest with a disgruntled observation that 'the term Prime Minister is not really appropriate, but is not a matter which calls for interference'. Several princes went one step further, creating government departments similar to those of Britain, some even appointing a 'Foreign Minister', and the state of Bahwalpur from 1928 had a 'Colonisation Minister', complete with a colonisation scheme.[16] On account of the virtually unlimited power vested in the monarch, a lot depended on the judiciousness of these men. Indeed, in an attack on the backwardness of the princely states, the eminent political scientist Harold Laski observed in the *Daily Herald* in 1933: 'It is seldom indeed that a civil service exists in the modern sense of the word. The prince's will is law, things like a habeas corpus act, a criminal code and an independent judiciary are still to be made.'[17]

The dewans were nevertheless statesmen notable, on the whole, for their brilliance, astuteness and competence, and some worked in several states successively during their careers. They included K. M. Panikkar of Patiala and Bikaner and Sir C. P. Ramaswamy Aiyer, who served as the Dewan of Travancore. Sir Mirza Ismail served as Prime Minister of Mysore, Jaipur and Hyderabad successively, three powerful and active states. Nawab Sir Liaquat Hyat Khan was Home Secretary in Patiala and then political adviser to the Nawab of Bhopal. Sir Manubhai Mehta, the Dewan of Baroda, served as Prime Minister of Bikaner, and then Home and Foreign Minister of Gwalior. Sir Colonel Kailash Narain Haksar began his career as the private secretary of Gwalior and became the Prime Minister of Bikaner and then of Kashmir. To Sir M. Vishweshwariya of Mysore goes the credit of modernising that state in the early twentieth century.

While these represent a few of the better-known ministers, each of the several hundred Indian princely states had dewans corresponding to their state's status, scale and, quite crudely, pay. They tended to be well-educated graduates from the new British-modelled universities, such as those in Bombay, Madras and Allahabad, with Panikkar graduating from Oxford. They were English-speaking and often literary, and at least one, Maharaja Sir Kishen Preshad of Hyderabad, was a renowned Urdu poet who exchanged letters with the great writer and fellow poet Sir Mohammad Iqbal. Maharaja Preshad could even trace a 'dewani' lineage of blue blood, as the descendent of Todar Mal, a minister of the Mughal Emperor Abkar (r. 1556–1605).[18] The men who circulated through the highest appointments possible within the princely states came from a very small social pool. They were either Brahmins (for example, Aiyer, Zutschi, Haksar, Krishnamachari and Vishweshwariya), Parsis or aristocratic Muslims – their background pointing to the very limited access most contemporary Indians had to education and patronage, as well as prevailing British prejudices. In a note on Nagar-Brahmins, a subset of Brahmins in Kathiawad, Captain Harold Wilberforce-Bell of the Foreign and Political Department remarked on 'their ability and shrewdness' and noted that they are 'found to be associated with the administration of nearly every important state'.[19]

In turn, this upper-class network of aristocratic Indians, British officers and Indian princes often facilitated a sense of jolly brotherhood. Requests were frequently made to 'borrow' a man from a neighbouring state. In 1917, for instance, the Maharaja of Jodhpur wrote to Sir John Wood of the Foreign and Political Department stating that his aged Parsi dewan lent to him by Jam Sahib of Nawangar wanted to return home and asking if there was a 'good man' to be 'spared'.[20] The dewans' high social status helped both their employment and their marriage prospects. Both Kailash Narain Haksar and Sir Mirza Ismail grew up with heirs to the throne, Madho Rao Scindia (1886–1925) of Gwalior and Krishnaraja Wodeyar IV (1894–1940) of Mysore, respectively, forming friendships which lasted until their deaths. Marriages between the princely families and the dewans were viewed as unions between equals and consequently not frowned upon. The daughter of the Nawab of Bhopal, Rabia, for example, fell in love with and married a nephew of Sir Mirza Ismail, Agha Mirza,[21] while Salar Jung I, the Prime Minister of Hyderabad, engineered the marriage of his daughter Amat-uz-Zehra Begum to the sixth Nizam of Hyderabad (1869–1911).

Unlike their British counterparts of the ICS (who worked in British India mostly), and the Political Department, the dewans were not as regulated and subject to bureaucratic control as other officials in India.

The freedom to administer often substantial territories also drew many ICS members, both serving and retired, into the Indian princely states. To stall this unexpected 'brain drain', in 1920 rules were codified so that appointment of an ICS officer to an Indian princely state became subject to the sanction of the Governor General's council as well as annual review.[22] Yet the state of Bhopal, for instance, would not dispense with Sir Oswald Bosanquet, an Englishman, and his term was renewed every year, provided that he did not advise the Nawab on any 'political matter', with the narrow definition of political being 'not affecting relations with the British'. On the whole, no one considered the practice of renewed appointments objectionable, least of all the British, who rather found it convenient for one of their own men to be working in the administratively dark interiors of the princely states. As well as the greater administrative freedom, the pay made working in a princely state attractive. The pay for appointees in a princely state was much higher than that of the ICS or the Indian Political Service. A dewan could easily receive Rs. 4,000 per month, a salary granted only to the ICS Residents of the biggest states, at the end of their career. Furthermore, there was no intimidating examination and interview as there was for both the ICS and Political Department, nor training for a new appointee to endure.

While many states copied the British system of administration and also changed the nomenclature of the senior official from Dewan to Prime or Chief Minister, others persevered with the old term, and at times spoke of a 'dewanship', a newly minted Indian-English word of the twentieth century.[23] Adding to the confusion was, of course, that 'Dewan' (along with other terms) was one of the titles bestowed upon Indians by their imperial British monarch. It was quite possible then to have a ruler, like that of Palanpur, whose string of titles included Dewan, but also for a Dewan to have the title of Maharaja, as was the case with Maharaja Kishen Preshad of Hyderabad. In everyday matters, however, where everyone knew their place in the order of things, this did not make much difference. The hereditary ruler, by his natural right, embodied both sacred and the temporal authority in his state, unlike a minister, who might move from state to state, looking for better opportunities.

The dewans stood at the intersection of personal and private ambition, the wide mandate of power in a princely state and in the British Empire. Ambitious they were: along with their competence and ability came the great attraction of employment in a princely state and such benefits as a free motor car, accommodation and a hefty salary. On the other hand, they often had to suffer a fickle and petulant ruler and could be dismissed at a moment's notice. The 'better' men were regularly fought over, and the more illustrious ones were constantly beseeched to come to the aid of a needy prince and reform a weak or rudimentary administration. To Colonel Bashir Hussain Zaidi of Rampur, for instance, goes the credit for energetically modernising that state in the 1930s after dispelling the nawab's notion that new factories 'swallow up' people.

Most crucially, dewans became indispensable. While absolute in theory, princely power was in practice hedged about with numerous checks and balances, with local aristocrats keen to influence the ruler and their subjects. The latter, as the decades passed, began to grow increasingly indignant about being 'ruled' as subjects and not as citizens. Moreover, rulers owed their position to powerful landowners of the state, who often tried to exert pressure on them. Having an 'outsider' settle these disputes was easier than having a biased state stakeholder do the same. Furthermore, the workload was impossible for a prince to manage alone, and, as a result, the Nawab of Cambay, for example, passed orders on broad policy issues only 'after consulting the dewan'.[24] When the Prime Minister of Bahwalpur, a rich and prosperous state in the Punjab, was fired, the competition for his replacement was fierce, with numerous able candidates, including serving ministers from other states, putting themselves forward. In the absence of a regulatory structure for appointments as in the ICS, candidates' assertion of self-interest was unabashed and naked. States which had minority administrations or had been penalised for maladministration often held a greater attraction on account of the degree of freedom available to a potential dewan.

The matter of appointment was nevertheless tricky and tedious. While the British administration 'advised' the prince on the choice of minister, multiple factors, including religion and caste, as much as individual competency, influenced the final selection. An application for the position of dewan of Indore by Rai Bahadur Pandit Hari Kishen Kaul, CSI, CIE – his having been decorated with the Star of India and the Order of the Indian Empire by the British seemingly an indication of his status – was rejected because 'he has no experience of a work in an Indian state and I have seen many men come to grief. Rai Bahadur Hotu Singh was far from a success and nor was Sir James Cleveland in Jaipur'.[25] Very often the greatest challenge for an efficient dewan determined to reform a creaky administration was a reluctant and petulant prince, who found it easier to fire the agent of change than undertake reforms.

Like a marriage, then, a lot of effort went into a successful appointment, which involved a sort of *ménage à trois* between the British, the Indian prince and the dewan. The dewans individually were also trying to carve out space for ministers, ostensibly to balance the overwhelming autocracy of the princes. In a few instances, dewanship even became hereditary. When the Nawab of Rampur married in 1920, he appointed his father-in-law, Masnad Khan, as dewan; keen to retain power within the family, Masnad Khan then appointed his son, Abdus Samad Khan, as the next dewan, who served for nearly two decades until the early 1940s. In Rajpipla, a small state in Gujarat, a Parsi, Khan Bahadur Pheroza Dhanjisha Kothavala, BA, LLB, worked as dewan for thirty-three years in the early decades of the twentieth century, having 'succeeded' his father, who had served the king for twenty-three years.[26]

Between these three groups – the British, the princes and the dewans – power configurations changed rapidly, and it was not unusual to find a minister who had been appointed by the monarch to later turn 'traitor'. The Nawab of Banganepalle, for instance, returned from a pilgrimage to find that his dewan, Humayun Mirza, had taken over as ruler.[27] The dewan had drawn the attention of the British to the 'misdeeds and misconducts' of the Nawab, who was questioned by them and eventually asked to 'reside outside his state'. Like several other princes who found themselves exiled from their own state, such as the rulers of Nabha, Banganepalle and Pudukottai, the dewan then assumed the 'conduct [of] the administration of the state with full powers under the [British] Resident'. At other times, however, the dewan and the monarch had to ally against the people of the state. When the Nawab of Rampur decided to cut down on the extravagant expenditure of his large extended family, the *khaandanis* (quite literally, 'family members'), the dewan, Colonel B. H. Zaidi, became increasingly unpopular with the locals and faced demands that he be evicted and replaced with a 'rampuriya' (i.e., a native of Rampur) dewan.[28] Of course, the larger issue, according to Lieutenant Colonel G. T. Fisher, Political Agent to the states of Benaras and Rampur, was that 'none of these positions can be held by Rampuris as none are fit for the position'.[29] Indeed, on the grounds of ability and education, outsiders constantly scored (or, rather, were believed to score) better than locals throughout the princely states. Finally, on occasion the British warned a prince whose administration was being wrecked by an unscrupulous minister. In 1928, the Dewan Bharat Singh of Barwani was fired indirectly, when the Agent to the Governor General advised the prince to do so.

When obtaining a position as dewan, quite often the challenge was not only to unravel the political configurations at play but to stay clear of malicious traps. At times, the prince himself obstructed good administration. For instance, Albion Banerjee (his Christian first name elicited more than a few wry remarks from British officials), found upon reaching Kashmir to take up the post of dewan there that 'the constitution had been altered and that he was not to occupy that position. During the whole two years he never once had a private interview with his Highness ... [and] his notes and minutes law [were] unheeded'.[30] This became the grounds for a searing criticism of the Kashmiri monarchy, but presumably one which made no difference to the ruler, Raja Hari Singh. Persisting in the belief that their opinion actually counted, many educated men, quite often retired from the ICS, wrote letter after letter to the Foreign and Political Department asking for employment in an 'Indian' state. On account of the enforced political isolation, the only way of getting into a darbar was via the British.

In a revealing letter about the networks of patronage in 1921, one Pandit U. N. Zutschi, a Kashmiri, wrote to Sir John Wood in the Foreign and Political Department, earnestly asking for a letter of introduction 'with a view to get[ting] employment in Bhopal'.[31] Zutschi's attached résumé illuminates the career trajectories of men like himself, competent, educated and ambitious figures who moved up the bureaucratic structures in princely states. Starting as a tutor to the Maharaja of Ali Rajpur in Indore residency, Zutschi moved to the judiciary, becoming a collector to the state of Bhilsa, the secretary to the dewan of Datia, the Chief Judge of Jhabua and finally making a pitch for what would quite clearly be the acme of his career, to become the Dewan of Bhopal. Explaining his credentials, or 'Family Respectability and Status' as he put it, Zutschi explained how he was a third-generation dewan. The Foreign and Political Department nonetheless refrained from facilitating such requests, impressing a change of dewan on a prince only on charges of proven maladministration or mischief. Indeed, true to their word, it was only in desperate times, from Alwar's refusal to administer well, to Bahalwalpur's financial recklessness, that the British insisted on their best English officers from the ICS as dewans. Sir Alexander Tottenham served in Pudukottai, Mr. F. V. Wylie in Alwar and Sir Penderel Moon in Bahawalpur, the latter offering valuable perspectives about Partition and the princely states in his works.[32]

By and large, however, the monarchs and their ministers muddled along, battling the growing political influence of the Congress whose vision of a democratic India posed a direct threat to the princely states, as well as India's growing participation in global politics. Indeed, the Congress was the fourth unsolicited partner in this alliance, rushing in and changing the delicate alliance between the British and the princes. Formed in 1885, the Indian National Congress was at first a mild pressure group. Early in the twentieth century, however, as the chant for representative democracy grew louder, the Congress became a political party, determined to shape the future of India. As India inched towards

Independence, it became evident that neither monarchies nor their men would have a place in independent India.

Ministerial and not-so-ministerial tasks

While the ministers of the more important states are better known, this chapter has examined them as a collective, and now focuses on the political practices which the dewans pursued between the princes and the British. The tasks of the dewan were varied and could be unexpected. In the more progressive states, such as Baroda, duties could include the routine matter of filing the annual administrative report to the Foreign and Political Department. From inspecting the site allotted to his state's ruler in the new imperial capital, New Delhi, as the Dewan to Nabha, D. M. Narsinga Rao, found himself doing, to constantly petitioning the Viceroy to grant the Mahadhiraja of Darbhanga a gun salute, as Aditya Prashad Sinha, Dewan to Darbhanga, tediously did in the 1920s, the dewan could be called upon to carry out a variety of tasks and jobs.[33] One of the most important recognised responsibilities was to speak in 'his master's voice'. As a representative of the prince, he often addressed his 'majesty's people' and in this capacity also reached out to the subjects as one of 'them'.

As the pressures to form constituent assemblies arose, many 'progressive princes', such as those of Baroda, Mysore and Indore, rose to the occasion and formed such bodies. The establishment of Dushhera Assembly, where the Dewan of Mysore addressed the people, was a much-feted occasion, and much like the European statesmen who circulated their well-written speeches, so did the dewans. It became a practice to send to the Crown Representatives the speeches made at this assembly, which were no less accounts of international and local events than those made by any statesman in Great Britain. Speaking in 1945, Sir Brojendra Mitter, Dewan of Baroda, addressed the Dhara Sabha, the representative body, starting with the victory of the Allied forces: 'His Highness Maharaja Saheb is in Europe. He has asked me to assure you that wherever he may be the progress and prosperity of his subjects will be his first concern.'[34] The majority of states, however, stumbled across the century without such an assembly, the dewan simply appointed the head of the 'executive council', a small coterie of influential and powerful men who maintained the delicate balance between landholders, the monarch and the people.

The minister served as a conduit between the ruler and 'his' people, between the prince and the British, and between 'home' and the wider world. As India's membership and participation in international organisations grew after the First World War, it was the ministers who stepped in to represent and speak on behalf of 'our empire', as the Maharaja of Bikaner rather ambitiously put it.[35] Dewans needed to be able to speak in many tongues, including English, as well as to employ the language of a certain political correctness. Even though none of the employment parameters specifically spelt it out, the dewan needed to pay political obeisance to his feudal lord. Even the much-admired Sir Mirza Ismail referred to the Maharaja of Mysore as 'my august master'.[36]

From a modern employment perspective, this hierarchical relationship was emblematic of the traditional ordered space of the kingdoms themselves. The dewans were deferential, and, as they realised later to their horror, they also symbolised the excesses of monarchical rule. As the clamour for freedom mounted, it was the dewans who were targeted as symbolic of autocratic excesses. Sir C. P. Ramaswamy Aiyer of Travancore narrowly escaped a murder attempt, and in the aftermath his bust in the Travancore Palace was viciously pulled down and broken to pieces.[37] The golden period lasted until it was clear that the Indian princes would not have the autonomy they had had under paramountcy. During this period though, the dewans glided smoothly, between states, and between governing their fiefdoms and representing the princely states at international summits, like the League of Nations, with princes looking down at such 'political activities'.

The father of the 'father of the nation', Mahatma Gandhi, was himself a dewan. Karamchand Uttamchand Gandhi served as the dewan of the states of Porbander, Wankaner and Rajkot. Like most dewans, he was no political radical, and certainly not an anti-colonial one. His generous salary allowed him to send his son abroad to study, changing the young Gandhi's life – and Indian history – altogether. Ironically, it was Gandhi's transformation of the Indian National Congress from an elite organisation to a mass-based popular nationalist party which threatened and eventually swept away the princely states – and the dewans like his own father who served them.

Imperial recognition

The dewans collectively influenced the spatial arrangement of the new imperial city. In 1911, the British shifted the capital of their Indian Empire from Calcutta to New Delhi and made space to fit in the princes and their dewans. Architecturally and aesthetically, the British made a political statement with the layout and structure of the new capital. Apart from imposing a British sense of order and decorum on this ancient city, they fashioned the city with imperial gusto. The city was designed to symbolise the essential unity of the three estates of India: the

Raj, the princes and Indian subjects.[38] The assembly hall of the Chamber of Princes, formed in 1921 as a consultative body in which all senior princes and a number of lesser ones had seats, was originally designed to be circular, but, given the princes' propensity to take umbrage at being seated hierarchically, Herbert Baker designed a horseshoe-shaped chamber, thus reducing the chances of rulers slighting each other (see Figure 2.1). The princes were also seated territorially. In a glittering ceremony held in the *Dewan-i-am* of the Red Fort, in 1921, the Chamber of Princes was inaugurated by the Duke of Connaught.

The artificial isolation between the states that had hitherto prevailed now ended, with the princes meeting together at the annual session held in New Delhi. Within the deep corridors of the Chamber of Princes, a separate room was created for the dewans as a quiet nod to the increasing importance and indispensability of these men. Not only did they prepare speeches and examine the most crucial and knotty areas of paramountcy at the annual sessions of the Chamber of Princes, they also served a pragmatic role as translators and go-betweens. The Raja of Kota, for instance, was quite deaf and needed an intermediary to bridge the gap between the Viceroy and himself.[39] Quite a few other princes did not speak English; fortunately, most ministers were fairly anglicised. Finally, many princes observed orthodox practice and refused to dine with Europeans, and it is presumably here that men like Sir C. P. Ramaswamy Aiyer, Dewan of Travancore, filled the social gap between the British administrators and the Indian monarchs.[40]

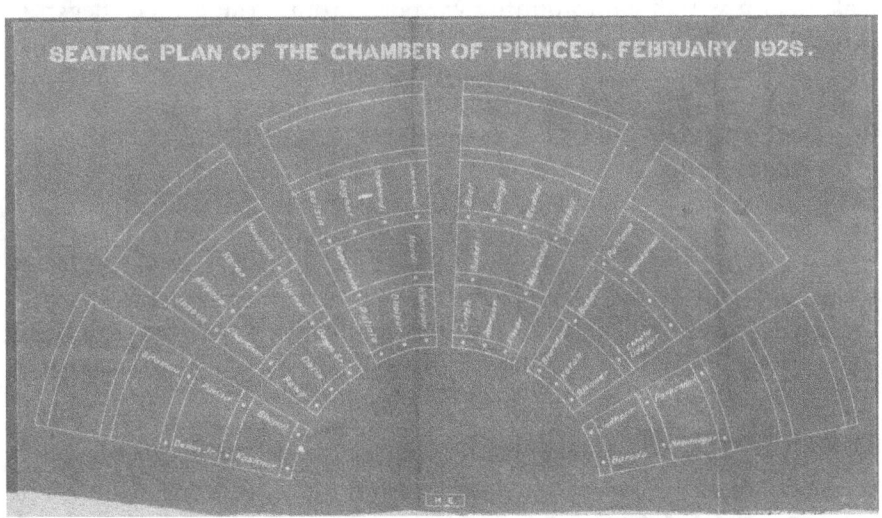

Figure 2.1 Seating Plan of the Chamber of Princes, February 1928

In the making of the new imperial city, territory was delineated for the princes. In a delicate process coordinated by three departments – the Foreign and Political Department, the Delhi Committee, the Engineering Department, as well as Sir Herbert Baker as architect – large swathes of land were allocated for each prince to build a residence in the 'Princes' Area' of New Delhi (Figure 2.2). With the kings came their men. The north of the area allotted to princes was set aside for the 'Dewans and Raises',[41] with at least one plot set aside for Sir Abdul Hamid, the illustrious Dewan of Kapurthala. Never before had land been granted exclusively to these mobile men. This deeply symbolic act was the recreation of the Indian empire at the heart of the new city.[42] Much like the miniature homes created by Dutch artisans, brought to life so magically by Jessie Burton in her novel *The Miniaturist*, the capital would embody the tiny princely palaces (in comparison to their stately ones) as a microcosm of the Indian empire.[43] In 1935, the Prime Minister of Indore, Rai Bahadur Colonel Dina Nath, too, requested that a plot be set aside for him. By 1939, however, in perhaps the first signs of 'winding' up the empire, policy changed and neither the princes nor their ministers were subsequently allotted land.

Between local and international, communalism and independence

The Paramountcy was a period of mutual dependence of the princes and the British. As the nationalist movement grew, however, the political cocoon which paramountcy wrapped around the princes began to be punctured. Communal organisations such as the All India Muslim League (1906), the All India Hindu Mahasabha (1915) and the Akali Dal of the Sikhs (1920) began 'infiltrating' the borders maintained between British and princely India. For a long time the princely states, of course, had prided themselves in embodying a secular and syncretic culture. 'So in the states generally,' opined Bikaner's Maharaja Ganga Singh in an address to mark the 1932 new year, 'the communal question does not really exist; and I cannot conceive of any prince – Hindu or Moslem – who would like to see this evil brought into ... the states.'[44] In the choice of dewan, the communal angle apparently mattered very little to the rulers, with Hindu kings appointing Muslim dewans, as when the Wodeyar Maharaja of Mysore appointed Sir Mirza Ismail. By the late 1930s, the Congress also decided to swoop in and openly target the Indian princes, most articulately by Nehru. The pressure on the princes was growing on all fronts and yet, just as their domestic prospects were diminishing, the Indian princes were relishing their greater international circulation and recognition. It was during this

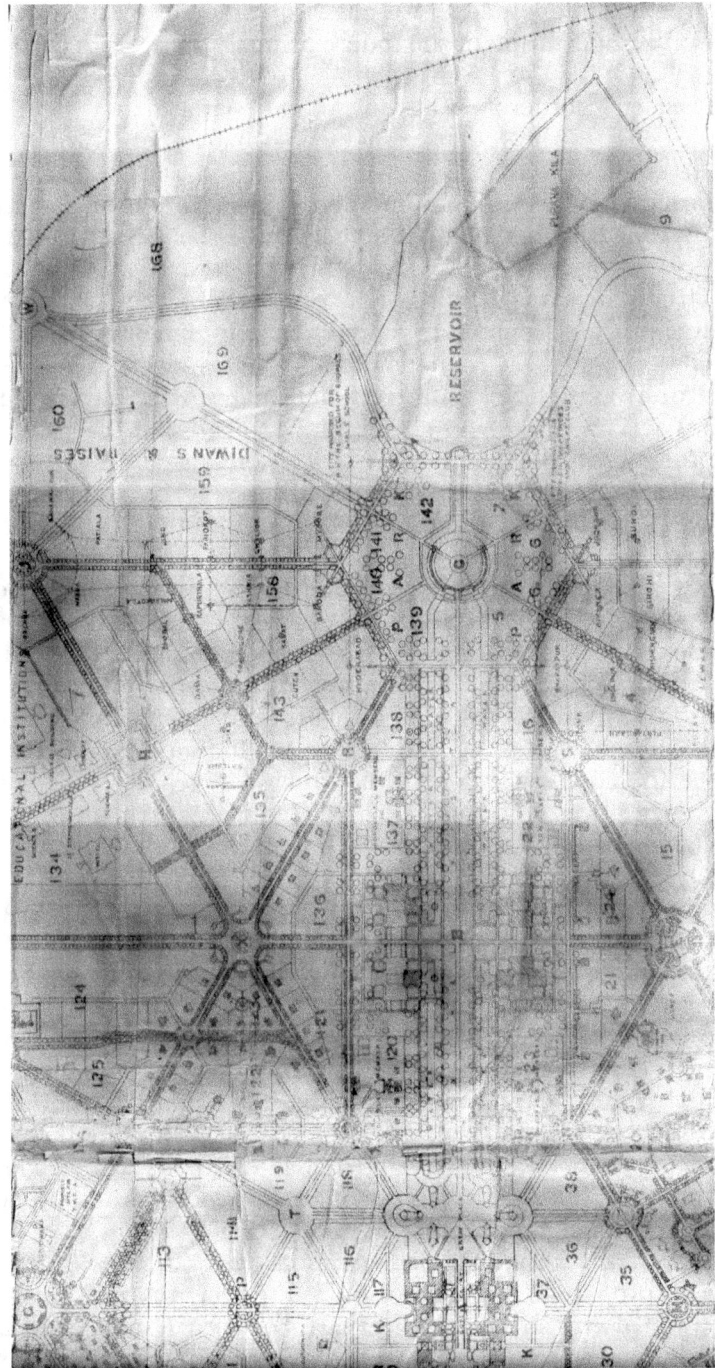

Figure 2.2 Detail of 1911 map of New Delhi, showing areas designated for maharajas and dewans

time that the ministers made a valiant effort to create 'Princestan', or the successful importation of the Indian princely states into independent India.

Already at the conference leading to the signature of the Treaty of Versailles (1919), the Indian princes had made their international debut and established that they were 'equal' to the British. As the Viceroy noted in 1926, 'India's membership at the LoN [League of Nations] is based on her being a signatory to the Versailles Treaty. That treaty was signed both by a British Indian and by ruling princes ... their status is equal.'[45] This only fuelled the righteousness of the Indian princes' demand to represent the Indian empire in global affairs. It also explains the Maharaja of Bikaner's audacious suggestion that 'territorial grants be made to Indian states who have rendered meritorious service in the war'; he helpfully added that these could be 'either in India or in the conquered portions of German East Africa or Mesopotamia'.[46]

When it came to the international representation of the British Empire, the British carefully selected Hindu, Muslim and Sikh representatives among both the princes and their ministers. The policy of equal representation of both Indias – British India and the princely states – also evaded a few sticky issues, the first being that the princes were unwilling to be 'led by an Indian' (i.e., a person of British India) and not princely India. Given their deep sense of local identity shaping their sense of self, being represented by an 'Indian', and therefore a commoner, an encompassing identity which evolved with the nationalist movement, was humiliating. It made sense, then, to send two delegations to conferences, representing British and princely India, respectively, with the latter headed by a royal. While a few Indian princes repeatedly made international appearances, such as Alwar, Kapurthala, Palanpur, Bikaner and Nawanagar, ministers soon began to serve in this role as well, fulfilling the British specification of having an 'impressive and able Indian'. Ministers were also more 'economical' to send to Europe than were princes, as a British officer of the Foreign and Political Department bluntly observed. An added benefit was that 'it might be that a dewan may have more practical knowledge of the working of a state' than the prince himself.[47] Sir Ali Iman of Hyderabad, Sir Abdul Hamid of Kapurthala, Sir Abdus Samad Khan of Rampur and Sir V. T. Krishnamachari of Jaipur were thus despatched to various international summits.

The communalism that had been introduced in the legislatures was transformed into a policy of delegation at the international level. The easiest way of doing so was to alternate between Hindu or Muslim princes or ministers to lead the delegation to the League of Nations.

Communalism also caused questions to be raised about representation, so much so that in 1934, an indignant member of the Central Legislative Assembly asked if a Sikh minister had been despatched to the League of Nations, and if not, why not. Clearly, ministers were representing themselves, as much as the layers of identity they embodied. For instance, on the selection of Sir Ali Imam as a representative in 1920, the Maharaja of Bikaner wrote a private letter to the Viceroy stating carefully that while one 'is prepared to accept Ali Imam, he will represent the princes primarily and only incidentally represent Mohmaden opinion. The delegation will presumably discuss questions affecting *our empire*. It should be absolutely clear that he represents the States and Princes in general and not the one he is at present serving.'[48]

Ironically, while rulers absented themselves from their states for long periods of time, concerns and eyebrows were raised about the princely administrations being neglected in the absence of their ministers. As Sir Charles C. Watson of the ICS noted in 1931, 'it is not desirable that Abdul Hamid should leave his state for Europe on account of the existence of political and agrarian agitation in the state and the necessity of strict control over its finances'.[49] By the middle of the twentieth century, the dewans were 'equivalent of a rajah, [going] on delegations and good-will missions, always in the best of hotels, all expenses paid, conveying comradely greeting[s] from one part of the world to another'.[50]

This period gave ministers the opportunity to carve out a space for their masters and inverted the position they held vis-à-vis those rulers. Previously, ministers filled in for their rulers *at home* when princes holidayed on the Riviera or travelled elsewhere in Europe, or when Muslim rulers fulfilled their religious obligation to perform the Hajj pilgrimage to Mecca. First mobile within South Asia, the ministers now formed part of an international league of official travellers.

The sense of an ending

It was not just the League of Nations that required international mileage of the princes and ministers. During this period, a series of investigations looked into the delicate relationship between the British and the princes as part of a wider review of British India, such as the Simon Commission, the Butler Commission (1928), the three Round Table Conferences in 1931–33 in London, as well as discussions leading to the Federation Act of 1935.[51] This meant plenty of paperwork, representation and keen understanding of constitutional matters. Ministers here played a vital role, as they always did when it came to negotiating with the British (in the 1920s, Sir Ali Imam was paid Rs. 1,000 *a day* to present Hyderabad's claim over the territory of Berar). During this period, a notable role was played by Colonel Haksar, the 'scholarly and urbane'[52] minister of Gwalior, who threw his weight behind appointing a barrister of reputation to represent the princely states in the Federation Act discussions. The barrister was to be paid the astounding fee of £60,000, with Haksar himself receiving initial payment of one and a half lakhs (about US$1,500), along with his salary of Rs. 8,000 per month. These figures indicate how high the stakes were. Indeed, the question of federation, India's very own Brexit in the 1930s, revolved around whether the princely states would be able to maintain their rights under paramountcy in independent India. The Butler Commission's pronouncement that the individual treaties signed between the princes and the British were not enough to assure them of a place in independent India killed hopes, but only briefly. Ahead of the Round Table Conference, negotiations between the Congress, the British and the Indian princes involved Haksar allied with his protégé K. M. Panikkar, who had left an academic career at Aligarh University to advise the raja of Kashmir. In *Federal India* (1930), Haksar and Panikkar argued elegantly for the future of the Indian princes in a federation. They also reached out to Sir Mirza Ismail of Mysore and Akbar Hydari of Hyderabad for support. Nonetheless, it was the states' inherent rivalry and suspicion that paralysed these attempts, and, as previously, the larger states were the first to pull out, afraid of what they might lose under the proposed federation.

After the failure of the Round Table Conferences and the inability of the Indian princes to lobby collectively for an Indian federation, Mirza made individual efforts to bring the British to the negotiating table with the Congress. Working with British officials, such as Arthur Lothian and Kenneth Fitze, Mirza made an attempt to reach out to both the Muslim League and the Congress. Gandhi, however, was clear about the impossibility of such a meeting: 'I cannot, I must not trust the British', he wrote, ruling out the princes being granted their kingdoms after independence.[53]

Eventually, however, distrust brought about by the communalisation of politics affected the princes first and foremost. By the early 1940s, these communal forces 'reserved their biggest guns for Mirza Ismail', serving as the Dewan of Jaipur.[54] The Hindu Mahasabha built up enormous pressure on the Maharaja of Jaipur to dismiss Mirza. In Mysore, his able ministership had earned the state a rare compliment from Gandhi, who described it as 'almost ram-rajya'.[55] Mirza himself was admired as an 'ideal Indian' by Abdul Gaffar Khan, a nationalist leader also known as 'frontier Gandhi'. But this was not good enough for the Hindu Mahasabha who saw the employment of a Muslim as dewan in an ancient Hindu kingdom as an opportunity to practise their divisive politics.

The pressure to fire Mirza was one of the very many pressures unleashed on the princely states. By 1946, Jaipur acquiesced and let Mirza go. Sir Abdul Hamid of Kapurthala and Mohammad Sadiq of Jind were fired as well. Datia's Muslim dewan, Khan Bahadur Ainuddin, was turned out, and in Pudukottai in 1947 the people openly stated their dislike for the Dewan Khalifullah and objected to a Muslim administering a 'Tamilian Hindu state'.

If it were not for the ignominy of being dismissed, it was the end of the princely states that eclipsed the dewans altogether. The old Political Department was taken over by a new Indian Ministry of States in 1947, and a new set of men – Indian, Congress and democratically elected – took over. Sardar Vallabhai Patel headed the new department and with his colleagues, V. P. Menon and M. K. Vellodi, took over the tedious correspondence and ultimately the 'merger' of the Indian princely states with independent India. As the states acceded to India, the darbars with their ministers and obsessive protocols gradually disappeared. While the Indian princes like the Nawab of Bhopal sulkily holidayed in Europe or took unexpected Hajj trips, their abandoned dewans languished in India. Sir Abdul Hamid of Kapurthala in 1949 wrote piteously to the Ministry of States about his pension not 'being paid for many months'.[56] The new Mysore Congress-led government embarrassed Mirza by their 'extraordinary and utterly untenable' claims of their inability to pay Mirza his pension, and in 1956, Cubbon House, the Mirza family's home for more than two hundred years, was occupied by the Ministry of Information and Broadcasting, never to be returned.[57]

Not all of the dewans, however, were so completely eclipsed. Quite a few were absorbed into the shiny new Congress-led independent India. Sir V. T. Krishnamachari ended his career as a member of the Finance Commission (1953–60), and K. M. Panikkar became a member of the Indian delegation to the United Nations, though as Mirza wrote privately to a friend, 'Muslims are not wanted by the government for any high posts ... I am now only a distant, disinterested observer.'[58] In the end, the Ministry of States did exactly what their British predecessors had done. Indian ICS officers were despatched as 'administrators' to a host of grumpy princes, such as C. M. Butch to Saurashtra and Ram Babu to Tonk.

Conclusion

Despite being connected intimately to the Indian princes, the dewans did not see themselves as a collective, independent political force. In 1941 the dewans organised the first annual conference of 'dewans'. Meeting every year until 1946, in Lahore, these men tried hard to ignore the collapse of the familiar world they knew so well. They carried on with the serious discussions on food supplies and concerns about the effects of the Second World War on their kingdoms. By 1947, their 'august masters' realised that it was all going to end too soon, and came to terms with the new political realities. But at least the Indian princes were granted the Privy Purse and privileges, which were only discontinued in 1971. The dewans were left out in the cold.

If games are indicative of the social context in which they are played, in the English version of chess, the most powerful piece after the king is the queen. In the South Asian version, it is the *wazir* (minister). Seated firmly beside the king, the wazir cruises across the board, while the king stays put, safe and snug in his castle, presumably free to indulge in royal pastimes. Much like their chess counterparts, ministers in princely India in the late colonial period were afforded unique circumstances which gave them a more legitimate and visible (or prominent) position in Indian princely states than ever before. In the loosening of territorial affiliations, the ministers were freer chess pieces, with the autonomy to move around. This was a task many dewans played splendidly, filling in for their monarchs ably and competently.

Notes

1 See Barbara Ramusack, *The Indian Princes and Their States* (Cambridge: Cambridge University Press, 2008).
2 National Archives of India, New Delhi (hereafter 'NAI'), Foreign and Political Department, Internal B, September 1918, No. 286. In 1918, the British government issued an 'intimation that motor vehicles belonging to Kashmir Darbar when brought into British India will carry a board with the name of the State and the serial number of the car printed on it'.
3 Dane Kennedy, *Decolonisation* (Oxford: Oxford University Press, 2016), p. 50.
4 Shail Mayaram, *Resisting Regimes: Myth, Memory and the Shaping of a Muslim Identity* (New Delhi: Oxford University Press, 1997). The princely states were feudal and autocratic. Even those considered liberal, such as Baroda and Mysore, were slow to reform and relinquish the concentrated authority vested in the rulers, leading to the fatalist argument that they were doomed in a democratic, modern and independent India.
5 The few explorations of the princely states taper off around the making of independent India in 1948. See Ian Copland, *State, Community and Communalism in Princely North India, 1900–1950* (Basingstoke: Palgrave Macmillan, 2005) and

more recently, D. A. Prasanna and K. Sadashiva (eds), *The Princely States and the Making of Modern India* (Manipal: Manipal University Press, 2017).
6   NAI, Ministry of States, File no. 85(14), PR Branch, 1947. The foolish counsel notwithstanding, Bhutto went on to Pakistan to change the course of that country's history and future as well. His son, Zulfikar Ali Bhutto, a firm champion of representative democracy, formed the Pakistan People's Party (PPP) in 1967 and served as Prime Minister (1973–97), changing Pakistan's political trajectory.
7   Ministry of States, File no. 85(14), PR Branch, 1947.
8   Philip Mason, *The Men Who Ruled India* (Rupa, New Delhi, 1992); Terence Creag-Coen, *The Indian Political Service: A Study of Indirect Rule* (Bombay: Allied Publishers, 1971).
9   Other branches included 'Frontier', which included states such as Afghanistan, and the External Branch amounting to states not coterminous with British India.
10 Regulating the princely states, given their sheer number, was quite a lot of work, as the areas allotted to this branch reveal: 'Political matters not specifically relating to the Indian states; employment in Indian states – excluding military employment; claims against ruling princes and chiefs, finances and loans to princes and chiefs, births, death, education, training, marriages, succession, adoptions, installations, abdications, depositions, investitures, powers of ruling princes, nazrana and tribute, famines, floods, mints, currency, coinage, amongst others.' *Guide to the Records in the National Archives of India, Part VIII*, Foreign and Political Department, National Archives of India: New Delhi, 1985, p. 17.
11 Robin Jeffrey, 'The politics of "indirect rule": types of relationship among rulers, ministers and residents in a "native state"', *Journal of Commonwealth & Comparative Politics*, 13 (1975), 262.
12 David Cannadine argues that the Paramountcy lasted as long as it did because the coded world of aristocratic hierarchy was celebrated by both the princes and the British. See David Cannadine, *Ornamentalism: How the British Saw Their Empire* (London: Allen Lane, 2001).
13 Literature on the dewans is limited; they figure most comprehensively and collectively in Ian Copland, *Princes in the Endgame of Empire* (Cambridge: Cambridge University Press, 1997). At least two of them wrote autobiographies. See Sir Mirza Ismail, *My Public Life: Recollections and Reflections* (London: G. Allen & Unwin, 1954); K. M. Panikkar, *An Autobiography* (Madras: Oxford University Press, 1977).
14 NAI, New Delhi, Foreign and Political Department [hereafter F & PD], Internal, 1131, 1–2, 1922.
15 Mayaram, *Resisting Regimes*, p. 69. Although *all* monarchs were aware of their religious identities, which were part of the divine and temporal claims to power, Alwar and Bharatpur most obviously aligned themselves with the emerging national organised Hindu religious organisation, the Hindu Mahasabha. Jai Singh (1882–1937) of Alwar also renamed his streets 'Kushmarg' and 'Raghumarh', in an attempt to recreate Alwar as the ancient Hindu city of Ayodhya, the key site in the epic *Ramayana*.
16 NAI, New Delhi, F & PD, Accounts, 31(4), 1926. This grand plan was to colonise the Masnuds, a tribe to the West to Bahawalpur, and encourage them to occupy vast tracts of unused agricultural land.
17 NAI, F & PD, Political, File no. 104, 1933.
18 Harriet Lynton and Mohini Rajan, *The Days of the Beloved* (Berkeley: University of California Press, 1974).
19 NAI, F & PD, Internal A, Proceedings, File no. 101–4, 1918.
20 F & PD, Deposit, Establishment, File no. 20, July 1918. And, of course, there was. Chajju Ram, CIE, who had done consistently good work as Dewan of the Dhar State was noted for his 'enlightened views and practical ability'. He was made a Diwan Bahadur in 1912, a CIE in 1916 and was in 1918 serving as the Dewan of Datia state.
21 Abida Sultaan, *Memoirs of a Rebel Princess* (Karachi: Oxford University Press, 2004).
22 NAI, New Delhi, F & PD, Political, File no. 164, 1929.

23 NAI, New Delhi, Ministry of States, Political Branch, File no. 17(11), 1949.
24 Copland, *State, Community and Communalism*.
25 F & PD, Political, File no. 114(14), 1926.
26 NAI, New Delhi, Ministry of States, Political, File no. 1–10, 1949.
27 NAI, New Delhi, Political Department, Political Branch, 3(11), Secret, 1946.
28 NAI, New Delhi, Political Department, Political branch, 39(3), Nos 1–12, Secret, 1940.
29 NAI, New Delhi, Political Department, Political Branch, 415 (Secret), 1937.
30 F & PD, 247, Political Branch, 1929.
31 F & PD, Deposit, Establishment Branch, No. 8 1921.
32 Penderel Moon (ed.), *Wavell: The Viceroy's Journal* (Karachi: Oxford University Press, 1998).
33 F & PD, General, Secret, 135, 1922.
34 Political Department, Political Branch, 129, 1945.
35 F & PD, Deposit, Internal, File no. 55, 1920.
36 Mirza, *My Public Life*.
37 Ministry of States, Political Branch, File no. 17(11), 1949. This was not unusual. As the nationalist movement from British India spilt into princely India, there were many popular demands and protests against the excesses of princely rules and the perceived meddling with local power structures. Aiyer was under attack from local groups from the late 1930s, specifically from the 'monied Syrian Christians, angry with the Dewan's patronage of the Nayar caste at their expense'. Copland, *Princes in the Endgame*, p. 162.
38 David A. Johnson, *New Delhi: The Last Imperial* City (New York: Palgrave Macmillan, 2015).
39 F & PD, Internal, File no. 770, 1923.
40 Ramachandra Guha, 'The strange case of Sir C. P. Ramaswamy Iyer', *The Hindu – Sunday Magazine*, 25 May 2008, www.thehindu.com/todays-paper/tp-features/tp-sundaymagazine/The-strange-case-of-Sir-C.P.-Ramaswamy-Iyer/article15401680.ece (accessed 18 February 2019).
41 The term *rais* is another word borrowed from the Urdu language, meaning wealthy and propertied. The allotment of land to dewans *and* some others could have been a way of accommodating wealthy property owners. In the 1930s, quite a few demands to reward large estate owners with 'princely autonomy and privilege' were made. Speculatively, this could have been a way of acknowledging their loyalty during the two world wars.
42 These princely palaces were taken over by the Indian Government after Independence and are presently being used for a variety of governmental purposes. They remain, however, in place, their sense of grandeur perhaps diminished. See Sumanta Bhowmick, *Princely Palaces in New Delhi* (New Delhi: Niyogi Books, 2015).
43 Jessie Burton, *The Miniaturist* (New York: Ecco, 2014).
44 Copland, *State, Community and Communalism*, p. 13.
45 F & PD, Special, File no. 36, 1930.
46 F & PD, Internal, Secret, File no. 36, 1919.
47 F & PD, Political Branch, File no. 183, Secret, 1929.
48 F & PD, Deposit-Internal, File no. 55, 1920.
49 F & PD, Political Branch, 321, 1931.
50 Doris Lessing, *The Sweetest Dream* (London: Harper Perennial, 2001), p. 133.
51 For a gripping, behind-the-scenes narrative on this, see Copland, *Princes in the Endgame*, ch. 4, 'A vision splendid'.
52 Ian Copland, *The Princes of India in the Endgame of Empire, 1917–1947* (Cambridge: Cambridge University Press, 1997), p. 66.
53 Letter from M. K. Gandhi to Mohammad Gaffar Khan, August, 1941, Sir Mirza Ismail Private Papers Collection, Microfilm No. 2, Nehru Memorial Museum and Library, New Delhi, India.
54 Copland, *State, Community and Communalism*, p. 114.

55 As we have seen, the *Ramayana* represented the ideal state, the *Ram-Rajya* (literally, the state of Ram). To Gandhi, ram-rajya with perfect communal harmony was the aim of the growing nationalist movement.
56 GoI, Ministry of States, Relief Branch, 1(2), 1949.
57 Mirza, *My Public Life*.
58 Ministry of States, Hyderabad Branch, 14(1), Secret, 1948.

CHAPTER THREE

Decolonised rulers: rajas, maharajas and others in post-colonial India
Jim Masselos

The winning of independence on 15 August 1947 brought immediate change to South Asia with the subcontinent split into the two rival nation-states of Pakistan and India. It was an ambiguous and difficult time, this confused advent of freedom. In much of what had been British India – in Bombay and Delhi, for instance – there was initially wild celebration and much joy, but in the Punjab, Bengal and parts elsewhere there was unparalleled rioting and mass destruction, not countrywide jubilation.[1] Concurrently, new India's leaders, Prime Minister Jawaharlal Nehru and his cabinet, were already at work restoring order and facing up to the huge challenge of building the nationalist dream of a sovereign and free united nation.

Among the many complex issues that had to be addressed was the critical one of how to handle the princely states and their proud rulers, monarchs who variously sported titles such as *raja, maharaja, rana, rao, maharao, nizam* or *nawab*, or had other honorifics specific to the custom of their territories. What was to be their place in the new order? As primal survivors of India's ruler warrior clans, the princes considered themselves the upholders of all the values associated with rulers and warriors; they were supposed to be (and often were) cultivated, judicious, brave, decisive and chivalrous. Along with their military ethos went lives spent in grandeur: an existence of privilege and luxury played out against the backdrop of magnificent palaces and grand mansions (*haveli*). The princely states were institutions equally appreciated by the new paramount British rulers of the nineteenth century who chose to view them in Orientalist terms and were delighted by, even if sometimes critical of, what they encountered. Thus, Lady Minto, wife of the fourth Earl of Minto, Viceroy of India from 1905 to 1910, was more than impressed on a visit to Alwar by what she considered was 'an unbelievable pageant of Eastern magnificence'.[2] It was not only Indian princes, however, who appreciated pageantry. Pageants were a regular feature of life under the British raj with three great Delhi Darbars (in 1877, 1903 and 1911) providing the grandest of all displays of pomp. Such displays were carried out on space that had once belonged to the great Mughals, where older spectacle was now matched or even surpassed by the foreigner's ostentation.[3] It was nevertheless display that drew on the Indian princes and their court practice for inspiration and more often than not relied on the princes' subordinate participation to establish the gravitas of official occasion and ceremonial.

As for the rulers themselves, each kingdom had its own story symbolised in lineages that folded back over the centuries. Some lineages asserted claims to a far distant past. Most impressive was the Guhilot/Sisodia dynasty that ruled over Udaipur, in Rajasthan, which claimed to go back at least to the eighth century, and in doing so vied with the Japanese royal family as the world's oldest hereditary monarchy.[4]

Proud the princes may have been, but their impressive lineages did not protect them from falling under British control during the course of the nineteenth century. Thereafter and through to independence in 1947, the princes functioned under British suzerainty, and being under indirect British rule meant that they could not engage in foreign relations or other external matters. In theory, the princes were internally autonomous, each administering his own state's affairs, though subject to the 'advice' and guidance of a British official, the Resident or Agent, who was usually stationed in the capital of the princely state or nearby, clearly and conveniently accessible. More often than not, he functioned as a de facto governor, though in practice, while subject to the Resident's advisory role, some maharajas exercised quasi-independent administrative functions and issued their own coinage and postage stamps, ran state railways, collected revenues and carried out other functions of governance.

A Chamber of Princes operated as a consultative chamber from 1921 to 1947, but it had only a limited function as a meeting point for the leading royal houses, though there was some suggestion it might form the basis for a future hereditary chamber of parliament and become the equivalent of what elsewhere was an upper house, a Senate or a House of Lords. By 1947 the Chamber encompassed 108 larger royal houses whose rulers represented themselves and spoke on their behalf in the Chamber. As well, the smaller kingdoms had as representatives twelve princes delegated to speak for 127 rulers of smaller territories.[5] A similar division had been evident in the composition of the London Round Table Conferences debating the future of India in the early 1930s, where one or two princes represented some 250 others.[6]

However, the Chamber of Princes did not become an upper house in an independent India. The logic of events and the impact of the Second World War took the princes in other directions. From the mid-1940s, the war seemed to be heading to a favourable conclusion for the Allies and presented a possibility that independence was likely to come soon. Some accommodation would need to be brokered with the princes in the changed *post bellum* order that seemed increasingly inevitable. It was not immediately obvious, however, what their place would be in the new nation and in a democratically elected parliament. That, in turn, depended on what policies the other actors in the endplay of empire would pursue. By 1947 it was clear that the Indian National Congress wanted the princely states to be part of the new nation – so that consequentially, over time, they would likely lose their separate identities and be absorbed into independent India. Such a policy would prevent India from becoming a balkanised moth-eaten entity of numerous independent kingdoms of varying sizes, something alien to the Congress ideal of a unified nation. The task of implementing party policy and persuading around 562 kingdoms[7] to join a unitary India before independence was taken up by the deputy prime minister, Sardar Patel, the most powerful and esteemed leader in the nation after Prime Minister Jawaharlal Nehru and Mahatma Gandhi. By his side was the highly capable and brilliant bureaucrat V. P. Menon, who had the role of dealing with the detail and the paperwork required of each prince in acceding to India.[8] Menon's account of what he saw and did would seem necessarily to privilege his own viewpoint on the accessions, but the signatures he managed to obtain in the limited time available represent a distinctive achievement. Also influential in the hectic days and hours before India's assumption of independence was the charismatic viceroy, Lord (Louis) Mountbatten, whose task it was to transfer power to the new dominion. Mountbatten's presence in the few months prior to the transfer of power added to the pressure on wavering and hesitant rulers and doubtless influenced their decision-making. The task was not easy. Mountbatten later commented, albeit perhaps self-servingly, on what he faced after he first formally met the princes, around 3 June 1947:

> Nothing had been said to me in London to prepare me for the gravity and magnitude of the problem of the States. I had been given no inkling that this was going to be [an issue] as hard, if not harder, to solve as that of British India.[9]

The states dramatically differed from one another in terms of size – some had enormous territories while others controlled tiny estates. They had different genealogies, different family traditions, varied social compositions and economies and separate notions of governance.

Given the complexity, it would thus not be easy to persuade the princes to accede to the new India and, what's more, to get them to do so quickly. Nor could the states be ignored – they represented a significant portion of the subcontinent, covering 48 per cent of the territory of pre-independent India and some 28 per cent of the population of the undivided subcontinent.[10]

Mountbatten announced, on 25 July 1947 in the Chamber of Princes, what had to happen in the three weeks before Independence on 15 August, and offered little joy to the princes with regard to the new order coming into being. Each ruler, no matter how small or important his kingdom, would have to sign a separate document of accession to either Pakistan or India and give up defence, foreign relations and communications (including transportation); a ruler was to retain his other roles and privileges. For most of the princes, the choice was limited given that the principle of contiguity would operate, and each state would join the nation in whose territorial space it was geographically located. Some ten states were in Pakistani space and would eventually formally accede to Pakistan, but not immediately – they had not signed the accession document by 14/15 August when independence came to the two new nations. It was not until the end of the 1940s and later that princes such as the rulers of Bahawalpur and Khairpur ceded their territories to the Pakistani central government; Dir held out until 1969, and Hunza and Nagar until 1973.[11]

Mountbatten's proposals created particular issues for Kashmir with its Hindu ruler, Muslim majority population and landlocked position. Nor did they suit Junagadh and Hyderabad, states also with Muslim rulers and Hindu majorities. The ruler of Junagadh denied the applicability of the principle of territorial contiguity, initially held out against joining India and refused to link his realm with small neighbouring states in western India. The Nizam of Hyderabad similarly held out for a separate state in the centre of India. The three rulers resisted the pressures and tried to retain a separate identity for their states. Their havering came to an end when the new government of India, under orders from Sardar Patel, mounted 'police actions' which forced first Junagadh and then Hyderabad to join India. The 'police actions' began on 13 September 1948 when Indian troops moved into Hyderabad; there was violence and killings, and four days later the Nizam capitulated and joined the Indian Union.[12]

The problem of Kashmir was not easy to resolve at the time and has continued to be contentious, especially because of the different religion of the maharaja and most of his subjects. Adding to the social complexity was the fact that Kashmir was contiguous with both Pakistan and India. The maharaja played a complicated game in 1947 in negotiating with the various players but the logic of what was happening and the speed of events forced him to accede to India, though under certain provisos. The decision was controversial and has continued to have long-lasting repercussions on relations between the players on the subcontinent. They remain the object of extensive debate and argument over the matter, reaching the United Nations; more drastically, India and Pakistan went to war over the issue in 1948 and 1965. There is an agreed 'line of control' between the opposing armies but from time to time hostilities along the line of control have gone from border skirmishing to virtual warfare.

Meanwhile, nation-building continued. Under the instruments of accession, the princes' states were integrated into India, but the rulers retained their royal titles. They were also accorded privy purses, payments of a stipend that was determined according to their importance. The purses were to total 8.5 per cent of a kingdom's annual revenues. Amounts ranged from as little as Rs. 5,000 p.a. for the smallest principalities to above Rs. 1,000,000 each for the six most important kingdoms. Even these amounts were to be progressively reduced, usually when heirs succeeded to the throne – Hyderabad, for instance, saw its privy purse diminish over time from Rs. 4,285,714 to Rs. 2,000,000.[13] In return for the privy purses, the rulers gave up property considered to belong to the state rather than to the family lineage, including assets such as palaces, land, museums, buildings, aircraft, railways, jewellery and cash. An estimate put the total value of public holdings transferred from the princes to the new Indian Union to be around 77 crores (or Rs. 770,000,000).[14] The princes nevertheless retained property and treasure deemed to be private and to belong to their families rather than to the kingdom.[15]

Decolonisation, as far as the princes were concerned, was somewhat problematic. Some princes were committed nationalists and welcomed the departure of the British and the creation of a new independent nation. Most rulers, however, were mortified by the loss of their positions and the ending of their dynastic powers. Initially, they retained a modicum of respect for their lineages. Although the 1947 accessions integrated the princely states into India and took over the princes' control of various aspects of internal government, they retained positions not all that different from what they had enjoyed under British suzerainty. The situation changed dramatically in 1949, however, when the Congress Party government decided to merge the states more fully into a refurbished Indian administrative structure. The consequence was that the princes would be deprived of their separate royal status as well as their enjoyment of the quasi-autonomous structure which they had still, at least partly, continued to enjoy after

Independence. Thus, in dissolving the former princely territories, the government began giving India a new appearance. Sardar Patel, in the Constituent Assembly, underscored the importance of what had happened as being nothing less than a 'bloodless revolution which has affected the destinies of millions of our people'.[16] Seventy years later, the measure retains its critical importance in setting up new parameters of change for India.

As for the princes, they were left with nominal titles and privy purses that would diminish over time. Even with their gradual reduction, the privy purses came under attack. In 1963, for instance, the controlling body within the Congress government, the All India Congress Committee (AICC), wanted to abolish the purses, but Prime Minister Nehru opposed the suggestion on the grounds that the Rs. 50 million paid to the princes would progressively diminish as successor rajas received lesser amounts. He also saw the matter as one of principle for the government since the government's word in 1947 to provide privy purses was at stake.[17] His daughter, Indira Gandhi, was less principled when she became prime minister, and in 1969 sought the abolition of the purses and indeed all princely privileges. She was nevertheless unable to get the required two-thirds majority in parliament for the measure to pass. In 1971, after a landslide electoral victory, Mrs Gandhi again moved parliament to amend the constitution, abolish the privy purses and cease all recognition that had been granted to 'Rulers of Indian States'.[18] By this measure, she effectively planned to abolish all those 'feudal' privileges that had surrounded the princes. This time she had the requisite majority in the two houses of parliament for the constitutional amendment to be carried. She later justified the action both in terms of her left-wing sympathies and her anti-colonial stance. In the late 1970s she explained:

> It was a very sensitive question. The princes had been on the side of the British. Many of them had been put there by the British in place of the former rulers. Some of them were not even the actual persons entitled to the benefits. I think it was a good thing that Sardar Patel came to an agreement with them at the time of independence and that there was no bloodshed. I don't believe for a moment that they would have fought. Had they done so, they would have been pulled to pieces by the people. What we were giving them [the princes] as privy purses was negligible ... But we realized that it was becoming more and more of a remnant of old situations and conditions; and our Party held strong views. That is why it became necessary to put an end to that system. What irritated people most was not the privy purse, but the rest of it, the fact that princes didn't pay water and electricity rates. The poor man had to pay but the

princes did not. They also had free medical treatment. Different states had different concessions and many of these small privileges were an irritant to the common man.[19]

It seemed as if an end had come to the long lines of India's hereditary rulers with the final stage in the decolonisation of the subcontinent brought about by Indian agency, and a democratically elected government at that. Technically, the princes were shorn of their surviving privileges and were no longer to use their regal honorifics and titles. They were henceforth commoners, to be addressed as plain Mr or Mrs Singh in a society whose dominant political rhetoric was now to be egalitarian in character. The privy purse legislation implicitly or even explicitly opposed the value systems that had been represented and utilised over the centuries by India's royals and that had provided the base on which their kingdoms rested.

Yet not all the new commoners – the former princes – found themselves reduced to anonymous invisibility. They were not necessarily irrelevant, but found a place in the new nation, as was demonstrated when they were inducted into positions in the foreign service of the Ministry of External Affairs. Thus the Maharao of Kutch was appointed ambassador in London, Norway and Chile, and Patiala became a member of various Indian delegations to the United Nations, UNESCO and other bodies, and later took up the ambassadorship in Rome in 1965.[20] The Raja of Sarila was another former prince who enjoyed a long span of public service in the Foreign Office from 1948 to 1985.

Despite Mrs Gandhi's reading of the attitudes of the rulers' former subjects, it was not at all a foregone conclusion that the princes could be wiped so easily from their memories or removed from their emotions or allegiances. An indication of the regard ex-subjects held was provided when princes stood for Lok Sabha (the Indian parliament) or in other elections. On these occasions the princes explicitly posed the symbolism of their lineages against the mechanisms and values presented by the new modern state and its refashioned democratic structures.

The results were mixed. In 1967, for instance, the Maharaja of Patiala won handsomely on an independent ticket in a contest for the Punjab legislature. On the other hand, the Nawab of Pataudi, a celebrated cricketer, contested a seat in Haryana in the 1971 elections on an anti-Congress ticket and in protest against the loss of his Rs. 48,000 privy purse. He had hoped to capitalise on his cricketing reputation as much as on what popularity he would garner from his regal role. He was disastrously unsuccessful and scored less than 5 per cent of the vote in his electorate. Twenty years later, Pataudi had become reconciled with the Gandhi family and had developed close ties with Rajiv Gandhi, prompting him to contest elections on a Congress ticket, though he did not win that vote either.[21] He may have been just unlucky or perhaps his principality was too small to give him numerical electoral security; there were not enough former subjects in the electorate to constitute an effective vote bank whatever his appeal as a test cricketer or whatever the charisma of his wife, the actor Sharmila Tagore. Their son, Saif Ali Khan, nevertheless had star quality because of his ancestry and later became a leading Bollywood actor, followed into acting in due course by his son and daughter.[22]

Other royals who decided to chance their luck on the hustings did better. Dr Karni Singh, maharaja of the prestigious Rajasthani desert kingdom of Bikaner, was elected five consecutive times to the Lok Sabha – but as an independent. Then there was beautiful and charismatic Gayatri Devi, Maharani of Jaipur, who joined the right-wing and pro-capitalist Swatranta Party and won record landslide victories in her electorate in 1967 and 1971. She became a strong opponent of the prime minister, Mrs Gandhi, who had her imprisoned in 1975 during the Emergency. Another maharani, Vijaya Raje Scindia, the wife of the ruler of Gwalior, began her political career in 1962 on a Congress ticket, which she relinquished after five years to represent the right-wing Jan Sangh party, another opposition party that also led to her being jailed as an opponent of Indira Gandhi during the Emergency.

Over the following years, the place of the princes in the political life of the country remained complex and problematic. The next generation of royals faced much the same issues their families had faced before them: what their place was to be in an officially egalitarian society. In 2008, for instance, a significant number of royals, wives as well as husbands, decided to stand in elections.[23] It would seem that the princes still retained a significant hold over the loyalties and allegiances of their erstwhile subjects. While some ex-rulers had links with the Congress Party, other royals remained hostile and joined opposition parties.

The process of decolonisation thus placed the princes in an ambiguous position in which they sought to maintain their positions through alternative avenues enabled by the new democratic structures of governance. But the results of elections at state and national levels indicated there was no clear consequence, no unambiguous reading of the impact of state integration: votes went both to some princes and against others. The long-term impact of decolonisation on the princes in this sense was still not clear-cut.

While it was harder for the first generation of princes in independent India to adjust to egalitarian, democratised living, it would seem to have been easier for their children. Some were able to enter the parliamentary arena and so ensure they survived as political figures along with their regal ethos. An early 1980s set of interviews – some eighteen years after the abolition of privy purses – illustrates how the royals had adjusted to their situation and the new circumstances they faced. Rajmata Vijaya Raje Scindia, for instance, commented: 'Ruler or not, you're accountable to the people', while another prince, the erstwhile ruler of Wankaner, was more reflective: 'The fact that we're princes is immaterial now', adding that what was important was their 'ability to stand up to time. Princes may slowly disappear, but the concept of dynasty stays'. An unnamed princess completed the interview: 'Dynasties never went out of fashion in India. So, what's changed? Everything and nothing.'[24]

Not all the former rulers indulged in politics or charitable work, and many occupied themselves trying to maintain their lifestyles and finances even after the abolition of princely privileges. They explored possible avenues to enable them to survive adequately, though any change in the way in which they lived was difficult given that the princes had led sheltered lives before Independence and wanted to continue to do so afterwards. For most, their former lives had not privileged commercial ventures or commercial values. As one prince commented:

> Dealing in money for the princes has been the hardest reality to accept. The commercial instinct was never particularly finely honed among ruling families – in fact it was plainly despised. Most of the princes had no business acumen ... Rulers were expected to be above money.[25]

Some former princes, like the maharajas of Baroda and Gwalior, successfully challenged prevailing attitudes. They ventured into commerce and built up significant investments in cotton mills located in their former territories. They did well and profited sufficiently to cope with the changed circumstances of the post-colonial years.

Other princes looked elsewhere for funds to support themselves and their lifestyles but were not necessarily particularly adept at handling finances or at developing and managing a money stream. Some chose to turn possessions into cash or income-earning assets. During the first decades of Indian rule a steady stream of artefacts and antiques thus flowed, presumably mainly from princely treasuries, out of India and onto world art markets. That trade was curbed in 1972 with the passing of the Antiquities and Art Treasures Act but was not eliminated. However, what the princes earlier had gained from the (possibly illegal) sale of precious objects could have provided only temporary and limited financial relief of their monetary troubles.

There were, however, other assets that the princes could access – those retained in their possession notably included royal buildings, such as palaces, lodges and outhouses. In the early 1970s these were sprawling and often neglected structures, many decrepit, decaying and urgently in need of restoration. Some maharajas confronted the mammoth task of repair skilfully and managed to turn palaces into museums and the grandest of hotels that became magnets to the affluent tourists who had begun flooding into India. Adding immensely to the attractiveness of princely palaces for foreign tourists was the visit of Jacqueline Kennedy, the US President's wife, to Jaipur in March 1962. Her visit was highly publicised and did much to put Jaipur and (by extension) other Rajasthani sites on international tourist's itineraries.

In restoring the palaces and turning them into heritage structures, the princes were privileging a past that was gone. It was this constructed and created past that had attracted tourists previously and it drew on much the same Orientalist imagery as had obsessed the nineteenth-century British imagination; it appealed to enthusiastic travellers more than satisfied by the grandeurs they encountered. In the twentieth century and up to the present, the restored palace hotels purveyed ideas of Oriental splendour and luxury as much as they carried notions of the codes of warrior rulers and the exotic grandeur of their reigns.[26] Much could be conveyed through the interior of the palaces and the way they became objects for refurbishment. What may once have been a darbar hall, a space for regal ceremonial, could become a bar or dining hall replete with regal memorabilia – so that the demands of the tourist became the prime concern.

To passing travellers, the princes epitomised the warrior values written up in guide books, and some rajas may well have played royal roles deliberately for the tourists staying in their hotels. But they also of necessity had to learn to cope with managing hotels and the staff employed in them, many of whom were retainers from former days. The current ruler of Udaipur, for instance, studied hotel management in the United States in the 1960s before returning home to take over the management of world-class landmark hotels, including the beautiful Lake Palace Hotel. His son, in turn, chose to be equally studious, though it was in Australia at a hospitality college in the Blue Mountains where he learned the hospitality trade.[27]

While the princes were operating within the confines of a post-colonial nation and were bound within its structures of governance, they were also operating within the demands of the value systems that attached to the princely states. Critical in the 1950s and 1960s was the way in which an emotional sense of approval, a pleasing attitude to the princes, was being created, not only within India but outside it. Large exhibitions in the major European and American museums devoted to the arts and crafts that the princes had once patronised further promoted princely India as a popular tourist destination and increased understanding of its cultural achievements.[28]

Back in India, a generalised sense of goodwill towards the princes had been spread widely through the impact of a public relations exercise. It centred around a mascot designed for Air India in 1946 by Bobby Kooka, the commercial director of Air India, and Umesh Rao, an artist with the advertising agency J. Walter Thompson. They had been working on a design for the cover of a notepad to be given to passengers, but a 'friendly and slightly mischievous looking maharaja'[29] took over their creative brainstorming. It was not long before the maharaja rose in the popularity stakes and became a beloved symbol of the airline (see Figures 3.1 and 3.2), remaining its mascot even after

Figure 3.1 Painted plaster of Paris figurine of a maharaja produced by Air India as a gift for passengers, c. 1970s–1980s

Figure 3.2 Printed set of Air India playing cards featuring a maharaja, c. 1970s–1980s

the airline was nationalised in 1953. Air India's maharaja, however, is an ambiguous figure, as Kooka suggested:

> We call him a Maharajah for want of a better description. But his blood isn't blue. He may look like royalty, but he isn't royal ... The Maharajah began merely as a rich Indian potentate, symbolizing graciousness and high living. And somewhere along the line his creators gave him a distinctive personality: his outsized moustache, the striped turban and his aquiline nose.[30]

Readings of what the mascot represented varied. Another commentator saw an underlying relationship between the princes and Air India's maharaja, one that served tourist interests with its witty insouciance but whose charm also aroused affection and widespread attachment:

> In my view, the mascot served its purpose during a certain period of time. India was perceived as the land of maharajahs for many years even after independence. Foreigners were fascinated by the palaces and the mystique associated with our royalty. While that is still a part of India's many attractions, I feel it is not the most dominant one. India has moved on and so has dominant perceptions about India among foreigners. Also, it is up to us to have a cohesive, single-minded messaging about brand India.[31]

The ambivalence inherent in the maharaja image surfaced at various times in sophisticated discussions throughout the country over just what was the message conveyed by the maharaja mascot. As one observer noted, the mascot 'was *about making the customer feel like royalty*. He isn't royal himself and hence took many avatars in the marketing communication'.[32] Air India today describes the company's maharaja figure as 'a world figure. He can be a lover boy in Paris, a sumo wrestler in Tokyo, a pavement artist, a red Indian, a monk ... he can effortlessly flirt with the beauties of the world. And most importantly, he can get away with it all. Simply because he is the Maharajah!'[33]

Just who was represented in these cartoon-like images and what they should be representing was raised in June 2014 when the then-new prime minister, Narendra Modi, suggested during a visit to the aviation ministry that the ordinary man, the *aam aadmi*, should replace the former mascot. The result was a young man, sporting spiked hair and a large moustache, and wearing jeans, cross-trainers and shoulder bag. He had none of the gentleness and self-deprecating humour that had marked his predecessor, nor the innocence. The change was immediately disliked, with tweets suggesting he looked like a tout or lout or a 'wannabe' (among other more colourful epithets).

The new version did not feature on the 2019 Air India home page and instead Air India has returned to earlier depictions of the maharaja.

He is a little more slick and mechanical but seems much as he had been before – replete with turban, handlebar moustache, formal Indian dress (sherwani), and with his typical wry sense of humour still much evident. There were also slogans on the home page which implicitly explained how the logo was to be understood. One slogan is simply 'Fly Like a Maharajah', a simple phrase suggestive of a bundle of pleasant attributes: safety, comfort, particularity, elegance, perhaps, and convenience. Another slogan is patriotic: 'Air India ... Truly Indian', and asserts notions of quality and service as well as pride in the nation. Both slogans extrapolated the maharaja as a symbol and as an expression of the national imaginary, but they also had important practical financial implications, given the maharaja's track record in advertising and in the promotion of international travel for Indian and foreign travellers alike. The maharaja somehow has the ability to invite affection and appeals not only to potential and former passengers but also those who may never fly with the airline, but who delight in the maharaja's connection with India.

The cartoons are characterised by their wry humour, their underlying sense of goodwill and their fondness for the ex-rulers. The Air India maharaja thus had a surprisingly extensive impact. He featured widely on posters and billboards throughout the country where his doings sparked many a discussion in teashops, coffee houses, bus stops and the like. In this sense, the cartoons transcended their ostensible primary role as advertising logos and had a cumulative effect that went beyond specific campaigns. The Air India maharaja brought a touch of humour – a humouresque addition – to wide national concerns but did not challenge or threaten the new order's status quo, far less did it query existing structures.

The maharaja as depicted on the posters had a memorable persona and a distinctive presence. Not only was he instantly recognisable, but he looked both likeable and trustworthy. He displayed features suited to an international travel company as well as being important for a government concerned with establishing a national presence. In this sense, he presented both as a domestic icon and an internationally recognisable logo – a writ that has had an extensive shelf life.

The ex-maharajas, the former ruling princes, have not had as untroubled an existence as the cartoon representations might suggest. Despite individual painful experiences and difficulties, the maharajas survived the processes of decolonisation in the 1940s and the reforms of the 1970s. Many retained much of the popularity, affection and loyalty that had been theirs when they had reigned. Individually and severally they survived in the new democracy with its more egalitarian ethos. They weathered disagreements with various governments and adapted to parliamentary democracy. In becoming skilled in working within the new structures of power, many princes benefited from the endeavours of the new nation. They gained from tourism, profiting as once little-known areas transmuted into enclaves of prosperity thanks to tourists who patronised royal palaces turned into luxury hotels. Some indeed retained or built up important positions in the public life of the country, including those who entered republican politics and others who found their place in the world of business. The process of accommodating to an independent and republican India was not limited to ex-royalty. But the royals, like other groups in society, had to find their own paths and their own places in the new nation.

Notes

1 See my '"The magic touch of being free": The rituals of independence on 15 August', in Jim Masselos, *The City in Action: Bombay Struggles for Power* (Delhi: Oxford University Press, 2007), pp. 321–37.
2 Cited by Ian Copland in Soumya Jain, 'India's historical luxury fables', in Glyn Atwal and Soumya Jain (eds), *The Luxury Market in India: Maharajas to Masses* (London: Palgrave Macmillan, 2012), p. 18. The Orientalist view of Rajasthan of course derived from James Tod's *Annals and Antiquities of Rajasthan, or The Central and Western Rajput States of India* and was published in London between 1829 and 1832. For an extensive analysis of the transition to independence with regard to the princes, see Ian Copland, *The Princes of India in the Endgame of Empire, 1917–1947* (Cambridge: Cambridge University Press, 1997).
3 For the Delhi Darbars, see my 'The Great Durbar crowds: the participant audience', in Julie F. Codell (ed.), *Power and Resistance: The Delhi Coronation Durbars* (Delhi: Mapin Publishing, 2012), pp. 176–203.
4 For Japan, see Caitlin Dewey and Max Fisher, 'Meet the world's other 25 royal families', *The Washington Post*, 22 July 2013 at www.washingtonpost.com/news/worldviews/wp/2013/07/22/meet-the-worlds-other-25-royal-families (accessed 20 March 2019); and 'The Economist explains, Why is the Japanese monarchy under threat?', *The Economist*, 2 June 2017, https://www.economist.com/the-economist-explains/2017/06/02/why-is-the-japanese-monarchy-under-threat (accessed 1 November 2019). For the Udaipur lineages, see www.historyfiles.co.uk/KingListsFarEast/IndiaRajputanaMewar.htm (accessed 20 March 2019).
5 The figures come from Philip Ziegler, *Mountbatten: The Official Biography* (London: Fontana, 1985), p. 404.
6 The Raja of Sarila, in his memoir, notes that Viceroy Irwin selected one or two princes to represent 250 princes at the Round Table Conferences in London at the beginning of the 1930s. See Narendra Singh Sarila, *Once a Prince of Sarila: Of Palaces and Tiger Hunts, of Nehrus and Mountbattens* (London: I. B. Tauris, 2008), p. 24.
7 Different sources give different figures for the number of ruling princes. For instance, Ziegler's 'official' biography of Mountbatten has a total of 565 (p. 494), while Copland gives 552 states that acceded to India (p. 263). Elsewhere Copland refers to '600-odd' princes (p. 269). In the extensive literature on Independence, various totals appear in the texts but none seems definitive. In some instances, the variation seems to depend on whether the states that sided with Pakistan are included in the count.
8 V. P. Menon, *The Story of the Integration of the Indian States* (London: Orient Longmans Green and Co., 1961).

9   *Report on the Last Viceroyalty*, cited in H. V. Hodson. *The Great Divide: Britain – India – Pakistan* (London: Hutchinson, 1969), p. 357.
10 The figures come from Arvind P. Datar, 'Who betrayed Sardar Patel?', *The Hindu*, 19 November 2013, www.thehindu.com/todays-paper/tp-opinion/who-betrayed-sardar-patel/article5366083.ece (accessed 22 March 2019).
11 Yaqoob Khan Bangash, *A Princely Affair: The Accession and Integration of the Princely States of Pakistan, 1947–1955* (Karachi: Oxford University Press, 2015), pp. 144, 153 *et seq*.
12 John Zubrzycki, *The Last Nizam: An Indian Prince in the Australian Outback* (Sydney: Pan Macmillan, 2006), ch. 8.
13 Jain, 'India's historical luxury fables', p. 19.
14 Datar, 'Who betrayed Sardar Patel?', p. 2. One British pound at Independence in 1947 was valued at Rs. 13.37 and one US dollar equalled Rs. 4.16. See www.quora.com (accessed 25 March 2019).
15 Datar, 'Who betrayed Sardar Patel?'.
16 Speech of 12 October 1949, quoted in Datar, 'Who betrayed Sardar Patel?'.
17 His general attitude to such matters of reliability and commitment is summed up in his letter, on a different subject, to India's High Commissioner in London on 3 April 1955: 'For the Government to break its own contract would be bad. Governments do not do this kind of thing.' As quoted in Nayantara Sahgal, *Indira Gandhi: Her Road to Power* (New York: Frederick Unger, 1978 and 1982), p. 59. A similar statement by Nehru in regard to the matter of privy purses appears in a letter to B. Ramakrishna Rao, dated 14 March 1953: 'There is such a thing as a Government's word and a Government's honour', quoted in Sarvepalli Gopal, *Jawaharlal Nehru: A Biography*, Vol. 2: *1947–1956* (Delhi: Oxford University Press, 1979), p. 79.
18 The Constitution (Twenty-Sixth Amendment) Act, 1971, www.constitution.org/cons/india/tamnd26.htm (accessed 17 November 2017).
19 Indira Gandhi, *My Truth* (New York: Grove Press, 1982), p. 147.
20 For Patiala, see www.sikhiwiki.org/index.php/Lieutenant_General_Maharaja_Yadavinder_Singh (accessed 18 April 2019).
21 Rasheed Kidwai, 'Twice he fought political battles against betrayals', *The Telegraph*, 23 September 2011, www.telegraphindia.com/india/twice-he-fought-political-battles-against-betrayals/cid/346372 (accessed 18 April 2019).
22 Mohnish Singh, '7 Bollywood celebrities who hail from royal families', Critics Union, 5 January 2019, https://criticsunion.com/2019/01/05/7-bollywood-celebrities-hail-royal-families/ (accessed 6 March 2019).
23 For a listing of some of them, see Rituraj Tiwari, 'Royal blood to prove dominance in election fray in Rajasthan', *The Economic Times*, 19 November 2008, https://economictimes.indiatimes.com/news/politics-and-nation/royal-blood-to-prove-dominance-in-election-fray-in-rajasthan/articleshow/3729989.cms (accessed 4 December 2017); and 'Post Independent India: princes in electoral politics', Self Study History, https://selfstudyhistory.com/2015/01/17/post-independent-india-princes-in-electoral-politics/ (accessed 4 November 2019).
24 Quoted in 'Royal families: the way we were', *India Today*, 31 May 1983, http://indiatoday.intoday.in/story/scions-of-erstwhile-indian-ruling-elite-get-a-hold-of-their-double-standard-lives/1/371649.html (accessed 18 April 2019).
25 Jaideep Singh, former maharaja of Baria and Congress MP, in conversation with Sunil Sethi, 'Royal families: the way we were', *India Today*, 31 May 1983 at http://indiatoday.intoday.in/story/scions-of-erstwhile-indian-ruling-elite-get-a-hold-of-their-double-standard-lives/1/371649.html (accessed 18 April 2019).
26 See Carol E. Henderson and Maxine Weisgrau (eds), *Raj Rhapsodies: Tourism, Heritage and the Seduction of History* (Aldershot: Ashgate, 2007).
27 See [Steve Meacham], 'Waiter, waiter there's an heir in my soup', *Sydney Morning Herald*, 7 June 2005, www.smh.com.au/national/waiter-waiter-theres-an-heir-in-my-soup-20050607-gdlgx5.html (accessed 18 April 2019).
28 See, among many catalogues of collections and theme-oriented exhibitions, Rosemary Crill and Kapil Jariwala (eds), *The Indian Portrait 1560–1860* (London:

National Portrait Gallery, 2010); Ramesh Chandra Sharma, Kamal Giri and Anjan Chakraverty, *Indian Art Treasures. Suresh Neotia Collection* (Delhi: Mosaic Books, 2006).
29 Ram Jethmalani, 'The dying Maharaja's last sigh', *Sunday Guardian*, 15 January 2012, www.sunday-guardian.com/analysis/the-dying-maharajas-last-sigh (accessed 18 April 2019).
30 'The Air India brand', Air India, www.airindia.in/the-air-india-brand.htm (accessed 21 May 2019).
31 'Of logos, mascots, Air India and brand preference', bhatnaturally, 18 January 2015, www.bhatnaturally.com/of-logos-mascots-air-india-and-brand-preference (accessed 18 April 2019).
32 Quoted in *ibid*.
33 See www.airindia.in (accessed 21 May 2019).

CHAPTER FOUR

The Himalayan kingdoms, British colonialism and indigenous monarchs after the end of empire
Robert Aldrich

On 25 November 1907, John Claude White – who spent thirty-two years as a British colonial official in the Himalayan region – set out from Gangtok, where he was posted as Political Officer in the princely state of Sikkim, for Punakha, in the neighbouring country of Bhutan.[1] His mission was to represent the British government at the installation of Ugyen Wangchuck, the *penlop* (governor) of the region of Tongsa, as first hereditary *gyalpo* of Bhutan – a title that the British understood as 'maharaja', the Bhutanese later as 'king'. White had met Ugyen in 1904, when Bhutan had provided assistance to the British during their invasion of Tibet, and White had been sent to Bhutan the following year to invest Ugyen as a Knight Commander of the Order of the Indian Empire (KCIE). For the 1907 mission, White was accompanied by the Assistant Political Officer, an intelligence officer, a consular official, an army captain, an escort of twenty-five soldiers from the 62nd Punjabi Regiment, a hospital assistant and what he terms the 'usual following' of servants and bearers (in charge of 264 mule- and pony-loads of baggage), as well as three pipers and two drummers. The party took two weeks to reach their destination, making their way through forests of larch and pine, up and down mountain slopes, through narrow passes and across perilous bamboo bridges, battling a 'veritable hurricane' of wind and temperatures that plunged lower than 30 degrees below zero.[2]

The enthronement of the new maharaja took place in the Punakha *dzong*, a fortress-monastery, painted in the white, madder red and gold characteristic of Bhutan. White described the ceremony in his engaging memoir (which, predictably, expresses the perspectives of a convinced imperialist of the late Edwardian age, and has been branded 'self-serving'[3]) and, as he was also an avid photographer, in pictures. A thousand people crowded into the hall, decorated with multi-coloured Buddhist images and hanging streamers and altar tables piled with offerings, as yak-butter lamps flickered and fragrant incense burned. Three thrones were erected: one for the maharaja, a second for the Buddhist patriarch of Bhutan, and, at a lower level, one for White. A long line of officials bowed and presented ceremonial gifts to Ugyen, clad in silk robes and wearing his KCIE decoration, as well as a crown surmounted by a raven, Bhutan's guardian deity. An official read a declaration stating that all of the local authorities, 'having discussed and unanimously agreed to elect Sir Ugyen Wangchuck, Tongsa Penlop, the Prime Minister of Bhutan, as Hereditary Maharaja of this State, have installed him, in open Durbar, on the golden throne'. The patriarch affixed his vermilion seal, and fifty-odd other officials their black seals.

White made a congratulatory oration, speaking of Ugyen's 'integrity, uprightness and firmness of character': 'his accession to the Maharajahship is not only a gain to Bhutan, but is of great advantage to the British government, who will henceforth have a settled Government, with a man of strong character at its head, to negotiate with'. That evening, White hosted a dinner for the maharaja, his court and British officers. He stayed on in Punakha for some days, participating in the first session of the maharaja's council and proffering advice on education, trade, roads and tea cultivation. Before taking his leave, White took photos of the new monarch. In one relaxed image, the ruler sits with the British envoys on rugs draped over rocks; in another, wearing an ordinary robe (*gho*), he stands beaming on the steps of a house, surrounded by family members; in yet another, he looks more regal than paternal, posed alone, wearing his KCIE collar, a breast badge and a ceremonial shoulder scarf (though he remains barefoot) (Figure 4.1).

White concluded his speech at the installation ceremony directly addressing the monarch: 'May your descendants be equally worthy to succeed you for many generations to come.' His prediction came true, and Ugyen's great-great-grandson, Jigme Khesar Namgyel Wangchuck, now reigns as the fifth 'Druk Gyalpo', the King of the 'Land of the Thunder Dragon'. He assumed the position on the abdication of his father, Jigme Singye, in 2006, after his thirty-four years on the throne. The handsome young king and his beautiful wife, the Druk Gyalsuen (Queen) Jetsum Pema, are parents to a young crown prince, who will take the throne in due course; Bhutan's constitution requires the king to abdicate by the age of sixty-five.

The Wangchuck dynasty has carefully and cautiously modernised Bhutan, a country that nevertheless retains a strongly rooted Buddhist culture and many old customs, such as the colourful traditional dress mandatory on official occasions. Jigme Singye promoted Western-style education, the building of highways and an airport, and a gradual

Figure 4.1 Ugyen Wangchuck in 1905 after his investiture with the Order of the Indian Empire

opening of the country to the outside world. (Bhutan first received television in 1999.) He gained international attention for a theory about the need for Bhutan and other countries to evaluate well-being in terms of 'gross national happiness' instead of simple gross national product. The incumbent king has continued to undertake reform, including the adoption of a new constitution and the institution of elections and parliamentary government in 2008. The monarchy over the twentieth century and since has been acclaimed as a pillar of stability, progress and wise governance. The king and his father remain revered figures, and Jigme Khesar's tours around the country dispensing *kidu* – honours, grants of land and sums of money – to the needy have further enhanced his popularity.[4]

The British did not create the monarchy of Bhutan, as Ugyen Wangchuck by 1885 had bested his rivals and unified his own central region of Trongsa with what became the other parts of the kingdom.[5] However, White's mission in 1907 provided the imprimatur of the British government and the Government of India, according Ugyen the style of 'His Highness' and a 15-gun salute. Bhutan remained a protected state until India became independent in 1947, though unlike other princely states, Bhutan was not subsequently merged into India. Three years later, India signed a treaty of friendship with Bhutan, reaffirming the small realm's sovereignty; in return, Bhutan agreed to align its foreign policy with that of India. Relations between Britain and Bhutan remain cordial, as seen in a visit to Bhutan by the Duke and Duchess of Cambridge in 2016 that provided fine opportunities for photographs of the glamorous British and Bhutanese royal couples against stunning natural landscapes and grand *dzongs*.

The trajectory of dynasties through the pre-colonial, colonial and post-independence periods in the Himalayas is no less varied than elsewhere on the subcontinent and the wider colonised world. According to one count, there were forty-eight Himalayan ruling princes immediately before the independence of India and Pakistan, though in earlier ages the rulers of small mountain polities – 'one-valley kings' – had numbered in the hundreds.[6] Only the monarchy of Bhutan remains in power, though the demise of others occurred in varying ways and periods, including after the departure of the British from South Asia. The examples of the neighbouring countries of Nepal, Sikkim and Bhutan (with some reference to Tibet) illustrate how the Himalayan dynasties weathered their engagement with the British, independent India and their own restive populations.[7] It is impossible to trace here the complicated history of these countries' dynasties through the past centuries, and the diplomatic history of Britain's relationship with Tibet, Sikkim and Bhutan is covered in a detailed and authoritative work by Amar Kaur Jasbir Singh.[8] There are, in addition, scholarly volumes on the history of each country. The aim in this chapter is to explore the different itineraries of the major Himalayan monarchies in the late colonial period, during decolonisation and afterwards, and to argue that the British played a major role in the confirmation and maintenance of the Himalayan monarchies, though the invasive legacy of colonialism helped to determine their post-independence fates.

The colonial Himalayas

With spectacular scenery, challenging access and picturesque traditions, the Himalayas have excited foreign fantasies from the time of pith-helmeted Victorians to contemporary backpackers nurtured by tales of Shangri-La, mystical Buddhist lamaseries and mountains on the 'roof of the world'. News that Sir Edmund Hillary and Tenzing Norgay had reached the summit of Mount Everest was released in London on the morning of Queen Elizabeth II's coronation in 1953. The announcement symbolised the hope that even if the Raj now lay in the past, a team led by a British subject was still capable of breathtaking conquests in the new Elizabethan age. That Hillary was New Zealand born and bred, and that scant credit was given at the time to Tenzing Norgay or the other 'Sherpas' on whom the expedition depended, provides some indication of changes and continuities in realities and perspectives.

In the colonial period and since, the Himalayas have represented a field for geopolitical manoeuvres. In the west, Britain and Russia in the late nineteenth century played the 'Great Game' for strategic influence in the mountains of Afghanistan and Kashmir, while in the east, Britain and imperial China faced off. Safeguarding the further reaches of its Indian empire, securing vital mountain passes for hoped-for trade with Tibet and entry to the coveted Chinese market, recruiting support for its *imperium*, and (at least ostensibly) bringing 'civilisation' to wild areas were Britain's priorities in the Himalayas. Developments in the wider area – continuing conflict in Afghanistan, the Indian 'Mutiny' of 1857, the completion of the British conquest of Burma in 1885 – underscored the stakes for the imperialists.

Britain asserted its powers in the Himalayas through warfare, as well as less violent encounters with local sovereigns. In 1815–16, the East India Company waged war on Nepal; the bravery of Gurkha fighters much impressed the British, who branded them an admirable 'martial race' and began to recruit Nepalese for their own forces, as the British army continues to do. The Sikkimese, targets for earlier invasion by Nepal, sided with the British, and Sikkim became a

British protectorate. Sikkim was forced to cede territory, and in 1864, after British troops marched on Bhutan, so was that country, though it did not come under British control and was then left largely alone. As for Sikkim, however, the British did not hesitate to flex their imperial muscle. In 1887, the British took Chogyal Thutob, the ruler since 1874, and the maharani of Sikkim into custody and exiled them to Kalimpong in West Bengal, where they were kept in detention for several months. Then, in 1891, John Claude White accused the returned Chogyal Thutob of using forced labour and threatened sanctions. The *chogyal* appealed to the viceroy, which incensed the arrogant and autocratic White. Thutob then attempted to repair to a Sikkimese enclave in Tibet, but he was captured by the Nepalese en route and turned over to the British. White announced to a resigned *chogyal* and his angry consort – who hurled abuse, White recalled – that they would be exiled to Kerseong, part of the Darjeeling region that the Sikkimese had been forced to cede in 1856. They remained in detention for two and a half years before being allowed to return to Gangtok, where the monarch, seemingly reconciled with the British, resumed his reign.[9]

Further British military action took place in 1904. The objective of Sir Francis Younghusband's infamous 'mission' to Tibet was to resolve border disputes as well as to investigate rumours (which proved false) of Russian influence at the court of the Dalai Lama in Lhasa. The mission turned into an invasion, the Dalai Lama driven to take refuge in Mongolia and then China before an agreement was signed by which Britain forced Tibet to cede territory, pay an indemnity that if discharged in full would have taken seventy-five years to acquit, and renounce any rights over its traditional tributary of Sikkim.[10] (Three years later, in a convention between Beijing and London, the British agreed not to annex any Tibetan territory or interfere in its affairs, in return for rights of trade.) 'Gunboat diplomacy', though an inappropriate phrase for the Himalayas, enforced imperialist will and established British primacy, making the Himalayas into a British sphere of influence (though of a restricted nature in Tibet). However, it also opened the way for alliances between the British and the Himalayans, as shown by Nepalese support during the 'Mutiny', and Bhutan's support for the Younghusband campaign against Tibet. Having forced their will on the Tibetans, the British later offered limited backing for the Dalai Lama, who temporarily fled to British India after the Chinese invaded Tibet in 1910 and deposed the ruler. The demise of China's Qing dynasty allowed the Dalai Lama to return to Lhasa, where in 1913 he issued a proclamation reaffirming Tibet's independence; that sovereignty was and is rejected by the Chinese. The eastern Himalayas, therefore, provided a chessboard on which local rulers – often with aspirations to aggrandisement of territory and influence – and outside powers struggled, in mutating alliances, for dominion. Central figures in these contests were the Himalayan monarchs.

The Himalayan populations are ethnically and culturally diverse because of centuries of migration from Tibet, China, India and Nepal. Religion has formed a key component of culture and of the ideas of governance. Hinduism predominates in Nepal (known in the final decades of the monarchy as the only remaining Hindu kingdom),[11] while further east Buddhism is the religion of the majority, though with various lineages of lamas and schools. Hereditary rule was the norm, though new dynasties occasionally usurped older ones, and the monarch almost always exercised autocratic powers. In Nepal, the Hindu king represented an incarnation of Vishnu, and in theocratic Tibet, the Dalai Lama was the reincarnation of his predecessor. In other Buddhist realms the ruler served as guardian and protector of the Buddhist creed, Dharma law and the *sangha* (the monastic community). The rulers of the mountain kingdoms over time wielded together realms from disparate lands and multi-ethnic populations. Standardising languages, promoting the legitimacy of dynasties credited with ancient origins, and creating a sense of common membership of moral communities have offered strategies for nation-building, consolidation of political rule and, in more recent times, opposing republicanism and radicalism.[12]

More secure dynasties emerged, with continued fission and fusion, though the Westphalian system of separate and territorially bounded nation-states long remained a novelty. The diminutive kingdom of Sikkim (about three times the size of Luxembourg) was established by the Namgyel dynasty in the seventeenth century.[13] Further west, the Gorkha (or Gurkha) Shah dynasty had unified much of what became modern Nepal (now a bit larger than Greece) by the 1770s, though subnational vassal hierarchs remained in place in such regions as Mustang as 'kingdoms within kingdoms'.[14] Bhutan (almost a third bigger than Belgium) was unified in the early 1600s under an expatriate Tibetan lama, the Shabdrung Ngawang Namgyal, who set up a dual form of government comprising a secular authority and an ecclesiastical one. After the Shabdrung's death in 1651 the country disaggregated into fractious local polities led by *penlops*. Not until the 1880s, under Ugyen Wangchuck, were the pieces once again put together, though reincarnations of the Shabdrung continued to challenge the monarch's status until the last officially recognised Shabdrung was assassinated in 1926. The chief abbot of Bhutan (the *Je Khenpo*) continues to hold a position of respect and influence second only to that of the king.

Parliamentary government existed in none of these countries, though in Nepal a codification of laws in 1854 outlined the rights of the monarch and the limitations of his authority.[15] Nepal indeed had a unique dual system of government from 1846 until 1951, though one different from the duarchy in Bhutan. After an extended time of troubles with warfare, palace coups and child monarchs, a military leader, Jang Bahadur Kumar from the Rana family, took power in 1846, solidifying his control with the massacre of several dozen rivals. Jang set himself up as hereditary prime minister, the position initially passing from brother to brother in the family. This reduced the monarch to a ceremonial and largely figurehead role while real authority lay with the Ranas, who ruled for nearly a century. Jang also persuaded the king to grant him the hereditary title of Maharaja of Keski. The Rana prime minister threw Nepal's valuable forces behind the British during the Indian insurrection in 1857 and personally commanded Gurkha soldiers in the relief of Lucknow. Three years later, he undertook a European tour, a still highly unusual voyage for an Asian statesman, and was received by Queen Victoria.[16] The British rewarded the prime minister and his successors with support and honours, turning a blind eye to familial in-fighting and dictatorial government. The Ranas derived great benefits from their position, not least the wealth put on show in a thousand-room palace built in Kathmandu in the early twentieth century.[17] They entertained travelling British royals on hunting trips during which hordes of animals were slaughtered.

Violent early confrontations thus, paradoxically, led to amicable relations between the British and the Himalayan kings. British and Western influence penetrated their realms to differing degrees; Bhutan remained largely closed off, and the Chinese tried, unsuccessfully, to keep Tibet off limits. The Thirteenth Dalai Lama (r. 1878–1933), after returning to the Tibetan capital in 1913, introduced innovations such as electricity, revised the legal system and established a police force. According to the British Political Officer Sir Charles Bell, his friend and biographer, the Dalai Lama was intrigued by foreign technology and customs, and open to new ideas.[18] The unexpected visit of four Tibetan youths to Britain and their presentation on behalf of the Dalai Lama of gifts to King George V disconcerted British diplomats, but signalled continuing ties between London and Lhasa, the British sovereign and the reincarnated Tibetan leader.[19] Foreign ways appeared elsewhere as well. One of White's photographs, for example, shows the Rani of Nepal in a remarkable full-skirted gown that would have been the envy of ladies in turn-of-the-century England. In Sikkim, the British in 1899 chose Prince Sidkyong (1879–1914) as heir to the throne, passing over his elder brother, who was considered unfavourable to

British interests – an example of naked British intervention in dynastic politics. Sidkyong was sent off to a British school in Darjeeling and then to Pembroke College, Oxford, after which he toured North America, Japan and China. In Beijing, he met the Dalai Lama, the young prince wearing monastic robes for the occasion since he was a reincarnated lama. With high hopes for the crown prince, the British placed Sidkyong in charge of education and forestry after his return to Sikkim, and he attended the 1911 Delhi Darbar at which King George V and Queen Mary were crowned Emperor and Empress of India. British officials also served as marriage brokers by trying to find an appropriate spouse; Sidkyong's father wanted him to remain chaste as a Buddhist monk, Sidkyong himself longed for a Japanese wife (having found Japanese women educated and attractive), and an exiled Burmese princess emerged as the leading candidate, though he ultimately wed a Tibetan. Despite intense grooming for the throne, Sidkyong reigned for less than a year in 1914, dying officially of disease, but in suspicious circumstances.[20]

Bhutan's future king Jigme Sigye, at a later time, was also sent to boarding school in Britain, as were a few other members of the Himalayan elite. Introducing royal figures to British ways and to British imperial practices in India – as occurred during a visit of the Bhutanese leader to Calcutta in 1906, and the Sikkimese ruler to Calcutta in 1935, as well as a visit by a second Nepali Rana prime minister to Britain in 1908 – formed an important part of the strategy of British domination.[21] In the British view, successful 'pacification' might lead to collaboration, with Anglophile indigenous monarchs bound by fealty and self-interest. The Himalayan kingdoms remained exotic borderlands of the British South Asian empire, home only to a handful of Europeans and with limited trade and involvement in world affairs, though Nepal sent soldiers to fight with the British in the two world wars, and took part in other British military actions. The Himalayas meanwhile continued to work their magic in the Western imaginary, typified by James Hilton's 1933 novel *Lost Horizon*.[22]

Decolonisation

Opposition to the British in the Himalayas developed alongside the Indian independence movement, though without the widespread support, leadership or militancy of the Indian campaign. However, there was also concern in the Himalayan countries about what would happen if and when the British 'quit India', leaving small territories and unprotected rulers in vulnerable positions. The coming independence of India and Pakistan in 1947 implied substantial change because of the desire of Indian nationalists to incorporate into India all of the princely states of the imperial age, as well as the remaining Portuguese and French colonies on the subcontinent. The victory of the Communists in China in 1949 added a new factor into the geopolitical equation as Mao Zedong reasserted centralised authority over the ethnically diverse borderlands of the old Chinese empire and spread an ideology of revolution and socialism anathema to conservatives in the mountain kingdoms. A new 'Great Game' was set in play across the Himalayas, pitting India against China, and the game turned into open warfare in 1962. Tension between India and China remained constant on the eastern Himalayan frontier, just as divided Kashmir in the western Himalayas was destabilised by incessant friction, and occasional violent skirmishes, between India and Pakistan.

The rulers of Sikkim and Bhutan lobbied Jawaharlal Nehru to retain their independence, and the Indian prime minister proved sympathetic.[23] The two states, after all, were too small to represent a threat to India and had majority Buddhist populations different from the majority Hindu and Muslim populations of India. They formed a useful buffer between India and China, as did Nepal; their rulers espoused few aspirations other than to be left alone to oversee a gradual evolution of their kingdoms. They also agreed to maintain close and deferential relations with India, which formally recognised the independence of Nepal and Bhutan. After Indian independence, an Indian Political Officer replaced the British officer in Sikkim, though with little other immediate change in the relationship between New Delhi and Gangtok.[24]

The major governmental changes in the years immediately after the Second World War occurred in Tibet and Nepal. In Tibet, the Chinese steadily increased their presence and authority in the 1950s, Maoist ideology and Beijing's geopolitics inspiring attacks on a 'feudal' regime and antiquated theocracy. A revolt against tightening Chinese control in the late 1950s precipitated a Chinese invasion in 1959 and the flight of the Fourteenth Dalai Lama to India, where he established monastic headquarters in Dharamshala, gathered a large diasporic community and ultimately sponsored a government-in-exile. China's violent reassertion of rule in Tibet thus removed the 'hereditary' head of its state and government, with the Chinese putting into place their own political and spiritual appointees.

Nepal in the late 1940s saw rising discontent, spurred by the Nepali Congress Party, directed against the strong-arm regime of the Rana prime ministers. In 1950, King Tribhuvan, who had reigned since 1911 but wielded little political power and was effectively confined to his palace by the Ranas, sought refuge from the prime minister's government in the Indian embassy in Kathmandu. The prime minister pronounced the deposition of Tribhuvan and proclaimed the king's four-year-old grandson, Gyanendra, as new monarch. Indian aeroplanes spirited the royal family (minus the newly crowned boy king) out of the country to a warm welcome by Indian authorities; Nehru announced that India would not recognise Gyanendra as king. Demonstrations against the Ranas soon broke out in Nepal, provoking negotiations among representatives of King Tribhuvan, the Rana prime minister, and the dissident Nepali Congress Party. These resulted in an agreement for Tribhuvan to reclaim the throne; on returning, he appointed a prime minister from outside the Rana family, bringing the near century-long rule of the Rana dynasty to an end. The fall of the Ranas, whose position had been continuously shored up by British support before 1947, restored the Shah dynasty to primacy (Figure 4.2). Tribhuvan continued to rule until 1955, when he died while in Switzerland, though in circumstances that remain unclear.

Over the next decades, the fates of the Himalayan dynasties diverged, although space allows only a bare outline here. The Wangchuck royal

Figure 4.2 General Sir Claude Auchinleck receives the Order of the Star of Nepal from King Tribhuvan, 1945

line thrived in Bhutan, despite the occasional crisis, as when one chief minister was assassinated in the 1960s. There was limited democratisation and little demand for change from the population; political, economic and social reform was driven from the top down, by the kings, from the 1950s onwards. In the early 1990s, the issue of Nepali migrants also came to the fore, and significant numbers of what the government termed illegal residents were forced to leave the country, a move that raised questions about human rights. The king then had to confront the presence in the south of armed guerrillas from a movement, using Bhutan as a base, that claimed independence for the Indian region of Assam; the king personally led a military operation that forced them out of Bhutan. King Jigme Singye also continued moderate reform, announcing in 1998 that ministers would be responsible to the National Assembly, which could also trigger the king's abdication by a no-confidence motion. Many Bhutanese were dismayed at the king's willingness to give up absolute power, and the National Assembly refused to accept the measures until pressured by the sovereign. The changes led the way, in coming years, for the writing of a constitution and a fully parliamentary system.

In exile, the Dalai Lama meanwhile became a figure of enormous spiritual authority and a symbol of Tibetan freedom, awarded the Nobel Peace Prize in 1989 (the year of violent Chinese repression of protesters in Tiananmen Square) while the Chinese government moved in Han Chinese migrants to Tibet, closed or destroyed many monasteries, and tried to efface or folklorise the country's traditional culture. The Dalai Lama in 1974 had nevertheless obliged renegade supporters to abandon an armed struggle to free Tibet, and in a declaration in 1998 he formally stated that his objective is Tibetan autonomy not independence. In 2011, the Dalai Lama relinquished his political role in the Tibetan diaspora movement, yet the Chinese Government accuses him of being a subversive 'splittist'. It is unlikely that he will ever be able to return to Tibet. The Chinese invasion of 1959 brought to an end the rule inside Tibet of an ancient dynasty, though paradoxically it gave the Dalai Lama the moral gravitas, spiritual influence and celebrity that he now enjoys around the world, as well as clandestinely among countrymen in Tibet.

In Sikkim, the reign of Chogyal Tashi, from 1914 to 1963, traversed the colonial and post-colonial divide. His successor, and the last monarch to reign, Palden Namgyel, attracted a rare moment of international attention for Sikkim when in 1963 he wed a glamourous young American, Hope Cooke (Figure 4.3).[25] The marriage caused controversy in Sikkim; the *chogyal's* enemies later accused her, with no evidence, of being an American spy. The ruler was unable to

Figure 4.3 Chogyal (King) Palden of Sikkim and Gyalmo (Queen Consort) Hope Cooke, with their daughter watch birthday celebrations, 1971

buttress his position against an Indian-aligned faction associated with his powerful *kazi*, the prime minister, who ironically had also wed a foreigner. By the early 1970s, discontent in the small kingdom – based, among other issues, on demands for greater democratisation and for redress of the grievances of the substantial Nepali population in Sikkim – was becoming more pronounced, and riots broke out in 1973. (The demonstrations prompted the maharani and her children to leave Sikkim, and she and the *chogyal* later divorced.) Indian Prime Minister Indira Gandhi, who had deprived the Indian princes of their titles and privy purses in 1971, was far less friendly to the *chogyal* than her father had been. With continuing local protest against the monarch, the *kazi* in 1975 asked the Indian parliament to intervene and to incorporate Sikkim into the Republic of India; the Indian army thereupon occupied Sikkim's capital. In a subsequent referendum, 97.5 per cent of Sikkimese voted to abolish the monarchy (though reservations were voiced about the conduct of the balloting), and later in 1975, Sikkim duly became a state of India. The last *chogyal* remained in Sikkim as a commoner, but died in exile in the United States, where he had gone for medical treatment, in 1982. The orthodox interpretation from the Indian perspective is that New Delhi legally intervened at the request of the Sikkim government, though over the *chogyal's* opposition, to restore law and order, and that Indian statehood fulfilled the wishes of an overwhelming majority of Sikkimese. Others, by contrast, have identified conspiracy and subterfuge in the way that Sikkim's affairs were managed for the benefit of India, and have interpreted the 'snatch and grab' by New Delhi as Indian colonialism.[26]

Nepal's dynasty outlasted that of Sikkim though with a limited lifespan. After the Shah restoration in 1951, kings continued to rule autocratically. A constitution was granted in 1955, but the king suspended the constitution, parliament and party politics in 1960 after the victory of the opposition Congress Party. Under a new 1962 constitution, the king resumed almost full powers though local councils were elected by corporatist bodies; a referendum in 1980 narrowly confirmed the system, with the king agreeing to elections of a national assembly on a non-party basis. Within a few years, the Congress Party began a campaign of civil disobedience and boycotted elections. King Mahendra in 1990 agreed to another new constitution, and Congress won elections in 1991, but four years later Congress lost power to a Communist government, which was dissolved by the king. In 1996 there began a decade-long armed revolt by Maoists. With nine governments in ten years, Nepal by 2000 was a country in chaos. In 2001, drama and tragedy struck when Crown Prince Dipendra, rumoured to be enraged at family opposition to his choice of spouse, opened fire in the royal palace during a party, killing his father King Birendra and Queen Aishwarya, among ten royal victims. Dipendra was himself wounded and soon succumbed, and Birendra's brother Gyanendra assumed the throne.[27] The incident hardly strengthened the throne in the contest with the Maoist rebels, and opposition grew yet stronger when the king dissolved parliament in 2002 and suspended the constitution in 2005. Though a peace accord was agreed in 2006, when parliament was reinstated, in 2007, it suspended the king. By 2008, Maoists dominated the government, and the monarchy was abolished (as were the positions of several subnational hereditary rulers in Nepal) and a republic was declared.[28]

The inability of the Nepalese kings to install and accept a working parliamentary system, growing opposition to royal autocracy and the success of the Maoist guerrillas account for the crisis in the Nepalese monarchy.[29] The anthropologist Anne T. Mocko also argues that underlying the other factors was a decline in the king's ritual power. Focusing on 'succession rituals' surrounding the transfer of kingship from one incumbent to another, and 'reinforcement rituals' that reproduce and reaffirm the king's position, Mocko suggests that ritualistic monarchy gradually unravelled and finally tore apart when King Gyanendra was unable to demonstrate the potency of royal rituals.[30]

Such an argument underlines the spiritual, ceremonial aspects of monarchy (and not just in the Himalayas) and the bond they form between king and subjects.

The contrast among the Himalayan countries is great. The Dalai Lama in Tibet and the Sikkimese *chogyal* lost power in foreign takeovers, though the last *chogyal*, Palden, had helped to undo his dynasty by seeming personal incapacities, and his disavowal by subjects contributed to the monarchy's demise. The Nepalese king had attempted on several occasions to reinforce his power, and even to resurrect autocracy, though obduracy in trying to re-establish the *ancien régime* played a great part in the dynasty's downfall. In Bhutan, paternalistic rule, slow modernisation and limited democratisation undertaken by King Jigme Singye paved the way for a fully constitutional monarchy.[31] The Bhutan monarchy thus succeeded – with considerable credit to the monarchs – in accomplishing what other Himalayan rulers had not managed.

Legacies of monarchy in the Himalayas

The fates of the Himalayan dynasts are varied, the Fifth King of Bhutan alone remaining on a throne. The deposed last *chogyal* of Sikkim died in exile, while the refugee Fourteenth Dalai Lama continues to be viewed as a spiritual leader and victim of Chinese repression. The deposed Gyanendra of Nepal lives as an apparently disgruntled commoner in Kathmandu, banished from the old royal palace, yet occasionally making critical comments on politics.[32] The end of dynasties does not mean the disappearance of pretenders to thrones, though the heir to the Nepali crown, a prince with a chequered personal reputation, can nurture few hopes of regaining his ancestral position. It is uncertain whether the current Dalai Lama will be reincarnated inside or outside of Tibet or, as he has hinted, perhaps not at all. The pretender to the Sikkim throne, the last *chogyal's* Harrow-educated son by a first wife, was installed as nominal new ruler in a ceremony in Gangtok in 1982, following his father's burial there, though without Indian recognition and no political status; he has been reported to be now living as a monastic recluse.[33]

Monarchy as an institution, however, has remained a significant part of the patrimony even where it no longer exists. In Tibet, while the Chinese have disavowed the Dalai Lama, they make ostensible public gestures of honouring the Buddhist religion and the monastic community intimately connected with traditional rulership, all the while undermining the country's distinct culture. Though even his image is banned in Tibet, the Dalai Lama retains great international stature, his brand of Buddhism attracting increasing numbers of foreigners and galvanising support for the Tibetan cause. In Sikkim, descendants of the royal family have been involved in a project under the auspices of the British Library to digitise the Namgyal archives.[34] The most recently constructed royal palace in Kathmandu, completed in 1971, has been turned into a museum, its displays offering a romantic and nostalgic picture of Nepal largely devoid of condemnation of the former regime.[35] The thousand-room Singha Darbar of the Rana family was nationalised in 1953, and was used for the national parliament and government offices; damaged in a fire in 1973, it was rebuilt, but so badly damaged in an earthquake in 2015 that most of the edifice will be demolished. Not surprisingly, in Bhutan, the legacy of the Wangchuck dynasty and the presence of the current king is manifest, in particular in a museum in Trongsa, the ancestral base of the royal family.[36]

Why some monarchies survive and others do not is a difficult question. Despite last-ditch efforts to secure their rule, neither the Sikkim *chogyal* nor the Nepali king was able to preserve his throne.[37] Upheaval in the local elite with (depending on one's perspective) an attempt by the Indian government to respond to local wishes or blatant neo-colonialist intervention saw the end of the Namgyal dynasty in Sikkim. A domestic rebellion and the results of a long drawn out civil war brought an end to the Nepali dynasty. Chinese invasion and neo-imperialism brought down the Dalai Lama. In the Himalayas, as in other regions, domestic or international pressures cause thrones to topple, though in neither Nepal nor Sikkim was this an immediate result of decolonisation. The *gyalpos* of Bhutan, by contrast with their peers, have proved adept, by carefully managing relations with India and measured political and social change, to assure the survival of their dynasty. In line with key characteristics of the persistence of small-state monarchies comparatively identified by one set of political scientists, the Bhutan rulers had inculcated a sense of 'institutional fidelity' to the crown and established a successful 'personalised' rule over their subjects, a task that in the long run the rulers of Nepal and Sikkim failed.[38]

Britain played an enormous part in the history of the Himalayan monarchies during the colonial period, even though Sikkim, of the four countries discussed here, was the only fully incorporated 'princely state' of the British Empire. Britain's actions ranged from warfare and coercion to the 'courting' and grooming of local rulers and heirs. Britain invaded Nepal, Sikkim, Bhutan and Tibet, with considerable loss of life to indigenous soldiers and civilians. The British forced cession of territory and payment of indemnities, and demanded the opening of trade and permission for the posting of colonial or consular agents to national capitals. What was effectively the kidnapping of Chogyal Thutob under John Claude White's administration stands as one of the most egregious actions against a local ruler, and British invasion of Tibet forced the Dalai Lama to flee to eastern Asia. The rulers of Bhutan, Sikkim and Nepal were expected to follow British directives in foreign relations, to repulse any political initiative from Russia or other European powers, and to engage in commerce with traders from British India. Violence, coercion and manipulation of monarchs provided strategies for the imposition of British will on the Himalayan kings.

Once their realms were 'pacified', Britain continued to wield great influence, and to curb national sovereignty, all the while providing support for autocratic dynasts. Britain's recognition of Nepal as a sovereign state occurred only in 1923; Bhutan and, in particular, Sikkim were kept under the watchful eye of the Viceroy of India and his deputies. Though appearing to recognise the Dalai Lama's 1913 proclamation of the independence of Tibet, Britain provided only limited back-up for the rulers' efforts to preserve that independence. British support for the sovereigns of the Himalayan kingdoms was British policy simply because it served British interests: maintaining peace on the Indian frontier, keeping other powers at bay, ensuring (London hoped) pliable and amicable rulers and Anglophile interlocutors, allowing trade between the subcontinent and China. Good relations with Nepal's king and prime minister also meant that Britain could recruit prized Gurkha soldiers, though many received limited reward for their services.[39] The British, and other foreigners, continued to view the Himalayas as an exotic, backward and mystical mountain region providing good terrain for the exploits of hardy expeditioners and manoeuvring diplomats.

When Britain quit the Indian subcontinent, partition in the western Himalayas left Kashmir in a parlous position, the conflict between the successor states of India and Pakistan enduring today. International recognition of Nepal's sovereignty (under the terms of the 1923 Anglo-Nepalese treaty) allowed that nation to maintain its sovereignty, but the overthrow of the British-backed Rana regime in the early 1950s manifested the fragility of the throne and exposed latent unrest with the restored Shah dynasty. In Sikkim, the British in 1947 left the *chogyal* in a position to negotiate the country's status with Nehru, but made little effort to sustain the dynasty. British support for Tibet and the Dalai Lama has been as convoluted and conflicted as that of other powers eager to win favour with Beijing. Bhutan perhaps came out of the colonial era in the best shape, the monarchy of a unified state reinforced.

THE HIMALAYAN KINGDOMS AND BRITISH COLONIALISM

The Sikkimese monarchy succumbed to the machinations of independent India and its allies, and the rule of the Dalai Lama ended with the efforts of Communist China to reaffirm the old imperial hold over Tibet. As Jonathan Gregson puts it, 'there is a bitter irony in the fact that both China and India, two great nations which suffered so at the hands of European colonialism and led the struggle for freedom, should end up acting as colonial powers on the Roof of the World'.[40] The civil war in Nepal and the overthrow of the Shah dynasty was the work of rebels employing ideologies, strategies and funding brought from China. Perhaps authorities in New Delhi and Beijing had learned a few strategies from the British experience. The old monarchies of Nepal, Sikkim and Tibet, which had accommodated European colonial masters, could not repulse the challenges of post-colonial Asian ones.

Notes

1 Some inconsistencies in the spelling of names of people and places in this chapter are explained by varying transliterations of Himalayan languages.
2 John Claude White, *Sikkim and Bhutan: Twenty-One Years on the North-East Frontier 1887–1908* (London: Edward Arnold, 1909); the account of his second mission to Bhutan, in 1907, comes from chs 18 and 19, and the 1905 mission is discussed in ch. 13. Kurt Meyer and Pamela Deuel Meyer's *In the Shadow of the Himalayas: Tibet, Bhutan, Nepal and Sikkim* (Ahmedabad: Mapin Publishing, 2005) is a collection of White's photographs; it also contains biographical information on him.
3 Alex McKay, '"That he may take due pride in the Empire to which he belongs": the education of Maharajah Kumar Sidkeon Namgyal Tulku of Sikkim', *Bulletin of Tibetology*, 39:2 (2003), 27–52; quoted p. 28. McKay also characterises White as 'mean, petty and dominating', one of the 'worst type of colonial official' (27), an opinion apparently shared by some of White's superiors.
4 His Majesty King Jigme Khesar Namgyel Wangchuk, *Bhutan through the Lens of the King* (New Delhi: Lustre Press / Roli Books, 2012) provides a collection of the king's excellent photographs. Ashi Dorji Wangmo Wangchuck, *Treasures of the Thunder Dragon: Portrait of Bhutan* (New Delhi: Viking, 2006), is the evocative memoir of one of the queens, a spouse of the current king's father, King Jigme Singye Wangchuck.
5 The authoritative study is Michael Aris, *The Raven Crown: The Origins of Buddhist Monarchy in Bhutan* (Chicago: Serindia Publications, 1994, reprinted with corrections, 2005). The most comprehensive history of the country is Karma Phuntsho, *The History of Bhutan* (London: Random House, 2013). See also Peter Collister, *Bhutan and the British* (New Delhi: UBS Publishers, 1987).
6 Jonathan Gregson, *Kingdoms beyond the Clouds: Journeys in Search of the Himalayan Kings* (London: Pan Macmillan, 2000); see also Barbara Crossette, *So Close to Heaven: The Vanishing Buddhist Kingdoms of the Himalayas* (New York: Vintage Books, 1995).
7 With their reign dates, the kings of Bhutan are Ugyen (1907–26), Jigme (1926–52), Jigme Dorji (1952–72), Jigme Singye (1972–2006) and Jigme Khesar (2006–). The kings of Nepal from the start of the twentieth century were Prithvi Bikram Shah (1881–1911), Tribhuvan (1911–55, with another king, Gyanendra, recognised by the Prime Minister 1950–51), Mahendra (1955–72), Birendra (1972–2001), Dipendra (nominally, for four days, 2001), and Gyanendra (2001–8). The rulers of Sikkim were Chogyal Thutob (1874–1914), Sidkyong (1914), Tashi (1914–63) and Palden

(1963–75). The Thirteenth Dalai Lama reigned from 1895 to 1933, succeeded by the Fourteenth and current Dalai Lama.

8   Amar Kaur Jasbir Singh, *Himalayan Triangle: Historical Survey of British India's Relations with Tibet, Sikkim and Bhutan, 1765–1950* (London: British Library, 1988).

9   Singh, *Himalayan Triangle*, pp. 203ff., gives a full account. White, rather coyly, explains that 'Government decided it would be to the advantage of the State to remove the Maharaja from Sikkim for a time' (White, *Sikkim and Bhutan*, pp. 25–6). See also Rajiv Rai, *The State in the Colonial Periphery: A Study on Sikkim's Relations with Great Britain* (Bloomington, IN: Partridge Publishing, 2015); and J. R. Subba, *History, Culture and Customs of Sikkim* (New Delhi: Gyan Publishing House, 2011).

10 Sam Van Schaik, *Tibet: A History* (New Haven, CT: Yale University Press, 2013), provides the best overview. For more detailed discussion of recent decades, see Lezlee Brown Halper and Stefan Halper, *Tibet: An Unfinished Story* (London: C. Hurst, 2014).

11 Vivienne Kondos, *The Kingdom of Nepal: An Analysis of Hindu Culture*, ed. Michael Allen (Kathmandu: Mandala Book Point, 2019).

12 Michael Hutt, 'The last Himalayan monarchies', in Gerard Toffin and Joanna Pfaff-Czarnecka (eds), *Facing Globalization in the Himalayas: Belonging and the Politics of the Self* (New Delhi: Sage, 2014), pp. 419–43.

13 Andrew Duff, *Sikkim: Requiem for a Himalayan Kingdom* (Edinburgh: Birlinn, 2015).

14 Gregson, *Kingdoms beyond the Clouds*, ch. 6.

15 Simon Cubelic and Rajan Khatiwoda, 'Nepalese monarchy in an age of codification: kingship, patriotism, and legality in the Nepalese Code of 1854', in M. Bannerjee et al. (eds), *Transnational Histories of the 'Royal Nation'* (London: Palgrave Macmillan, 2017), pp. 67–86.

16 John Whelpton, *Jang Bahadur in Europe: The First Nepalese Mission to the West* (Kathmandu: Mandala Book Point, 2016), which contains a translation of a contemporary Nepalese account.

17 Mark Liechty, 'Selective exclusion: foreigners, foreign goods, and foreignness in modern Nepali history', *Studies in Nepali History and Society*, 2:1 (1997), 5–68.

18 Charles Alfred Bell, *Portrait of a Dalai Lama: The Life and Times of the Great Thirteenth* (London: Collins, 1946).

19 Emma Martin, 'Fit for a king? the significance of a gift exchange between the Thirteenth Dalai Lama and King George V', *Journal of the Royal Asiatic Society*, Series 3 (2014), 1–28.

20 On this fascinating figure, see McKay, '"That he may take due pride in the Empire to which he belongs"'; Emma Martin, 'Sidkyong Tulku and the making of Sikkim for the 1911 Delhi Durbar', *Bulletin of Tibetology*, 48:1 (2012), 7–31; Berthe Jansen, 'The monastic guidebook (*bCa'yig*) by Sidkeong Tulku: monasteries, sex and reform in Sikkim', *Journal of the Royal Asiatic Society*, 24:4 (2014), 597–622; Pema Abrahams, 'A royal proposal of marriage', British Library Endangered Archives Blog, 20 January 2017, https://blogs.bl.uk/endangeredarchives/2017/01/sikkim.html (concerning Sidkyong's plan to marry an exiled Burmese princess), (accessed 21 May 2019).

21 On the Rana's visit, Sam Cowan, 'The maharaja and the monarch: two visits to the United Kingdom in different eras', *The Record*, 14 April 2005, www.recordnepal.com/wire/maharaja-and-monarch/; and 21 April 2015, www.recordnepal.com/wire/maharaja-and-monarch-0/ (the second tour was that of King Mahendra in 1960) (accessed 21 May 2019).

22 James Hilton, *Lost Horizon* (London: Macmillan, 1933). For a fine study of how Tibetans, Westerners and Chinese have conceptualised and constructed an image of Tibet, and how it is portrayed in various museums, see Clare E. Harris, *The Museum on the Roof of the World: Art, Politics, and the Representation of Tibet* (Chicago: University of Chicago Press, 2012).

23 Singh's *Himalayan Triangle* provides valuable detail about the period of decolonisation.
24 Although India gained independence in 1947, it did not become a republic until 1950; in between those dates, the British monarch remained the nominal head of state, represented by a governor general.
25 The former queen published her memoirs as Hope Cooke, *Time Change: An Autobiography* (New York: Simon & Schuster, 1980).
26 Sunanda K. Datta-Ray, *Smash & Grab: Annexation of Sikkim* (Tranquebar: Westland, 2013).
27 John Gregson, *Blood Against the Snows: The Tragic Story of Nepal's Royal Dynasty* (London: Fourth Estate, 2002).
28 This chronology is taken from www.bbc.com/news/world-south-asia-12499391 (accessed 21 May 2019).
29 A more positive assessment of King Birendra is provided by Francis G. Hutchins, *Democratizing Monarch: A Memoir of Nepal's King Birendra* (Kathmandu: Vajra, 2007).
30 Anne T. Mocko, *Demoting Vishnu: Ritual, Politics, and the Unravelling of Nepal's Hindu Monarchy* (Oxford: Oxford University Press, 2015).
31 The interviews with the king recorded by Gregson in *Kingdoms beyond the Clouds*, chs 9–10, provide much insight into his views on monarchy and governance in Bhutan.
32 See, for example, Reuters News Service, 22 December 2016, www.reuters.com/article/us-nepal-politics-idUSKBN14A1R2 (accessed 21 May 2019).
33 *Hindustan Times*, 23 April 2017, www.hindustantimes.com/india-news/from-monarch-to-monk-scion-of-sikkim-dynasty-who-became-a-spiritual-recluse/story-S7KTrhIxzuN33QdtJhhb4K.html (accessed 21 May 2019).
34 https://iias.asia/the-newsletter/article/sikkim-palace-archive-digitisation-project (accessed 21 May 2019).
35 Bryony R. Whitmarsh, 'Staging memories at the Narayanhiti Palace Museum, Kathmandu', *Himalaya, the Journal of the Association for Nepal and Himalayan Studies*, 7:1 (2017), 83–97.
36 Christian Schicklgruber, *The Tower of Trongsa: Religion and Power in Bhutan* (Ghent: Snoeck, 2009).
37 See, for example, Jackie Hiltz, 'Constructing Sikkimese national identity in the 1960s and 1970s', *Bulletin of Tibetology* (2003), available at www.repository.cam.ac.uk/handle/1810/243140; Michael Baltutis, 'Advertising royalty: popularizing the monarchy for Kathmandu's middle class', *South Asian Popular Culture*, 9:2 (2011), 191–204.
38 Jack Corbett, Wouter Veenendaal and Lhawang Ugyel, 'Why monarchy persists in small states: the cases of Tonga, Bhutan and Liechtenstein', *Democratization*, 24:4 (2017), 689–706. On Bhutan, see, for instance, Thierry Mathou, 'The politics of Bhutan: change in continuity', *Journal of Bhutan Studies*, 2:3 (2000), 250–89; and A. Sinpeng, 'Democracy from above: regime transition in the Kingdom of Bhutan' (2007), available at www.dspace.cam.ac.uk/handle/1810/226946.
39 Until 2007, retired Gurkha soldiers were not given equal pay to British veterans, nor were they given right of abode in the United Kingdom. After much lobbying and several court cases, the situation was rectified; the British actor Joanna Lumley, daughter of a British military officer in colonial India, helped to raise the profile of the Gurkhas' case.
40 Gregson, *Kingdoms beyond the Clouds*, p. 360.

CHAPTER FIVE

Conflict and betrayal: negotiations at the end of British rule in the Shan States of Burma (Myanmar)

Susan Conway

The Shan States together comprise 160,000 square kilometres, about one quarter of the country known today as Myanmar, but in the period covered by this chapter, known as Burma. The main ethnic group in the Shan States call themselves Tai and are part of a wider network of Tai in Assam, Thailand, Laos and Yunnan. In political terms the Tai of the Shan States are often referred to as Shan. Other ethnic groups who interact with the Shan include Karen, Kachin, Chin, Danu, Pa-o, Wa and Palaung. The Shan States are bordered by China to the north, Laos and Thailand to the east, and Burma to the south and west. Over the centuries the number of Shan principalities and chiefdoms has fluctuated. Power centres formed under powerful *saopha* (princes) supported by *myosa* (governors) and *ngwegunhmu* (hill chiefs) and then often split into smaller units, re-forming at a later date as political circumstances changed.[1] At the end of the nineteenth century, British colonial authorities estimated the population of the Shan States to be over one million.[2]

Traditional Shan politics and culture

This complex network of principalities and chiefdoms operated under a traditional Tai *muong* system – that is, a Tai power centre or sphere of influence, usually a city-state ruled by a prince with people in outlying areas and in the hills controlled by their own leaders but paying tribute (tax) to a prince. He, in turn, paid tribute to Burma, China or Siam (Thailand). As observed by officials from those countries, and later colonial officers from Britain and France, the inland states appeared as a complicated world of fragmented ethnic categories. One linguistic surveyor described this unflatteringly as 'a dish cloth which has traces of everything it has wiped'.[3] In reality, it was a land where extremely sophisticated political networks and alliances operated. Through these networks the Shan were able to repel or seriously undermine many incursions, including by the Chinese, who invaded via Yunnan. The Shan hired hill groups living in the mountainous terrain that invaders had to cross. They attacked columns of soldiers and cut supply lines by killing their pack animals. The Shan were subject to raids from Tai neighbours in Lan Na (north Thailand) who captured and forcibly resettled whole villages on the Thai side of the border and in towns like Chiang Mai. The *muong* system more or less collapsed following the military coup of 1962.

What held the Shan together as a people was a unique culture. They practise a distinct form of Theravada Buddhism and have a belief system that incorporates spirit religion, astrology, cosmology, numerology and a belief in the power of nature and sacred objects.[4] Shan identity is expressed in language, literature and poetry, and in written scripts, some of which are now under threat of extinction. The most powerful Shan princes ruled over principalities the size of small European countries and lived in grand style. They supported the construction of monasteries, sponsored manuscript production and funded rituals. Weavers, dyers and embroiderers, goldsmiths, silversmiths and lacquer workers were commissioned to provide furnishings for the interiors of teak palaces, and to make court dress and regalia for ceremonial use. Their skill and artistry was widely admired and the beautiful objects they created can be found in museum collections throughout the world.[5]

Styles of dress and regalia were not merely symbols of wealth but signalled the complex *muong* system referred to earlier. On certain formal occasions, princes appeared in dress and regalia that signified tributary and sumptuary laws associated with China, Burma and Siam. Later in colonial times and leading up to independence, British forms of dress and regalia were added. Minor princes and leaders in outlying settlements generally wore more modest forms of dress on ritual occasions that reflected regional affiliations and ethnic loyalties. At all levels of society, importance was attached to rank, ethnic identity and tribute relations.

The Shan states after British conquest of Burma

When the British expanded their empire eastwards from India to Burma at the beginning of the nineteenth century, they created conflict with King Bodawpaya (ruled 1819–53) that led to the first Anglo-Burmese War of 1824–26. The ensuing peace treaty, ratified at Yandabo forty-five miles from the then Burmese capital of Ava, gave the British the southern province of Tenasserim, control of the port of Moulmein and the states of Assam and Manipur. In addition to these large territorial concessions, the Burmese paid a crippling indemnity. Defeat in battle and British presence at the mouth of the Salween River weakened the king, a situation the Shan were quick to exploit by flouting tributary obligations to Burma. A second Anglo-Burmese War in 1852 further undermined the Burmese, although the accession of King Mindon (ruled 1853–78) following the death of Bodawpaya led to a period of relative calm and negotiations with the British government of India in Calcutta. British officials in India looked upon countries east of India with a certain amount of aloofness, and the comprehensive term 'Further India' was often used to categorise them, suggesting they had no individual identity.[6] King Mindon was aware of this slight and resented the fact that he was not able to negotiate directly with Queen Victoria and her government in London. In 1872 he was offended when his chief minister visited London and was introduced to the Queen by the Secretary of State for India, and not by the British Foreign Secretary, as he had expected. Following King Mindon's death, any goodwill that existed between the two nations was lost. His successor at the Mandalay court was the weak King Thibaw, and during his reign the Shan princes set up independent states and confederations and freed themselves from the taxes imposed by the Burmese court. Some chiefs began to engage in banditry. Marauding bands of men, grouped around local leaders, took a share of the spoils.

In 1885 the British intervened to oust King Thibaw and end the Kon-baung dynasty. A Shan chronicle describes the arrival of the British (*gala ingalik*) by steamer, an event predicted by Shan astrologers.[7] The chronicle states that twenty thousand English soldiers surrounded the palace. King Thibaw, his consorts and their attendants were taken prisoner. They boarded a river steamer, going by stages to Rangoon (Yangon) and then on to exile in Ratnagiri, India. The forcible removal of King Thibaw created a disastrous power vacuum and, to make matters worse, the British showed little respect for Burmese court culture. The sacred Royal Audience Hall at the Mandalay court became the British army's garrison church, gilded palace apartments were whitewashed to become offices for British army personnel and the dress and regalia of the king was looted and shipped to London.[8] It was said that when news of this vandalism reached Lord Curzon, who would go on to be appointed Viceroy of India in 1899, he was appalled.[9]

The power vacuum the British created in Burma provided further opportunities to Shan princes who had taken advantage of the weakness of King Thibaw. They embarked on a mission to replace him with a compliant relative. Not all Shan rulers agreed with this decision and a power struggle followed that led to fighting, looting and pillaging across the country. Into this chaos marched Colonel Sir Edward Stedman with a column of British troops. By 1887 he had established a degree of order. In contrast to their strategy in Lower Burma, the British adopted an enlightened policy towards Shan and minority rulers. They agreed to respect the culture and customs of the Shan princes and other ethnic groups in Upper Burma, in so far as they were considered just and not contradictory to the laws of British India. In return, rulers agreed to swear allegiance to Queen Victoria. British officials issued patents of appointment. Each *saopha myosa* and *ngwegunhmu* was to administer his own state. In powerful states, prime ministers, departmental ministers and state judges were appointed. British administrators and local rulers formed a Governing State Council. The role of the British was to maintain civil order and control foreign affairs.

A real effort was made to accommodate local custom. Grand wooden bungalows built on stilts in local style and referred to as *haw* (palaces) were provided as formal residences when the princes attended sittings of the Shan State Council established in the town of Taunggyi. British officials went on tour to hold a series of darbars with the *saopha, myosa* and *ngwegunhmu*. Following local tradition, *tawmaw* (temporary buildings) were constructed for these meetings.[10] In a private letter, Sir George Scott wrote that the mere fact of getting the chiefs together was beneficial and after having met once he thought they might be less likely to fight.[11] It is interesting to note that football and music were used to create a friendly atmosphere. In his journals Scott describes team matches and military band performances.[12]

The British respected existing hierarchical tribute systems practised among the *saopha, myosa* and *ngwegunhmu*. The domestic lives of local rulers were not immediately changed by British presence, although gradually they came under the cultural influence of Empire. Wealthy princes began replacing traditional Shan wooden palaces with buildings that were an assimilation of Shan and Indo-European style. But not all succumbed. Out of respect for the ritual significance of old palaces, many princes stayed put. Others maintained their palaces for use on ceremonial occasions, keeping a few retainers in residence to take care of the building and grounds while moving to new palaces with modern amenities, including running water.

Meanwhile, in the formal atmosphere of the Administrative Headquarters in Taunggyi, the British drew up a 'List of Order of Precedence'. The Shan rulers were not coerced into adopting this order because the British authorities adhered to existing hierarchies that the Shan princes wished to maintain.[13] British imperial style was evident at formal banquets held at the end of Parliamentary sessions. Sao Noan Oo (Nel Adams), daughter of the Prince of Lawksawk, wrote:

> It was a tradition that on the last night of the Durbar [Parliamentary Session] the Commissioner would give a banquet for all the members of the Shan State Council. ... As it was one of the grandest social occasions, everyone dressed up in their best attire. The Sawbwas [princes] wore long embroidered robes over their suits, decorated with medals and silk turbans.[14]

On official occasions the rulers wore ethnic dress that was a symbol of identity, while acknowledging in displays of medals and ribbons their allegiance to the British crown. It could be argued that this display sent out a more subtle message. Court dress symbolised local tributary systems, while British medals were pinned-on additions that could be easily removed. As the British formalised relations with local rulers, those who were loyal to the crown were given titles, regalia and privileges according to sumptuary laws, operated by the court of Queen Victoria through her colonial representative, the Viceroy and Governor General of India. The prince of Yawnghwe was knighted as Knight Commander of the Indian Empire (KCIE). He received a Delhi Darbar medal and was entitled to a salute of nine guns. The Prince of Keng Tung received a King's Service Medal (KSM), a Delhi Darbar medal and also a salute of nine guns. Less powerful *saopha, myosa* and *ngwegunhmu* received titles and medals graded according to rank.

In December 1903, Lord Curzon staged a grand darbar in Delhi to mark the accession of King Edward VII following the death of Queen Victoria, and princes and senior officials from all parts of the British Empire attended. The display of exotic dress, military uniforms and caparisoned animals was the greatest visual spectacle of the age.[15] Rulers from the Shan States and representatives of ethnic minority rulers were photographed in exotic court dress and regalia that reflected historical and cultural connections with China and Burma, tribute systems that existed long before the British arrived (Figure 5.1). Pinned onto these exotic forms of dress were the medals and ribbons more recently awarded by Queen Victoria. There was no monarch to represent the Burmese because the British had banished King Thibaw and destroyed the Kon-baung dynasty.

In a continuing effort to exert soft power in the Shan States, the British arranged for the sons of Shan princes to attend British public schools, and they were invited to court ceremonies and introduced to members of the royal family.[16] The British also established a school in Taunggyi where sons of the elite not sent abroad were educated. Relationships with British royalty continued to be cordial even as calls

Figure 5.1 Shan sawbwas (princes) at the Delhi Darbar, 1903

for independence were gathering momentum. In 1947 Sao Nang Hearn Kham, wife of Sao Shwe Thaik, Prince of Yawnghwe, was invited to the wedding of Princess Elizabeth and Prince Philip in London. She was photographed in Burmese court dress, an elaborately embroidered silk blouse and sash and an ankle-length skirt woven in a *luntaya* pattern.[17]

As the relationship between the British, the Shan and minority hill groups was played out, in the background other power brokers operated in the area, particularly the Chinese.[18] In the northern and eastern Shan states, long-standing trade relations with China continued. Chinese merchants were key agents in trading companies owned by Shan princes and their families. This relationship was to become an important lifeline in the future.[19] Meanwhile British businesses set up extraction companies to harvest rich natural resources in the Shan States and Frontier Areas.[20]

The Second World War and the move towards Burmese independence

The political order and stability that the British claimed with some justification to have created collapsed when the Japanese invaded, in 1942, during the Second World War. In 1943 Japanese soldiers occupied Burma and the Shan States with the cooperation of the Burmese Independence Army under Bogyoke (Major General) Aung San. Eventual British success in defeating the Japanese was in part due to employing the same tactics used by Shan princes in their defeat of the Chinese in the nineteenth century. The British army hired hill dwellers, mostly Karen soldiers who were familiar with and able to fight in mountainous terrain. Initially the Burmese Independence Army inflicted terrible losses on the Karen. Four hundred villages were destroyed, and an estimated 1,800 Karen slaughtered. Eventually the tide turned, and in December 1944 Japanese forces were driven into retreat.[21] Armed Karen units were crucial in bringing about that defeat. British officials made promises to Karen leaders that after the war they would recognise their sacrifice and major contribution to the war effort.

Japanese occupation, and the battles that followed as the Allies regained territory, left deep psychological scars on the people of the Shan States and Frontier Areas. Allied bombing reduced some towns and villages to ruins. In 2018, while on a teaching assignment at Shan State Buddhist University, I witnessed the effects of an Allied bombing raid that had hit a township in the southern Shan States, one and a half hours' drive from Taunggyi. The township was set in a prosperous agricultural valley of rice fields surrounded by hills and mountains. Shan and Burmese anthropology students surveyed a Buddhist monastery, interviewed the abbot, monks and lay members of the community about the history, art and material culture of the monastery and history of the township. They reported that the area had been occupied by Japanese troops and later bombed by the Allies to drive them out. There was a direct hit on the site of an ancient and revered Buddhist monastery in the middle of town. Its grounds were hallowed as they were also a burial site for local Shan princes. This bombing was viewed as a catastrophic omen of bad luck and many rituals were held to cleanse and drive away the evil that was generated. Two buildings survived: an ordination hall built in ancient Shan style and a stupa that was partially damaged, causing it to lean precariously. With local donations, restoration work began at the end of the war and today the site is protected and lovingly cared for by local inhabitants. It is a symbol of resilience in the face of a war fought across their land by foreign forces and a mark of survival of an ancient culture.

After the Allies achieved victory over Japan, a new British governor, Sir Hubert Rance, was appointed. A desire for independence led the Shan princes to come together in 1946 in the township of Mongkung, where they aimed to establish a path to autonomy.[22] The conference was not a success as they were unable to agree on policies to amalgamate the smaller states into a Shan federation. They then sought negotiations with the Burmese and in March 1946 invited British officials to attend what they called a *pwe* (festival) to discuss future relations between the Shan and Burmese nationalists. According to *The Times* of 28 March 1946, an unofficial agreement was reached.[23]

Meanwhile, Burmese nationalists in the Independence movement were gaining authority under their leader Bogyoke Aung San, leader of the Anti-Fascist People's Freedom League (AFPFL). He had initially collaborated with Japanese forces, but changed sides when it became clear the Allies were gaining victory, and he intended to negotiate independence with them. He became the figurehead of Burmese nationalism and featured as a major player at the conference held in Panglong in February 1947. Its aim was to negotiate independence from Britain. In the Burmese version of events, Aung San convened the conference in the Shan town of Panglong because he wisely and benevolently recognised the interests of minorities.[24] In a display using dress as a symbol of his commitment to inclusiveness, Aung San had himself photographed with smiling groups of hill people wearing ethnic dress. The Shan version of events is quite different. They claim that Aung San did not organise the Panglong Conference. It was the Shan princes under their leader Sao Shwe Thaik, prince of Yawnghwe and Leader of the Supreme Council of the United Hill Peoples, who convened the Conference.[25] Sao Shwe Thaik was afraid that following victory in the Second World War the British would forget the promises they had made and abandon the Shan and hill peoples. His aim was to protect the rights and privileges that had been granted by the British in the late 1880s. His concern increased with the results of the British elections in 1945. Sir Winston Churchill was perceived as sympathetic to the cause because he recognised that Shan and hill groups had fought loyally with the Allies. It is unlikely, however, that Churchill would have supported their cause given his inclination to keep the empire together. When he lost the election, the new prime minister was Clement Attlee who, to the Shan, was an unknown force. They felt Attlee could not be relied on for support in future negotiations.

Those who attended the Panglong Conference included Shan princes, governors, hill chiefs and other ethnic minority leaders. The agreement protected the rights of the people of the Shan states and populations in the Kachin and Chin Hills. They were to be represented by a counsellor and deputy counsellor. Full autonomy in terms of internal administration was accepted in principle. The Panglong Agreement also stated that a separate Karen state would be established with consent of the Constituent Assembly. This was in recognition of the contribution made in the defeat of the Japanese. Citizens of all the Frontier Areas were to enjoy the rights and privileges regarded as fundamental in democratic countries. The pact recognised financial arrangements agreed between the Shan States and the Burmese federal government and similar arrangements for the people of the Kachin and Chin territories. The Panglong Agreement was binding for ten years.[26]

Recent accounts of events leading up to independence have been written by women, in particular female relatives of the Shan princes. The atmosphere at the Panglong Conference was described by Nel Adams, daughter of the Prince of Lawksawk, in her memoirs.[27] From their residence nearby, she and her mother listened to the cries of 'Out, Out British Out' erupting from the conference hall. She describes her father as sympathetic to the independence movement because he felt that times were changing, and it was now the moment, after sixty years of rule, for the British to go. Although the family had many British friends, her father agreed with Aung San, who was an inspiring orator. In his speeches he stressed that British companies had not used profits from the extraction industries they controlled to improve the local economy or provide a decent education for ordinary people.[28] If returned to local ownership, he argued, profits could be used to benefit the whole country and its people. Sao Sanda, eldest daughter of Sao Shwe Thaik, first President of the Union of Burma, described the visit of Aung San to their palace in Yawnghwe where he discussed the terms of the newly signed Panglong Agreement. Aung San had come to Yawnghwe to allay fears that Shan and citizens of the Frontier Areas were expressing about their status in future negotiations.

Aung San consented to representatives of the Shan and other Frontier rulers being present at future talks with the British, but he did not honour that commitment. Aung San went alone to London when summoned by Prime Minister Attlee in 1947. The ever-vigilant Sao Shwe Thaik, as leader of the Supreme Council of the United Hill Peoples, cabled Attlee to make clear that Aung San did not represent them: 'Neither the Honourable U Aung San nor any of his colleagues has any mandate to speak on behalf of the Frontier Areas. Whether and when the Frontier Areas will amalgamate with Burma is a matter for the people of the Frontier Areas alone to decide.'[29] This intervention led Attlee's staff to add an objective to the talks aimed at achieving unification of the Frontier Areas and Ministerial Burma with the free consent of the inhabitants. The Shan and other minority groups resented Aung San's sole presence at the talks, and it became clear there were major flaws in the resulting agreement, flaws that would come back to haunt politicians. They felt their views and vision of rule after independence were not represented. Many were completely left out, including the Karen, Karenni and Rohingya; and the Chin, Wa and Naga were not represented.[30]

In recognition of this dissatisfaction with the Panglong Agreement and continuing concern over representation of hill peoples, the British established a Frontier Areas Commission of Enquiry (FACE) in April/May 1947. The commission was chaired by David Rees-Williams MP (later first Baron Ogmore) with Shan, Kachin, Karen and Chin members. Witnesses from all the Frontier Areas were invited to testify before the Committee. The remit was to establish the best method of including the Frontier peoples in the process of writing a new constitution. Reading the report gives a sense of urgency in the short time available. Commission members made great efforts to reach all minority groups, with an extensive travel schedule organised for them. There were many problems. Although the area covered by the enquiry represented 47 per cent of the land mass of Burma, the population was only 16 per cent, so that the number of seats they could expect to be given in government was below their expectations. As had been the ambition of the Shan princes at the *pwe* held in Mongkung in 1946, enquiry members hoped some groups would amalgamate, recording that 'these amalgamations should reduce the craziness of the patchwork quilt which the present administration of the Frontier Areas resembles'.[31] During the enquiry it became clear that many groups interviewed were totally ignorant of the principles of electoral roles and the ballot box. Hugh Tinker, a historian at the School of Oriental and African Studies, wrote in 1957: 'The Committee has often been criticised for the cavalier way in which it appeared to dispose of the future of the hill peoples but in reality, the whole issue had been prejudged under the Attlee–Aung San Agreement.'[32]

Based on the report presented by the FACE committee and the agreements made at Panglong, a Union Constitution was framed. In the opinion of H. N. C. Stevenson, director of the Frontier Areas Administration (FAA), from the safe distance of London, government officials completely underestimated the depth of feeling among the minorities.[33] Stevenson described them as 'abysmally ignorant'.[34] In the following elections the AFPFL under Aung San won 176 out of 210 seats in the Constituent Assembly. In July 1947, however, Aung San was assassinated along with several members of his cabinet by a gang led by U Saw, leader of an opposition party, and six of his colleagues, including the Shan prince of Mongpawn. The vice president of the Union, U Nu, continued with preparations for independence celebrations that took place in January 1948. He was appointed prime minister. The Shan prince Shwe Thaik of Yawnghwe became the first President of the Union of Burma.[35] Burma joined the United Nations, but chose to leave the Commonwealth.

The Shan in independent Burma

The government of U Nu was unstable and internal unrest led to armed rebellion. The rebels included Karen and ethnic groups from the Frontier Areas who were either ignored in the Panglong Agreement or not given the level of recognition they had hoped for following the FACE enquiry. White and red flag communist factions, and some mutinous army regiments, also rebelled. The Shan princes continued to be dissatisfied because they felt Burmese nationalists belonging to the AFPFL had hijacked all the negotiations. At a mass rally held in January 1949 to mark the first anniversary of Independence, President Shwe Thaik[36] issued a warning to the nation:

> Co-operation and understanding cannot come about so long as the element of violence or threat of violence exists, for violence has no counterpart in freedom, and liberty ends where violence begins. The progressive retreat of democracy in the world today is due to the worship by nations of the cult of physical force.[37]

The government of U Nu survived internal unrest but was severely weakened. Elections were held, and the Shan princes took their seats in the newly established Parliament. Among their number was the active Sao Nang Hearn Kham, consort of President Shwe Thaik, who served as MP for the constituency of Hsenwi between 1956 and 1960. Unrest continued and, as had happened throughout the history of the Shan States, China and Burma were competing for supremacy in the area. The Chinese Kuomintang army under Chiang Kai-shek had been driven out of Communist China and now attempted to gain a stronghold in the northern Shan States by pushing south from their base in Yunnan. In an effort to prevent a Kuomintang invasion, the Burmese army under the leadership of General Ne Win, appointed Chief of Staff and Supreme Commander of the armed forces, took control.[38]

Continuing ethnic insurgencies and government instability led Ne Win to temporarily take over prime ministerial duties from U Nu in 1958. He managed to restore a semblance of order. General elections were held in 1960 and U Nu was re-elected. Ne Win was unhappy with the election result, and in March 1962 led a coup, and captured and imprisoned U Nu. Ne Win established the Revolutionary Council of the Union of Burma, with members drawn almost exclusively from the military.[39] The Shan princes were in conflict with Ne Win's military dictatorship and they decided to secede from the Union. They were within their rights to do so because the Panglong Agreement was beyond the binding period of ten years. In response, Ne Win forced them to relinquish their power and hereditary rights.

On 2 March 1962, the army stormed government buildings where Parliament was in session and, at gunpoint, arrested and imprisoned the president, prime minister and his cabinet, Shan princes and many of their relatives. Some princes and senior officials, including President Sao Shwe Thaik, died in prison in suspicious circumstances. One of the president's sons, a boy of seventeen, was killed on the day Parliament was stormed. Other Shan leaders disappeared, and those who survived were released but not allowed to return home to their states and people. The Burmese army ransacked Shan households and confiscated all weapons.

As the British had deposed the King of Burma, and with his deposition destroyed the culture of kingship in Burma, so the Burmese military now destroyed the power of the principalities and the traditional relationship that existed between the Shan people and their rulers. Buddhist religious institutions survived and continued to thrive, but the Shan rulers did not. The dynamic Sao Nang Hearn Kham, wife of Sao Shwe Thaik, fled with her family to Thailand in October 1963. Others took refuge in Thailand and in Europe, Canada and Australia. Today their descendants are scattered across the world. The story is not complete without mentioning the rulers of small states who managed to stay on and live in their modest palaces without coming to the attention of the authorities. They probably survived because they posed no threat to the military regime. The last *saopha* to rule in the township of Wan Yean, southern Shan States, was Sao Sein Nyunt, who passed away in 2018. He was the son of Sao Khun Yoong, who was a signatory to the Panglong Agreement of 1947. A copy of the Agreement is on display in the reception area of the modest teak palace where the elderly sisters of Sao Sein Nyunt continue to live.

The military have dominated the country now known as Myanmar since 1962. They have managed to represent their version of the country to the outside world. It is their identity and historical narratives that dictate and colour our understanding. Independent journalists are prevented from investigating an alternative view. In order to erase evidence of the Shan as an independent people with a distinct culture, they have systematically destroyed Shan palaces or confiscated them for use as offices for officials in the military regime. More recently, an important collection of court regalia, dress and court records has disappeared from a famous Shan palace museum. The military have hidden behind a smokescreen of religion by reinventing the palace as a Buddhist Museum. It is an irony not lost on many observers that the destruction of Shan culture and history has been foiled by a legacy from the colonial period. British diplomats and explorers, colonial administrators and travellers were great record-keepers, both in the written word and in photographs. Archives supply us with reports on the day-to-day running of a colonial regime and reveal the lifestyle of the Shan, including farmers, traders, artisans, village markets and the customs and pastimes of inhabitants of grand palaces. Photographs give insight into religious rituals and show interaction between British officials and the Shan people on formal and informal occasions. The records provide statistical data on local populations, ethnic identity, health and trade. This legacy, most of it now in the British Library, Cambridge University library, the British National Archives in Kew, and other British offices and museums in London and the provinces, has enabled scholars to conduct research up to and beyond the coup of 1962. Members of Shan royal families have added to this wealth of data with records and photographs that they carried with them when they fled abroad and some with published memoirs.

While living in exile, Sao Nang Hearn Kham, widow of the first president, together with her son Chao-Tzang Yawnghwe, formed the Shan State War Council (SSWC) and the Shan State Army (SSA), which were amalgamated in 1964. She died in exile in Canada in 2003, and her son, Hso Khan Pha, took up the cause of liberation. Currently there are armed Shan insurgent groups that have not signed peace agreements and engage in guerrilla warfare against the Burmese army. Shan civilians are often burned out of their villages and forced to flee. Young men are forcibly conscripted into the Burmese or minority armies and Shan men and women used as slaves in construction work, road-building and repairs for no pay and little food. Many have fled over the border into neighbouring Thailand, where they are not given refugee status and work as undocumented labourers. Young Shan women are trafficked and forced into prostitution.

How should we judge the behaviour of the British in the Shan States at the end of Empire? They helped establish a Parliament but did not intervene to prevent the Burmans under Aung San from dominating independence negotiations with Prime Minister Attlee. The Shan believed the British had failed them. The Karen, Kachin and Chin felt let down and resented the power of the Burmese army that exploited and continues to exploit their land, natural resources and habitat. The policy of the British government is to continue support for Myanmar through the Department for International Development (DFID). The department website states that food security, health and humanitarian aid are among its top priorities. A statement says: 'Now is not the time to turn our backs on a population which has suffered through decades of military dictatorship. A third of the population lives in conflict-affected areas, many out of the reach of the Burmese state.'[40] It is hoped that the DFID is able to give equal support to the Shan and other minorities, a policy that, as is argued here, was not achieved during negotiations at the end of empire.

Notes

1. *Myosa* were known locally as 'eaters of the town' because of the taxes they levied.
2. James G. Scott, *Burma, A Handbook of Practical Information* (London: 1906, reprint Orchid Press, 1999).
3. Sir George Grierson, quoted in J. G. Scott, *Burma and Beyond* (London: Grayson and Grayson, 1932), p. 26.
4. Susan Conway, *Tai Magic: Arts of the Supernatural in the Shan States and Lan Na* (Bangkok: River Books, 2014).
5. Susan Conway, *The Shan: Culture, Arts and Crafts* (Bangkok: River Books, 2006).
6. This term was adopted by cultural institutions in Britain, including the Victoria and Albert Museum which catalogued its Southeast Asian collections as 'Further India'.
7. Sao Saimong Mangrai, *The Padaeng Chronicle and the Jengtung* [Keng Tung] *Chronicle Translated* (Ann Arbor: The University of Michigan, Center for South and Southeast Asian Studies, 1981).
8. Some artisans found new patrons at the Shan courts, others survived by producing goods for the Burmese middle class and, as their numbers grew, British colonial officers and their families.
9. Lord Curzon took a great interest in preserving, not vandalising, Burmese monuments. (Rangoon, Office of the Superintendent Govt Printing Office, *List of Ancient monuments in Burma Mandalay Division*, 1910).
10. The British Library, India Office Library Collections, Sir George Scott photographed the Shan rulers at many darbars. The Colonel James Henry Green Collection, Brighton Pavilion and Museums, Brighton. Colonel Green photographed similar events from 1918 to 1935.
11. James G. Scott, *Burma and Beyond* (London: Grayson and Grayson, 1932), p. 260.
12. *Ibid.*
13. Published in the Shan State Manual of 1925. Rangoon: Superintendent Government Printing and Stationery, 1933 (p. 1v) National Library of Australia online catalogue.
14. Nel Adams, *My Vanished World* (Cheshire: Horseshoe Publications, 2000), p. 32.
15. *Coronation Durbar Illustrated* (Madras: Wieland Klein, 1903).
16. This mirrored earlier times when the princes had been sent to the court of Ava, and later to Mandalay, to learn the ways of the Burmese.
17. *Luntaya* is a type of tapestry weave pattern woven with many small shuttles.
18. Susan Conway, 'Shan tribute relations in the nineteenth century', *Journal of Contemporary Buddhism*, 10:1 (2009), 31–7.
19. These trading relationships became of great importance after the coup of 1962. Members of the Keng Tung royal family who fled to Chiang Mai were able to draw on their connections to establish successful businesses there.
20. The term 'Frontier Areas' was used to identify outlying lands where ethnic minority groups lived.
21. The Allies inflicted damage on the Shan States when they bombed Japanese positions. Monasteries and schools were among the casualties.

22 The period from the end of the Second Word War to 1948, when Burma gained independence, is called the Independence period.
23 Taihei Kikuchi, 'Shan Sawbwa's requirements in the Independence period of Burma/Myanmar (1945–1947)' *Journal of Tai Studies*, 2 (July 2018), 104.
24 Stanley A. Weiss, 'Did Aung San lead at Panglong – or follow?' *The Diplomat*, 21 July 2017, https://thediplomat.com/2017/07/did-aung-san-lead-at-panglong-or-follow/ (accessed 4 December 2018).
25 Information provided by Harn Yaungwhe, son of Sao Shwe Thaik, to S. A. Weiss (2017).
26 Taihei Kikuchi, 'Shan Sawbwa's requirements', pp. 101–11.
27 Adams, *My Vanished World*.
28 British companies were attacked over teak logging. This was an issue that had festered since a rebellion took place in the 1930s, which involved workers in the Shan States who were demanding the nationalisation of colonial companies.
29 Hugh Tinker, No. 156, IOR:M/4/2804 'Director Frontier Areas Administration to Secretary of State for Burma Telegram No 1447FA (2.1.1947), India Office Records, British Library, London.
30 The Rohingya are still not recognised legally as a minority group.
31 This reflects an earlier comment made by Sir George Grierson, who used the term 'dishcloth' rather than 'patchwork quilt'.
32 Hugh Tinker, *The Union of Burma* (London: Oxford University Press, 1957), p. 161.
33 Martin Smith, *Burma* (London: Zed Books, 1999), p. 75.
34 Quoted in Sao Sanda, *The Moon Princess* (Bangkok: River Books, 2008), p. 161.
35 Donald M. Seekins, *Historical Dictionary of Burma (Myanmar)* (London: Rowman & Littlefield, 2006), pp. 410–11.
36 After his term as president, Sao Shwe Thaik became speaker of the Chamber of Nationalities from 1950 to 1962.
37 Sao Shwe Thaik, Presidential Address to the Nation on the First Anniversary of Independence 4th January 1949 (Sarpay Beikman 1952, quoted in Patricia Elliot, *The White Umbrella* (Bangkok: Friends Books, 1999) pp. 206–7.
38 Ne Win was one of the Thirty Comrades who in 1941 had travelled to Hainan, China, to receive military training from the Japanese. He became an officer in the Japanese-sponsored Burma Independence Army.
39 Ne Win was president from 1974 to 1981. His policies turned Burma into one of the poorest nations of the world, with widespread government corruption and continuing unrest.
40 Department for International Development, Government of the United Kingdom, Policy paper: *DFID Burma Operational Plan 2014*, www.gov.uk/government/publications/dfid-burma-operational-plan-2014 (accessed 4 December 2018).

CHAPTER SIX

Malaysia's multi-monarchy: surviving colonisation and decolonisation
Anthony Milner

Modern Malaysia is characterised by its elaborate monarchy, as well as by its sharply plural society – a Muslim-Malay majority, but with very large Chinese and Indian minority communities. There is not just one royal ruler: apart from the country's King (or *Yang di-Pertuan Agong*), nine of the states in the federation (which consists of thirteen states and three federal territories) have Rulers (seven with the title 'Sultan'). Every five years, the Rulers choose one among them to be King. The country, not surprisingly, has many royal family members with the titles 'Tengku' and 'Raja'; and many royal subjects from every ethnic group are awarded royal titles – such as 'Datuk', 'Datuk Seri', 'Tan Sri' and 'Tun'. Royal ceremonies, especially royal birthdays, are glittering affairs, with crowds of participants – often dressed in sumptuous *songket* (brocade fabric), and seated largely according to rank – witnessing royal speeches and the bestowal of royal titles.

Malaysia is not the only Asian country where monarchy has survived, but it is unique in being a multi-monarchy state. It is also true that things might have turned out differently – as they did in Burma, Indonesia, India and many other countries. This chapter argues that the tenacity of monarchy in Malaysia was due not only to the particular colonial experience but also to specific qualities in the institution itself, and in the practice of Malay diplomacy.

Before the British and Dutch established their authority across the Malay Archipelago, mainly in the nineteenth century, there were numerous monarchies – often called *'kerajaan'* – not only on the Peninsula but also on Sumatra, Borneo and other islands. Many had populations of only thousands or tens of thousands, and they tended to rely on trade. They had converted to Islam one after another, commencing in the thirteenth century, and were defined by the personal relation between ruler and subject, rather than by territorial boundaries. Today, the Peninsular monarchies tend to be referred to as 'Malay Sultanates', but in the pre-modern period, as I will discuss, race appears not to have been the marker of identity it became in later years.

In the early part of the nineteenth century the British and Dutch divided the archipelago between them, initially as spheres of influence, and gradually began to sign treaties with the rulers, bringing them under various degrees of European control. The Dutch eventually made rulers formally subject to Dutch sovereignty, but also allowed them responsibility in numerous administrative and legal areas and sought to encourage respect for 'native customary law'. In the British sphere – in the southern portion of the Peninsula – the rulers retained sovereignty but agreed to accept the advice of British advisers. Although the Peninsula rulers now lost powers, especially in economic administration, they gained funding for new and substantial palaces. They also obtained greater authority vis-à-vis major chiefs, who had once possessed strong powers in their particular districts. The Peninsular monarchies certainly did well from the British by the standards of the once-powerful Burmese monarchy. When the Burmese king fought the British in 1886, he was sent into exile; moreover, the monarchy was abolished and direct rule was implemented.

European imperial power in Southeast Asia never recovered from the 1941–42 conquests by Japan. Most local rulers held on to some authority during the occupation, but in both British and Dutch regions they confronted new dangers in the immediate aftermath. In the Dutch regions they were removed, sometimes through revolutionary violence. There are still some sultans in Indonesia – the modern state which inherited the Dutch-governed territories – but they are much diminished in importance. On the Peninsula, despite a degree of tension with the nationalist leadership (including the United Malay Nationalist Organization, UMNO, which ruled from 1957 to 2018), and some other elements in Malaysian society, monarchy has proved resilient. The particular colonial experience with the British is one factor in explaining this, but it is also important to acknowledge the agency of the rulers themselves.

The British period

The fact that the British were convinced to work with the existing Malay monarchies rather than opt for direct rule, as they had in Burma (after the abolition of its monarchy), is of critical significance. Difficulties certainly arose in the state of Perak, where the British replaced the ruler, having decided he was involved in the murder of the first British Resident. In general, however, the Malay rulers and the British achieved an accommodation.

MALAYSIA: SURVIVING COLONISATION AND DECOLONISATION

Although the British established a colony in the Straits Settlements (that is, the coastal port cities of Penang, Melaka and Singapore) in the late eighteenth and early nineteenth centuries, their authority in the Peninsular kingdoms was based on treaties with rulers, especially with the 1874 Pangkor Engagement with Perak. One senior British commencing official explained in 1903 that 'these are protected Malay States and not British Colonies', and British officials were there to 'advise and assist and not to supersede the rulers in the administration of their own states'.[1] In fact, great change took place on the Peninsula, especially with the development of a new plantation and mining economy, largely involving the Chinese and Indian communities, as well as Europeans. The Malay states began to look like a dual society, with new urban centres, such as Kuala Lumpur and Ipoh, largely dominated by foreigners, and Malays remaining mostly in rural areas. To some observers, British-protected Malaya seemed, on the one hand, to be a 'bustling commercial outfit', and, on the other, a 'Malay museum'.[2] Although this exaggerates the extent to which the Malay communities were shielded from modernisation, Governor Hugh Clifford, even in 1927, could speak of the Peninsular states as 'Muhammadan Monarchies' – adding that the British had received 'no mandate' from the 'Rajas, Chiefs or people to vary the system of Government which has existed in these territories from time immemorial'.[3]

The institution of monarchy, therefore, was in a sense endorsed by the British. This could not have been the case, however, if the Peninsular rulers had responded to the expansion of British power as the Burmese king had done. The flexibility of the Malay rulers is important, as will be discussed below. Also, the British moved forward slowly on the Peninsula. After establishing the Straits Settlements, they were for many decades reluctant to assume further governmental responsibilities, seeking only informal influence over the different monarchies. As they became increasingly entangled in the economies and political strife of these states (all the more challenging because of immigration from China and elsewhere) – and as other European powers, including Germany, began to express an interest in the region – the incentives for greater intervention grew.

These developments took place in the 1870s, however, and it was only in the following decades that the pace of European colonial competition and expansion into Asia and Africa accelerated. The Pangkor Engagement provided only for the appointment of a British adviser (Resident); and it also left 'Malay Religion and Custom' in the hands of the Sultan. From a Malay perspective, this was highly significant. Custom, or *adat*, was so significant in Malay society that these reserve powers must have seemed substantial. According to a Malay maxim, 'life is contained within custom [adat]'; and it was also said: 'let the child die but not the *adat*'.⁴

The first Resident of Perak – against the wishes of the British government – was not cautious. He conveyed that he intended to move the Sultan aside altogether, and assume direct government over the country.⁵ As a result, he was murdered and a short war followed. Though victory over Perak was easy, the cost of the war made the British government all the more opposed to annexation or even to 'government of [Perak] by British officials in the name of the Sultan'.⁶ A few years later, in the state of Pahang, British officials again moved ambitiously, and another brief but expensive war occurred. In 1893, the leading official on the Peninsula, Frank Swettenham, concluded that 'annexation is impossible'.⁷

The British were not merely influenced by Malay resistance; they also realised that monarchy was a critical institution in Malay society. Without the Sultans, remarked one official in 1927, the 'Malays would become a mob'.⁸ It is possible he was influenced by the counterexample against annexation which British policy in that other Southeast Asian country, Burma, had offered. The removal in 1886 of the Burmese monarchy – which appears to have been as pivotal as Malay monarchy in social, political and religious organisation – was followed by violent anarchy and 'ideological crisis'.⁹ From a Burmese perspective and in the words of a Burmese poem, the country had entered an 'Age of Nothingness'.¹⁰

In the years between the 1870s and 1941, the British did bring far-reaching change to the Peninsular states, especially in the Federated Malay States (FMS) (Perak, Selangor, Negeri Sembilan and Pahang), where a united British-led bureaucracy was developed. It was primarily the Chinese and Indians in the country who engaged in the modern economy – the number of Chinese was almost equal to the Malay population in the FMS by 1900 – but Malays also engaged in the cash economy, especially in rubber growing, and an elite began to receive modern education.¹¹ Some commentators have argued that the rulers were reduced to symbolic significance in the British period, with 'the substance of power' passing into British hands.¹² Nevertheless, a number of legal decisions acknowledged that they retained their sovereignty, and as 'rulers-in-council' they continued to be the source of authority in their states. Their retention of power in the critical area of 'Malay Religion and Custom', as one would predict, gave them a major role in Malay society, including control over religious teaching and publishing in many areas.¹³ Also, as John Gullick demonstrated in his careful examination of the details of British administration, an important 'balance of power and influence' was developed.¹⁴ The

Malay Ruler had 'influence', because of a 'tacit bargain by which the colonial regime secured his support and advice'.[15]

In the British period, therefore, Malay monarchy was not drained of significance, and it can be argued that this was at least partly due to the character of the institution, the *kerajaan*, and the diplomatic traditions which the rulers inherited. It was not just a matter of defending an old institution; the sultanates had to be radically reformed to survive.

The monarchies

At the outset, it must be stressed that Malay monarchy was not merely an important political institution in the societies of the Peninsula and Archipelago. The monarchs, not surprisingly, were believed to possess supernatural powers (*daulat*); more importantly, monarchy was the *essential* institution in these societies. The Malay, like the Burmese case, in fact offers support for anthropologist Louis Dumont's reflections on the centrality of monarchy across Southeast Asia. Despite the strong Indian cultural influence in the region, he pointed out, the caste system, with its superior Brahmin, was not adopted. Nowhere in Southeast Asia was the ruler 'dispossessed of his religious prerogatives', and in this sense kingship could be said to have fixed 'a limit to Indian influence' in the region.[16]

Although Malay monarchy was remoulded over the years, such a deep ideational heritage in itself is likely to be a factor in that monarchy's survival. The essentialness of monarchy is conveyed time and again in Malay writings of the pre-modern era.[17] The term used to describe the polity, '*kerajaan*', means literally 'the condition of having a raja'. Understood in terms of ruler–subject not ruler–territory, the duty of those who 'live under Rajas', according to one famous Malay text, was to 'do whatever work we have to do as diligently as possible', and keep in mind that 'it is good to die with a reputation [*nama*] which is good'. The spiritual aspect of the ruler–subject relation is also suggested in the statement that a 'just Raja and the Prophet of God' are like 'two jewels in one ring': when you do loyal service for the 'Prophet of God it is as if you do it for God himself'.

Nothing expresses so clearly the Malay ruler's significance as the way a community possessing no ruler is portrayed. In the absence of a ruler, one text explains, 'customs and orders of procedure' no longer existed; and there was 'utter confusion' (*huru-hara*).[18] In a further case, related in the renowned *Hikayat Hang Tuah*, a sultan is removed from his palace by a traitor, and the chaos that follows involves mass killings and rape.[19] The 'property of this world', explains this same text in another episode, can have no real purpose (*guna*) in a raja-less state.[20]

The ruler's centrality was obvious in royal ceremonies, which were often elaborate. Participation in ceremonies might be compared with undergoing border immigration procedures today. Engaging in the *kerajaan* through ceremony, the rank you held would be evident in your dress or the position you occupied. All rank, all social structure, was articulated around the ruler. Similarly, the laws of the polity were said (in a text from Melaka) to be in the ruler's 'possession', and are described as having been 'laid down' by the first Muslim ruler of the state. A later text describes the Sultan of Pahang as 'disseminating both Islamic and customary law'.[21]

Even in narratives about Islamisation, the monarch is presented as central. The adoption of the new religion, so the texts make clear, did not entail the overthrow of rulers and their dynasties. Rather, the rulers, who had previously been Buddhist leaders described as *bodhisattva*-like, led the way in reconstructing their polities, appropriating Islamic titles and legal arrangements.[22] The Malay Annals describes Sultan Mohammed Shah as the first in his state to be converted, and as then 'commanding' his subjects to become Muslims.[23] Christian missionaries in later years, understanding the rulers' centrality, hoped to make use of them. If a ruler 'ordered' his subjects to do so, observed one missionary, they would 'be of any religion good or bad'.[24] In fact, although rulers talked earnestly with Christian clergy, seeking to understand their point of view,[25] there was no conversion. Other facets of Western civilisation, including style of dress, faced less resistance.

Whether dealing with Islam or the West, Malay rulers played what might be termed a teaching role, and to this end attempted to keep up to date with doctrines that might be of use to their people. Dependence on trade must also have encouraged monarchs who needed to be open to aspirations and viewpoints from many quarters. Cultural diversity was a long-term feature of these *kerajaan*. A Chinese account of Srivijaya, a large kingdom based in Sumatra and dating back to the seventh century, noted that 'traders from all countries' stopped there; and an Arab visitor reported that the domestic parrots in the place could speak Arabic, Persian, Greek and 'Hindu'.[26]

The earliest records also indicate that these Malay monarchs were accustomed to look up to China and other major states, and were comfortable seeing themselves as small polities. Far from aspiring to sovereign equality, they appear to have seen opportunities as well as threats in hierarchical relations. In the case of China, the rulers of Srivijaya and later (in the fifteenth century) Melaka, gained status on the basis of their China connection. They received noble titles and seals of investiture from the emperor, and such recognition would seem to have helped in their struggle with local rivals, including struggle over trade. The number of missions sent to the Chinese emperor testifies to the rulers' enthusiasm for Chinese recognition, and there is plenty of evidence of competition for that recognition.[27] Similar manoeuvres took place in later centuries with respect to Siam. The ruler of Kedah might rise in the Siam-centred hierarchy, obtaining a higher Siamese title than the Terengganu ruler, and this would be a result of perceived loyal service to the Siam king. The new rank would be symbolised by a royal 'grand dress-set' and new ceremonial arrangements.[28]

With respect to the skills the Malay rulers required to operate hierarchically, court texts stress a detailed knowledge of rituals and letter-writing, and also a talent for manoeuvring between one polity and another. The ingenuity this required conjures up the image of a creature in Malay folk literature – the wily mouse-deer, who uses all types of ruse to 'frustrate bigger and stronger animals'. The mouse-deer, it has been observed, is capable of teaching 'the small man how to survive among the physical giants by using his wits'.[29] The contrast here with the Burmese monarchy is instructive. Although kingship was the essential institution in both cases, the kings of Burma were less inclined to mouse-deer diplomacy. They called themselves 'king of kings, the lord supreme ... the mighty universal monarch'. In the nineteenth century, one of these rulers expressed amazement and anger when shown the small size of his country on a foreign-made map of the world.[30] Early in the nineteenth century, the Burmese Konbaung dynasty of Burma was probably the strongest power in Southeast Asia. The dynasty's proud founding monarch had boasted to a visitor: 'see these arms and this thigh (drawing the sleeves of his Vesture over his Shoulders, and tucking the lower part up to his Crutch) ... amongst 1000 you won't see my match ... I have carried my Arms to the confines of China'.[31] There is no record of Malay rulers making such claims. What chroniclers stress time and again is their fine manners and gentle (*lemah lembut*) personal style – and this is sometimes affirmed in European accounts.[32]

The further aspect of rulership (alluded to above) which may have proved valuable was the absence of strong ethnic identification. I have been writing of 'Malay rulers', as that is how they tend to be described today, but they could be described more accurately as just 'rulers'. The royal genealogies around the Archipelago suggest a wide range of ethnic input. The Melaka royal line claimed descent from Alexander the Great; the Sultan of Deli in Sumatra traced his ancestors back to an Indian; the Raja of Perlis on the Peninsula possessed

Arab origins. Senior officials in royal service included Hakkas from China, Indians and Peguans (from the Burma region). The people in a polity or *kerajaan* tended to be called just *rakyat* (subject). When the term 'Malay' began to gain circulation – stimulated partly by European preoccupation with racial classification – it was initially resisted by the royal courts.[33] In the colonial period, it is true, the ruler gained a special position with respect to the Malay community, but the residue of trans-ethnic rulership remained significant.

Strategies and tactics

The nineteenth and twentieth centuries were sharply challenging for the Malay monarchs – but not only because of Western imperial intervention. Even before the Pangkor Engagement, the British could be threatening. In 1862 their navy bombarded Terengganu, attempting to force the ruler to remove another sultan from his state. Certainly, in these years, the different rulers communicated with one another, and also with the King of Siam, deliberating on how best to deal with the British, the rising power in the region.[34]

When the rulers did accept British Residents, beginning in the 1870s, there is no indication they did so with enthusiasm. In some cases, they kept British officials waiting a long time before accepting the arrangement, and they appear to have agreed only when assured continued control over the customs of their states. When Residents then tried to implement reforms, the rulers were often reluctant. In Perak, there were rumours just before the Resident's assassination that the state was to be annexed, and that the Resident would intervene deeply in the state.[35] In 1891 in Pahang, the British found it difficult to discern whether the sultan was supporting the rebels, but there was evidence of collusion, and again plenty of examples of British interference in the state administration.[36] The Perak and Pahang uprisings had no chance of success, but the turmoil they caused may have assisted Malay monarchs to gain the 'tacit bargain' with the British.

Opposition to interference in the domestic affairs of a *kerajaan*, it should be noted, was deep-seated in Malay political thinking. Although hierarchical relations were not seen as a problem, pre-modern Malay texts contain strong injunctions against interfering in the customs (*adat*) of a state. There are often warnings that customs differ from one community to another, and that they must be respected. Even when one ruler gained superiority over another, the higher ruler was warned not to interfere in the local *adat* of his new vassal. In the case of relations between Malay states and Siam, the sending of tribute did not seem to trouble Malay rulers, but there was strong opposition if the Siamese ruler interfered with local customs.³⁷ This aspect of Malay political culture suggests how British promises not to interfere with 'religion and custom' would have reduced a ruler's anxiety about accepting a Resident.

To perceive rulers as always resisting change – defending the 'Malay museum' – would be misleading. Some were clearly conservative. Sultan Ahmad of Pahang (d. 1914) wanted no interference 'with the old customs of this country which have good and proper reasons', and seemed to turn away from changes taking place, withdrawing up river surrounded by male and female retainers. Such negative behaviour required skill, if one were to avoid British retaliation.³⁸ Other rulers employed their talents in embracing change, some reconstituting their polities along modern (Western) lines, as centuries earlier their ancestors had engaged in the Islamisation of their *kerajaan*.

Sultan Abu Bakar of Johor (d. 1895), based adjacent to the bustling British-governed Singapore, had his state properly surveyed – defined territorially – and created a police force and other bureaucratic institutions. His courtiers wrote books focused on the 'state of Johor' (its physical characteristics and its people) and not just – in the manner of the texts of pre-modern times – on the monarch's actions and orders. These writings convey a more active, development-oriented, approach to government – to the 'organizing of the affairs of the country and its tributaries'. The Sultan himself is said to have acted with 'diligence and energy', encouraging his subjects to open up plantations.

Abu Bakar also left his state with a constitution, and the Malay words used for 'constitution', '*undang undang tuboh kerajaan*', convey the idea of the constitution being the 'body' (*tuboh*) of the *kerajaan*. Like the surveying of the physical territory of Johor, this reinforced the impression of Johor being a state or entity existing independently of the person of the ruler.³⁹

In terms of diplomatic skills, the Johor ruler knew how to impress Westerners, with a palace conforming to English taste, and well laid-out roads. One female visitor in the 1880s commented that in Siam civilisation was 'potential': in Johor, 'it is at work'.⁴⁰ In his personal style, as some saw it, Abu Bakar seemed like an English gentleman, and he even took pains to cultivate Queen Victoria. Gaining high royal awards from the British and other European monarchs, he used these foreign credentials in much the way the Kedah ruler exploited the Siam hierarchy: to advance his local status vis-à-vis his close neighbours. Knowing that Johor was not a large or populous state, Abu Bakar in this way practised mouse-deer diplomacy.⁴¹

A number of Perak rulers also saw advantages in joining, not resisting, the hierarchy around English monarchy. Under Sultan Idris (d. 1916), in the words of a later Malay account, Perak was 'organized in the manner of civilized states'.[42] Idris also said he liked 'belonging' to the British Empire, noting that 'none of my forebears enjoyed the greatness that is mine, in that I am a portion of something so very great'.[43] He, too, this comment suggests, was operating in the long Malay tradition of hierarchy diplomacy. In the 1930s, another Perak ruler who won British respect and helped modernise his state was Sultan Abdul Aziz. In a brochure issued at the time of his coronation, he is portrayed as a senior bureaucrat rather than a sultan of the past. His administrative experience (including a period as an Assistant District Officer) is listed, and he is described as being 'careful and conscientious'. Reading this brochure, including the section on the 'History of Perak', underlines the way the state was now constituted separately from its ruler. The new sultan is presented not so much as the linchpin of the raja-polity as servant of the state, helping to promote economic and political development.[44]

In these British years, the rulers confronted three other challenges, as well as that of reconstructing their states in European style. First, there was the change underway in the religious life of their subjects. What are sometimes referred to as Salafi (or Fundamentalist) doctrines gained influence in the nineteenth century, and involved both a critique of Malaysian monarchy and advocacy of religious scholars (*ulama*) as the real leaders of the community. In this context, a sultan had to demonstrate his piety[45] but also be careful to counter or censor religious criticism. In 1915 in Kelantan, for instance, the Sultan set up a Council of Religion and Custom, led by loyal officials, in an attempt to reduce the influence of the state *mufti* (jurist), who appeared hostile to royal authority.[46] In Perak it was made clear that the administration of religious law was 'in the hands of' the ruler.[47]

The second type of challenge to the rulers arose from the new 'Malay' movement. Influenced by eighteenth- and nineteenth-century European stress on race in the classification of humankind, the promotion of a concept of a specifically 'Malay' identity and loyalty had the potential to compete with allegiance to a ruler. Royal courts on the Peninsula (and also in the Dutch East Indies) initially resisted the formation of Malay associations. Then, in the late 1930s, a form of compromise was reached, when they began to accept associations with such titles as the 'Selangor Malay Association' and the 'Pahang Malay Association'.[48] In Perak, in the case of Sultan Abdul Aziz, official proclamations made clear he had taken on a special responsibility to 'unite our race [*bangsa*]', and to make sure the Malay people were not left behind as the state was modernised.[49]

As the Peninsular sultanates headed towards the independence period, they demonstrated flexibility by increasingly presenting themselves as 'credible and respectable champions and guardians of the Malays'.[50] At one level, they were competing against a growing non-royal elite which claimed to speak on behalf of an incipient Malay nationalism. At another, they were making the 'adaptation to nationalism' which the political scientist Benedict Anderson considered essential for the survival of any monarchy.[51]

The third challenge concerned the growing number of non-Malays in the Peninsular states. Here we need to put aside the description 'Malay ruler', and recall how the ethnicity-blind heritage may have helped these monarchies when faced with great demographic change. One Malay text praised Abu Bakar of Johor for 'looking after the Chinese subjects living in his state';[52] he certainly rewarded his Chinese subjects with royal titles.[53] At his coronation, Abdul Aziz of Perak declared he had 'always been friends' with all the different races because he 'had not forgotten the help these races have given in making Perak wealthy'.[54] In post-independence times, in fact, one ruler after another has declared a commitment to be a monarch for all racial groups, and not just the Malays.

To portray the rulers as merely passive or impotent during the British period, therefore, is misleading. They led both in the reform of their polities and in positioning them advantageously in the British hierarchy, and in doing so drew upon the *kerajaan* political heritage. The Japanese Occupation may have been more damaging to them. The institution of monarchy was retained, but commoner political leaders were given new opportunities in administration and began 'throwing their weight around'.[55] Furthermore, as Kobkua Suwannathat-Pian has observed, it would have been a 'cultural and politically shocking experience' for the 'average Malay' to see 'his Ruler performing self-demeaning exercises such as bowing in the direction of the Imperial palace as a mark of homage to the [Japanese] Emperor'.[56]

The sharpest challenge to Malay monarchy occurred immediately after the Japanese surrender. Although the British, following the Pangkor Engagement, had a duty to 'protect' Perak,[57] they had failed to do so in the Pacific War. Nevertheless, on resuming control following the Japanese occupation, they began investigating which rulers had shown signs of disloyalty. Taking advantage of this threatening atmosphere, and only weeks after the Japanese capitulation, they also sought to impose on the Peninsular states a new and radical constitutional structure. The so-called Malayan Union reversed decades of British policy, ushering in a unitary state structure in which the sultans would no longer hold sovereignty and the Malay community would lose its privileged position. Nervous of British reprisals, the rulers assented to the new order, but with great reluctance.[58]

An influential narrative in post-independence Malaysia suggests the rulers let their people down, and that it was UMNO which overthrew the Malayan Union. This is an exaggeration. The threat of the Union did promote Malay unity along ethnic grounds – the cry of 'Long live the Malays' was often heard. But the rulers also campaigned strongly against the Union, and Sultan Abdul Aziz of Perak has even been credited with proposing the 1948 federal scheme, introduced to replace the Malayan Union, and destined to become the structure on which independent Malaya would be based (Figure 6.1).[59]

These post-war years were also troubling for the Peninsular monarchs because of developments in Indonesia. In East Sumatra, Malay royal houses not unlike their own were being overthrown in the social revolution. Although the Sumatran rulers prospered financially under the Dutch, they did not, as noted already, retain sovereignty, and for various reasons failed to achieve accommodation with the Indonesian nationalist movement.[60] In Indonesia, Sukarno overcame state or regional loyalties, and asserted a national sovereignty based on Dutch colonial sovereignty.

In the years between 1948 and 1957, the Peninsular rulers went on defending their position, against UMNO, as well as the British. As one British official saw things (in 1946), the British had 'not weaned' the rulers from an 'active and dominating role in the political field'.[61] Another official commented (in 1951) that they were not yet 'fully

Figure 6.1 Signature of the Federation of Malaya Agreement by the Sultan of Perak, at King's House, Kuala Lumpur, 1948

constitutional rulers'.[62] Certainly, in the preparations for the 1957 Independence Constitution, the rulers did not play 'second fiddle' to UMNO.[63] They made interventions, first, in the deliberations of the Reid Commission (formed to advise on the constitution), and second, in the Working Party (created to deal with unresolved matters in the Reid report). They gained extra powers for the Conference of Rulers and an increase in the financial distribution to the states. They also insisted they were no mere constitutional monarchs in the religious sphere. They boycotted the Working Committee when they did not get their way – possessing the advantage, one assumes, of having the sovereign right to approve or not approve the constitution.

When the rulers emphasised 'their personal position as titular founts of the temporal and spiritual authority in their respective territories' and the 'ties of personal allegiance' with their 'subjects in the states',[64] they invoked their pre-modern historical role. It is a role picked up in the Constitution with the declaration that, 'subject to the provisions of this Constitution', the 'sovereignty, prerogatives, powers and jurisdiction of the Rulers ... as hitherto had and enjoyed shall remain unaffected' (Article 181, 1). In Lord President Raja Azlan Shah's view, it is a mistake to assume that a monarch's role is 'confined to what is laid down by the Constitution', and this complements well Prime Minister Mahathir bin Mohamad's judgement that the rulers have exercised 'considerable influence, being backed by strong Malay traditions'.[65]

Malaysia's first prime minister, Tunku Abdul Rahman, had hoped that the rulers of independent Malaya (and Malaysia) would not be involved in politics. Various attempts have been made since then (particularly by Mahathir) to cut back their role, but the rulers remain significant political players. Mahathir himself has observed that Chief Ministers in Malaysian states find it 'difficult to say "no" to their Sultans'.[66] With respect to the Malay community, the rulers have legal control over the critically important constitutional provisions regarding the 'special position of the Malays'; on the other hand, the rulers have consistently invoked their trans-ethnic credentials to speak up on behalf of all Malaysians, not merely Malays. In 2008, the Conference of Rulers spoke inclusively, describing the institution of monarchy as a 'protective umbrella ensuring impartiality among the citizens'.[67]

In 2018, when the Government of Malaysia passed out of the hands of the UMNO-led coalition for the first time since 1957, monarchy, together with other national institutions, played a key role in ensuring a stable transition. Rumours of behind-the-scene tensions were rife, but the King (Agong) and Deputy King implemented a constitutional mechanism which transcended day-to-day, year-by-year, political battle.

Conclusion

Debate about the future of monarchy has taken place from time to time since 1957 and has occurred again during the political upheavals of 2018. But monarchy seems embedded in modern Malaysia, even though this has been portrayed as departing from 'present-day notions of parliamentary democracy'.[68] Going back to pre-modern times, monarchy was the foundational institution in the organising of political and social life – more important, for instance, than it had been in Indian contexts. Modern Malay monarchs benefited from this *kerajaan* heritage. They have gained also from a tradition of flexibility – a degree of comfort operating in hierarchies (sharing sovereignty, so it might seem). A third element in this ideational heritage has been alertness to fresh ideas and trends in the wider world, seeking out what might be of benefit to their rule.

The Peninsular monarchs were willing, certainly by contrast with the kings of Burma, to seek compromises with British imperialism. Some even renovated their polities along Western lines, as they had reconstructed their *kerajaan* in earlier centuries, when entering the Muslim world. In the nineteenth and twentieth centuries, the rulers adapted as well to the rising commitment to ethnic loyalty, now presenting themselves, in the words of a coronation album from Pahang, as a 'branch of Malay culture'.[69] In a further danger area, the rulers took advantage of the special role they maintained, even in the British period, with respect to Islam, making sure they could defend themselves against hostile religious doctrines.

The Malay rulers behaved shrewdly, especially in convincing the advancing British of the benefits of retaining rather than overthrowing monarchy. Even the resistance movements in Perak and Pahang, which rulers appeared quietly to foster, served a purpose. They helped to convince the British to leave sovereignty in the rulers' hands, not insisting they become subordinate, as their fellow rulers in Sumatra had become, under Dutch sovereignty.

In the creation of independent Malaya, the rulers benefited from having retained this sovereignty, and, partly as a result, a continuing loyalty from many of their Malay subjects. They also inherited a tradition of trans-ethnic allegiance which helped them to accommodate, in one way or another, the rapidly growing number of non-Malays entering the country. At least at the elite level, these non-Malays could gain titles and other benefits offered by Malaysia's elaborate monarchical architecture.

When the Malay monarchs began to carve out a position for themselves in Malaysia's turbulent political and social life, they drew, first, on a pre-modern institutional and diplomatic heritage and, second, on an assemblage of skills refined in the heat of British colonialism.

Acknowledgement

The author would like to acknowledge the advice of Abdul Rahman Embong, Astanah Abdul Aziz, Peter Borschberg, Philip Koh, Claire Milner and Mohd Annuar Zaini.

Notes

1 J. P. Rodger, cited in Donna J. Amoroso, *Traditionalism and the Ascendency of the Malay Ruling Class in Colonial Malaya* (Petaling Jaya: SIRD, 2014), p. 60.
2 C. Harrison, quoted in A. J. Stockwell, *British Policy and Malay Politics during the Malayan Union Experiment* (Kuala Lumpur: MBRAS Monograph, 1979), p. 31.
3 William R. Roff, *The Origins of Malay Nationalism* (Kuala Lumpur: Oxford University Press, 1994), p. 11.
4 Quoted in Anthony Milner, *The Malays* (Chichester: Wiley-Blackwell, 2011), p. 67.
5 Anthony Milner, 'Malay kingship in a Burmese perspective', in Ian W. Mabbett (ed.), *Patterns of Kingship and Authority in Traditional Asia* (London: Croom Helm, 1985), pp. 168–9.
6 *Ibid.*, p. 170.
7 *Ibid.*, p. 174.
8 Anthony Milner, *The Invention of Politics in Colonial Malaya* (Cambridge: Cambridge University Press, 2002), p. 195.
9 E. Sarkisyanz, quoted in Milner, 'Malay kingship in a Burmese perspective', p. 165.
10 From Zibani Sayadaw, and quoted in Ni Ni Myint, *Burma's Struggle against British Imperialism (1885–1895)* (Rangoon: The Universities Press, 1983), p. 42.
11 Milner, *The Invention of Politics*, pp. 91–2.
12 Eunice Thio, *British Policy in the Malay Peninsula 1880–1910* (Singapore: University of Malaya Press, 1969), p. xvii.
13 Milner, *The Invention of Politics*, p. 194; Anthony Milner, *Malaysian Monarchy and the Bonding of the Nation* (Bangi: Penerbit Universiti Kebangsaan Malaysia, 2011), p. 10.
14 J. M. Gullick, *Rulers and Residents: Influence and Power in the Malay States 1870–1920* (Singapore: Oxford University Press, 1992).
15 *Ibid.*, p. vi.
16 Louis Dumont, *Homo Hierarchicus* (London: Paladin, 1970), p. 262.
17 For textual references regarding the *kerajaan*, see Milner, *The Malays*, pp. 66–9. See also Anthony Milner, *Kerajaan: Malay Political Culture on the Eve of Colonial Rule* (Petaling Jaya: SIRD, 2016).
18 Milner, *The Malays*, pp. 68–9.
19 Kassim Ahmad (ed.), *Hikayat Hang Tuah* (Kuala Lumpur: Dewan Bahasa dan Pustaka, 1968), p. 307.
20 *Ibid.*, p. 70.
21 Anthony Milner, 'Islam and Malay kingship', *Journal of the Royal Asiatic Society*, 1 (1981), 49.
22 *Ibid.*, pp. 50–3.
23 *Ibid.*, p. 51.
24 Quoted in Milner, *The Invention of Politics*, p. 154.
25 *Ibid.*
26 Milner, *The Malays*, p. 26.

27 O. W. Wolters, *Fall of Srivijaya in Malay History* (Ithaca, NY and London: Cornell University Press, 1970), chs 5 and 11.
28 Kobkua Suwannathat-Pian, *Thai–Malay Relations. Traditional Intra-regional Relations from the Seventeenth to the Early Twentieth Centuries* (Singapore: Oxford University Press, 1988), p. 63; J. M. Gullick, 'Kedah 1821–1855: years of exile and return', *Journal of the Malaysian Branch of the Royal Asiatic Society*, 56:2 (1983), 62.
29 Muhammad Haji Salleh, *Romance and Laughter in the Archipelago: Essays in Classical and Contemporary Poetics of the Malay World* (Pinang: Universiti Sains Malaysia, 2006), p. 200.
30 S. J. Tambiah, *World Conqueror and World Renouncer: A Study of Buddhism and Polity against a Historical Background* (Cambridge: Cambridge University Press, 1978), p. 81; James S. Olson and Robert Shadle (eds), *Historical Dictionary of the British Empire* (Westport, CT: Greenwood, 1996), p. 215.
31 *Reprint from Dalrymple's Oriental Repertory, 1791–7 of portions relating to Burma* (Rangoon: Government Printing, 1926), pp. 151–2.
32 Milner, *Kerajaan*, p. 44.
33 Milner, *Malaysian Monarchy*, pp. 31–6. The British, in particular, were responsible for racialising the monarchs. Early in the nineteenth century, Thomas Stamford Raffles and John Leyden envisaged a 'general Malay league', and at the time of signing the Pangkor Engagement the British stressed the ruler's role with respect to 'Malay custom'. *Ibid.*, pp. 33–4.
34 See, for instance, the correspondence in Raimy Che-Ross (ed.), *The Royal Letters of Baginda Omar, Sultan Terengganu Darul Iman IX Marhum Baginda (1806–1876)*, vol. 1 (Kuala Lumpur: Yayasan DiRaja Sultan Mizan, 2015).
35 Milner, 'Malay kingship in a Burmese perspective', p. 169.
36 *Ibid.*, pp. 170–2.
37 Anthony Milner, *Will ASEAN Continue to be the Cornerstone of Malaysian Foreign Policy: The 'Community-building' Priority* (Kuala Lumpur: ISIS Malaysia, 2016), pp. 29–30.
38 Milner, *The Invention of Politics*, pp. 209–10.
39 *Ibid.*, ch. 8.
40 Thio, *British Policy*, p. 115.
41 Milner, *The Invention of Politics*, ch. 8.
42 *Ibid.*, p. 239.
43 *Ibid.*, p. 210.
44 *Ibid.*, ch. 9.
45 *Ibid.*, pp. 216–19, 245.
46 *Ibid.*, p. 218.
47 *Ibid.*, p. 245.
48 Milner, *The Malays*, pp. 135–6.
49 Milner, *The Invention of Politics*, pp. 242–3.
50 Kobkua Suwannathat-Pian, *Palace, Political Party and Power: A Story of the Socio-Political Development of Malay Kingship* (Singapore: NUS Press, 2011), p. 183.
51 Benedict Anderson, *Useful or Useless Relics: Today's Strange Monarchies* (Shiga: Ryukoku University, Afrasian Centre for Peace and Development Studies, 2007), p. 7.
52 *Ibid.*, p. 214.
53 *Ibid.*, p. 261.
54 *Ibid.*, p. 244.
55 Paul Kratoska, *The Japanese Occupation of Malaya: A Social and Economic History* (London: Hurst, 1998), p. 110.
56 Kobkua, *Palace, Political Party and Power*, p. 109.
57 C. Northcote Parkinson, *British Intervention in Malaya* (Kuala Lumpur: University of Malaya Press, 1964), p. 323.
58 Simon C. Smith, *British Relations with the Malay Rulers from Decentralization to Malayan Independence 1930–1957* (Kuala Lumpur: Oxford University Press, 1995), pp. 62–4.

59 Kobkua, *Palace, Political Party and Power*, p. 149. See also Smith, *British Relations*, pp. 65–6, 170–3.
60 Ariffin Omar, *Bangsa Melayu: Malay Concepts of Democracy and Community, 1945–1950* (Kuala Lumpur: Oxford University Press, 1993).
61 Milner, *Malaysian Monarchy*, p. 14.
62 Smith, *British Relations*, p. 146.
63 Joseph P. Fernando, 'Defending the monarchy: the Malay rulers and the making of the Malayan constitution 1956–1957', *Archipel*, 88 (2014), 166; Joseph M. Fernando, *The Making of the Malayan Constitution* (Kuala Lumpur: MBRAS Monograph, 2007), ch. 5.
64 Fernando, 'Defending the monarchy', p. 156.
65 Milner, *Malaysian Monarchy*, pp. 18–19.
66 Mahathir Mohamad, *A Doctor in the House* (Petaling Jaya: MPH, 2011), pp. 452–3. On the rulers' different interventions in Malaysian state and national politics, see also Kobkua, *Palace, Political Party and Power*; Andrew Harding, '"Nazrinian" monarchy in Malaysia', in Andrew Harding (ed.), *Law and Society in Malaysia* (London and New York: Routledge, 2018), pp. 72–95; Milner, *Malaysian Monarchy*.
67 Milner, *Malaysian Monarchy*, p. 38.
68 H. P. Lee, *Constitutional Conflicts in Contemporary Malaysia* (Kuala Lumpur: Oxford University Press, 1995), p. 37.
69 Milner, *Malaysian Monarchy*, p. 38.

CHAPTER SEVEN

Celebrating the 'world's most ideal state': Sarawak and the Brooke dynasty's centenary of 1941

Donna Brunero

The week of 20–28 September 1941 marked the centenary of the Brooke dynasty rule in Sarawak. The anniversary proclaimed an opportunity to celebrate the 'world's most ideal state', one free from crime, poverty, exploitation and subjection. A common refrain in such English-language newspapers as the *Sarawak Gazette* and the *Straits Times* depicted the centenary as evidence that Brooke rule was resoundingly 'Well Done'. The year 1941 was, however, a watershed for the dynasty as it faced external and internal challenges. In 1940 and again in 1941 the Raja had dipped into Sarawak's treasury to make substantial gifts to the British government's war effort.[1] He also introduced a constitution altering the nature of the Brooke dynasty's position as it abandoned absolute rule over Sarawak. This chapter explores the representations of Sarawak under its 'White Rajahs' as a model of imperial benevolence and examines how the ideals of the Brooke raj were conveyed through the centenary festivities.

The history of Sarawak has often been linked to the exotic, from indigenous headhunters and sea raiders to the White Rajahs.[2] The Brooke family produced a dynasty which held power and shaped Sarawak's economy and administration for more than a century. How then, towards the end of their reign, did they view themselves? The centenary year was momentous for the Brooke administration; locally, the ruling family had been mired in inter-family feuding revolving around the marriage of heir-designate (or *Raja Muda*), Anthony Brooke. Global concerns meant that attention was directed to the ongoing war in Europe and Japanese aggressions in Asia, and wartime precautions were taken in Sarawak. Celebrations thus took place against a backdrop of dynastic problems and security concerns, and they provide a way to consider how the Brookes represented and described their rule, for the act of governing was also about how rule was performed and experienced by communities within Sarawak. This gives a valuable understanding of Brooke rule at the edge of formal empire, in territory held up as an idyllic place, nurtured by the White Rajahs and liberated from worries or violence.

By studying how the centenary reflects on the Raja's 'self-fashioning of rule', through rituals, iconography and parades, the chapter draws inspiration from David Cannadine's *Ornamentalism*, and demonstrates that such self-fashioning of rule was an ongoing practice at a time when the British imperial system was in decline. Following a brief overview of the history in Sarawak, of Brooke rule and the place of rituals in empire, it will discuss events of the centenary week, the popular culture expressed at bazaars and competitions, parades and performances, speeches and demonstrations, and analyse how each reveals the crafting of Brooke rule.

Borneo before Brooke rule

Sarawak, on the northwest coast of Borneo, came under the suzerain rule of the Brunei Sultanate prior to James Brooke's arrival in the late 1830s. The Brunei Sultanate had established a settlement in Kuching for officials and their followers, their development of the town largely motivated by interest in the potentially lucrative income from antimony mining (in Upper Sarawak), with the demand driven from Singapore.[3] Despite the tropical rainforest giving an appearance of fecundity, the soil conditions in Sarawak were generally poor; the coast's swampy riverine networks often resulted in mangroves, tidal swamps and marshlands where it was difficult to cultivate crops. Beyond the coast the interior is hilly. Sarawak's eco-friendly environment is lauded today as an unrivalled regional tourist attraction. However, Sarawak remains sparsely inhabited. In colonial times, its neighbours were the Sultanate of Brunei and British North Borneo (now Sabah) to the northeast, and Dutch Borneo (now Indonesian Kalimantan) to the south and southeast.[4] In the early 1800s, Sarawak's inhabitants included Malays and Land Dayaks who came under the rule of the Malay *datu* (chief), as well as a Chinese community of miners.[5] Malay traders supplied Kuching with goods, the Chinese miners (many of them Hakkas) moved from Dutch Borneo to operate in Upper Sarawak, and Bruneians tenuously exercised suzerainty over the territory. Land Dayaks practised subsistence cultivation, and some indigenous communities engaged in raiding and headhunting. Sea Dayaks (maritime raiders) lived on the coast. These were the 'pirates' James Brooke vanquished with Captain Henry Keppel of the British Navy in the 1840s – exploits that made him a household name in the metropole. The term 'Dayak', it should be noted, encompassed a plethora of ethnic subgroups whom the Brooke raj would regard as the indigenous inhabitants.

British involvement in Borneo, but more specifically Sarawak, came about through the adventures of James Brooke, who was been described as a 'freelance' imperialist.[6] Brooke was valorised as a hero of the Victorian age, his 'Rafflesian vision' an expansion of British interests in Southeast Asia.[7] His connection to Sarawak and the region began in the1840s when, in receipt of a good inheritance, the former English East India Company man bought a ship, *Royalist*, and sailed to Singapore to gather intelligence, and then to Borneo. By aiding the local ruler, Sultan Omar Ali Saifuddin II, and intervening to subdue a rebellion of Sarawak Malays against their Bruneian overlords, Brooke was publicly installed as raja in Kuching in September 1841. Brooke, described by biographer Nigel Barley as 'desperate as ever for distinction', used his ambiguous position – his arrival in the heavily armed ex-Royal Yacht Squadron vessel with the privileges of a man-of-war – to promote his own interests. Brooke further impressed local people through his right to wear semi-naval uniform, creating uncertainty among Malay chiefs as to whom he represented (although he claimed to be in Sarawak in a private capacity).[8] With his new status of raja, Brooke intervened to curb maritime raiding by the Sea Dayaks (the 'pirates') and headhunting, allowing him to further strengthen his position and negotiate treaties extending the territory under his control. Herein rested an irony: the Brunei rulers had 'no idea' they were entering into a political alliance 'not with a government but with a spoiled young man from Bath squandering his inheritance'.[9] Not only did Brooke establish his political dominance, but through his 'raj' he created the basis of what became a personalistic and family-based Sarawak dynasty. Subsequent territorial expansions took place (at the expense of Brunei) under the second raja, Charles (James's nephew), with Sarawak encompassing just over 124,000 square miles by 1905.[10] The nature of Brooke's early rule focused on ensuring security and stability for the different ethnic communities, at the same time eliminating potential opposition to his authority. Major instances of unrest (piracy, for instance) were put down with the assistance of the British Navy.[11] An important distinction that shaped the Brooke raj was his characterisation of the Sea Dayaks – whom he suppressed – as warlike, while the Hill (or Land) Dayaks were deemed pacific and warranting protection from other tribes *and* exploitative Europeans.[12]

Raja James Brooke's ascent to power was described in the centenary accounts as 'an accident' of circumstances and not of his own choosing.[13] This brings to mind Sir John Seeley's famous lecture series *The Expansion of England* in which he proposed the idea that the British

Empire was gained in a fit of absent-mindedness.[14] We should be cautious, however, about such apparent indifference to empire, as Philippa Levine notes that while there seemed to be no singular characteristic policy driving the expansion of the British Empire, this does not mean it grew in an accidental or random manner.[15] Likewise, the takeover of Sarawak was hardly accidental, but an intentional acquisition by James Brooke. The important distinction is that, while making a name for himself as a 'Victorian hero' through his actions in supporting the Sultan of Brunei during revolts and in suppressing the Sea Dayaks, Brooke acted in a personal capacity. Robert Payne's history of the Brookes rather feverishly sums up James Brooke's story: 'There were perhaps ten thousand young Englishmen like him ... Yet a fire burned in him, blazing with such heat that it drove him nearly out of his mind and sent him to places on earth, to become the sole possessor of a land of raging rivers and haunted forests.'[16] The number of scholars, who, like Payne, were swept into the 'romance' of Brooke's great adventure has been balanced by more recent critics of the Brooke dynasty and the embarrassment it caused to British imperial interests.[17] For instance, R. H. W. Reece argues that there was something 'inherently feudal' and self-serving in Brooke rule, and that the rajas instinctively resisted any change because they sensed it would undermine their status as 'paternalistic rulers'.[18] James Brooke's rule as Raja of Sarawak set the tone for a charismatic (or, perhaps 'personalised') family dynasty of absolute monarchs. Barley points out that the family's involvement with the English East India Company and India itself was formative in shaping the Sarawak Raj – if only in how a colony should *not* be run.[19] Brooke believed that the British administration in India was 'too large, too professional, not based on a loyalty that was purely personal', and hence in Sarawak the emphasis would be on a raj which could foster a loyalty that was almost familial.[20] Brooke's letters, written to his friend and confidant John Templer and to his mother, illustrate how he saw his actions as bringing British civilisation to Southeast Asia. Brooke saw that he was embarking on a grand experiment, 'which, if it succeeds, will bestow a blessing on these poor people, and their children's children will bless my name'.[21] Here was an inkling of the familial and personalised underpinnings of the Brooke raj. This rule would vary as the personalities of successive Rajas dictated.

While James Brooke produced no heir, his nephew Charles Antoni Brooke became the second White Rajah in 1868, reigning until his death in 1917. In ruling over the indigenous population, the Brooke administration adopted and reinforced existing chieftains or created new political authorities, creating a dual system where government-appointed indigenous chieftains operated alongside 'District Officers'.[22]

While the Brookes were autocrats, they ruled with the advice of native chieftains – they recognised the Malay leaders (or *datus*) as the governing race.[23] This system of indirect rule, established by James, continued under Charles. The Raja thus served as governor but also as paramount local chief with final authority over local inhabitants. Indirect rule was facilitated through a small European civil service and reliance on local Asian elites.[24] Sarawak's various ethnic groups had their own leadership (such as a *kapitan* for the Chinese) – reflecting the belief of all three Brooke rulers that 'divide and govern' was most appropriate for an ethnically heterogeneous population.[25] From the outset, Malay chiefs were paid regular salaries; this salary system meant that the *datus'* traditional source of support – extortion of revenue from the Dayak peoples – was brought to an end.[26] The *datus* retained their symbolic leadership over the Malay and Dayak peoples. This arrangement relied heavily on the *datus*, and has been described as symbiotic in that by drawing on traditional local leaders the Brooke dynasty's own prestige was enhanced. The administration's promotion of local elites was not dissimilar to practices in British Malaya where Malay elites preserved and reconstructed royal ceremonial roles (often making them more opulent) as a means of maintaining their positions in a colonial structure of authority.[27]

In spite of creating a seemingly 'harmonious' relationship between a European ruler and local elites, the Brooke administration unsettled (and at times frustrated) the British colonial office. Nicholas Tarling's *Britain, the Brookes and Brunei* describes the Brookes' increasingly fraught relationship with the British government and official policy in the region.[28] Tarling considers the 'anomalous' position of the Raja and of Sarawak as a whole within the larger British imperial project.[29] (The first Brooke is aptly described as a 'benevolent despot' by some scholars.)[30] The relationship between Charles, the second Raja, and the British administration was uneasy, and Charles's attempt to take over Brunei and what became British North Borneo was thwarted by the British government.[31] The British government disliked the idea that a subject of the Queen could also be an independent raja.[32] Officials felt torn because, even though they disapproved of Charles, they could also not resist requests for naval support and other assistance even if providing them might be seen as countenancing his authority. The government instead tried to justify such support in terms of the usual protection afforded to British subjects and their property.[33]

Under Raja Charles, territorial expansion continued and so did the development of Sarawak's economy, administration and infrastructure. Despite these efforts, Charles's attempts to develop Sarawak as a coaling station and a major trading centre did not come to fruition.

One other initiative in Kuching was a set of infrastructure projects; in particular, the creation of roads and a rail system, providing an alternative to the slow and often dangerous riverine routes into the interior.[34] But despite experimentation with crops and agriculture, the territory lacked major economic resources. Charles Brooke's rule, in sum, conferred the benefits of law and order, but it did not create a modern state.[35] In 1888 Sarawak acquired protected state status from Britain, whereby it remained an independent state with absolute rights of self-government but was bound to conduct foreign relations through the British government.[36]

It was under the third and final Raja, Charles Vyner Brooke, who succeeded his father Charles in 1917, that the Brooke dynasty celebrated its centenary milestone but also came to an end in 1941, when the territory fell to the Japanese.[37] Although Vyner, unlike the other rajas, left few writings explaining his political philosophy, he was regarded as conservative, and cautious in undertaking reform.[38] Vyner has also been regarded as less autocratic in manner (and he spent less time in Kuching); under his rule there occurred a gradual decentralisation of power as the administration, including a municipal government, oversaw more of the day-to-day concerns with Kuching and the Districts.[39] Family rivalries beleaguered Vyner's rule: a poor relationship with his father, sometimes strained relations with his brother Bertram, who assisted him in ruling Sarawak, and disputes with his heir presumptive (declared *Raja Mudah* in 1939), Anthony Brooke, who was Bertram's son. (Vyner fathered three daughters and therefore named his nephew as heir. This caused much consternation for Ranee Sylvia who had hoped her eldest daughter, Leonora, would be named heir, and these hopes were the subject of scheming by Sarawak administrative cadet Gerard O'Brien, who hoped to not only alter the line of succession to the female line but to marry into the family and secure power through this means.)[40] By 1930, Sarawak remained relatively 'isolated', relying on a weekly steamer service from Singapore and with no hotel accommodation; it appears casual visitors were not encouraged.[41] The few who did come, such as British Labour MPs in the 1920s, charged that Sarawak could be developed more quickly and not just in aid of the Brooke family's coffers.[42] In 1941, Sarawak's economy remained based on subsistence agriculture, with some cash crops of rubber, sago and pepper. Jungle produce, such as resins, edible birds' nests and hornbill ivory, provided another source of revenue. The Chinese (who had arrived in increasing numbers during the 1800s) dominated trade and commerce, complemented by a few European agency houses. Western enterprises – deliberately restricted out of concern that the native populace would be exploited – involved themselves in oil, timber and rubber plantations. Sarawak was thus regarded as a relatively peaceful but also backward territory due to both Brooke raj policies and the natural limitations posed by resource endowment.[43] By 1939, the total population stood at just over 490,500 inhabitants; Europeans constituted just 704 people, a tiny 0.2 per cent.[44] Considering Sarawak's much-lauded ethnic diversity, its limited development and relative isolation, the 1941 centenary offered a rare glimpse into the state, and an opportunity for the ruling family to demonstrate to the world the benefits of Brooke rule.

On pageantry and empire

David Cannadine's observations in *Ornamentalism* concerning rituals and notions of class and race in the British colonies are relevant to understanding this territory on the fringes of Britain's formal empire. Cannadine argues that the empire was not exclusively concerned with the creation of otherness but as much – and possibly more – with finding affinities with the colonised peoples, and the way that the exotic could be domesticated, re-ordered and recognised.[45] Cannadine's interest in the 'world-view' of those who dominated and ruled the empire is relevant to Brooke rule.[46] While Sarawak did not become a British crown colony until 1946, the centenary sheds light on the thinking of the Raja and his administration, and the ways the Brookes fashioned family rule and employed ceremonies, honours, iconography and visual culture to secure the dynasty. It is important to remember that the British Empire was shaped around a cult of monarchy, as Cannadine argues.[47]

The Brooke rulers revealed how a cult of monarchy was adopted and fashioned to the local situation. The centenary celebrations in Sarawak, like royal and imperial festivities in Britain and other parts of the empire, provided opportunities for the involvement of local elites and communities. Iconography, military parades, festivals, the granting of honours and public festivities helped create a 'collective identity'. The young and many others were brought in to enjoy local festivities and at the same time were actively involved in creating a broader engagement and responsibility.[48] This affiliation was enhanced further through imperial tours by members of the British royal family,[49] which reinforced the importance of the monarchy. For if, as Charles Reed argues, British imperial culture was made and remade through the planning and the reception of royal tours,[50] similar creative efforts also took place on the outskirts of empire, where notions of rule, pageantry and power were also articulated.[51] In fashioning their dynasty, the Brooke rulers adopted some elements of 'Malay rule' in that they resided in a palace, the Astana in Kuching, and they enjoyed the trappings of state including royal titles, gun salutes and parades. In 1872, Ranee Margaret (wife of Raja Charles), who professed a love for wearing Malay dress,[52] composed an anthem, 'Gone Forth Beyond the Sea', which captured the essence of the Brooke administration being 'called to bear the sword and crown', bring justice, and save the 'creatures in jungles deep'.[53]

Other markers of royal status, privilege and duties also appeared, combining British and local cultural symbols with an emphasis on the personal, familial link between rulers. In his 1918 coronation ceremony, for instance, while seated with his consort Sylvia under a canopy of gold brocade, the Raja was presented with a ceremonial cutlass (first used by James Brooke) by two Malay chiefs as a symbol of his sovereignty in Sarawak – while a traditional *kris* might have seemed more apt, Ranee Sylvia emphasised the ritual handing over of the cutlass to reaffirm Brooke rule.[54] The use of gold is significant as its association with Malay royalty can be traced back to the *Sejarah Melayu* (*Malay Annals or Sulalat al-Salatin*) and the *Tuhfat al-Nafis* (*The Precious Gift*).[55] Ranee Sylvia often wore Malay dress and, in particular, the colour yellow which was considered her royal prerogative.[56] Through rituals, objects and even music, the Brooke raj thus fashioned aspects of its visual, imperial culture, a process that reached its apogee during the centenary. We should not be entirely surprised at such a regal fashioning: Ranee Sylvia was the daughter of the influential Reginald Brett (second Viscount Esher), prominent in British Liberal politics and a senior adviser to the Royal Household; he had indeed been instrumental in shaping the triumphal and imperial aspects of Victoria's Diamond Jubilee in 1897. Brett's 'stage management' of pageantry and empire was thus unrivalled.[57] (The connection to Sarawak proved lucrative for the Ranee, when in the late 1930s she toured the United States giving talks as 'Queen of the Head Hunters'.)[58]

The centenary

In September 1941, a week of festivities marked a century of Brooke rule in Sarawak, with 24 September a public holiday throughout the country.[59] The emphasis fell on the 'cult of monarchy', including the co-opting of local elites and the broader community to enjoy the pomp and pageantry of Brooke rule. There was much evidence of a cult of personality around the Raja and his family, as well as a focus on grand events to celebrate the milestone. A conscious effort was made to create a sense of occasion: flags adorned buildings and ships, with a liberal use of yellow standards and umbrellas – traditional symbols of royalty in Asia – to signify the importance of the event. Military rituals such as guards of honour, processions by youth, and models of *Royalist* (the ship in which the dynasty's founder arrived in Sarawak) recalled devices employed very effectively in the Empire Day celebration and occasions across Britain and the British Empire.[60] Dignitaries travelled to Sarawak to join in the events, while others sent their good wishes; those of King George VI were received with particular appreciation by the Raja. A K.N.I.L.M. Netherlands Indies airplane was chartered to carry government officials directly from Singapore to Sarawak. Other passengers on the reportedly fully booked flight included two newspapermen, one from an American newspaper, and cameramen, one of whom, a Mr Fisher, would capture events using the novelty of 16 mm colour film.[61]

Bazaars and competitions

In the capital, a Centenary Grand Fancy Bazaar was held from 24 to 27 September. The grounds of the Sarawak Museum, an institution initiated by Charles Brooke in 1888 and housed in a building opened in 1891, provided the site; it stood in Kuching's central *padang* and the collections showcased Sarawak's natural and cultural diversity.[62] The bazaar's organisers had sent out a call for goods, helpers, booths, sheds and theatres, and the *Sarawak Gazette* reported that 'the result was a Fancy Bazaar which eclipsed any of its kind ever held before'.[63] The Ranee and Raja arrived at 11.30 a.m. to receive good wishes from the community, and the Ranee opened the bazaar with a ribbon-cutting ceremony and planted two trees.[64] Visitors enjoyed competitive displays and events. An agricultural show displayed cereals, vegetables and other food crops competing for prizes.[65] A baby show boasted sixty-one infants and toddlers, also vying for prizes. A fancy-dress competition proved a highlight (with one contestant dressed as Hitler – a reminder that the war in Europe was never far away from the public consciousness), and the Ranee assisted other judges in awarding prizes. Numerous raffle prizes were available including a motorcar, sewing machine, bicycle, table, chairs, clocks, lamps and, biggest of all, a house contributed by the Raja – all the trappings of the modern home, representative of British technology and a Westernised lifestyle.[66] Intermittent rain did not deter large crowds, and merrymakers stayed on into the evening to enjoy acrobatic shows and puppet plays. There was a fundraising aspect to the bazaar as well, with 30,000 people paying admission over the three days, providing a profit of over $30,000, the money raised reportedly split between the War Effort and the China Relief Fund (the latter fund prompted by the Chinese in

Sarawak).[67] Districts outside Kuching also held festivities; for instance, Simanggang (the Second District) held a regatta day, the racing of boats considered dear to the hearts of the Dayak community.[68] In Miri, a Chinese lion procession was accompanied by a display of portraits of the three Rajas. Schools were decorated for the festivities, bands gave performances, and the police erected a stand in imitation of a fort.

Competitions were widespread, related to agricultural products and sport. The idea of sports and empire, demonstrations of masculinity and good sporting values, came to the fore.[69] Sports in Sarawak, as elsewhere in the British Empire – in particular, cricket – were used as a way of transmitting imperial values such as discipline, teamwork and restraint.[70] They also provided a way of ordering people through decisions about who could and could not play certain sports.[71] Thus the centenary regattas, which proved a highlight of the festivities, appeared reserved largely for the indigenous population, with races of 'native prahus' and sampans cheered on by supporters.[72] Focus on water sports reaffirmed the strong maritime and riverine identity and connections of indigenous communities in Sarawak. More 'colonial' sports, which always attracted large audience, such as horse races, were also held. The press laid emphasis, however, on the high spirits in which all joined in the games, rather than on the 'purity' or discipline of traditional sports. The *Illustrated London News* devoted a full page to photographs illustrating the hundred years of Brooke rule (Figure 7.1).

Parades and performances

Each district witnessed extensive parades during the celebrations. For instance, in Simanggang a large-scale model of the ship *Royalist* paraded through the streets; illuminated from within, on the bridge 'were cleverly drawn pictures of the three white rajahs'.[73] School children performed in marching bands and dance groups. In Miri a large illuminated sign flashed '1841 Brooke 1941' to add to the grandeur.[74] The night parades nevertheless took place when precautionary blackouts had been ordered, and Ranee Sylvia later lamented, 'little did we know that the Japanese attack was only three months away'.[75]

The celebrations were captured on film for a wider Western audience. *Sarawak Centenary*, a British Movietones short film of 1941, captured impressions of the centenary. The Raja and Ranee appear, accompanied by umbrella bearers, crossing the Sarawak River in Kuching and receiving a 101-gun salute from 'ancient weapons'. The viewer is able to see the diverse population of Sarawak, many performers and spectators dressed in military uniforms or indigenous dress.[76]

MONARCHIES AND DECOLONISATION IN ASIA

Figure 7.1 'Sarawak's hundred years of rule under the White Rajahs', *Illustrated London News*, 4 October 1941, p. 22

(All those entitled to wear uniforms were expected to do so.)[77] The emphasis on ethnographic displays highlighted the 'exotic' in contrast with the modern and Western. This film highlights contrasts between the indigenous tribes adorned in traditional dress with the ceremonial order, and styles of dress of the rulers, the Raja in a Western suit and the Ranee in a Malay sarong greeting their subjects and reviewing uniformed Indian troops and the Sarawak Constabulary.[78] Once again, viewers' attention is drawn to the contrast between the formal militaristic rituals such as a gun salute and the 'natives'.[79] In particular, the documentary shows a fascination for the Dayaks, described as not too long ago a 'head-hunting race'. In one scene, tribal leaders are pictured on board a British Navy vessel investigating the guns – according to the narration, the modern 'head-hunting weapons of the white man'. Some of the night-time processions, including one involving the model of *Royalist*, are also captured, evidence of the way in which the first Brooke's arrival has been built into founding (origin) narratives of the state and how this 'journey' was now re-enacted. It is noteworthy that a British naval vessel was present; those familiar with the James Brooke story could have drawn parallels between the current and the first Raja, who had relied on the support of Captain Keppel and HMS *Dido* in the 1840s. The cult of the British Navy offers a subject of scholarly interest in the way that naval imagery helped to shaped imperial identities and create easily recognisable images that could be circulated globally.[80] Here the presence of the British Navy served as a reminder of its long relationship with the Brooke family and Sarawak.

In a contemporary interview, Ranee Sylvia reflected on the centenary celebrations, revealing a clear sense of the crafting of an idyllic picture of Brooke rule. In an article titled 'The world's most ideal state', one paper echoes the Ranee's pride in the events. Reuters' special correspondent, D. P. Wagle, who interviewed the Raja and Ranee, described Sarawak in glowing terms: 'Probably nowhere in history has a corresponding period of 100 years of family rule been more congenial to the people and worked more for their real happiness.'[81] The rulers spoke of a country free from exploitation, underscoring the Sarawak people's progress from 'primitive to modern' and from 'jungle to roads' under the watchful care of the Brooke administration.

Brooke rule and the new constitution

In a speech during the centenary week the Raja explained the principles of a new constitution proclaimed to coincide with the celebrations, tracing its genesis to the efforts and original vision of the first Raja, Sir James Brooke.[82] Raja Vyner drew attention to the significance of the place where he gave his address – the very same location where the first English Raja was proclaimed. He observed: 'Much has happened in Sarawak since that day, turmoil and trouble, fear and insecurity, have given place to peace, prosperity and happiness.'[83] The Raja expressed satisfaction with Sarawak's progress, and belief that a second century of Brooke rule could bring further benefits. In fact, he made the point that he did not want to dwell on the past, but was looking to the future and anticipating new successes. He thanked those present for the celebration, both the civilian and military representatives from overseas (including Britain and Singapore), and District Officers who had travelled from outstations. The Sarawak administration had its own order of merit and so the commemorative medal for the centenary added to the decorations worn by District Officers. A commemorative stamp featuring all three of the Brooke Rajas was commissioned, though ironically the stamps were not available in Sarawak until 1946, after the Japanese occupation and surrender.[84]

As some scholars have observed, however, the motivation for the new constitution which would lead the people of Sarawak to self-governance was not as altruistic as it first appears. Certainly there was an international climate of colonial reform but, apart from *Raja Mudah* Anthony Brooke, few Brookes seemed interested. It seems that as Bertram, brother of the Raja, was in poor health, Vyner's willingness to shoulder the 'burden' of governing Sarawak was dwindling. From 1938 the Raja had been in talks with representatives of the British government about taking over Sarawak, with £5,000,000 in payment reportedly mentioned. But at this point, the British were more concerned about finding out how the internal administration of the territory operated. Vyner appeared torn between bringing in a British adviser and still keeping a role as an 'absentee sovereign'.[85] Sylvia was reportedly also looking to secure her future; Philip Eade's biography of the Ranee points to her and her daughters' financial extravagance, and suggests that this gave further impetus to the ceremony – a last hurrah – as Vyner negotiated for a settlement of funds to provide for the family. In exchange there would be no further demands on Sarawak's coffers. A payment was made to the Brookes (to the tune of £200,000, from the treasury with additional concessions of allowances and loans being paid off) in return for constitutional reform; this was seen as having 'rather shattered' the reputation of the Raja.[86] (The Raja also disposed of some property, selling the 'Sylvia Cinema' to a Chinese consortium in what was thought undue haste.)[87] The constitution was unsurprisingly not a polished document, but 'hurriedly written', and it 'attempted too much'; there was no real intention of granting votes to 'the primitive Dayaks', but for the first time Malays,

Dayaks and Chinese were represented in considerable numbers in the State Council.[88] Reece captures the decline and confusion of the Brooke administration through Bertram's own words: 'The "Sarawak side" was wilfully blind to the fact that internally it was on the downgrade.' Bertram cited administrative officers trapped in 'old duties' and a ruler who enjoyed personal popularity but had stopped taking real interest in administrative affairs, merely following any 'adviser' who held his attention and interest at the time.[89]

Despite the shady nature of the negotiations, the end of autocratic rule was presented as the fulfilment of James Brooke's ambitions. The Raja explained that the Brooke dynasty's aim had always been to 'protect the natives of Sarawak, the real but backward owners of this land, from exploitation and oppression, until such time that they could govern themselves'.[90] Members of the Committee of Administration took this responsibility seriously, assuring the Raja that they would formulate measures for constitutional reform that would take into account the hundred years of Brooke rule; such statements gave little inkling of the feverish behind-the-scenes negotiations. The Committee of Administration originated in the 1870s as an interim measure to administer the territory while the Raja was away and was installed in 1915 as a permanent body with three Residents and five other members. The Committee of Administration oversaw the secret agreements securing Vyner's financial situation in exchange for transferring most of his powers to the Committee in March 1941.[91] Members of the Committee now swore to respect the benevolent gesture of the Raja in establishing a degree of self-government:

> We solemnly declare to Your Highness that Your people will always look back with heartfelt gratitude to the years of absolute rule by the three rajahs which has led them to the day, on which Your Highness is able to feel assured that a measure of democratic freedom may be extended to them and yet all will remain well with Sarawak.[92]

The Committee of Administration furthermore pledged to uphold the tradition of the Brooke family.[93] Similar sentiments were echoed by the Chief Secretary of the committee, C. D. Le Gros Clark, who in a visit to Singapore to meet with its Governor, Sir Thomas Shenton, explained that 'the peoples of Sarawak are extremely happy under the rule of the Brookes, and they realise that the magnificent gesture on the part of their Rajah [in granting a constitution] is for their own eventual good'.[94] Even with the institution of a new constitution, the Raja remained a constitutional monarch.[95] In her memoirs, the Ranee reflected that the absolute rule of the Brooke Rajas had turned Sarawak from savagery and barbarism to prosperity, but conceded that in Britain the idea of one-man rule was an anachronism. Critics had described Vyner as a tired man; and she described him as becoming the one thing he had averred – a puppet king.[96] But beyond this, his 'indecent haste' in clearing funds to Singapore caused consternation in the administration and many believed that Vyner's actions were at best a means of 'forestalling British pressure' for more regular governance to take place and at worst simply an act of self-preservation.[97]

Conclusion

Finally, all rose as the band played 'God Save the Rajah'.[98]

The parallels between 'God Save the King' and 'God Save the Rajah' are clear. The week-long festivities commemorated and celebrated monarchical Brooke rule and also signalled a new era. While centenary celebrations and the new constitution marked a turning point for the dynasty and country, the idyll was short-lived. Sarawak fell to the Japanese military within months of the festivities, and, crucially, at a time when no Brookes were present: the family members were all overseas.[99] Raja Vyner had been en route to Brisbane on holiday when news came of the attack on Pearl Harbor; he intended to return to Sarawak and reached Surabaya by air in December 1941, only to discover that Kuching had fallen three days earlier. Part of Sarawak's government regrouped in exile in Sydney.[100] The Ranee was also in Australia and devised nothing short of a 'crack-pot' plan to land two Sarawak officers into Sarawak via submarine to gather intelligence while she masterminded a rebellion against the Japanese.[101] Bertram (the Raja's brother) was in England and the *Raja Muda*, Anthony, arrived in England in mid-January 1942 and volunteered for active service.[102] This absence of the Brookes at a critical juncture casts some doubt over the strong paternalistic instincts of the Brooke raj, for surely, when the threat of war was imminent, the leadership should have been present.

After the war, Sarawak returned to Vyner Brooke; by 1946 he agreed to cede it to the British in what was seen as a fairly hasty move, but one that allowed for a generous payment for his family's upkeep.[103] Again, whether finances were at the heart of this decision is debatable; rumours of payments abounded. Moreover, Vyner had no confidence in his successor and was convinced that Brooke rule should end.[104] The Brooke dynasty's rule in Sarawak thus drew to a close. Cession was not a simple affair, however, as there was a protest from Anthony Brooke and resistance on the ground, as the *datu*s and Dayak chiefs objected to this transfer of power.[105] Uncertainty surrounding the status of Sarawak culminated in the stabbing of Duncan Stewart, the first British governor of the new colony of Sarawak, while he was attending a public event in Sibu in December 1949. The assailants, two Malay men, were initially thought to have been inspired by conspirators desiring a return to Brooke rule, but recently released official British documents reveal that their intention was to secure Sarawak's incorporation into the Republic of Indonesia (the former Netherlands East Indies, declared independent by nationalists in 1945) instead of it remaining a British colony.[106]

The legacies and memories of the 'White Rajahs' continue to run deep, and the Brooke name is still visible on statues, buildings and tourist-oriented attractions in Kuching. The centenary celebrations, while brief, had reaffirmed ways in which the Brooke rulers and administrative elites wanted to project themselves as 'personal and personable rulers' by hosting community-oriented events that showcased different cultural traditions, but always with the Brooke name at the forefront. In particular, an emphasis on water, in the form of replica boats and regattas, reaffirmed the identity of the Sarawak raj as governing the seas, riverine networks and jungles. The image of the Brooke Rajas is often depicted as a 'paternal presence' guiding and protecting the people of Sarawak; and the centenary, with a new constitution, was fashioned as a 'coming of age' for a fledging territory that could still expect 'protection' and concern from the ever benevolent Brookes, even though the British had now become the paramount power. The use of the ship *Royalist* as part of the 'founding story' speaks to the importance of origins and how a cult of personality had grown around the Rajas. To foreign onlookers and some scholars, the appeal of the White Rajahs appears irresistible. For instance, it is telling that in a history of Sarawak written as late as 1960, Steven Runciman (a scholar perhaps best known for his writings on the Crusades and the Byzantine emperor) was undoubtedly moved by the story of the Rajas:

> The White Rajahs had their faults. They suffered mishaps, they sometimes made mistakes, but their achievement was extraordinary. In an age when colonial methods were not always pretty, when the lust for power or for commercial gain too often dictated policy, they showed how a few Europeans could bring peace and contentment to a fierce and lawless country, with the goodwill and even the love of its peoples.[107]

This quotation echoes sentiments expressed by the Brooke administration during the centenary celebrations twenty years earlier. Clearly, the cult of personality revolving around the Brooke family endured beyond their tenure.

There were other, less rosy views of Brooke rule and the Rajas. Economic policy under the Brookes was deliberately self-limiting, and

Sarawak was far from a 'modern state' when compared to neighbouring regions even in 1946. For instance, under the second and third Rajas, infrastructure development was partly delayed, in keeping with the belief that Malays would never really 'leave the riversides', nor would Dayaks willingly live in an urban setting.[108] Moreover, the rivalries, jealousies and excesses of the extended Brooke family made for tabloid news and much criticism. Sensational reports followed all three Rajas. In the case of James, Victorian norms and morality were unsettled, and contemporary biographers such as Spencer St John skirted over James's sexual ambiguity, his romantic entanglements with a series of young male protégés, the lack of an heir and clear preference for the company of young men.[109] These same protégés often moved into service with the Sarawak administration as District Officers.[110] The second Raja, Charles, was involved in disputes regarding his choice of heir, and the third Raja, Vyner, and Ranee Sylvia and their family became the stuff of tabloid news for eccentricities, extravagant parties and sexual exploits.[111] Anthony Brooke, nephew to Vyner and the *Raja Muda*, but never Raja of Sarawak, represented himself as a self-appointed peace ambassador travelling the globe to promote peace. His grandsons created a Brooke Trust in 2010 as a charitable organisation with the aim of uncovering Sarawak's heritage in a bid to 'inform, enrich, and inspire' the people of Sarawak and a broader public. The Trust has two key projects, one to build a replica of the *Royalist* in Britain, and the other to rebuild James Brooke's original dwelling in Sarawak.[112] The Trust has also been instrumental in establishing a Brooke Gallery in Kuching, focusing less on the 'personalities' of the Brookes than on material culture relating to Ranee Margaret.

The centenary of the Brooke administration in 1941 provides a snapshot of a frontier of empire and a glimpse of how imperial ceremonial practices, such as parades, festivals and the show of the military, could all be brought into play to celebrate the origins and identity of a hereditary ruling dynasty, its subjects and a British presence (with a distinct flair for Malay notions of elite rule resulting in a hybrid ceremonial style). The centenary represented the celebration of a family who, perhaps uniquely in British colonial history, had conquered a territory and made their family its rulers. At the same time, the centenary marked an apparently decisive shift in the family's status: the transformation of the White Rajahs' absolutist monarchy into a constitutional one. The festivities represented an attempt to capture something of the ideal – perhaps a seductive fantasy – of 'benevolent rule' in a territory 'emerging' from its primitive state. The realities were murky as 1941 was less a 'coming of age' than the culmination of family feuds, indifferent administration and a Raja considering how and when to leave the territory. The imperial project at the frontier was still unfolding and in Sarawak in the anniversary year, the pageantry, rituals and iconography of empire were deliberately intertwined with more personal images of the Brooke family and their claims to have 'created' this territory.

Notes

1 See, for instance, *Sarawak Gazette*, 1 August 1941.
2 See Steven Runciman, *The White Rajahs: A History of Sarawak from 1841 to 1946* (London: Cambridge University Press, 1960) as an example of how the term 'the white rajahs' was in popular use. See also R. H. W. Reece, 'Sir James Brooke', *Oxford Dictionary of National Biography*, online edition, www.oxforddnb.com/view/10.1093/ref:odnb/9780198614128.001.0001/odnb-9780198614128-e-3549 (accessed 13 May 2019); and Reece, 'Sir Charles Anthoni Johnson Brooke', *Oxford Dictionary of National Biography*, online edition, www.oxforddnb.com/view/10.1093/ref:odnb/9780198614128.001.0001/odnb-9780198614128-e-32092 (accessed 13 May 2019).
3 Ooi Keat Gin, *Of Free Trade and Native Interests: The Brookes and the Economic Development of Sarawak, 1841–1941* (Oxford: Oxford University Press, 1997), ch. 1.
4 *Ibid.*, p. 5.
5 *Ibid.*, p. 10.
6 'Inventing Southeast Asia with Dr Farish Noor, Episode 2: Kings and Pirates', Channel NewsAsia, 6 September 2016, https://video.toggle.sg/en/video/series/inventing-southeast-asia-with-dr-farish-noor/ep2/444776 (accessed 8 May 2019).
7 The Byron-esque Brooke was said to have inspired Rudyard Kipling's 'cautionary' novella, *The Man Who Would be King*.
8 Nigel Barley, *White Rajah* (London: Little Brown Book Company, 2002). See chapter 4 for an account of how James Brooke capitalised on the uncertainty of his appearance in Sarawak since there was little clarity as to how 'official' he might or might not be.
9 *Ibid.*
10 Gin, *Of Free Trade and Native Interests*, pp. 4–5.
11 Donna Brunero, 'Maritime goes global: the British maritime empire in Asia', in Donna Brunero and Brian F. Farrell (eds), *Empire in Asia: A New Global History*, Vol. 2 (London: Bloomsbury, 2018), pp. 266–8.
12 Barley, *White Rajah*, ch. 4.
13 D. P. Wagle, 'Accident gave to Brookes Sarawak', *Malaya Tribune*, 24 September 1941, p. 3. Brooke's activities in Southeast Asia are described as 'accidents' or by chance in this overview of the history of Sarawak.
14 John Robert Seeley, *The Expansion of England* (Cambridge: Cambridge University Press, 1883).
15 Philippa Levine, *The British Empire: From Sunrise to Sunset* (London: Routledge, 2013), p. 92.
16 Robert Payne, *The White Rajahs of Sarawak* (Oxford: Oxford University Press, 1986), p. 16.
17 Reece discusses the embarrassment and frustration that the Brooke administration posed to the British colonial office, culminating in the cessation of 1946. R. H. W. Reece, *The Name of Brooke: The End of White Rajah Rule in Sarawak* (Oxford: Oxford University Press, 1982), pp. 94–127.
18 *Ibid.*, p. xxvi.
19 Barley, *White Rajah*, ch. 1.
20 *Ibid.*

21 Brooke to his mother from Kuching Sarawak, 27 September 1841, *The Private Letters of Sir James Brooke K.C.B. Rajah of Sarawak, Narrating the Events of his life from 1838 to the present time*, Vol. 1, ed. John C. Templer (London: Richard Bently, 1853), p. 121.
22 Amarjit Kaur, '"The babbling Brookes": economic change in Sarawak 1841–1941', *Modern Asian Studies*, 29:1 (1995), p. 72.
23 Ooi Keat Gin, 'The attitudes of the Brookes towards education in Sarawak 1841–1941', *Journal of the Malayan Branch of the Royal Asiatic Society*, 70:2 (1997), pp. 53–67.
24 Craig A. Lockard, 'The evolution of urban government in Southeast Asian cities: Kuching under the Brookes', *Modern Asian Studies*, 12:2 (1978), 245–67. See also Gin, 'The attitudes of the Brookes towards education in Sarawak'.
25 Lockard, 'The evolution of urban government', pp. 246–7.
26 *Ibid.*, p. 248.
27 *Ibid.*, p. 248. For a discussion of the Malay elites and their co-opting into the British colonial world in general, see Donna J. Amoroso, 'Dangerous politics and the Malay nationalist movement, 1945–47', *Southeast Asia Research*, 6:3 (1998), pp. 253–80.
28 Nicholas Tarling, *Britain, the Brookes and Brunei* (London: Oxford University Press, 1971).
29 Nicholas Tarling, 'Britain and Sarawak in the twentieth century: Raja Charles, Raja Vyner and the Colonial Office', *Journal of the Malayan Branch of the Royal Asiatic Society*, 43:2 (1970), pp. 25–52.
30 Lockard, 'The evolution of urban government', p. 247.
31 Reece, 'Sir Charles Brooke', *Oxford Dictionary of National Biography*.
32 Tarling, *Britain, the Brookes and Brunei*, p. 547. Further to this, Tarling describes the Colonial Office as depicting the second Raja's rule as one marked by 'chicanery and violence'. Tarling, 'Britain and Sarawak', p. 33.
33 Tarling, *Britain, the Brookes and Brunei*, p. 547.
34 Gin, *Of Free Trade and Native Interests*, pp. 43–4.
35 Tarling, *Britain, the Brookes and Brunei*, p. 551.
36 Kaur, '"The babbling Brookes"', p. 68.
37 *Ibid.*
38 Gin, *Of Free Trade and Native Interests*, pp. 47–8.
39 Lockard, 'The evolution of urban government', pp. 246–9.
40 Payne, *The White Rajahs of Sarawak*, pp. 176–7. Reece, *The Name of Brooke*, pp. 19–29 gives insight into the complex intrigues and scheming at play.
41 Reece, *The Name of Brooke*, p. 95.
42 *Ibid.*
43 For an excellent assessment of the economic development of Sarawak, see Gin, *Of Free Trade and Native Interests*, pp. 317–28.
44 Population of Sarawak in 1939: Dayak: 167,710; Chinese 123,626; Others 4,579; Malay 92,709; Land Dayak 36,963; Melanau 36,772; Other indigenous 27,532; and Europeans 702. Gin, *Of Free Trade and Native Interests*, p. 10.
45 David Cannadine, *Ornamentalism: How the British Saw Their Empire* (Oxford: Oxford University Press, 2001), p. xix.
46 Cannadine, *Ornamentalism*, p. xx.
47 *Ibid.*, pp. 105–6.
48 Jim English, 'Empire Day in Britain, 1904–1958', *The Historical Journal*, 49:1 (2006); 247–76.
49 Charles V. Reed, *Royal Tourists, Colonial Subjects and the Making of a British World, 1860–1911* (Manchester: Manchester University Press, 2016).
50 *Ibid.*, p. xix.
51 Donna J. Amoroso chronicles how such practices were encouraged by the British in the Malay states, and Malay elites became exceedingly 'visible and extravagant' in appearance and in their rituals, in *Traditionalism and the Ascendancy of the Malay Ruling Class in Colonial Malaya* (Singapore: NUS Press, 2014), ch. 3.

SARAWAK AND THE BROOKE DYNASTY'S CENTENARY OF 1941

52 Margaret Brooke, The Ranee of Sarawak, *My Life in Sarawak* (Oxford University Press, 1986 [1913]).
53 Lyrics for 'Gone Forth Beyond the Sea'. https://ipfs.io/ipfs/QmXoypizjW3W knFiJnKLwHCnL72vedxjQkDDP1mXWo6uco/wiki/Gone_Forth_Beyond_The_ Sea.html (accessed 15 January 2019).
54 Philip Eade, *Sylvia: Queen of the Headhunters: An Outrageous Englishwoman and her Lost Kingdom* (London: Phoenix, 2007), pp. 125–6.
55 Raja Ali Haji Bin Ahmad, *The Precious Gift (Tuhfat al-Nafis)* (Oxford: Oxford University Press, 1982); and *Sejarah Melayu or Malay Annals* (Oxford: Oxford University Press, 1970). The *Malay Annals* was originally known as the *Sulalat al-Salatin* or *Genealogy of Kings*. (With thanks to my colleague Kelvin Lawrence for his advice regarding these sources.)
56 Reece, *The Name of Brooke*, p. 98.
57 William M. Kuhn, 'Brett, Reginald Baliol, second Viscount Esher', *Oxford Dictionary of National Biography*, online edition, www.oxforddnb.com/view/10.1093/ref:odnb/9780198614128.001.0001/odnb-9780198614128-e-32055 (accessed 13 May 2019). Viscount Esher did not approve of Sylvia's marriage to Vyner Brooke (nor did Charles Brooke approve of his son's choice of wife).
58 Sylvia Lady Brooke, *Queen of the Head-hunters, the autobiography of the H.H. the Hon Sylvia Lady Brooke Ranee of Sarawak* (London: Sidgwick & Jackson, 1970), pp. 135–7.
59 *Straits Times*, 16 September 1941, p. 10. 'Forthcoming centenary celebrations', *Sarawak Gazette*, 1 August 1941, p. 144 detailed some of the plans that were underway.
60 Empire Day was created in 1904 as a way to celebrate the empire and to create an awareness among the youth in particular. See English, 'Empire Day in Britain', pp. 247–76.
61 'Special place for Sarawak', *Malaya Tribune*, 19 September 1941, p. 5 and 'Special flights for Sarawak centenary', *Singapore Free Press and Mercantile Advertiser*, 20 September 1941, p. 5.
62 For a timeline of Sarawak's (Brooke) history, see the webpage of the Brooke Heritage Trust, www.brooketrust.org/history-of-sarawak (accessed 13 May 2019).
63 'The Centenary Grand Fancy Bazaar', *Sarawak Gazette*, 1 November 1941, pp. 231–4.
64 Ibid.
65 *Sarawak Gazette*, 1 August 1941, p. 141.
66 'The Centenary Grand Fancy Bazaar', *Sarawak Gazette*, 1 November 1941, pp. 231–4.
67 Ibid., pp. 231–4.
68 Ibid., p. 236; 'Simanggang centenary celebrations' (A report from Simanggang, 2nd district), *Sarawak Gazette*, 1 November 1941, p. 235.
69 Brian Stoddart, 'Sports, cultural imperialism, and colonial response in the British Empire', *Comparative Studies in Society and History*, 30:4 (1998), 649–73.
70 Ibid., pp. 660–3.
71 Ibid., p. 663.
72 'Simanggang centenary celebrations', p. 240.
73 *Sarawak Gazette*, 1 November 1941, p. 236.
74 Ibid., p. 240.
75 Eade, *Sylvia: Queen of the Headhunters*, p. 142.
76 *Sarawak Centenary*, British Movietone film (2 minutes 04 seconds), 17 November 1941. Story number: BM41548, www.aparchive.com (accessed 18 October 2018).
77 *Sarawak Gazette*, 'Programme of the celebrations', 1 September 1941, pp. 171–2.
78 This procession is also described in detail by D. P. Wagle, Reuters' Correspondent, 'Sarawak's centenary: today's ceremony described', *Malaya Tribune*, 24 September 1941, p. 12.
79 For instance, Iban traditional dress consisted of a loincloth (*sirat*) made of bark cloth or cotton, sometimes with distinctive ikat weaving. Body tattoos, or

pantang, were also important. *Gajong* was the Iban warrior costume that included a loincloth, vest (possibly of animal skins) and headdress (*labung*). For a contemporary account of Iban customs, see Janggang, 'Iban traditional clothing and attire', Iban Customs & Traditions, https://ibancustoms.wordpress.com/iban-traditional-clothing-and-attire/ (accessed 13 May 2019). (This online article is by Janggang, an Iban based in Miri.) For a discussion of the colonial anxieties relating to dress, see Philippa Levine, 'States of undress: nakedness and the colonial imagination', *Victorian Studies*, 50:2 (1998), pp. 189–219. The Ranee later described her choices of dress to an American publisher for a series of lectures as a choice of something 'super Oriental' and that her 'full Malay Sarong' was very effective in bringing a 'Ranee element' to her appearance. Eade, *Sylvia: Queen of the Headhunters*, p. 297.

80 Jan Ruger, 'Nation, empire and navy: identity politics in the United Kingdom 1887–1914', *Past & Present*, 185 (2004), pp. 159–87.
81 'Sarawak the world's most ideal state', *Malaya Tribune*, 25 September 1941, p. 2.
82 'Cardinal principles of Sarawak Charter', *Straits Times*, 26 September 1941, p. 10.
83 Ibid.
84 Eade, *Sylvia: Queen of the Headhunters*, p. 282.
85 Reece, *The Name of Brooke*, pp. 101–3.
86 Eade, *Sylvia: Queen of the Headhunters*, pp. 218–19.
87 Ibid., pp. 220–1.
88 Payne, *The White Rajahs of Sarawak*, pp. 172–3.
89 Reece, *The Name of Brooke*, p. 69.
90 'Rajah of Sarawak proclaims end of absolute rule', *Singapore Free Press and Mercantile Advertiser*, 8 April 1941, p. 7.
91 Reece, *The Name of Brooke*, pp. 76–7.
92 'Absolute rule ended in Sarawak', *Straits Times*, 8 April 1941, p. 7.
93 *Malaya Tribune*, 25 September 1941.
94 'Sarawak impressed by Rajah's decision', *Straits Times*, 9 April 1941, p. 10. Cyril Le Gros Clark worked for many years in Sarawak and had been the Secretary of Chinese Affairs from 1929 to 1941. He produced influential reports on conditions in the Sarawak Service and recommendations for change. Reece, *The Name of Brooke*, p. 48.
95 Runciman, *The White Rajahs*, p. 251.
96 Eade, *Sylvia: Queen of the Headhunters*, pp. 142–3.
97 Reece, *The Name of Brooke*, pp. 82–3. There is much speculation as to whether the Raja really needed monetary compensation and whether it motivated his actions. The counter-argument is that he was not only tired of the almost constant feuding but that he had no faith in his successor.
98 *Sarawak Gazette*, 1 November 1941, p. 240.
99 Runciman, *The White Rajahs*, p. 253.
100 Reece, *The Name of Brooke*, pp. 166–7.
101 Ibid., p. 100. These plans were kept secret from the Raja but the Ranee reportedly hinted to friends that she had 'big plans' afoot.
102 Ibid., pp. 170–1.
103 Max Seitelman, 'The cession of Sarawak', *Far Eastern Survey*, 17:3 (1948), pp. 35–7.
104 See Reece, *The Name of Brooke*, for the best discussion of this. Vyner left little documentation of his motivations.
105 Payne, *The White Rajahs of Sarawak*, pp. 177–80. Both Anthony and his father Bertram questioned whether the Raja had the right to surrender the state to Britain.
106 Mike Thomson, 'The stabbed governor of Sarawak', *MMC Magazine*, 14 March 2012. www.bbc.co.uk/news/magazine-17299633 (accessed 13 May 2019).
107 Runciman, *The White Rajahs*, p. 266.
108 Gin, *Of Free Trade and Native Interests*, p. 209.
109 Nigel Barley discusses Brooke's sexuality in some detail – for instance, his attachment to and admiration of a young Malay Prince, Badrudeen. Barley, *White*

Rajah, ch. 5. See also Robert Aldrich, *Colonialism and Homosexuality* (London: Routledge, 2003), pp. 89–91 for a discussion of Brooke's private life and his romances in Sarawak, in particular.
110 Aldrich, *Colonialism and Homosexuality*, pp. 89–91.
111 Eade's fast-paced popular history of the Ranee details her extramarital dalliances and those of her husband and daughters. See, for example, Eade, *Sylvia: Queen of the Headhunters*, pp. 294–6 for the Ranee's reflection on her acceptance of the Raja's continued need for new women in his life.
112 Brooke Heritage Trust, www.brooketrust.org.

CHAPTER EIGHT

Refashioning the monarchy in Brunei: Sultan Omar Ali and the quest for royal absolutism

Naimah S. Talib

The survival of Brunei as the only ruling absolute monarchy in Southeast Asia has been attributed to the statesmanship of its former Sultan, Sir Omar Ali Saifuddin.[1] Credited as the 'architect' of modern Brunei, Sultan Omar Ali's reign, from 1950 to 1967, coincided with a period in post-war colonial Southeast Asia marked by tumultuous change. The Japanese occupation of Southeast Asia during the Second World War highlighted the inequities brought about by colonialism, and the end of the war provided opportunities for colonised peoples in the region to question more vociferously the legitimacy of colonialism. Throughout the 1950s and 1960s, Brunei, like other British colonial dependencies in the region, was confronted with imminent British withdrawal as well as the rising tide of nationalism.

Brunei occupies two small enclaves on the northwest coast of Borneo covering a land area of 5,769 square kilometres. The population of Brunei today is 428,000 with the Malays, who comprise around 66 per cent of the population, dominating the political and bureaucratic life of the country.[2] Important minority communities include the Chinese and several indigenous groups. Islam is the official religion of Brunei and the religion of the majority Malay community as well as members of indigenous groups who have embraced the faith. Before the discovery of oil in 1929, the Sultanate's revenue was dependent on a range of duties and monopolies on goods such as coal and cutch.[3] The revenue from oil grew rapidly especially from the 1950s and, with accumulated surpluses, Brunei soon became a very wealthy country. The sultan is descended from a long line of hereditary rulers that has governed Brunei since the fourteenth century. Brunei became a British protectorate in 1888, with the Sultan retaining internal control while the British took responsibility for foreign relations. This arrangement was expanded in 1906 when a Residential system was put in place, with a succession of British officers appointed to advise the Sultan and manage the state's internal administration; this undermined the sovereignty and independence of the Sultanate. Self-government was achieved in 1959, and Brunei gained full independence from Britain in 1984.

Exhausted by the Second World War, the British drew up a 'Grand Design' to gradually withdraw from their colonies in Southeast Asia and prepare them for eventual self-government within the Commonwealth.[4] Apart from the local challenges of restoring damaged infrastructure, providing social welfare services and meeting the needs of the local population, the British also had to deal with the rising tide of nationalism and the ideological appeal of communism in post-war Southeast Asia. Once Burma was granted independence in 1948, the British became more preoccupied with preparing the remaining territories for independence – Malaya, Singapore, Sarawak, North Borneo (later Sabah) and Brunei. In order for these states to be robust and sustainable after independence, the British favoured the amalgamation of the territories into bigger units; Singapore with Malaya, and the Borneo states into a North Borneo Federation. The British territories were expected to move in the direction of constitutional democracy in preparation for independence; all remaining monarchies would retain symbolic but not real power, and sovereignty would pass on to each state after independence. These pressures for change made the reign of Sultan Omar Ali an especially challenging one. And yet, while the neighbouring Malay monarchies lost real political power except as custodians of Malay custom and religion, the Brunei monarch during the period of British withdrawal from the region managed to reclaim royal powers lost when Residency rule was established in 1906. Brunei, a small British protectorate with a royal dynasty intact, was also the only British territory in Southeast Asia that managed to circumvent strong British pressure to merge with its neighbours into Malaysia in 1963 (although Singapore would later secede from Malaysia in 1965). Sultan Omar Ali was a master strategist who was quick to seize opportunities to regain power for the monarchy, consolidate its conservative institutions and ensure its survival after independence.

Omar Ali, born in 1914, was the son of Sultan Muhammad Jamalul Alam II, who reigned from 1906 to 1924. Omar Ali's elder brother, Ahmad Tajuddin, succeeded as Sultan upon their father's death. As a child growing up, there was no expectation that Omar Ali would succeed to the throne. Apart from receiving a traditional Islamic education, he was one of the few royal family members sent to Malaya for a Western type of education at the Malay College in Kuala Kangsar, a residential school that prepared the sons of Malay nobility and elites for a career in the British administrative service. On his return in 1936, he was encouraged by the British Resident, R. E. Turnbull, to join the administrative service briefly as a cadet officer in the forestry department. Turnbull, who had experience in Malaya for nearly five years before being appointed as Brunei Resident from 1934 to 1937, was keen for Omar Ali to be exposed to the workings of British colonial bureaucracy. After a few months, Omar Ali was transferred to the Legal Department and within two years he was promoted as an administrative officer.[5] Omar Ali also managed to cultivate relationships with important British officials, including Malcolm MacDonald, who became Governor General of Malaya in the immediate post-war period. During the Japanese occupation, Omar Ali was given the opportunity to serve at a senior rank in the administration and was seconded to the Japanese Governor's office. Upon the death of his uncle in 1943, Omar Ali became the Pengiran Bendahara, the second highest royal office after the Sultan, and in this capacity he attended State Council meetings. Since his brother, the new sultan, Ahmad Tajuddin, was often away in Sarawak, Omar Ali was left to manage the royal responsibilities.[6] He also won the trust of British Residents such as L. H. N. Davis, who was British Resident in Brunei in 1948, and was increasingly seen as a firm supporter of British interests in Brunei as well as in the region. When Ahmad Tajuddin died unexpectedly in 1950, leaving no male heir, British officials strongly supported Omar Ali's accession to the throne as the next Sultan.

British interests in Brunei

Sultan Omar Ali was the twenty-eighth ruler of a Sultanate that had reached its zenith from the fifteenth to the seventeenth centuries, when it was a formidable regional power exercising suzerainty over the whole of Borneo and the southern Philippines.[7] However, a century of bitter internal rivalry turned into a long civil war in the early nineteenth century, resulting in the gradual and inevitable decline of the dynasty. The entry of the British and Dutch colonial powers into Southeast Asia shifted the regional power dynamics and further undermined the Sultanate. The arrival of James Brooke, a British adventurer, in Borneo in 1839 further aggravated the dismal fortunes of Brunei; James Brooke carved out his own kingdom, Sarawak, from Brunei territory, and together with his successor continued to nibble at Brunei land, so that by the turn of the early twentieth century, Brunei was reduced to two small non-contiguous enclaves. If not for the propitious intervention of the British, Brunei might have been completely absorbed by Sarawak.[8]

The accession to the throne in 1885 of Sultan Omar Ali's grandfather, Hashim Jalilul Alam, heralded the beginning of British influence in Brunei. Following the signing of an agreement in 1905–6, the Brunei Sultan was obliged to take advice from a British Resident on all questions of government other than those affecting religion. The Residential system established in 1906 emulated the one put in place in the Malay Peninsula states. Decisions were made by the State Council, whose members were not elected, and which was dominated by the Resident and supported by his officials. Although the Sultan and senior members of the nobility sat on the Council, the Resident, as representative of the British authorities in Malaya, was able to exercise undue influence. British-influenced legislation was nevertheless passed and legitimised in the name of the Sultan.[9]

A centralised, bureaucratic system of government was gradually established under the Residency. This represented a departure from the previous system of traditional administration that depended on power relationships and balancing networks of authority among the Brunei nobles. In a 1904 report, M. S. H. McArthur claimed that Brunei did not have a 'system of government in the usual acceptance of the term', but only 'ownership', by which he meant control of communities and the right to tax them.[10] Under British rule, however, the Sultan presided over a centralised administration and his power as the head of a traditional nobility was undermined.[11] The Residency also marginalised the networks that supported the monarchy in the past, including the highest ranking Brunei nobles, known as *wazir* (vizier), the equivalent of noble ministers. An important outcome of the establishment of the Residency was that the power relationship between the Sultan and his nobles shifted in his favour. The British policy of emphasising the prestige and dignity of the office of the Sultan slowly eroded the power of the various royal advisers and nobles. Nevertheless, during the regency of Sultan Omar Ali's father and brother, who both ascended the throne at a young age, the local royal advisers found an opportunity to exercise some temporary influence. In his interactions with the British, Sultan Omar Ali had the advantage of another source of leverage: the discovery of oil in 1929 and its subsequent commercial exploitation. By 1935, Brunei had become the third largest oil producer in the British Empire.[12] Oil revenue allowed Brunei to cope with the difficulties of the Depression years, and by 1936 Brunei's revenue was in surplus.

The Second World War and the subsequent Japanese occupation of Brunei from December 1941 to June 1945 ended the brief period of prosperity. The British offered no resistance to the invading Japanese troops, who immediately took over the oilfields and equipment. Sultan Ahmad Tajuddin and his family had no option but to cooperate with the Japanese and continued to rule during the occupation. The local government officials and oilfield employees continued working and provided support for the Japanese administration. However, shortages of food and medicine towards the end of the war affected the daily lives of Bruneians. After the war ended, the British prioritised the restoration of oil production, and Brunei's revenue increased to a level that allowed it to extend a loan to Malaya in the 1950s.

Dealing with the British

When Omar Ali (Figure 8.1) ascended the throne in 1950, Brunei was still struggling with post-war rehabilitation; the expansion of public works and the extension of public utilities had to proceed slowly due to a lack of skilled personnel. Politically, it was clear to Omar Ali that there were impending changes on the horizon. The immediate post-war period saw Britain taking over Sarawak and North Borneo as Crown Colonies in 1946, and it soon became apparent that British post-war planning envisaged closer cooperation and eventual amalgamation of the three British territories in Borneo in preparation for independence.[13] The new circumstances also presented challenges that needed to be resolved through a new treaty between Brunei and Britain.

The Sultan's attempt to assert his power and authority during the 1950s was undermined by the British Resident, who was answerable to the High Commissioner, based in Kuching as Governor of Sarawak. The cession of Sarawak to the British crown in July 1946 resulted in an overhaul of the government with the first colonial governor, Sir Charles Arden-Clarke, appointed in October. The priority of the British in Borneo was to restore public services and infrastructure destroyed by the retreating Japanese troops. The British maintained that Brunei was too small to stand on its own and it would be wise to amalgamate the Sultanate with Sarawak and North Borneo. To this end, the Governor of Sarawak became simultaneously the High Commissioner for Brunei. The Brunei Resident would report to the Sarawak Governor, and Sarawak administrative officers would be seconded to Brunei. The new Sultan, Omar Ali, viewed with alarm the power of the Resident, as the 1905–6 Agreement allowed the Resident both power and authority to control every aspect of government administration even though decisions and actions taken were legitimised in the name of the Sultan.[14] However, according to a Colonial Office legal authority, J. C. McPetrie, the Sultan was an absolute sovereign and the State Council and the 'law-making power must be vested in him'.[15] The Sultan and the local members of the State Council were determined to limit the executive role of the Resident. The Sultan's Private Secretary, Pehin

Figure 8.1 Sultan Omar Ali Saifuddin

Ibrahim Jahfar, had served for many years as a trusted administrator, and, encouraged by the Sultan, he closely scrutinised all legislation brought before the Council.[16] Rather than being a mere rubber stamp, the local members of the State Council were encouraged by the Sultan to participate actively in debates on any legislation.

The State Council had a majority of local members appointed by the Sultan in consultation with the British Resident and the Sultan realised that this executive body could be manipulated to push his interests vis-à-vis the Resident and other British officials.[17] From the early 1950s, the Sultan urged the State Council to call for more regular meetings and all decisions and legislation were meticulously examined by the Sultan, his able Private Secretary and other local members in order to ensure that the interests of the sovereign would be taken into account. With a Council dominated by the Sultan's nominees, the Sultan-in-Council clearly held a dominant and influential role. One area in which there was competition for power and authority was responsibility over financial management. In 1953, the Resident attempted to pass legislation that would widen the authority of the colonial State Treasurer, giving him powers to regularise financial administration and minimise ad hoc financial decisions.[18] Ibrahim bin Jahfar argued that the legislation gave 'unfettered discretion' to the Treasurer; the legislation was not supported and was subsequently defeated. With time, the Sultan realised that the State Council could be manipulated to limit the authority of the Resident. In doing so, he also managed to expand his 'de facto sovereignty' and influence the future direction of political change.[19]

Resisting the amalgamation of British Borneo

For Brunei, the greatest change experienced in the immediate post-war period lay in a policy adopted in 1948 by the British to streamline administration by placing Brunei's affairs under the supervision of authorities in Sarawak. This had resulted in the Governor of Sarawak concurrently serving as High Commissioner of Brunei.[20] Under the agreement, a senior British administrative officer would be seconded to Brunei as the Brunei Resident, though he effectively remained under the direct control of the Sarawak Governor. Many in Brunei viewed the arrangement as an attempt to treat Brunei as another administrative district of Sarawak, while others speculated that Brunei would eventually be absorbed by Sarawak. The administrative association of Brunei with Sarawak was perceived by both the Sultan and the local population as politically insensitive given the loss of former Brunei territories to Sarawak. Yet the link between the administration of Brunei and the Governor of Sarawak was only terminated in 1959 when Brunei achieved internal self-government.[21]

Apart from fostering close administrative links between Sarawak and Brunei, Malcolm MacDonald, then Commissioner-General for Southeast Asia, suggested in 1948 that plans for the consolidation of Brunei, Sarawak and North Borneo should be accelerated, and that closer cooperation and the pooling of resources among the British Borneo dependencies should begin as soon as possible. The underlying assumption was that the Borneo territories could merge into a single unit with 'administrative economies that would result from giving them a common administration'.[22] At a meeting of Governors convened by MacDonald in 1948, it was decided to take steps to gradually advance towards the goal of closer integration and coordination in all fields. The British Secretary of State for the Colonies, Arthur Creech Jones, stated that no opportunity should be lost to further the ultimate aim of full administrative union. Various initiatives were consequently implemented, such as the setting up of a common Geological Survey Department and the establishment of a single Supreme Court for the Borneo territories in 1951. An inter-territorial Borneo conference was also held twice annually from 1953 onwards to discuss coordination of policies and common services.[23] Malcolm MacDonald convened the first Inter-territorial Conference, and set up a standing body to review the implementation of decisions. The secondment of Sarawak officers to Brunei was also implemented as a result of the 1948 agreement.

Sultan Omar Ali, however, was concerned that the moves to bring Brunei closer to Sarawak and North Borneo would eventually result in Brunei losing its identity as a Muslim monarchy since the populations of the other two colonies were dominated by non-Muslim communities. The changes also gave the impression that it might not be too long before Brunei would be absorbed into a British Borneo entity, which would prejudice the Sultan's status as an independent sovereign. The trend towards amalgamation ran against Sultan Omar Ali's determination to reclaim the rights and power that were lost or undermined by the treaty of 1905–6. A further issue was Brunei's reluctance to share its enormous oil wealth with Sarawak and North Borneo. Hence, Sultan Omar Ali was reluctant to welcome positively moves towards closer association of the Borneo territories.

MacDonald nevertheless found a way to persuade Sultan Omar Ali to respond more favourably to closer cooperation among the territories. He impressed on the Sultan that before any negotiations on constitutional changes, Brunei should first attempt to work more cooperatively with Sarawak and North Borneo. As a compromise, MacDonald proposed that the administrative arrangement by which Sarawak officers were seconded to Brunei and the Governor of Sarawak concurrently served as Brunei High Commissioner would be terminated. In return, Brunei would agree to become a member of the proposed standing joint council which would replace the inter-territorial conferences. The standing joint council would be vested with executive power, and its establishment would signal a move towards closer integration of the three territories. However, before these proposals could be formally presented to Brunei, the Sultan made a public announcement that he firmly rejected the plan.[24] The Colonial Office did not pursue the matter until two years later, in 1950, with the arrival of Anthony Abell as the next Governor of Sarawak and High Commissioner of Brunei. Abell tried to convince the Sultan of the benefits of integration but he was unsuccessful. The idea of closer association and perhaps eventual federation of the Borneo territories, in short, proved to be too difficult an idea to sell to the Sultan, who was suspicious of any attempt to undermine Brunei's status as an independent state and British Protectorate and to share her oil wealth with Sarawak and North Borneo.

Rise of nationalism

The Sultan and the British authorities meanwhile had to contend with another issue that began to challenge the status quo. The Japanese wartime occupation of Brunei had raised political awareness among younger Bruneians. With time, they began to question the legitimacy of British rule and privileges. The strong nationalist movement that swept Indonesia before and during the war had also influenced people in Brunei to question whether the British colonial authorities were safeguarding the interests of the local community. In particular, these early stirrings of 'proto-nationalist sentiments', especially among the Malays, focused on their lack of progress in education and lack of participation in the economy.[25] However, rising political consciousness did not evolve to become a political movement until the mid-1950s. The increase in oil wealth led only to a marginal improvement in the standard of living and welfare of the Malay community as most of the oil revenue went to the British colonial authorities. The British policy of avoiding too much development and 'over-education' helped to sustain conservative attitudes and loyalty to political traditions to which people were accustomed.[26]

Opportunities for education increased only gradually after the end of the war, and most Malays had access only to vernacular education which did not equip them with the skills needed for the oil industry. A number of Malay students were sent to the premier teacher training institution in Malaya, the Sultan Idris Teachers' College, where they were exposed to the political developments in Malaya in the late 1940s with the emergence of Malay opposition to the Malayan Union proposal that would give equal citizenship rights to migrant communities. One young student, Shaikh A. M. Azahari, however, did not experience his political awakening in Malaya. During the Japanese occupation, he was instead sent to Bogor in Indonesia to study veterinary science. He remained in Indonesia after the war, met a number of the leaders of the Indonesian independence movement and joined the war against the Dutch. A charismatic speaker, Azahari returned to Brunei in 1952, and very soon attracted a large following, especially among the lower ranks of the civil service. He soon spread anti-colonial propaganda and taught the local Malays to agitate and organise themselves to participate in mass demonstrations in defiance of the colonial authorities. The British were suspicious of Azahari's activities and his pro-republican stance, while the Sultan was wary of Azahari's political ambitions.

Managing constitutional change

Sultan Omar Ali was aware that the 1905–6 Agreement had to be renegotiated but was also suspicious of Britain imposing constitutional change that would undermine his position in the long term. As early as 1953, Sultan Omar Ali declared that he was in favour of a written constitution for Brunei. While the British ultimately desired to curtail the powers of the Sultan through such a constitution, Omar Ali instead saw the constitution as a vehicle for promoting his own power. In mid-1957, Alan Lennox-Boyd, the Secretary of State for the Colonies, during a visit to Brunei raised the possibility of negotiations for a constitution. Two periods of lengthy talks ensued in September 1958 and in March 1959. Negotiations focused on preparations for independence, and the introduction of universal suffrage and democratic institutions for the eventual shift of power from the colonial authorities to elected local leaders. However, during these discussions, the Sultan demonstrated his unwillingness to embrace democratic reforms; he wanted instead a constitution that would guarantee his dominant role in politics in perpetuity. Another important issue for the Sultan was to push for the removal of any connection with Sarawak in the administration. The outcome of the negotiations was a new treaty, signed in 1959, that effectively granted internal self-government with the Sultan given a dominant role in politics. The Sultan was vested with extensive executive power and control over a partially elected legislature. Britain would retain jurisdiction over defence, external relations and internal security.[27] The administrative ties with Sarawak were severed, and the High Commissioner of Brunei now had no formal executive role in the administration.

The Sultan's success in gaining concessions from the British could be attributed to the formation in 1956 of a political party, the Parti Rakyat Brunei (PRB, Brunei People's Party). Led by Shaikh A. M. Azahari, the party was strongly opposed to colonialism. The party was also in favour of establishing a democratic government and a merger with North Borneo and Sarawak, with Brunei playing a dominant political role. Both the British and the Sultan were extremely concerned with the aims of PRB, as Britain had envisaged granting self-government to leaders who would continue a positive and close relationship with Britain. The Brunei High Commissioner, Abell, described Azahari as

> an irresponsible opportunist seeking power at all costs. His ultimate aims are removal of British influence, destruction of the Sultanate and replacement by a Government headed by himself. Our information is that his political associates in Singapore and Malaya are Indonesian Nationalists and Communist fellow travellers.[28]

The Sultan was similarly wary of Azahari for fear that he would have no executive authority or role in a democratic Brunei. Perhaps the Sultan's fears were well founded because soon after the independence of Malaya in August 1957, and while Sultan Omar Ali was himself in the midst of negotiations with the British, Azahari, without the Sultan's knowledge, led an unofficial mission to London to negotiate for Brunei's independence.[29] The mission was doomed to fail but went ahead anyway despite the British advising Azahari that it would be a waste of time to proceed with the mission without the Sultan's blessing.

Throughout negotiations with the Sultan, the British entertained hopes that by their accepting the Sultan's proposals on the constitution, the Sultan would be more amenable to joining a merger of the British Borneo territories. Hence the British gave in to the Sultan's demands not to guarantee citizenship rights to recent immigrants, especially to members of the growing Chinese community. The Sultan was determined to extract maximum concessions from the British in order to 'establish his supremacy as the de facto local sovereign'.[30] The British soon discovered that in agreeing to the Sultan's sovereignty, the 1959 constitution left them with 'responsibility without power'.[31] Britain stood to gain by continuing its hegemony over Brunei as oil revenue was channelled through the British Malayan Petroleum Company, which held rights to the oilfields.

The new constitution was promulgated in September 1959 and vested the Sultan with executive authority as head of an Executive Council, which later became the Council of Ministers. It also restored the Sultan's traditional prerogative of appointing his own ministers and key administrative personnel.[32] The Council was responsible for approving the government budget and met only when convened by the Sultan. The Sultan had to consult the Executive Council but could, in theory, ignore its advice by providing reasons for doing so. The constitution also provided for a partially elected Legislative Council with eight ex-officio members, six official members, three nominated non-official members and sixteen elected members chosen from the district councils; the Sultan held authority to nominate a majority of the members.[33] (The first district council elections would be held two years after the promulgation of the constitution.) The Council's responsibilities included passing laws and acting as a check on the Executive Council. Saunders argues that the constitution provided the Sultan with tremendous power without any serious check on his authority;[34] the outcome of difficult negotiations with the British can be seen as a major victory for the Sultan.

The constitution gave Sultan Omar Ali responsibility to appoint senior government officials as well as members of the Executive Council, the successor to the former State Council, which was responsible for advising and formulating policy. In practice, the Sultan could make appointments on the basis of patronage. He thus appointed his trusted private secretary, Ibrahim Jahfar, as the first Menteri Besar (Chief Minister) and other local dignitaries to his government. Because of the shortage of qualified personnel, Sultan Omar Ali turned to the Prime Minister of Malaya, Tunku Abdul Rahman, for assistance in providing key staff. Sultan Omar Ali then was keen to cultivate a positive relationship with Tunku Abdul Rahman and had extended a substantial loan to Malaya in 1958. The Tunku obliged but, before long, tension developed between seconded Malayan officials and local Brunei civil servants. Azahari was quick to exploit the grievances and accused the Malayan officers of colonising Brunei. The British High Commissioner, unfortunately, was constitutionally not allowed to intervene in domestic affairs.

Rejection of Malaysia

In 1961, the Prime Minister of Malaya, Tunku Abdul Rahman, publicly announced a scheme for amalgamation of Malaya, Singapore, Sarawak, North Borneo and Brunei into a single state. The British, for their part, were keen to have the smaller territories in Borneo come together in a larger entity that would be more sustainable. The Sultan was willing to seriously consider the Malaysia proposal due to two key factors. First, with a population of only 84,000 in 1961, Brunei was too small to stand on its own as an independent state. Second, owing to its oil wealth, Brunei would need the security and protection of inclusion in a bigger political entity. The Malaysia proposal was set against looming local elections in Brunei planned for August 1961. In order to win over the PRB, its leader, Azahari, was appointed a member of the Legislative Council, which allowed him the opportunity to participate in the Malaysia talks. However, Azahari rejected the Malaysia proposal; he was more interested in advancing his agenda of forming an independent Northern Borneo political unit with the Brunei Sultan as the focus of its loyalty.[35] When his motion proposing the establishment of an independent union of the Northern Borneo states was defeated in the Legislative Council, Azahari resigned.

The long-delayed Brunei elections were eventually held in August 1962. The PRB campaigned on Brunei independence through a union of Northern Borneo states and also highlighted 'gross inefficiencies' of the Sultan's government.[36] Azahari himself was not able to contest the elections because he had been born in Labuan, an island off the coast of Brunei that became a British naval outpost in 1846, and did not qualify for Brunei citizenship. His party nevertheless won an overwhelming victory, capturing all but one seat. However, the elected seats in the Legislative Council were outnumbered by the government-appointed seats and so the PRB was not able to pass resolutions easily.[37] Unlike the PRB's strong mandate in the 1962 elections, the parties allied to the government performed dismally and failed to win any seats. With a high voter turnout of 90 per cent, it can be deduced that public opinion was against Brunei's integration into Malaysia. After several delays, the first session of the new Legislative Council was convened. Azahari's party unsuccessfully tabled a motion to form a union of Northern Borneo states and reject integration into Malaysia. The PRB, behind the scenes, had already begun planning for an armed revolt if amalgamation with Malaysia occurred, and Azahari had hoped that support from the Philippines and Indonesia would be forthcoming; both countries publicly denounced the Malaysia scheme as a neo-colonialist plot.

A revolt in Brunei broke out on 8 December 1962, though it was swiftly quelled by the British. Azahari and his deputy, Zaini Ahmad, were both in the Philippines at the time of the insurrection, leaving the PRB Secretary-General, Jasin Affandy, in charge on the ground.[38] According to some reports, the revolt did not receive the strong support from the Malay community that the PRB had expected.[39] The Sultan declared a state of emergency and suspended the constitution. The rebellion disrupted the government as many of those implicated were employees of government agencies. Shaken by the revolt, the Sultan was now more determined to avoid liberalising the government and pursuing democratic reforms.[40] The Sultan, under pressure from the British, then continued with negotiations on the formation of a united Malaysia.

By March 1963, it became clear that Brunei was not willing to compromise on exclusive control of its oil revenue, except perhaps to provide a fixed annual contribution to the Malaysian federal government.[41] The

Sultan's royal precedence relative to the other Sultans in Malaya also became a contentious issue. Under the Malaysia proposal, the Sultan of each state would take turns to become the Yang di-Pertuan Agong (supreme head or king), or head of state, of Malaysia. Furthermore, the Sultan preferred a partial surrender of his sovereignty, retaining independence over internal administration, while Malaysia required a full surrender of sovereignty. Since Sultan Omar Ali continued to remain intransigent about committing to joining Malaysia, Tunku Abdul Rahman decided to proceed with establishing Malaysia without Brunei. The Malaysia agreement was signed on 31 August 1963 by Malaya, Singapore, Sarawak and North Borneo but without Brunei. Tunku Abdul Rahman then took retaliatory measures against Brunei including the immediate repatriation of hundreds of Malayan teachers and civil servants. Their departure en masse created a serious short-term personnel problem in Brunei.

After Brunei's refusal to join Malaysia, the British put enormous pressure on Sultan Omar Ali to embrace democratic reforms and undertake steps to allow for more meaningful popular participation. However, the British authorities were only able to provide advice, having lost the opportunity to influence directly the course of political developments as a result of the 1959 agreement.[42] Sultan Omar Ali agreed reluctantly to hold elections and gradually increase the number of elected seats in the Legislative Council. Since the PRB was banned, only a number of small independent parties contested elections in March 1965. Of the ten elected candidates, nine were independents, seven of whom were former members of the PRB. Sultan Omar Ali increasingly distanced himself from smaller new political parties formed just before and after the 1965 Legislative and District Council elections, many of which began to push for Brunei's independence. By the end of 1965 and early 1966, Sultan Omar Ali had become convinced 'not to relax his supreme hold on the government' and even resisted attempts by parties loyal to him to share power.[43] The Sultan was determined to disregard British advice to include elected members as part of the Council of Ministers. Further talks with the British on Brunei's independence ensued and the British continued to insist on democratic reforms as a condition for independence.[44] Rather than give in to the British, Sultan Omar Ali decided to abdicate in 1967 in favour of his eldest son. The Crown Prince, Hassanal Bolkiah, was not legally bound to the British to make the constitutional changes. He was young, at twenty-one years old, and inexperienced, and was attending Sandhurst Military Academy in Britain when he ascended the throne. At the time of Sultan Omar Ali's abdication, Brunei was effectively self-governing and relied on the British for protection and security, which it would continue to do until independence was achieved in 1984. By abdicating, Sultan Omar Ali was freed from his legal obligations to the British. That gave him more time to mould Brunei politically into a viable, authoritarian monarchy by providing advice to his son, the new Sultan.

Legitimising an absolute monarchy

During the reign of Sultan Omar Ali, much thought was focused not only on the nature of the Brunei state but also on building a nation that would reflect the interests of a monarchy determined to survive and rule in the post-colonial era. Under the British Residency, the Brunei monarchy went through a major overhaul. The power and authority of the monarchy in Brunei on the eve of the accession of Sultan Omar Ali in 1950 was dramatically different from the time of his grandfather and father. In 1906, the declining Brunei monarchy was on the brink of being absorbed by an expanding Sarawak; if not for British intervention, it might not have survived another century. Sultan Omar Ali was determined to ensure that decolonisation would not undermine his sovereign right. He was careful to reclaim his power and authority and reinvent the monarchy as an institution. In trying to resuscitate the monarchy, Sultan Omar Ali attempted to ensure the legitimacy of the Brunei Sultanate by reinventing aspects of Malay culture and tradition that would support continued loyalty to a paternalistic sovereign.[45] In the process, Sultan Omar Ali laid the foundations of a political culture that would provide sustenance for an absolute monarchy.

In an attempt to revive the glory of the Sultanate in the 1950s, royal loyalists, in particular, Pehin Jamil al-Sufri and his associates, worked in tandem with Sultan Omar Ali to systematically collect documentation regarding royal customs and traditions. Sultan Omar Ali explained that these could be adjusted and developed so as to remain relevant to changing times.[46] Within a few years of his accession, Sultan Omar Ali established a department of customs and traditions (*adat istiadat*), religious affairs and social protection; by 1962, the department of customs and traditions had become a separate department, underscoring its growing importance. Rituals and ceremonies that can be traced to the foundation of Malacca in the early fifteenth century were observed in the coronation and enthronement of Sultan Omar Ali and his successor, Sultan Hassanal Bolkiah. Similar ceremonies were also practised by sultanates on the Malay Peninsula and were marked by recitations by a senior Muslim cleric. Symbolic colours, and in particular yellow, derived from Theravada Buddhist tradition, were reserved for the sovereign.[47] In addition, religious ceremonies, such as the procession to celebrate of the birth of the Prophet (*Maulud Nabi*), were regularly held and led by the royal elite and joined by commoners. Lavish royal processions, as seen during the coronation of Sultan Omar's Ali's successor, Sultan Hassanal Bolkiah, promoted the idea of a royal family that was not only privileged but also occupied a special status in Brunei society.

During the 1950s and early 1960s, Sultan Omar Ali, in trying to elevate the monarchy through a revival and celebration of royal customs and traditions, was in effect also reminding people that the monarchy formed an integral part of the Bruneian Malay identity.[48] While the national ideology of *Melayu Islam Beraja* (Malay Muslim monarchy) was only formalised from 1984 onwards, it was Sultan Omar Ali who promoted the idea of an official ideology based on three important components of Brunei culture and identity[49] that should be aligned to Brunei's national destiny. The strong emphasis placed on Malay culture, Malay religion (i.e., Islam) and the monarchy supported the interests of the royal family.[50] With the monarchy inextricably intertwined with the national culture and identity of the Brunei state, it would be difficult to question the legitimacy of this long-running dynasty.

Conclusion

Sultan Omar Ali's reign was marked by major political challenges that could have severely limited the role of the monarchy in Brunei. The establishment of the Residency in 1906 eroded the traditional authority and power of the Brunei sovereign; the patronage networks that propped up the declining monarchy were replaced by a centralising bureaucracy that curtailed the ability of the nobility to take an active part in administration. The early days of the State Council which was dominated by the British Residents did not allow the Sultan and the nobility to have a meaningful role in decision-making. While colonisation subverted the institutions and authority of the Sultan, British rule also provided new opportunities for the monarchy. The development of infrastructure and the discovery of oil, which made Brunei a very wealthy country by the late 1950s, enabled Sultan Omar Ali's resolve and determination to revive not just the glory of the Brunei monarchy but also sovereign power and authority that was once part of royal tradition. During the chaotic period of British decolonisation, which was marked by the introduction of representative institutions and elections, Sultan Omar Ali not only skilfully avoided the introduction of democratic reforms and meaningful popular participation but also consolidated and entrenched the monarchy in Brunei society.

Notes

All translations by the author, Naimah S. Talib.

1. B. A. Hussainmiya, *Sultan Omar Ali Saifuddin III and Britain: The Making of Brunei Darussalam* (Kuala Lumpur: Oxford University Press, 1995).
2. Prime Minister's Office, Economic Planning and Development, Brunei. web.archive.org/web/20161111141102/; http://www.depd.gov.bn/SitePages/National%20Statistics.aspx (accessed 15 November 2018).
3. Cutch (or catechu) is an extract from the acacia plant which can be used as an astringent, dye, food additive or tannin.
4. A. N. Porter and A. J. Stockwell, *British Imperial Policy and Decolonization, 1938–64* (London: Macmillan, 1987).
5. Hussainmiya, *Sultan Omar Ali Saifuddin III and Britain*, p. 57.
6. *Ibid.*, pp. 55–60.
7. See Graham Saunders, *A History of Brunei* (Kuala Lumpur: Oxford University Press, 1994); A. V. M. Horton, *The British Residency in Brunei, 1906–1959* (Hull: Centre for South-East Asian Studies, University of Hull, Occasional Paper no. 6, 1984); Naimah S. Talib, 'A resilient monarchy: the Sultanate of Brunei and regime legitimacy in an era of democratic nation-states', *New Zealand Journal of Asian Studies*, 4:2 (2002), 134–47.
8. Horton, *The British Residency in Brunei*; Hussainmiya, *Sultan Omar Ali Saifuddin III and Britain*.
9. B. A. Hussainmiya, '"Manufacturing consensus": the role of the State Council in Brunei Darussalam', *Journal of Southeast Asian Studies*, 31:2 (2000), 325.
10. M. S. H. McArthur, *Report on Brunei in 1904* (Athens, OH: Monographs in International Studies, 1987).
11. David Leake Jr., *Brunei: The Modern Southeast-Asian Islamic Sultanate* (Kuala Lumpur: Forum, 1990).
12. Horton, *The British Residency in Brunei*, p. 27.
13. Nicholas Tarling, *The Fall of Imperial Britain in South-East Asia* (Singapore: Oxford University Press, 1993).
14. Hussainmiya, '"Manufacturing consensus"', p. 323.
15. Cited in *ibid.*, p. 342.
16. Hussainmiya, *Sultan Omar Ali Saifuddin*, pp. 70–1.
17. *Ibid.*, p. 71; Hussainmiya, '"Manufacturing consensus"', p. 9.
18. Hussainmiya, '"Manufacturing consensus"', p. 344.
19. *Ibid.*, p. 345.
20. Naimah S. Talib, *Administrators and Their Service: The Sarawak Administrative Service under the Brooke Rajahs and British Colonial Rule* (Kuala Lumpur: Oxford University Press, 1999), pp. 139–41.
21. *Ibid.*, p. 141; Horton, *The British Residency in Brunei*, p. 44.
22. Talib, *Administrators and Their Service*, pp. 152–3.
23. *Ibid.*
24. *Ibid.*, p. 154.
25. Hussainmiya, *Sultan Omar Ali Saifuddin III and Britain*, p. 80.
26. Hussainmiya, *The Brunei Constitution of 1959: An Inside Story* (Bandar Sri Begawan: Brunei Press, 2000); Tarling, *The Fall of Imperial Britain*, p. 131.
27. Hussainmiya, *The Brunei Constitution of 1959*.
28. Hussainmiya, *Sultan Omar Ali Saifuddin III and Britain*, p. 185.
29. Saunders, *A History of Brunei*, p. 138; A. J. Stockwell, 'Britain and Brunei, 1945–1963: imperial retreat and royal ascendancy', *Modern Asian Studies*, 38:4 (2004), 793.
30. Hussainmiya, *Sultan Omar Ali Saifuddin III and Britain*, pp. 166–8.
31. Stockwell, 'Britain and Brunei', p. 795.
32. Donald E. Brown, *Brunei: The Structure and History of a Bornean Malay Sultanate* (Brunei Museum Journal Monograph No. 2, 1970), p. 127.

33 Saunders, *A History of Brunei*, p. 137.
34 *Ibid.*, pp. 137–8.
35 *Ibid.*, p. 147.
36 Simon Francis, 'Brunei Darussalam: stresses and uncertainty 50 years on from the 1959 agreement with Britain', *Asian Affairs*, 40:2 (2009), 198.
37 Hussainmiya, *Sultan Omar Ali Saifuddin III and Britain*, p. 270.
38 Harun Abdul Majid, *Rebellion in Brunei: The 1962 revolt: Imperialism, Confrontation and Oil* (London: I. B. Tauris, 2007).
39 Saunders, *A History of Brunei*, p. 151.
40 Stockwell, 'Britain and Brunei', p. 802.
41 Isa bin Ibrahim, *Brunei and Malaysia: Why Sultan Omar Ali Saifuddin Refused to Join the Federation* (London: I. B. Tauris, 2013), p. 37.
42 Saunders, *A History of Brunei*, p. 159.
43 Hussainmiya, *Sultan Omar Ali Saifuddin III and Britain*, p. 353.
44 Eussoff Agaki Hj Ismail, 'Brunei Darussalam: its re-emergence as a sovereign and independent Malay-Muslim Sultanate (1959–1983)', MPhil dissertation, University of Hull, 1991, p. 135.
45 Eric Hobsbawm, 'Introduction', in Eric Hobsbawm and Terence Ranger (eds), *The Invention of Tradition* (Cambridge: Cambridge University Press, 1983); Siti Norkhalbi Haji Wahsalfelah, 'Traditional woven textiles: tradition and identity construction in the "New State" of Brunei Darussalam', PhD dissertation, University of Western Australia, 2005.
46 Pehin Mohd Jamil al-Sufri, *Adat Istiadat diraja Brunei: Brunei Royal Customs and Traditions* (Bandar Seri Begawan: Jabatan Adat Istiadat Negara, 2002).
47 Marie Sybille De Vienne, *Brunei: From the Age of Commerce to the 21st Century* (Singapore: NUS Press, 2015), p. 255.
48 De Vienne, *Brunei*, p. 255.
49 *Ibid.*, pp. 262–4.
50 Ann Black, 'Ideology and law: the impact of the MIB ideology on law and dispute resolution in the Sultanate of Brunei Darussalam', *Asian Journal of Comparative Law*, 3:1 (2008), 7.

CHAPTER NINE

Colonial monarchy and decolonisation in the French Empire: Bao Dai, Norodom Sihanouk and Mohammed V

Christopher Goscha

The Vietnamese emperor Bao Dai has gone down in history as a colonial puppet. He lies today beneath a black, nondescript tombstone in a Parisian cemetery. Meanwhile, millions of visitors stream through ornate monuments in Rabat and Phnom Penh to pay homage to the fathers of the Moroccan and Cambodian nations, Mohammed V and Norodom Sihanouk. The French had crowned them all as their colonial monarchs during the colonial period, but only two became the national icons of their post-colonial states. This raises the simple question at the heart of this essay: why did some colonially conceived monarchs survive decolonisation while others did not? To answer that question, I use a comparative framework to consider four main factors: the nature of French colonial monarchy in each of these protectorates; the specific local, national and international circumstances; the individual personalities of each sovereign; and the strategies they used. I proceed in three separate acts, one for each monarch, before returning to Bao Dai to conclude.

Act I. Bao Dai

During the second half of the nineteenth century, the French conquered and colonised the Vietnamese kingdom ruled by the Nguyen dynasty since 1802.[1] By the turn of the twentieth century, they had divided the country into three parts, a colony in the south, Cochinchina, and two protectorates located to the north, one in the central part of the country, Annam, the other covering the Red River delta, Tonkin. This truncated Vietnam was in turn part of a wider colonial state known as French Indochina, which also included Laotian and Cambodian monarchies. In theory, as a protected state, the Nguyen monarchy would continue to administer local affairs from its imperial capital in Hue while the French would take care of diplomatic, security and military matters. In practice, however, French Residents held the real power.[2]

The French may have taken control of the Nguyen monarchy, but they never trusted their kings.[3] When, in 1888, they captured the young emperor, Ham Nghi, who had been escorted by his protectors to the nearby hills to rally the people to the anti-colonialist cause, they quickly exiled him to Algeria and appointed a new, docile emperor to take his place. The French still worried that their monarchs would turn on them and, thanks to a Confucian-based administration premised on loyalty to the emperor, mobilise the people against the foreign invaders. More than one French administrator at the time spoke admiringly of a deep-seated royalist patriotism in Vietnam. Fears were rekindled in 1907, when Emperor Thanh Thai, and then his son Duy Tan a decade later, tried to escape the French to join anti-colonialists circulating outside Indochina. The French captured both, deposed them, and shipped them off to La Réunion.[4]

Paradoxically, this simultaneous distrust and respect for the Vietnamese royalty proved seductive – so much so that a core group of influential colonial administrators in charge of the Annam and Tonkin protectorates came to believe deeply that precisely because the Confucian monarchy retained its patriotic force, it and its living emperor, if handled adeptly, could serve as a powerful instrument for ruling the 'masses'. Several administrators who had arrived in the protectorates at the turn of the twentieth century immersed themselves in the history, language, culture and traditions of 'ancient Annam', and became some of Indochina's most adamant royalists. They included such men as Pierre Pasquier, Léon Sogny, Eugène Charles and Jean Cousseau. The first three had personally witnessed the Thanh Thai and Duy Tan revolts. Their long service in Vietnam and work with the monarchy in Hue and its mandarins made them indispensable advisers to governors general.

It was in this context that the Governor General during the 1910s, Albert Sarraut, joined forces with Pierre Pasquier and Eugène Charles to fashion the crown prince Bao Dai and the throne into reliable instruments of indirect rule.[5] Together, they convinced their latest emperor, Khai Dinh, to entrust his nine-year-old boy to them. He did. The idea was then to mould the prince into a tame monarch from a young age, to educate him directly so that he would be able to understand the French and their ways, all the while remaining rooted in his own royalist 'tradition'. As Residents to Annam, Pasquier and Charles were particularly influential. Pasquier was an erudite man who knew the protectorate and the monarchy on which it turned in minute detail. In 1907, he published *L'Annam d'autrefois*, an erudite history of the Vietnamese monarchy. He also worked closely with Annam and Tonkin's mandarins and was always keen to use them to rule more effectively. In 1907, after having led a special delegation of mandarins to France, he advised the government to introduce these Vietnamese elites to 'progress' by sending more of them to study in France, for 'they will thereafter be able to grasp our thinking, the meaning of our acts. They will be useful auxiliaries between the thinking of the popular masses and the directing idea of our Protectorate'.[6] He also insisted that French administrators had to immerse themselves in Vietnamese culture, tradition and language (and Jean Cousseau did precisely that). Charles had also served as Resident to Annam and knew the monarchy intimately.

With nationalism and communism on the rise after the First World War, Sarraut, Pasquier and Charles went to work. This meant removing the crown prince from his imperial household and entrusting him to the Charles family for his Franco-Vietnamese upbringing. In 1922, Pasquier issued instructions that would serve as the blueprint for the future emperor's education:

> He must acquire during the five or six years he will spend abroad, not only a purely bourgeois edification but in particular an *education* leading him to understand and to feel all that is harmoniously civilized in French society and its traditions – all that is artistic, beautiful in all domains, in all the arts, this 'gentle country that is France'. Let him be caressed by the elegant breezes of the Ile de France, but that he not have the time to drink too long from the overly strong air of liberty. We must have the prince acquire a sense of French politeness in our ways and spirit, by bringing him into contact with young people who have maintained the ways that have always made us in the eyes of foreigners the most polite people of the world ... and make of Vinh Thuy [Bao Dai] an elegant, gracious, prince, gifted in the arts, and understanding of the French soul, speaking our language clearly, capable of understanding our civilization but also for the same reason incapable of rejecting his own past. As such he will be tomorrow the sovereign who will move the evolution of his country in the French direction. This is the goal to attain.[7]

And so it was. Under Pasquier and Sarraut's careful guidance, the Charles family raised Bao Dai in the finest aristocratic ways, first in Hue, then in Paris. They initiated him into modern sports, including horse-riding and football, all the while steering him away from dangerous 'isms' in his studies. Except for a brief return to Hue to be crowned emperor in 1926 following his father's death, Bao Dai spent the most formative years of his life in France – in the Charles family under the watchful eye of his colonial minders. He soon spoke French with a perfect accent and frequented elite Parisian circles. Sarraut and Pasquier's trust in their new colonial monarch was such that in 1931 they seated him at the centre of the opening ceremony of the famous International Colonial Exhibition at Vincennes. Bao Dai did not speak that day; he had no subjects. He was the symbol of the French Empire on display for all the French to see (Figure 9.1).

A year later, as nationalist and communist revolts rocked Tonkin and Annam, the French rushed the young emperor back to Indochina to accomplish the most important part of what Sarraut called the Bao Dai 'experiment'. This meant taking over the throne and winning over the support of the people tempted by new leaders and novel forms of socio-political organisations. The young emperor had only to leave the palace, his colonial handlers said. He had to tour the countryside in order to establish contact with his subjects. Pasquier's team duly presided over a series of imperial tours sending Bao Dai into the countryside between 1932 and 1934.

Figure 9.1 Former Emperor Bao Dai of Vietnam at the Elysée Palace, Paris, 1948

Like his counterpart in Morocco, Bao Dai was willing to work with the French. But in exchange for his collaboration, the modernist-minded emperor expected the French to make good on reform promises and respect the protectorate treaty. This meant returning a certain number of governing powers to the monarchy, promoting the economic development and modernisation of the country and improving the well-being of the people in these troubled times. Confident that their sovereign would toe the line and under pressure to make concessions in light of the revolts of the early 1930s, Pasquier allowed Bao Dai to form a government in the imperial capital of Hue, propose several policy measures, and recruit promising elites like the Catholic reformer and nationalist Ngo Dinh Diem. However, when the monarch's desire for change appeared to infringe on colonial rule, Pasquier immediately backtracked. Diem resigned, the reforms failed and with it the chance to transform the protectorate into an autonomous form of local government.

Bao Dai could have rebelled at this point, like others in his family had before him. He withdrew instead into a world of solitude, taking long hunting trips in the central highlands and flying his airplane into the blue skies. Introverted, the emperor hated public speaking. And when he did, he was always more at ease speaking in French than in Vietnamese. The idea of walking among crowds intimidated him. Unlike his counterparts in Morocco and Cambodia, who embraced Islam and Buddhism as essential parts of their nationalist transformations, Bao Dai was reluctant to play the part of a Confucian Son of Heaven. Well aware of what the French were doing, he preferred to resist passively. He stopped signing papers or let others do it for him. His withdrawal from 'public affairs' continued under Vichy's rule of Indochina during the Second World War. He carefully avoided the royalist-minded governor general, Jean Decoux, who wanted to use the crown, imperial tours and Confucian tradition against the Japanese, as well as Vietnamese nationalists and communists.

But when the Japanese overthrew the French in Indochina in March 1945, before surrendering to the Allies a few months later, Bao Dai acted. While he never thought of leading an independence crusade, he did something just as significant: he abdicated, and in so doing finished off the centuries-old Vietnamese monarchy. To the ire of the French, he turned over the dynasty's ceremonial seal to the Republic forming rapidly around the person of Ho Chi Minh and then became a private 'citizen' and a 'supreme adviser' to the nationalist government. This was in stark contrast to Norodom Sihanouk, who never dreamed of giving up his throne.

COLONIAL MONARCHY IN THE FRENCH EMPIRE

Act II. Sihanouk[8]

With the outbreak of the Second World War, the French needed to expand their colonial monarchy beyond its Franco-Vietnamese mould. Worried by the Japanese occupation of all of Indochina starting in 1940, followed by the Japanese-backed Thai annexations of western Cambodia and Laos a year later, Vichy's governor general, Jean Decoux, incorporated Lao and Cambodian kings into what became for the first time a truly Franco-Indochinese monarchical project: 'The need to use in every way possible the royal instrument wherever present', he later wrote, 'revealed itself to me imperatively.' In perfect continuity with his predecessors working on Bao Dai earlier, Decoux ordered his men to build up the 'prestige' of the Cambodian and Lao monarchs.[9]

Docility was always the essential prerequisite for becoming a colonial king. If Bao Dai had been *gentil* ('nice') for Sarraut, Decoux saw in Sihanouk, as he wrote later, his 'prince charmant'.[10] In 1941, in an elaborately organised coronation, weaving the French into the sacred royal temples of Angkor Wat and Phnom Penh, Decoux crowned Sihanouk the new King of Cambodia. Sihanouk soon embarked on imperial tours, lit the torch in Angkor Wat for the Indochinese cycling race of 1943, sang the praises of Franco-Khmer collaboration, and warned of the dangers of Thai expansionism. Unlike Bao Dai, who was more at ease in French than in Vietnamese, Sihanouk had grown up speaking Khmer and had not been subjected to the same level of colonial re-programming as had his Vietnamese counterpart in Paris. Sihanouk was at ease performing royal rituals, switching into traditional costume and embodying the sacred role of a Buddhist king. He was much more extroverted, animated and jovial by nature than his Vietnamese and Moroccan counterparts. The latter were certainly modern, to be sure, but Sihanouk had an extraordinary passion for things related to public speaking, entertainment and the media. Bursting with energy, the young Khmer king was always on the move. He loved jazz and played the saxophone. His passion for cinema was real. For the first time in Indochina, arguably in the history of the French Empire, colonial king-makers had wrapped up in one royal being their 'tame', 'modern', 'mobile', 'human' yet equally 'divine' monarch (Figure 9.2).

With the Thais playing up the racial and religious unity of Laos, Cambodia and Thailand, Decoux used inter-royal travel to consolidate closer links among France's three Indochinese monarchies in Laos (Sisavang Vong), Cambodia (Sihanouk) and Annam (Bao Dai). Sihanouk visited his counterpart in Hue before moving on to see Tonkin for the first time. He was a favourite in the Lao court in Luang Prabang, and the Lao king visited his counterpart in Phnom

Figure 9.2 King Sihanouk of Cambodia, c. 1949

Penh. Like Pasquier working with Bao Dai, Decoux saw in Sihanouk a precious intermediary through which the French could ensure the loyalty of the Cambodian peasant majority. In charge of the monarchy was a tightly knit group of French administrators with long service in the protectorate. The Resident, Georges Gauthier, accompanied Sihanouk on his travels across the protectorate, putting modern communications and media technologies at the sovereign's disposal. Moving from provincial capitals to remote villages by car, Sihanouk presided over sacred rituals and ceremonies in provincial and district capitals. He took to public speaking in Khmer with self-confidence, addressing peasants in ways unprecedented for any Indochinese king of the time. During trips to small villages, he distributed rice, salt, clothing and medicines. Leaving the palace and walking among his subjects came to him naturally. As he later told a French journalist:

> The Gauthier plan allowed me to present myself to those of my compatriots located in faraway regions, who, of their own admission, had never seen the king. They knew that their country was a monarchy but they confessed to me that never had a sovereign visited their districts and villages. To reach these remote places, I had to use cars, boats, oxen-drawn carts, horses and elephants ... In villages and hamlets lost in distant valleys, I handed out rice, salt, cloths, and medicines. The people, very poor but very dignified, showered me with prayers and brought me wild fruits, the only gifts they could offer me. These are unforgettable and moving memories.[11]

But unlike Bao Dai and Mohammed V, it never occurred to Sihanouk, as French Indochina crumbled in mid-1945, that he might find himself on the wrong side of the colonial–national divide. He collaborated closely with Vichy's Jean Decoux until the Japanese overthrew the French in March 1945. On Japanese orders, he declared Cambodia's independence like Bao Dai did, but he never thought of opposing the re-establishment of the French protectorate when the Japanese capitulated a few months later. Instead, Sihanouk welcomed de Gaulle's commander-in-chief to Phnom Penh in October 1945 and his High Commissioner to Indochina. In early 1946, he was the first of the Indochinese leaders to sign a *modus vivendi* making Cambodia part of the Indochinese Federation and a member of the emerging French Union.

Sihanouk had competition, however, from one of Cambodia's first modern nationalists, Son Ngoc Thanh. Born in the Vietnamese Mekong Delta, this motivated Khmer man did so well in school that he won a scholarship to study in France in the early 1930s. He returned to Indochina in 1933, completed his law degree, moved to Phnom Penh and joined the colonial civil service. He helped reform the Buddhist church, schools and teachings. He worked closely with French Buddhist specialists at the *Ecole française d'Extrême-Orient* who opposed Thai attempts to draw Khmer monks to Bangkok. He joined the French in creating the Buddhist Institute in Phnom Penh in 1931. He also helped run Cambodia's first modern newspaper of nationalist design, the *Nagara Vatta*.[12]

Print media, Buddhist connections and excellent speaking skills made Thanh an influential nationalist leader. In 1942, the French cracked down on a demonstration he and his associates had organised. The Japanese protected Thanh from colonial arrest, but returned him to Phnom Penh following the March coup of 1945 which overthrew the French. Thanh then established Cambodia's first nationalist party and served as the country's prime minister until the French returned and exiled him to France. However, for many students, monks, peasants and even several anti-colonialist royalists, Son Ngoc Thanh had come to symbolise the father of a future, independent Cambodian nation. Sihanouk had competition for the hearts and minds of the 'masses'.

Relations between Sihanouk and the nationalists deteriorated in the post-war years as the king turned to the French to help him curb the rise of political liberalism. Cambodia's first constitution of 1946, to which he initially agreed, allowed for the formation of political parties and the creation of a National Assembly based on universal male suffrage. It also guaranteed the right of assembly and freedom of speech. Spared the colonial and civil conflicts tearing Vietnam apart, Cambodian nationalists, mainly civil servants, teachers and students, but also Buddhist monks and a few members of the royal family, formed the Democrat Party. Its members vowed to serve the king and the people, but a growing number of its members increasingly wanted to empower the National Assembly, the people it represented, and push for full national independence. The Democrats established party chapters at the provincial and district levels, working with urban elites and monks. The party nominated candidates with real support in the countryside to run for Assembly positions. In the first election of 1946, the Democrats won fifty of the sixty-seven available seats. The rise of parliamentary republicanism in Cambodia was real. The French could live with such colonial democracy as long as the protectorate remained a part of the French Union.

But things began to change as the Democrat Party increased in popularity, further developed its national organisation and advanced its call for full independence. In so doing, the Democrats challenged French efforts at the imperial level to hold the French Union together and reinforced an already close alliance between French authorities and their Cambodian monarch, each of whom saw their interests coming under threat from the Democrats. Unlike their negotiations with Bao Dai, the French easily convinced Sihanouk to sign off on the creation of the Associated State of Cambodia within the French Union in 1949. However, an increasing number of Democrats refused 'Indochinese Association', knowing that it and the imperial Union it preserved put a brake on full Cambodian independence. So it did.

COLONIAL MONARCHY IN THE FRENCH EMPIRE

The French decision to allow Son Ngoc Thanh to return to Cambodia in 1951 put Sihanouk in a particularly difficult position concerning the question of independence. The French returned this famous nationalist on the apparent understanding that he would help build up support for the Cambodian Associated State against the communist threat, including the parallel set of associated states Ho Chi Minh had just created for Laos (the Pathet Lao) and Cambodia (the Khmer Issarak). The plan backfired, however, when it became clear that Thanh remained a formidable political threat not just to Ho's communist-minded allies in Cambodia, but also to the French hold on Cambodia and its king. Waiting to meet Thanh at the airport was an estimated crowd of twenty thousand people, many of whom called him a 'national hero'. They included enthusiastic civil servants, teachers, students and monks. Also present were many of the Democrat Party's leaders, who increasingly worried Sihanouk. The monarch was further shocked when Thanh made a spectacular nationalist tour of the countryside, travelling from the temples of Angkor Wat to Phnom Penh, speaking favourably of full Cambodian independence and implicitly casting the king as a colonial creature. Several hundred thousand people lined the roads, raising banners proclaiming him 'our hope' and 'national hero'. Although the Democrats had tried to tone down the tour, knowing that it could provoke Sihanouk's jealousy and potentially hurt their cause, Thanh marched to his own drum. A few months later, he went into opposition along the Thai border.

Thanh's popularity and the rise of the Democrats nevertheless convinced Sihanouk that he was in trouble. He also realised that the Democrats were not the only ones pushing the French to let go of the French Union and its 'Associated States' in favour of a commonwealth of fully independent nation-states based on the British model. By the early 1950s, resistance to the French Union had emerged from French Indochina to North Africa as Tunisians, Moroccans, Vietnamese and, increasingly, Laotians pushed for complete independence. This is why, starting in 1952 and not before, Sihanouk began to backpedal fast on his earlier support of the 'Associated State' and started making plans to recast himself as a nationalist king, the enemy of Indochinese 'association' and of the French Union.

While Sihanouk could not know at the outset where his Royal Crusade for Independence would take him, by 1952 he was determined to seize the nationalist mantle. He would have to stop the Democrats, frustrate their negotiations with the French and transform himself into the defender of Cambodian independence before the Democrats did and before they might put a republic in the monarchy's place. Unlike in Morocco, there would be no anti-colonialist alliance between the king and nationalists. In 1952, Sihanouk began preparing a de facto *coup d'état* against the Democrats in favour of creating something closer to an absolute monarchy. In order to get rid of his republican rivals, however, the king still needed the French. (The French, at war with Ho Chi Minh, ran the army.) Unaware of what Sihanouk's ultimate intentions were, the French supported his coup against the Democrats, happy to stop Cambodia's nationalists from destroying 'association' and possibly bringing down the French Union by setting off a chain reaction. On 15 June 1952, the French deployed Moroccan troops to take control of Phnom Penh as Sihanouk dismissed the Democrat cabinet, began dismantling the party and arrested its leaders. He named his own prime minister as French Union troops surrounded the National Assembly and French 'tanks rumbled up and down Phnom Penh's principal streets'.[13] As one French official commented, 'we must move rapidly for all Cambodians want true independence'.[14]

What the French did not see coming was Sihanouk's immediate transformation into *the* defender of Cambodian independence. In early 1953, with the Democrats out of the way and having consolidated his internal hold on power, the king immediately launched his independence crusade by casting himself as a fierce opponent of the 'Associated State' and of Cambodia's continued membership in the French Union. In February, he travelled to Paris, where he asked to meet President Vincent Auriol to discuss the Union and begin negotiations to secure full Cambodian independence. Deeply involved in building the Associated States and holding the French Union together against a wider assault coming from other parts of Indochina and the Maghreb, Auriol listened politely, but gave a non-committal promise to look into matters. Sihanouk interpreted this (correctly) as a 'no' and took his crusade to the other side of the Atlantic. However, his desire to pressure the French from Ottawa and Washington proved just as unsuccessful. John Foster Dulles wondered why he was pressing the French on independence now – he never had before – when the real problem was the communist threat to Southeast Asia and his own country as Ho Chi Minh's divisions struck deep into Laos.

When Paris and Washington failed to support his cause, Sihanouk took his crusade back home, not to Phnom Penh, but to the ancient temples of Angkor Wat. This was the heart of Khmer civilisation, home to the first great kings of the Angkorian Empire, the source of all that was 'Cambodian'. To force the French hand, Sihanouk began mobilising popular support in the countryside. His team mobilised modern media, radios, microphones and pamphlets. The king mobilised all of his communication skills. Photographs and portraits of him popped up everywhere. In late June, he and his allies called upon former scouts, youth, peasants and soldiers to join royalist militias. Sihanouk walked among his subjects, all the while presenting himself as the defender of the Buddhist faith and, above all, the defender of national independence. He bound the two together in his royal person. He turned on the coloniser all that they had taught him about the power of modern kingship.

Popular support for Sihanouk was real and deserves more treatment than I can give in a comparative essay. International factors also worked in his favour. First, Sihanouk was anything but alone in his crusade against the French Union in 1953. A wide range of Indochinese and North African anti-colonialists in favour of full independence had already been attacking the French Union. Ngo Dinh Diem from Vietnam and Habib ben ali Bourguiba from Tunisia were two examples among several Indo-Maghrebin ones. Second, the movement of Ho Chi Minh's troops into Laos in 1953 and soon into northeastern Cambodia convinced French strategists that they could ill afford to alienate Sihanouk at this critical juncture in their war against Ho's already independent Vietnam. Moreover, by mid-1953 the French had already agreed that once they scored a major battle victory against Ho's army, they could negotiate a favourable end to the war. This is why in October and November 1953, as the battle of Dien Bien Phu shaped up, the French gave in to most of Sihanouk's demands. However Machiavellian he was, Sihanouk had nonetheless engineered one of the most rapid transformations of a colonial monarch into a defender of the nation in the history of the French Empire. And in so doing, he had also struck a devastating blow against Cambodian republicanism and sent many young nationalists down even more radical roads than republicanism.[15] French colonialists looked on in dismay as the empire's most loyal monarch recast himself as the father of Cambodia's independence. 'Messieurs, the King is a madman', said the commanding officer of French troops in Cambodia, 'but he's a brilliant one!'[16]

Act III. Mohammed V[17]

Mohammed V may have presided over a very similar royalist crusade in Morocco, culminating in the country's full independence in 1956, but his transformation into a nationalist monarch occurred over a longer period of time and did so in ways very different to what had occurred in Cambodia. Like Bao Dai and Sihanouk, nothing at the outset indicated that this pious man would topple the French protectorate established over Morocco in 1912. By all accounts, the future Mohammed V was, in his youth, introverted, frail, shy, even something of a loner. As a boy, he apparently roamed the streets of Rabat, unsupervised and unrecognised. His dress was always simple. His Arabic was fluent. He went about unnoticed, content to do so.

That changed, however, upon his father's death in 1927, when the French saw in the seventeen-year-old Sidi Mohammed ben Yusef the required passivity they needed to continue operating the protectorate on their terms. Finding a malleable monarch was all the more important given that the French had just helped the Spanish smash the rebel Rif Republic in northern Morocco in 1925 and arrest its legendary leader Abd el-Krim (the Spanish had maintained control of northern Morocco, including Rif, after 1912). This charismatic man had called upon Muslims to rise up and implored the Sultan of Morocco to join the struggle. Hubert Lyautey, one of the main architects of the Vietnamese and Moroccan protectorates and the man who stood next to Bao Dai during the opening ceremony of the colonial exhibition of 1931, agreed with the French Resident in Morocco that Sidi Mohammed ben Yusef was the right man to be their colonial monarch. The French duly made him Sultan in 1927 and, following a rain-soaked coronation with few present, sent him on his way to the Grand Palace in Rabat where one Resident after another tended to his education, movements and daily schedule.

As in Indochina, the crowning of the new sultan coincided with the rise of modern nationalism in North Africa. Though captured and exiled to La Réunion, Abd el-Krim's protracted battle against the 'infidel Christians' in the Rif had captured the imagination of the Muslim faithful and budding Moroccan nationalists. Significantly, many of them began to see their sultan less as a colonial collaborator than as prisoner of Christian foreigners. Efforts by French missionaries, sometimes with official support, to convert tribes to Christianity only reinforced the connection between a nationalist idea of Morocco based on Islam, its law, and the sultan as its protector. It helped that the young sultan was a deeply religious man. He attended Friday prayers, maintained close relations with the *ulamas*, who, like the Buddhist monks in charge of pagodas in Cambodia, marshalled an impressive religious network of mosques and Quranic schools. He embraced his role as the defender of the Islamic faith, as did Sihanouk the Buddhist one.

Moreover, French Morocco was not the territorially unified national body we recognise today; its northern and southern tips had remained under Spanish control. French efforts to administer non-Arab tribal groups independently of the protected monarch and Islamic law further irritated Moroccan nationalists and religious leaders intent on creating a territorially bounded nation with the sultan at its centre and in charge of the tribal lands. Unsurprisingly, nationalist-minded elites started to use the word *Marocains* for the first time to describe this new national body,[18] just as their counterparts in Annam began to use the words 'Vietnamese' to capture a unified Vietnam uniting Cochinchina, Annam and Tonkin into one 'Vietnam'.

In the early 1930s, Mohammed V got his first real taste of change as these nationalist winds swirled. In May 1930, the French Resident had the sultan sign a decree or *dahir*, protecting customary law codes for the non-Arab, Berber tribes. This move was in part designed to tame their unruly areas, but it also allowed the French to remove these areas from pre-existing Islamic sharia codes that had placed them under the sultan and *ulama* administration. Controlling the 'tribes' would also help the French check the rise of Moroccan nationalism and pan-Arabism in the wake of the Rif War. Naively, Mohammed V signed the *dahir*, triggering an outcry from nationalists opposed to this French attempt to administer these territories independently of the protectorate and, more importantly, the Moroccan nation and central government they were imagining. Nationalist leaders such as Mohammed Allal el-Fassi criticised the king for signing this document, leading the French to remove el-Fassi from his teaching position in a Quranic school. In what became a pattern, the sultan bowed to French pressure but received nationalists in private audiences to reassure them of his sympathy. In a meeting with el-Fassi, the sultan recognised his error, saying: 'I will relinquish no more of our country's rights.'[19] He did not necessarily mean political independence, but rather that he would fight to consolidate all 'Moroccan' territory in the form of the protectorate.

Mohammed V remained committed to the protectorate. He joined colonial authorities to make imperial tours across the country, singing the praises of French deeds and modernity. But here again, nationalists knocked on the sultan's door. In May 1934, on his way to participate in holy prayers in Fès, the ancient royal capital and home of Moroccan nationalism since the Rif War, dozens of young nationalists greeted him in the street, hailing him with the words 'Yehia *el-Malik*', meaning 'god-King' in Arabic. Although such royalist sympathies moved him, like Bao Dai and Sihanouk, Mohammed V let others take the nationalist lead. The first modern political party came to life as such in 1934, the Comité d'action marocaine led by el-Fassi and others. This party forced the French to backtrack on the infamous *dahir* of 1930. Its leaders elaborated a series of reforms they submitted to the protectorate authorities at exactly the same time as Ngo Dinh Diem joined Bao Dai's reformist-minded protectorate government. The sultan supported these projects designed to promote economic modernisation, restore and modernise Muslim institutions, and push back against de facto direct colonial rule in favour of increased local rule.

But the reforms went no further than in Vietnam. The French still ran the show.

Mohammed V was not necessarily unhappy to see his nationalist competitors forced into exile in the 1930s. Like Sihanouk in Cambodia, the sultan was wary of the rise of political republicanism in North Africa, especially during the Popular Front period. In 1936, for example, el-Fassi created the Moroccan National Party, while Mohammed V continued to collaborate with his Resident. He did nothing when the French dissolved the Comité d'action marocaine in 1937 and exiled el-Fassi. However, during the 1930s, Mohammed V did something Bao Dai avoided: the *malik* slowly but surely consolidated his throne and its control over tribal lands in favour of an inclusive, unified Moroccan territorial unity. He pushed back against local powerholders, whereas Bao Dai did nothing to stop the French from administering the central highland peoples separately from the protectorate. The arrival of General Charles Noguès as Resident in 1936 and this man's commitment to the protectorate dovetailed with the sultan's plans to increase his prestige and control over Moroccan territory via this colonial entity.

As in Indochina, the Second World War profoundly changed Mohammed V and his relationship with nationalist elites. Until 1940, the sultan had been quite content to work with Noguès. When war broke out in 1939, many Moroccans joined the French army, including nationalists. Mohammed V pledged his loyalty to the Third Republic in its hour of greatest need and he kept that promise. When forced to choose, he chose the Allied cause in 1942, whereas the Resident, Noguès, opposed the Allied landing in North Africa. Ludicrous charges that the sultan went over to the Germans never stuck. As a result, Mohammed V's prestige emerged greatly strengthened from choices he made of his own volition during the war. Neither Bao Dai nor Sihanouk ever stood up like this to Vichy authorities in Indochina.

Particularly important, the war reshaped the balance of power in the Maghreb as in Indochina. The Allied liberation of North Africa, and the presence of their armies and leaders, opened up new contacts and possibilities for Moroccans. In what would have been unthinkable only a few years earlier, Mohammed V personally dined with President Franklin D. Roosevelt in early 1943 in Casablanca as his exiting Vichy and newly arriving Gaullist advisers watched from the side lines. For the first time, the sultan interacted with a foreign head of state as if he were one himself. Roosevelt's vision of a postcolonial world and economic modernisation tantalised. An avid follower of world events, Mohammed V was well aware of the Atlantic Charter and its mention of self-determination. A few months later,

Charles de Gaulle met the Moroccan king as he set up his own government in exile in Algiers:

> This young, proud, personal sovereign did not hide his desire to be at the head of his country as it marched towards progress and, one day, independence. On seeing and listening to him, sometimes ardent, sometimes prudent but always adept, one felt that he was ready to get along with anyone who would help him play this role and capable of deploying a great deal of stubbornness against those who would oppose him on that count.[20]

These monarchs were not the only ones taking advantage of the changes generated by the global war. Just as Ho Chi Minh in 1941 created the Vietnamese Independence League, the Viet Minh, Moroccan nationalists established in 1943 the Hizh al-Istiqlal or Independence Party. Significantly, Moroccan nationalists looked to the monarch to help lead the independence movement. Never, to my knowledge, did Ho Chi Minh entertain such an alliance. In January 1944, a group of nationalists including el-Fassi submitted an independence manifesto to the sultan which Mohammed V intentionally forwarded to the new Resident with the monarch's implicit approbation. To no avail. The 'new French' had no intention of decolonising. The protectorate remained in force. Mohammed V deferred again and called on nationalists to avoid pronouncing the word 'independence' for the time being. He also looked the other way as the French clamped down on the Istiqlal. The sultan was no more ready to lead an independence crusade in 1944–45 than Bao Dai or Sihanouk. Nor did he take to the *maquis*. However, like Sihanouk, and unlike Bao Dai, he never considered abdicating his throne.

The sultan remained committed to the French and welcomed the arrival of the Fourth Republic's reformist-minded Resident, Erik Labonne, in 1946. The Moroccan leader was still hopeful that reforms, including eventual independence, could be achieved via a partnership and peacefully. That said, Mohammed V resumed his efforts to build up his power at the expense of those regional and tribal leaders who opposed the throne's more centralised control. He sought to affirm the unity of the country and let it be known that he considered the southern and northern strips, administered by the Spanish until 1956, to be a part of his Morocco. In his famous imperial tour of Tangiers in 1947, the sultan wanted to demonstrate his internal supremacy and proposed to make an important speech to mark the occasion. Labonne liked the idea. An imperial tour would respect the protectorate and strengthen the prestige of the king who would help the French to rule more effectively, as in the past. It would also send the right signal to

Spain. The sultan promised to show his texts to the French before going public, including the required mention of good French deeds (*bienfaits*), the signifier of the king's loyalty to the French. Labonne agreed, but things took an unexpected turn when Senegalese troops fired on civilians and set off violent protests. Passions suddenly ran high as newspaper front pages and radio bulletins beamed the news across the country. The sultan, upset, decided to omit the promised phrase thanking the French. But what made Tangiers unique compared to Bao Dai's tours in the early 1930s was that the Istiqlal was secretly working the crowds, labour unions, scouting organisations, student associations and religious halls in Tangiers. When the sultan appeared to speak, a flood of people met him with cries of joy and pleas for action. In the heat of the moment, the monarch embraced the crowds, approved their calls for independence, evoked a glorious Moroccan past, applauded pan-Arabism and endorsed the unification of the country, though he carefully pulled back from saying 'independence'.

For the French, however, Mohammed V had crossed a line. The Tangiers speech cost Labonne his job and set reformism back as hardliner settlers and colonial administrators came together to call for a military man to take over, someone who would not be afraid to move against the sultan and the nationalists if need be. Agreed, Paris sent General Alphonse Juin to Rabat in 1947 and gave him orders very similar to those sent to Indochina: there could be reforms, but there could be no independence within the confines of the French Union established by the 1946 constitution. French legal experts entered into complicated legal arguments in the Maghreb, as in Indochina, over how *not* to say 'independence'. 'Inter-independence' became the preferred term in Morocco, while 'association' was the buzzword in Indochina. Pushed by nationalists and aware of similar anti-colonial opposition in the French Empire, Mohammed V became increasingly involved in negotiations over the French Union and his country's position in it.

French settler hostility to the sultan grew, pushing him into an ever closer alliance with the anti-colonialists. So, too, did French support for tribal leaders, most notably the Pacha Glaoui (the chief of the Glawa tribe in southern Morocco). The latter saw an opportunity to use French settler and colonial anger at the sultan to promote his own local interests and territorial autonomy instead of having to incorporate his lands into a potential Moroccan nation-state run by the sultan. That a stand-off was in the making was clear when the Glaoui felt safe enough to tell the sultan famously to his face: 'You [*tu*] are no longer the sultan of Morocco, you are the sultanate of the atheistic, communist Istiqlal.'[21] The sultan dug in his heels and, as he did, nationalist support coalesced around him. In turn, French opposition to his rule only increased. This was clear when Juin made his famous threat to Mohammed V in terms as threatening as those of the Glaoui: 'Either you disown the Istiqlal or you abdicate. If not, I will depose you myself. I'm leaving now for Washington. You have the time to think about what I have just asked of you. We will see what we will do upon my return!'[22] The problem was not communism; it was nationalism and the spectre of independence that troubled the Glaoui and the French Resident. When Juin threatened to depose Mohammed V if he did not sign the protocols of 1950 respecting continued French rule, the sultan signed but claimed he did so only to stop the bloodshed. Nationalists immediately closed ranks behind him. Nothing of the sort ever occurred in Vietnam. Nationalists led by Ho Chi Minh saw in Bao Dai a colonial puppet.

After Juin came another general as Resident, Augustin Guillaume, brandishing the same threats. The situation worsened dramatically in the early 1950s as verbal French insults, humiliations and thinly veiled insinuations rained down on the sultan as he refused to budge. Mohammed V sent his colonial handlers into rages. Present in several meetings between the French and the sultan, the sympathetic French journalist Jean Lacouture described the sultan's passive resistance memorably: 'With a beard working his face, black sunglasses hiding his face, a folded hood over his forehead, it was a ritual of sovereign antipathy, symbolic of the aversion that would have delighted a specialist of court intrigues and royal moods like [the Duc de] Saint Simon (in the court of Louis XIV).'[23] Mohammed V, almost in spite of himself, came to embody nationalist unity, pushed as much by the Istiqlal in this direction as by French and tribal leaders terrified that he was indeed a nationalist monarch, when, in fact, that was arguably not yet the case. But when French settlers, administrators and the Glaoui began to attack Mohammed V with an avalanche of insults and crude humiliations, they forgot how Moroccan nationalist and religious minds might interpret these affronts. They certainly underestimated how their assault on the royal person could telescope a range of social, nationalist, religious and even feminist frustrations into massive support for the sultan. It did.

And the sultan did act. He increasingly welcomed alliances with newly formed workers' unions. He told the Communist Party that he embraced all social classes into the larger Moroccan family, based on greater democracy. He visited industrial establishments and renewed his visits to popular quarters of Rabat and elsewhere. Like Sihanouk, he was at ease walking among large crowds. He touched his people and allowed himself to be approached by them. He visited the families who had lost loved ones during the violence in Casablanca, Fès and Rabat. His confidence grew rapidly and, as it did, he warmed to public speaking. In his speeches, he carefully wove together the fabric of the nation into his person as the king and defender of the country's religion, Islam.[24]

In 1952, overcoming the timidity Bao Dai never conquered, Mohammed V went on the offensive. He overtly associated his monarchy and his royal being with the nationalists and the people. He condemned the French state of siege, and the attack on workers, and called for negotiations over the future of the French Union. During his visit to Casablanca that year, thousands of people came out to welcome him, greeting him with cries of *'malik'*. During his speeches, microphones were carefully placed to make him heard, and portraits were distributed at every gathering. Nationalists and settlers inevitably clashed as the monarch called the colonial order into question. The resulting violence further charged the atmosphere as the French prepared to move against their very royalist creation. The growing Moroccan crisis came to a head in February 1953 – just as Sihanouk prepared to launch his crusade to free Cambodia. Desperate, the French Resident, settlers and officials agreed to bring a new collaborator to power in Morocco and depose the existing sultan in order to do so. Morocco had to remain in the imperial hold even if it meant that Mohammed V had to go.

It was a fateful decision. On 20 August 1953, French tanks, jeeps mounted with machine guns, and security officers entered the palace compound as troops took up their positions. A few minutes later, General Guillaume arrived in the sultan's quarters and told him either to abdicate or leave. The sultan refused. Guillaume's men forcibly escorted the monarch out of the country with his two sons and exiled them all to Madagascar. In so doing, the French action triggered a nationalist outcry. Although they were hardly monarchists, el-Fassi and other nationalists threw their support behind Mohammed V and the common struggle for the complete independence of Morocco.

Thinking they were saving their protectorate and preserving the Union, the French only accelerated the decline of both. The new French-backed sultan certainly enjoyed the support of the tribal leaders, but that support did not go much further. There was no popular acclaim for the new sultan when he entered Rabat – just silence, except for the settler press and the tribal troops whom the French had brought in, who hailed him as a saviour. Meanwhile, people in the streets said that they had seen Mohammed V in the stars. Religious leaders and increasing numbers of Muslims interpreted the French action as sacrilege and an offence against Islam. As even a settler in Casablanca recognised at the time: 'The Sultan has emerged from this trial with added greatness, and more than ever worthy of the attachment of his people. He has remained their sovereign and supreme Imam, in whose name they will continue, in their innermost hearts, to recite their prayers.'[25] Despite being outlawed, Moroccans placed portraits of the legitimate sultan in their homes as signs of defiance. In many ways, in forced colonial exile, Mohammed V assumed nationalist powers, which he had never previously possessed. In the end, the French had no choice but to return the exiled sultan to calm the situation or undertake violent repression and risk war. As in Cambodia, they capitulated, and on 16 November 1955 Mohammed V made his triumphant return to Rabat before hundreds of thousands of Moroccans who poured into the streets to welcome him. There was no going back now. Mohammed V was no longer a colonial king. By deposing and exiling the sovereign, the French had made a nationalist martyr of him. His return was the turning point at which this initially timid man finally transformed himself into a national monarch and the defender of Moroccan independence, formally acquired in 1956.

Bao Dai: The failed decolonisation of a colonial monarch

But why does Bao Dai rest in a Parisian cemetery and not in Vietnam today? To a considerable extent, the answer to that question lies in the very different nature of Vietnamese decolonisation and the international context in which it occurred. Let us pick up on Bao Dai's case where we left it, after 1945. In early 1946, worried by the communist hue of Ho Chi Minh's Democratic Republic of Vietnam and convinced that the French had no intention of letting go of Vietnam, Bao Dai went into self-exile in Hong Kong and began working with fellow non-communist nationalists to carve out a third way between the 'French colonialists' and the 'Vietnamese communists'. From his position of exile, Bao Dai gambled that he could rally non-communist nationalists around the prestige of his person, garner American support in light of their growing anti-communism, and play the Vietnamese 'communists' against the French 'colonialists' in order to win the independence Ho had failed to achieve when full-scale war broke out in late 1946.

The High Commissioner for Indochina in the late 1940s, Léon Pignon, saw things differently. He was convinced that the French could win the emperor back and, as in the past, use him and his royal person to keep an associated state of Vietnam within the French Union, all the while drawing support away from Ho's Vietnam. Not only had Pignon started his career as an administrator under Pierre Pasquier in the early 1930s, but he was also working with many of the same men who had been involved in Sarraut and Pasquier's first Bao Dai 'experiment', in particular Jean Cousseau. In 1947, Pignon sent Cousseau to Hong Kong to meet with Bao Dai. Arduous negotiations followed over the nature of a future Vietnamese state and its position within the Union. Bao Dai wanted independence but the French argued in favour of 'association' in order to keep Vietnam within the wider French Union. In the end, Bao Dai got little further in his negotiations than Ho had before him, other than the fact that the French finally agreed to allow the unification of Cochinchina with the two northern protectorates to form the 'Associated State of Vietnam' in 1949.

Unlike the situation in the Maghreb, international changes in 1949–50 greatly weakened Bao Dai's hand, in particular the Chinese communist victory in 1949 and Mao Zedong's decision to recognise and support Ho's Vietnam. The French, however, saw in the Chinese communist victory an opportunity to convince the heretofore-reluctant Americans to support them in Indochina as part of Washington's attempt to contain the spread of communism any further into Asia. The French would stay in the war for the anti-communist cause but they expected American military assistance as well as support for the 'Bao Dai solution'. It worked. Instead of pushing the French to decolonise as they did in Indonesia, the Americans supported French efforts to build a less than independent, non-communist Vietnamese state around Bao Dai in order to contain what they perceived as the greater Sino-Soviet communist threat to Southeast Asia via Ho Chi Minh's Vietnam. The French thus accepted the unification of Vietnam under the ex-emperor, but, in exchange, Bao Dai had to join the French Union and return to Vietnam. He did both things in 1949 but it cost him dearly. He lost his leverage.

Sihanouk and Mohammed V never faced combined Franco-American pressure the way Bao Dai did. Nor did they have to compete with a nationalist state at war with them and their association with the colonisers. The Istiqlal party in Morocco was independence-minded, but it was *not* run by communists or supported by Mao. As long as the French remained committed to fighting the Indochina War, the Americans were reluctant to push them too hard on independence, as they did the Dutch over Indonesia. The French successfully used American fears of communism to maintain their colonial hold on Indochina and thwart efforts by Bao Dai, Ngo Dinh Diem and others to free a non-communist Vietnam from the French Union like Morocco's Mohammed V and Cambodia's Sihanouk did. When Bao Dai returned to Vietnam in 1949, the High Commissioner, Léon Pignon, flatly refused to turn over to him the governor's palace in Saigon, the seat of power of Vietnam. Bao Dai could have done in 1949 what Mohammed V and Sihanouk would do a few years later – he could have turned the monarchy on the French to force decolonisation. He could have transformed the largely French-invented Confucian 'tradition' and the imperial tour into a modern crusade for national independence before Ho turned his guerrilla forces into a seven-division-strong professional army capable of bringing down the French at Dien Bien Phu in 1954. Bui Diem, a famous non-communist nationalist, recalled his efforts to win over Bao Dai in 1949:

> We realized that there was one way to break the French lock step, and that was for Bao Dai to turn on them. If the emperor would not ask but demand the immediate implementation of French promises, the colonialists would be in a dangerous dilemma themselves. They badly needed the Bao Dai government to provide a Vietnamese alternative to the Vietminh and to marshal all the anti-Communist sentiment he could. But just as they were using Bao Dai, there was no reason he could not use them.[26]

But Bao Dai did not have it in him. In the end, he let events and others push him to the side lines. Passive resistance was not enough. Ultimately, the Vietnamese nationalist who had refused to sign off on the 'associated states' arrangement in 1949 and who travelled to France in 1953 and the United States to push for Vietnam's exit from the French Union was none other than Ngo Dinh Diem. This was the man with whom Bao Dai had collaborated briefly in the early 1930s. He was also the one – not Ho Chi Minh – who would run the last emperor out of Vietnam in 1955 for good in order to create the Republic of Vietnam. This is how the last emperor of Vietnam came to rest in a Parisian cemetery, while the tombs of Sihanouk and Mohammed V still attract millions of visitors each year as the men who secured Cambodian and Moroccan independence, the fathers of their nations.

Notes

All translations by the author, Christopher Goscha.

1. For general histories of colonised Vietnam, see Christopher Goscha, *The Penguin History of Modern Vietnam* (Milton Keynes: Allen Lane, 2016); Ben Kiernan, *Viet Nam: A History from Earliest Times to the Present* (Oxford: Oxford University Press, 2017); and Pierre Brocheux and Daniel Hémery, *Indochina: An Ambiguous Colonization, 1858–1954* (Berkeley: University of California Press, 2009).
2. The Resident-General (often referred to as the Resident) was the senior French administrative official in the protectorates, such as Vietnam and Morocco.
3. See Nguyen Thé Anh, *Monarchie et fait colonial au Viet-nam (1875–1925): le crépuscule d'un ordre traditionnel* (Paris: L'Harmattan, 1992); Bruce Lockhart, *The End of the Vietnamese Monarchy* (New Haven, CT: Yale University Press, 1993); and Oscar Chapuis, *The Last Emperors of Vietnam: From Tu Duc to Bao Dai* (New York: Praeger, 2000).
4. On the exile of colonial monarchs, see Robert Aldrich, *Banished Potentates: Dethroning and Exiling Indigenous Monarchs under British and French Colonial*

Rule, 1815–1955 (Manchester: Manchester University Press, 2018); see in particular ch. 4: '"Dragons of Annam": the French and three emperors in Vietnam', pp. 117–77.
5   The emperor's autobiography gives his own perspective: Bao Dai, Le Dragon d'Annam (Paris: Plon, 1980).
6   Archives nationales d'outre-mer (ANOM), Indochine nouveau fonds 27, 'Pierre Pasquier au résident supérieur d'Annam', Hanoi, 16 January 1907, p. 5. My thanks to Charles Keith for sharing this reference.
7   ANOM, dossier 2326, box 858, fonds AFOM, nouveau fonds, 'Note au sujet de l'éducation en France du Prince Vinh Thuy', Hue, 18 February 1922, signed by Pierre Pasquier.
8   I rely, in this section, on the following: David Chandler, The Tragedy of Cambodian History: Politics, War, and Revolution Since 1945 (New Haven, CT: Yale University Press, 1997); Milton Osborne, Sihanouk: Prince of Light, Prince of Darkness (Sydney: Allen & Unwin, 1994); Nasir Abdoul-Carime, 'Le verbe sihanoukien', Péninsule, 2 (1995), 79–98; Norodom Sihanouk, La Monarchie cambodgienne et la croisade royale pour l'indépendance, Phnom Penh, Ministère de l'éducation nationale, n.d. For the earlier reign of King Sisowath and his relations with the French, see John Tully, Cambodia under the Tricolour: King Sisowath and the 'Mission Civilisatrice', 1904–1927 (Clayton, Vic.: Monash University Press, 1996).
9   Jean Decoux, À la Barre de l'Indochine, 1940–1945 (Paris: Plon, 1949), pp. 270, 274.
10 Ibid., p. 287.
11 Sihanouk, Souvenirs doux et amers (Paris: Hachette, 1981), pp. 87–8.
12 Penny Edwards, Cambodge: The Cultivation of a Nation, 1860–1945 (Honolulu: University of Hawai'i Press, 2007).
13 Chandler, The Tragedy of Cambodian History, p. 61.
14 Ibid., p. 63.
15 Ibid., p. 72.
16 Norodom Sihanouk, L'Indochine vue de Pékin (Paris: Le Seuil, 1972), p. 54.
17 I rely, in this section, on Daniel Rivet, Le Maroc de Lyautey à Mohammed V, Le Double visage du protectorat (Paris: Denoël, 1999); Daniel Rivet, Le Maghreb à l'épreuve de la colonisation (Paris: Hachette, 2002); Jean Lacouture, Cinq hommes et la France (Paris: Le Seuil, 1961); Rom Landau, Moroccan Drama, 1900–1955 (San Francisco: American Academy of Asian Studies, 1956); on the dethroning and exile of Mohammed V and other Moroccan sultans, see Aldrich, Banished Potentates, pp. 255–60 and 265–71.
18 Charles-André Julien, L'Afrique du Nord en marche, 3rd edn (Paris: René Julliard, 1972), p. 135.
19 Lacouture, Cinq hommes et la France, p. 187.
20 Ibid., p. 193.
21 Ibid., p. 211.
22 Ibid., pp. 211–12.
23 Ibid., p. 205.
24 Rivet, Le Maroc de Lyautey à Mohammed V, ch. 11.
25 Landau, Moroccan Drama, pp. 324–5.
26 Bui Diem, In the Jaws of History (Bloomington: Indiana University Press, 1999), pp. 67–8.

CHAPTER TEN

Loyalism and anti-communism in the making of the modern monarchy in post-colonial Laos
Ryan Wolfson-Ford

The last king of Laos, Savang Vatthana (r. 1959–75), opened the National Assembly on 11 May 1967, Constitution Day in the Royal Lao Government (RLG) era (1945–75). But it was hardly business as usual. For the first time in seven years, parliament was functioning normally. The King had only recently revived democracy after a period (1958–64) when it seemed a dictatorship might arise. Early in his reign, Savang considered supporting ambitious Royal Lao Army officers. He and his father, Sisavang Vong (r. 1904–59), had a complicated relationship with democracy, especially during the Issara independence movement (1945–49). Yet now Savang entered parliament, followed first by Crown Prince Vongsavang and only after by Prime Minister Souvanna Phouma.[1] Savang served a ceremonial but nonetheless crucial role. This was not a given; two decades earlier there had been not a single, but rather several monarchies across Laos. This chapter examines how the modern Lao monarchy was made (and unmade) by partisan struggles. More deeply, it considers questions about what role kings had in a post-colonial democracy and how this was influenced by intellectual, cultural and political tensions.

Monarchy in Laos

Modern Laos, the landlocked nation at the heart of mainland Southeast Asia, derives its name from the ethnic Lao who long inhabited the middle Mekong River. Its central location made it significant to regional contests for centuries. It remains one of the most ethnically diverse countries in the area. The ethnic Lao make up less than half the population, which in 1974 was 3,257,000 (and today has grown to 7,234,171). The old Lao kingdom of Lan Xang has existed since the thirteenth century. Over time, a uniquely Lao monarchy evolved, supported by Buddhism. In the eighteenth century, the kingdom broke up into smaller kingdoms before falling under Thai vassalage. In 1893, Auguste Pavie inaugurated the French colonisation of Laos that lasted until the Second World War. Laos nevertheless remained marginal within the French Empire; underdevelopment would be a rallying cry of later independence movements. In 1904, Sisavang Vong took the throne, and during his fifty-five-year reign he worked closely with France; his generation was the first to be French-educated and to travel abroad. In 1959, Savang Vatthana succeeded as king while delaying his coronation until peace returned amid the outbreak of the Second Indochina War (1959–75). Yet, just as monks foretold that Luang Prabang would not fall to the communist-aligned Pathet Lao in 1953, so they prophesied, rightly, that Savang Vatthana was to be the last king of Laos.

There were other royals besides the main line. In the north at Luang Prabang a secondary branch held the post of viceroy or 'second king', who traditionally was next in line for the throne, but who had lost that function in the nineteenth century. In 1893, Viceroy Boun Khong initially resisted French colonisation before deciding to collaborate actively. His sons Phetsarath Rattanavongsa, Souvanna Phouma and Souphanouvong went on to play leading roles in politics. Phetsarath was the top Lao official in the colonial administration before leading the Issara independence movement to resist French colonialism in September 1945.[2] Both Souvanna and Souphanouvong joined him along with many others across Laos. A democratic government was established that sought Allied recognition and, failing that, resisted French reconquest in 1946 after the Second World War and Japanese occupation. Defeated, the Issara went into exile in Thailand while their followers stoked guerrilla war for years. In 1949, the Issara split over a loyalist offer of amnesty. Souvanna and others returned to work with the French while Souphanouvong joined the North Vietnamese-backed Pathet Lao. Phetsarath, meanwhile, remained in exile before returning to Laos in 1957.

Multiple royal lines complicated the formation of a modern monarchy. Before 1945, Sisavang Vong, ruling the northern Luang Prabang kingdom, was only one of several kings. There were southern kings (the Champassaks), eastern kings at Xieng Khouang (the Phouan), and aristocratic families from the old Vientiane kingdom. Under colonialism Luang Prabang cooperated with France, while Champassak and Xieng Khouang secretly supported ethnic-minority anti-French revolts.[3] By 1941 the French granted Sisavang Vong the Vientiane and Phouan domains to compensate for the loss of Sayabouri (and its royal teak forests) to Thailand. While France favoured Sisavang Vong until 1947, it was not certain that he would become the sole monarch. This was only resolved when Champassak Prince Boun Oum renounced his claims, instead becoming 'Inspector of the Kingdom' for life. Luang Prabang kings never matched the Champassaks' popularity in southern Laos. Phouan royals did intermarry with the Luang Prabang dynasty but remained distinct. Ultimately, other royal lines thus limited the monarchy's popularity across post-colonial Laos.

During the 1950s, politics further fragmented into factions: right, left and neutral. Princes Savang Vatthana, Souphanouvong and Souvanna Phouma led opposing factions. Souvanna sought to neutralise Laos to be non-aligned in the Cold War, before leading the RLG in the Second Indochina War. Souphanouvong led the Pathet Lao, which aimed to liberate Laos from foreign rule; it co-opted Issara remnants but was controlled by North Vietnam. Early in his reign, Savang Vatthana quietly supported the Comité pour la Défense des Intérêts Nationaux (CDIN), a virulently anti-communist, nationalist movement loyal to the state.[4] After the collapse of the Geneva Accords all attention turned to the escalating war from 1964 as neutralists and rightists reconciled. In April 1964, Western ambassadors called on Savang to denounce a coup. The King approved but when hearing their draft statement, which included a vow not to interfere in Lao internal affairs, he 'laughed and exclaimed, "*Vraiment?*" [Truly?]'.[5]

The pivotal role of kings in post-colonial Laos has not always been appreciated. Timothy Castle was not alone when he claimed that 'the last sovereign, Savang Vatthana, exercised little power and influence'.[6] However, all sides in the Second Indochina War, even the Pathet Lao, pledged loyalty to the monarchy. This misunderstanding arises partly due to a lack of sources on the monarchy. The most important study has been Grant Evans's *The Last Century of Lao Royalty*,[7] and Evans in particular revealed the many ways the monarchy was modernised. There nevertheless remain unaddressed, but defining, issues: specifically, how loyalism and anti-communism made (and unmade) the monarchy.

Although Lao historiography largely concerns politics, nonetheless the role of partisanship in making the modern monarchy remains obscure. In the period 1945 to 1949 the monarchy was defined by the loyalist movement. (I define a 'loyalist', a label the movement never used, as one who supported France's return to Laos after 1945.) Loyalists were just as ardent nationalists as were the Issara.[8] Since 1953, anti-communism provided a key platform for the monarchy, especially in Savang's early reign (1959–64). Savang indeed expressed personal anti-communist views in 1946 – well before such positions guided US foreign policy in Asia.[9] Two cases illustrate the place of partisanship in the making of the modern Lao monarchy; ultimately the monarchy was overthrown in 1975 due to its partisan stance in the Second Indochina War.

First, the late 1940s was a formative time, when Sisavang Vong led the loyalists. He was no mere figurehead but used the movement to cultivate support. He bent the movement to his will, equating loyalty to France with loyalty to himself; this represented a deft political move. He guided the loyalist-dominated Constitutional Assembly that wrote the 1947 constitution – a unique political document in Southeast Asian history that was amended but not replaced until 1975. From his efforts emerged a single monarchy for the whole country, including the south, and Sisavang Vong carefully navigated a regional split among loyalists. The loyalist movement presents a case study of Sisavang Vong's unification of the monarchy and reassertion of precedence over democracy amid his support for the return of colonial France.

In the second case, the chaos of Savang Vatthana's early reign overshadowed his efforts to remake the monarchy. Nevertheless, Savang undertook a programme to instil nationalism and loyalty in the masses. Starting with the youth, he created the Lao Scout movement in 1947,[10] and by 1963 he had also moved to put his stamp on schools. The Scout movement engendered loyalty to the throne, and to the king personally. In a newly independent country, still in the process of unification, politically divided and subject to intensifying foreign meddling, the Scouts constituted an important nation-building force. Yet Savang's youth movement was inextricably linked to earlier Vichy fascist undertakings from the Second World War period.[11] Moreover, his promotion of civics in the school curriculum reveals his uneasiness with democracy to the point that he justified the monarchy by recourse to religion. The Scout movement shows Savang Vatthana's efforts to rally right-wing nationalism even as he negotiated the place of the monarchy in a democracy. This same partisanship led to the unmaking of the monarchy during the revolution of 1975.

Loyalism unifies the monarchy (1945–49)

After the French reconquest of Laos, Sisavang Vong and Savang Vatthana began to negotiate with the colonisers. On 12 May 1946, one day before the French entered the city of Luang Prabang, Prince Savang received a letter in which the former French High Commissioner of Laos, Jean de Raymond, spoke of a renewed alliance in which 'France hoped to see Laos united under the high authority of King Sisavang Vong'.[12] The next day, Sisavang Vong personally welcomed the returning French officials to Luang Prabang in the 'usual manner'.[13] The following day, the King declared that he would accept France's offer and establish a democratic constitution.[14] In June, a committee drafted a new *modus vivendi*, signed on 27 August, restoring the colonial bond severed by war. More significant, however, was the rise of loyalism.

Loyalism was a unique movement that appeared nowhere else in the French Empire. Only in Laos did a sizeable indigenous force fight to safeguard French lives and restore French rule. Moreover, a unified monarchy only arose at the height of the loyalist movement. Loyalism is thus vital to understanding the context of the rise of the modern monarchy. Yet what role did Sisavang Vong and Savang Vatthana have in the new movement? Were they active agents or mere bystanders? While many sources attest to the loyalist attitude of the King and Crown Prince, how did they relate to other loyalists, such as Prince Boun Oum of Champassak?

The loyalists emerged after the Japanese coup of 9 March 1945 against Vichy-controlled Indochina, when Lao had to decide whether to aid the French or accept Japanese-mandated independence. Japan, fearing Allied victory, forced out its putative ally, Vichy France. Hundreds of Lao followed the French into the jungles in opposition to the Japanese. The King and Crown Prince gestured to the anti-Japanese movement, delaying the declaration of Lao independence that Japan demanded; as punishment, Savang was taken to Saigon as hostage. But as the Issara movement led Laos onwards to independence, conflict with the King emerged. On 20 October, the Issara dethroned the King, putting him at odds with the nascent democracy, and ultimately the King and Crown Prince were arrested. Negotiations followed, and eventually the 'ex-King' recognised the Issara on 10 November and pledged not to make treaties with France.[15] His support 'willingly or unwillingly' given, he agreed on 20 April 1946 to be re-enthroned in a ceremony held three days later. The following day, Vientiane fell to the Free French forces, by which time it was clear the whole country would be reconquered.

On 15 March 1947, Sisavang Vong convened a constitutional assembly to draft a new constitution that would re-establish the primacy of the monarchy.[16] The monarch was closely involved in the composition of the forty-four-member assembly, of which thirty-five members were officials in an administration dominated by northerners.[17] While the King was not present at deliberations, Crown Prince Savang oversaw the constitutional assembly.[18] One participant noted with irony that the democratic principles enshrined in the preamble of the constitution were ones that most Lao did not understand.[19] The loyalist constitution was distinctly elitist and monarchical compared to the one drafted by the Issara movement. The key passage in the preamble of the new constitution was: 'The populations of Laos affirm their fidelity to the monarchy, their attachment to democratic principles, and proclaim as Sovereign of Laos, His Majesty Sisavang Vong.'[20] Democracy was subordinated to the monarchy and the new constitution removed certain democratic elements from the Issara version, raising the King above the National Assembly.

In his message promulgating the constitution on 11 May 1947, Sisavang Vong conflated his own wishes with the 'aspirations of Our Lao People', posing as the people's arbiter, and thus reclaiming the role the Issara wrestled from him. He spoke of modernisation while presiding over a conservative, elitist constitutional monarchy. However, his speech hinted at how the events of 1945 caused 'the people' to become a new political force, entering into the political discourse for the first time:

> On this occasion, *we report to our people that Laos counts on them for its renovation, its stability and its prosperity*. We undertake a difficult and delicate work, we must undertake it with wisdom, with conscience, with energy, with faith. We do not forget that our goal is to make our country, within the great family of the French Union, a place worthy of its glorious past. (Emphasis added)

This passage is striking because the King placed himself in a subordinate position to the people: it is the King who reports to the people and who pledges to work hard, with the people implicitly standing in judgement of his actions. In the previous age, the King, never the people, had been the source of 'renovation', 'stability' and 'prosperity'. By 1947, the world had fundamentally changed, and the King openly acknowledged that change. He could no longer wield absolute power but had to compete with the new forces of politicians and political parties. As a result, he now spoke in a language never used by any previous Lao king. The monarchy was thus in transformation. The 1947 constitution, printed and distributed widely, provided potent propaganda against the Issara and undercut their demands. The text contained an image of the constitution placed on an offering bowl, just as palm leaf manuscripts, the sacred texts of the Lao, had traditionally been depicted. Years later, the elite continued to revere the constitution for having been introduced by the great King.[21]

In drafting a new constitution, southern regionalism remained prominent. Recalling the privileged position enjoyed by Luang Prabang in the colonial era, southerners were loath to cede sovereignty. Agreements made between Luang Prabang and Auguste Pavie had been the pretext for French colonisation in 1893 – even though the Luang Prabang authorities had no authority outside the north of the country. However, in a secret protocol the Champassak dynasty renounced its centuries-old claim to central and southern Laos. Luang Prabang's king was being elevated to become sovereign over the whole country. Not all southerners accepted this development easily, despite the secret agreements made by the Champassaks. Southern Lao continued to fear northern domination in a unified kingdom and called on France to remain as a paramount power to serve as neutral arbiter.[22] Boun Oum was a loyalist not solely because of his anti-Japanese and anti-Issara stance, but in order to seek French protection for the south. As the new national government formed, the southern intellectual, Thao Nhouy Abhay, complained of regional favouritism in appointments of ministers, leading him to question the 'promises of equality' regarding selection of officials whose qualifications were supposed to be based 'solely on their merit and not at all on their origin'.[23] But Luang Prabang's long collaboration with the colonial administration and its protectorate governments enabled it to muster more experienced officials than did other regions.

Southerners remained uneasy with incorporation of their region into a unified kingdom. One of the first acts of the new government was to debate regional autonomy. A noted intellectual and *député*, Pierre Somchine Nginn, explained that while Laos had been unified until the eighteenth century, it was subsequently divided for centuries. All Lao, he conceded, could see the need for unification, but how to go about the process was uncertain. The Champassak claim was the source of tension. Nginn put it diplomatically: 'If the necessity of unification was recognized by all, it nonetheless raised some difficulties when the modalities of application were examined.'[24]

Opposing unification, unnamed southern deputies 'requested' that the Champassak line be 'restored'. They wanted to undo a 1935 French decision to abolish any rights for the Champassak ruler (even in the diminished role of 'governor'). *Députés* from the south called for the new government to 'recognise' Prince Boun Oum. They made much of the fact that Boun Oum himself had 'rendered ... invaluable services to the French cause' in the Resistance. Supporters of Boun Oum argued, moreover, that he was the real leader of the loyalists, having actually fought for France during reconquest. They again spoke of a 'traditional distrust of the populations of the south [who] fear being led by functionaries [who] come from elsewhere and are ignorant of the country'. 'Country' in the southerners' lexicon still meant the south rather than the unified kingdom as a whole. As the first national government formed, a move was made to decentralise power. Some even proposed a different form of government entirely: a diarchy. Ultimately, the matter was resolved in favour of Sisavang Vong. Boun Oum ceded his rights, as Laos was unified under an unprecedented constitutional monarchy.[25]

After resolving the crisis, Sisavang Vong exchanged letters with French President Vincent Auriol in November 1947 in which he expressed support for the new Union Française – a kind of commonwealth of France and its overseas territories created in the 1946 constitution of the Fourth Republic, but one in which France effectively retained paramount power in its territories and newly recognised 'associated states' such as Laos – and boasted of RLG delegates' influence over the Union Française. While defending 'the liberty of internal administration', the King approved of common foreign relations and especially defence. He agreed to Lao soldiers serving in Union Française armies, and to the free movement of French forces and retention of French military bases in Laos. In part, the monarch was concerned with the expanding Issara guerrilla movement, though in 1948 he would offer amnesty to Issara 'rebels'. Positioning himself as an early supporter of the Union Française, the King gained a measure of political autonomy and economic and defence aid with comparatively greater ease than what was given by France to the other Indochinese states of Vietnam and Cambodia.[26]

By the time the General Conventions between Paris and Luang Prabang were signed on 19 July 1949, granting Lao autonomy within the Union Française, Sisavang Vong could speak as the unquestioned loyalist leader. To France he proclaimed: 'When, after a year of hardship, We have found, with all the Lao people, the liberty which France contributed to Us, We have loudly proclaimed our fidelity to the friendly nation, hoping that with its help and as part of the Union Française, We could give the necessary satisfaction to the legitimate aspirations of Our people.' He spoke proudly of endowing the kingdom with a constitution, while France recognised 'our internal sovereignty'. For the last three years he had worked 'to fix the basis on which We could set down our sovereignty'. The agreement with France 'sets the stage to permit Us to take our place in the great community of free nations'. Finally, the King hoped the agreement would satisfy the aspirations of all Lao 'of good faith'. As for the Issara, the King stated that he had 'never haggled Our clemency'.[27]

For all their accomplishments, the loyalists might be seen as merely following in the Issara's footsteps. After all, the Issara had been the first to create a parliamentary democracy, write a constitution and establish a unified Laos; their efforts must be regarded as a watershed in modern Lao history. Yet while the loyalists were conservative and monarchical, they nonetheless consolidated the Issara's gains. While the constitution granted wider powers to the monarchy than those contained in the Issara constitution, it did not do away with representative government, nor dispense with the fundamental civil and political rights considered the hallmark of Western democracies. As for King Sisavang Vong, he unified the loyalists even as they unified Laos under a monarchy, and he gave the movement potency with his support. He negotiated with France to preserve internal autonomy while making the most of its financial, administrative and technical support. He realised the dangers confronting newly independent post-colonial states as well as the threat of continued insurgency. Though hostile to more radical change and elitist in outlook, the King did not dispense with democracy as he navigated the transformation of the monarchy into an era of constitutions, nationalism and popular sovereignty. Sisavang Vong thereby created the modern monarchy of Laos despite serious opposition from several quarters.

On their return to Laos from exile, the ex-Issara formed political parties that swiftly won the parliamentary elections in 1951. Several ex-Issara prime ministers then dominated politics during the 1950s. But one episode shows the monarchy's political power in the new democracy. An Issara ideologue and future prime minister, Katay Don Sasorith, was forced into 'exile' in Saigon for several years,[28] punished for publishing 'anti-monarchy' pamphlets that mercilessly criticised the monarchy. Prince Savang Vatthana was also mocked in several biting political cartoons. Katay was only able to return after publishing an apology, writing articles praising the political system: 'Finally, Laos has regained its unity and independence ... The results obtained are still very important. These results were not obtained without the spirit of abnegation and without the sacrifices of some and others.'[29] While praising Issara soldiers who died on the battlefield, and Prince Boun Oum's own sacrifice, he nonetheless acknowledged national unification by the King's hand.[30]

Aid the king: echoes of fascism in Savang Vatthana's early reign

The chaos of the late 1950s partly derived from anxiety surrounding the transition of the monarchy. Sisavang Vong's long reign had been a source of stability, and when he died, on 29 October 1959, he was reputedly the longest reigning monarch in the world. After capturing the national imagination by steadfastly refusing to evacuate his capital during the March–April 1953 Vietminh invasion, Sisavang Vong faded from public life as his health declined. Savang Vatthana took on more duties, finally becoming regent in August 1959. Sisavang Vong's death nevertheless shocked the nation, and, coming within a month of Prince Phetsarath's death, it signalled the end of a generation. Katay died not long afterward, in December, during the first of several military coups which destabilised Laos.

While Savang Vatthana was actively involved with the political right, he undertook a concerted programme to remake the monarchy in the first years of his reign. He remoulded major institutions after his ideas and created several new ones, with the aim of spreading nationalism among the masses and cultivating loyalty to himself. He thereby forged a nationalism which promoted loyalty to the state in order to combat the subversive activities of North Vietnam and the Pathet Lao. His programme included creation of a mass youth movement, a new educational curriculum to disseminate nationalism in the schools and the replacement of French with Lao as the language of instruction. Yet Savang's programme, especially where it targeted youth, ominously mirrored the fascist movements of the Second World War, reviving techniques of authoritarianism in Cold War Laos.

Savang created the Lao Scouts at the height of the loyalist movement, long before he acceded to the throne. The organisation was formed in 1947 at the Luang Prabang royal palace by Savang and two French instructors (the Lao word for scout – *sakut* – is a French loan word).[31] The Lao Scout handbook makes clear that Savang was its leader, employing royal language to denote the Prince's actions: 'Crown Prince Savang Vatthana deigned to be leader of the Lao Scout organization.' The organisation subsequently expanded throughout the country, under the future neutralist Pheng Phongsavane, who stood with Savang and his father in late 1945, as administrative head. French officials, including spymaster Jean Deuve, served as advisers. The scouts then set about 'building goodness and rightness for the nation'.[32]

The new movement held several rallies, culminating in the first national rally at Savannakhet in 1956, and by 1958 it counted 2,385 members. To increase membership further the organisation began accepting girls; membership increased even more dramatically when Savang decreed in July 1963 that every public school student must participate in what was then called the 'youth movement'. Furthermore, the Lao Scouts established training grounds for its members and forged close links to the military; a camp opened in 1953 on the outskirts of Vientiane in an area of military bases included 'drill masters' for the young Scouts. The Scout handbook boasted of a new physical exercise regime devised by Sourith Don Sasorith, a high-ranking military officer.

With the Scouts, Savang succeeded in creating a mass movement loyal to the king, a unique organisation in Laos during the 1950s–60s. Savang had personally observed the French-sponsored mass movement,

Lao Renovation (1941–45), and the Vichy-era youth movements as well as the anti-colonial Issara, and Lao Pen Lao militias.[33] Symbolising these connections, Savang adopted the Lao Renovation symbol which was prominent in the Scout uniform, especially the pledge insignia. Moreover, the King promoted loyalty, and every new Scout pledged 'to serve the Nation, the King'. The first principle that a 'Lao Scout takes pride in, observes [as an] ideal and defends as long as [he] lives' was 'the Scout respects the King and the Nation'. Illustrations in the Scout handbook pictured youth saluting portraits of Savang.[34]

The King attended the annual mass rallies, at the centre of activities. Moreover, Savang regularly appealed to the youth of Laos in his speeches. Just before the outbreak of war, Savang began to hold 'youth rallies' emphasising national unity – for instance, in February 1959 at Wat Phou in southern Laos.[35] This rally followed an earlier one in Luang Prabang that was said to 'resonate all through the Kingdom and beyond its borders'. Savang's speech was not printed, but the press reported on the rally: 'It had given back courage and a new ideal to the youth, the future elite of the nation, the future of the nation on the move, on the move towards progress, on the move towards grandeur, on the move towards glory, the glory of a Great and New Laos.' Savang personally awarded top prizes to the scouts chosen for 'dress', 'discipline'. and 'team spirit'. The youths who attended the rally were reportedly deeply affected, their 'heart[s] filled with courage, confidence, and enthusiasm'. The rally had awakened them to 'a new spirit, towards a new destiny'.[36]

As Laos descended into war, Savang stirred up the youth, exhorting them directly: 'Lao youth, without apprehension, without reticence, we confide to you the future of our country and our race'[37] Savang's Lao Scouts are comparable to Prince Norodom Sihanouk's own Vichy-era Cambodian youth movement formed in 1941.[38] Both promoted nationalism and martial spirit, complete with uniforms and rallies, while indoctrinating loyalty to the king amid external threats. Anne Raffin notes that youth movements were used to promote monarchy and maintain social order, and as a tool for social control of youth.[39] Savang started modestly, but when the prospect of war loomed, he turned the Scouts into an instrument of government. His efforts recalled Vichy wartime promotion of loyalty and obedience to the state. Just as the French had competed with the Japanese for popular support, now Savang was locked in a struggle with the Pathet Lao and North Vietnam. Finally, as the Second Indochina War escalated in 1964, scouts were told to die for the nation. In a broadcast over Radio Lao on the 'Duties of a Lao Boy Scout', the Scouts were exhorted to heed the call of duty: 'We nation of men, without regret, give [our] lives for the restoration of our Lao nation.'[40] The youth were drawn to take sides in the anti-communist struggle by Savang's denunciation of the Pathet Lao as 'traitorous rebels', 'enemies' (*satou*) of the nation.

Savang next implanted the youth movement in the schools. The Department of Youth and Sports moved from the Ministry of Education to Defence in 1958, presaging later developments.[41] By royal order on 30 July 1963, Savang revised the entire public school curriculum so that schools were 'no longer an academic institution but a system in the service of the country's economic and social development'.[42] For every primary school student, five hours per week were designated for 'organisation and activities of the youth movement'. Activities included 'morals in action, religion, practical hygiene and singing'. Another report explained the objectives of the movement: 'the spirit of civic responsibility is encouraged and developed in each class; the pupils elect their own chairman and take turns at filling various offices'.[43] In secondary schools, time for 'youth movement activities' was nevertheless reduced to a still significant three hours and forty-five minutes.[44] For the 1963–64 school year there were 119,986 primary school and 3,226 secondary school students, offering a large pool from which to create a mass movement,[45] and by the 1973–74 school year, numbers had grown to 245,857 primary school students and 9,774 in secondary schools.[46]

Savang's creation of a youth movement overlapped with his project to remake the curriculum by introducing civics instruction to promote nationalism. As one 1960 Ministry of Education report stated: 'The primary [school] syllabuses at present in use were drawn up in 1938 by the educational services of the protectorate ... The department has been studying since October 1959 the basic reforms to be made in the content of these syllabuses which are now old.'[47] Elsewhere the report complained of the existing curricula 'which have not been revised for more than twenty years'.[48] Civics was the first secondary school course taught in Lao by Lao instructors. Ethics was also introduced, focusing on Buddhism, 'especially the life of the Buddha'.

Civics instruction was designed not just to promote nationalism, but specifically loyalty to the King. Savang thus co-opted the expanding education system to engender mass loyalty to the monarch across Laos. This allowed the sovereign to project his influence into regions where loyalty to the throne was low, such as the south. The first citizenship textbook appeared in 1960, and further texts for students were produced later, including for years 1, 2 and 4.[49] Included in each was a photograph of Savang. In fact, every classroom had its portrait of the King just as every movie house played the national anthem while the audience saluted an image of the King. Civics texts, too, were designed for more than just use in schools, as the Minister of Education, Nhouy Abhay, stated: 'This book is not only a teacher's handbook ... [It] may yet be a handbook for the village-head, the district-head and citizens, persons who have a desire to study and know the duties of a citizen.'[50]

The teaching of civics raised deep questions about the place of the monarchy in a democracy. The textbook stated that 'the Lao nation is governed by a democracy with a King, lord of life, as leader of the nation'. This contrasted with republics, which merely had presidents. While noting that the King was 'the supreme leader of the nation' and was 'maintained in a status of being revered [sakkara]', a position which none could challenge, nonetheless the King could not exercise authority alone, as 'power of every type derives from the people according to the provisions of the constitution'. The Lao liked the monarchy because they 'respected and worshiped [bouxa] and believed [suathu] in the King always'.[51]

At this point, the textbook took a religious turn. It continued, with allusions to Hindu as well as Buddhist conceptions of monarchy, that the Lao

> believe [the King] is the venerable lord sitting on the head, that is lord Brahma of the Lao because [the King] has the four perfect states of the god (phrathai): compassion, mercy, kindness, [and] equanimity to the Lao people. [He] is the god (thevada) of the Lao combined with divine law: shame of demerit and fear of demerit. Stealing, shame, fear, demerit, bad actions – no evil of any kind can be done to the Lao people. [The King] will raise the Lao to the cool shade of peace, in happiness always.

When faced with the quandary over the place of monarchy in a democracy, King Savang was not above invoking religion to justify his rule, even going so far as to claim divine status. Pupils were instructed that they had a duty to know and respect the system of rule and to 'respect, believe, and worship the leader of the state truly'. They had a duty to 'elevate the system of rule to prosper permanently' and to hold it 'sacred [saksit]'.[52]

In the final analysis, Savang's partisan stance during the Second Indochinese War, which he viewed as an existential struggle against China and North Vietnam, as much as his strong anti-communism, led to the unmaking of the monarchy after 1975. His polarising stance on the war – despite foreign and Pathet Lao claims that he remained above the conflict – set up an untenable position for the monarchy in post-revolution Laos. There seems little doubt that the monarch would eventually have been pushed aside to make way for new power-holders, but not necessarily sent to a concentration camp to die with his wife and son, as was his fate.[53]

Unfinished business: diaspora calls for a royal funeral

The monarchy remained a powerful institution even in early 1975, the year in which it was abolished. No one seriously thought the King would be removed, nor did anyone openly call for the overthrow of the monarchy. The revolution was not anti-monarchical, since the Pathet Lao publicly pledged to uphold the monarchy. The most popular leader of the Pathet Lao was a (minor) member of the extended royal family, Souphanouvong, the 'Red Prince', who proved to be a figurehead of the movement, but a very popular one.[54] The monarchy was not swept away in a popular revolution but was destroyed in a calculated move by the Pathet Lao – now unmasked as the Lao People's Revolutionary Party (LPRP). Protests organised by the LPDR against the monarchy began on 12 October 1975 – the thirtieth anniversary of the Issara's promulgation of a Constitution and establishment of a Provisional Assembly – and during these demonstrations the King issued arms to the palace guard. However, in late November 1975 King Savang Vatthana was dethroned at the height of the revolution. His son, Crown Prince Vongsavang, delivered the King's abdication speech, paving the way for the creation of the Lao People's Democratic Republic on 2 December 1975. On 11 March 1977, the King, Queen and Crown Prince were arrested for allegedly contacting the resistance (and seeking rescue) and sent to 're-education' – a concentration camp in Viengxai near the Vietnamese border (Figure 10.1). The royal family was imprisoned with ministers, ambassadors and thirteen top generals, allowing the LPRP to decapitate the RLG in one stroke. Surviving for several years on starvation rations and without medications, the King died in March 1980 and, not long after, the Crown Prince succumbed. Queen Khamphoui died later, in 1982, in a camp for common criminals.

In retrospect, monarchs were key agents who actively shaped post-colonial Laos. The monarchy succeeded in remaking itself in the democratic-era of popular sovereignty after the Second World War as a constitutional monarchy, but it could not survive a communist revolution so closely linked to its enemies, China and North Vietnam. While Sisavang Vong had remade the modern monarchy during the loyalist movement immediately after the war, Savang Vatthana linked it to right-wing nationalism, best exemplified by the Lao Scouts, taking sides in the Second Indochina War and thereby unmaking it after 1975.

In 1960 the RLG had made elaborate arrangements for Sisavang Vong's cremation, but Savang Vatthana, his wife Queen Khamphoui and Crown Prince Vongsavang have never received this final rite, or

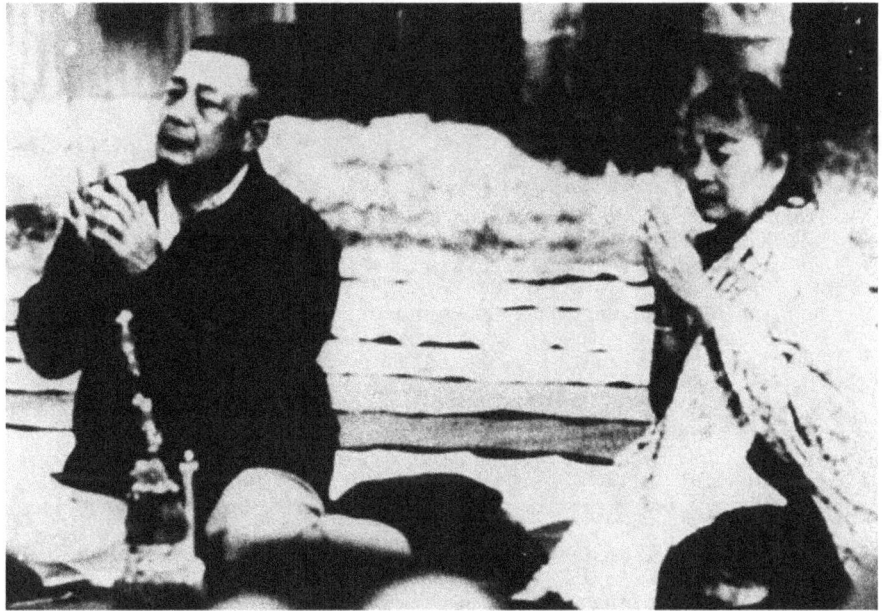

Figure 10.1 King Savang and Queen Khamphoui in internal exile after the overthrow of the Lao monarchy

even had their deaths officially recognised by the Lao government. The King's and Crown Prince's remains were left buried in an unmarked grave north of a re-education camp in Viengxai, though burial rather than cremation is offensive for any Buddhist Lao, much less the King. Nevertheless, the absence of the monarchy has cast a long shadow over the post-1975 period. At times, this tension is voiced explicitly by some Lao, as exiles in the diaspora have called for the proper funeral of King Savang Vatthana. In a speech in 2018, the head of the Royal Lao Government-in-Exile, Khamphoui Sisavady, compared US and Vietnamese efforts to repatriate war dead with that of Laos:

> But what about Laos? For 42 years the bones of RLG Lao leaders ... have been left rotting in the jungles all but forgotten. The remains of the Royal family, a 600-year [old] dynasty, including the King, Queen and Crown Prince have never been found, or even searched for, by anyone. Who should be responsible? And who even cares or pays attention to this issue?

Khamphoui concluded by calling on those who believe in justice to challenge 'the ongoing oppression in Laos today'. To some in the diaspora, the monarchy is not gone and buried but remains unfinished business. It remains a symbol around which to rally those opposed to the present government, a one-party state ruled by the LPRP.[55]

Notes

All translations by the author, Ryan Wolfson-Ford.

1. 'Pamouanpapkhao', in *Lokpatchuban*, special edition (1967), 2.
2. Soren Ivarsson and Christopher Goscha, 'Prince Phetsarath (1890–1959): nationalism and royalty in the making of modern Laos', *Journal of Southeast Asian Studies*, 38:1 (2007), 55–81.
3. Ian Baird, 'Millenarian movements in southern Laos and northeast Siam (Thailand) at the turn of the twentieth century: reconsidering the involvement of the Champassak Royal House', *South East Asia Research*, 21:2 (2013), 257–79.
4. The fathers of leading CDIN members, Khamphan Panya and Kouprasith Abhay, sat on the Privy Council. Another CDIN member, Prince Sopsaisana, was Palace Secretary.
5. Perry Stieglitz, *In a Little Kingdom* (Armonk, NY: M. E. Sharpe, 1990), p. 98.
6. Timothy Castle, *At War in the Shadow of Vietnam: United States Military Aid to the Royal Lao Government, 1955–1975* (New York: Columbia University Press, 1995), p. 4.
7. Grant Evans, *The Last Century of Lao Royalty: A Documentary History* (Chiang Mai: Silk Worm Books, 2009).
8. Anne Raffin notes that loyalists in Savannakhet and Khammouane welcomed French reconquest because they blamed the Issara 'for essentially turning over the country to the Viet Minh'. See Raffin, *Youth Mobilization in Vichy Indochina and Its Legacies, 1940 to 1970* (Lanham, MD: Lexington Books, 2005), p. 226.
9. Evans, *The Last Century of Lao Royalty*, p. 165.
10. On the Lao Scouts, see Simon Creak, *Embodied Nation: Sport, Masculinity and the Making of Modern Laos* (Honolulu: University of Hawai'i Press, 2015), p. 94.
11. Eric T. Jennings, *Vichy in the Tropics: Pétain's National Revolution in Madagascar, Guadeloupe and Indochina, 1940–1944* (Stanford, CA: Stanford University Press, 2001).
12. Frank Lebar, *Human Relations File 23: Laos* (New Haven, CT: Human Relations Area Files Inc., 1955), p. 41.
13. S. Virasan, *Nangsupavatsatlao* [History Book] (Vientiane: Modern Lao Publishing House, 1957), p. 83.
14. 'Proclamation de Sa Majesté Sisavang Vong, Roi du Laos', in Royaume du Laos, *Constitution Lao* (Saigon: Impr. Mai-Linh, 1947).
15. Katay Sasorith, *Le Laos: Son évolution politique, sa place dans l'Union française* (Paris: éditions Berger-Levrault, 1953), p. 61.
16. See Martin Stuart-Fox, 'The Lao constitution of 1947/1949: Creating a nation-state', in Kevin Y. L. Tan and Ngoc Son Bui (eds), *Constitutional Foundings in Southeast Asia* (Oxford: Hart Publishing, 2019).
17. Lebar, *Human Relations File 23: Laos*, p. 42.
18. Pierre Nginn, 'La Constitution', *Kinnari*, 6 (November 1947), 9.
19. Ibid.
20. *Constitution Lao*.
21. Ibid.
22. Charles-Henri Duparc, 'Le problème politique laotien', *Politique Etrangère*, 12 (1947), 542–3.
23. Lebar, *Human Relations File 23: Laos*, p. 42.
24. Nginn, 'La Constitution'.
25. Ibid.
26. Sasorith, *Le Laos*, p. 112.

27 'Allocution prononcée par S.M. Sisavang-Vong, roi du Laos, répondant à l'allocution précitée de M. le Président Vincent Auriol', cited in Sasorith, *Le Laos*, p. 129.
28 Mongkhol-Katay Sasorith, 'Les forces politiques et la vie politique au Laos', PhD thesis, Panthéon-Sorbonne University, 1973, p. 161.
29 Katay Sasorith, 'Le Laos depuis l'arrivée des Français', *Sud-Est*, 14 (July 1950), 16.
30 Katay Sasorith, 'L'évolution politique du Laos avant l'occupation française', *Sud-Est*, 13 (June 1950).
31 An earlier Lao Scout Association created in 1941 was small and largely Vietnamese. Raffin, *Youth Mobilization*, pp. 72, 139.
32 See *Phuansakut* [Scout Friends] (n.p., n.d.), pp. 9–16.
33 Søren Ivarsson, *Creating Laos: The making of a Lao space between Indochina and Siam, 1860–1945* (Copenhagen: NIAS Press, 2008).
34 *Scout Friends*, pp. 24–5.
35 Vichy rallies used ancient sites. See Jennings, *Vichy in the Tropics*, pp. 149, 195.
36 *Lao Hakxa Sat*, 9/10 (February 1959), 'Succès sans précédent de la "journée de la jeunesse" à wat-phou', p. 1. Hereafter cited as LHXS.
37 *LHXS*, 17 (June 1959), p. 1.
38 Jennings, *Vichy in the Tropics*, p. 190.
39 Raffin, *Youth Mobilization*, p. 4.
40 Kingdom of Laos, *Vitthanyuhonghian* [Radio School] (Bangkok: Light of Arts Publishing House, 1964), p. 37.
41 UNESCO, *International Yearbook of Education, Vol. XX 1958* (Paris: UNESCO, 1959), p. 218. Hereafter cited as IYB.
42 *IYB* (1963), pp. 221–2.
43 *IYB* (1964), p. 197.
44 *IYB* (1963), p. 222.
45 *IYB* (1964), p. 196.
46 Service national de la statistique, *Bulletin de Statistique: 1er Semestre 1974* (Vientiane: Kingdom of Laos, 1975), p. 13.
47 UNESCO, *International Yearbook of Education, Vol. XXII 1960* (Paris: UNESCO, 1961), p. 255.
48 *IYB* (1964), p. 196.
49 *Nathiphonlamuang* [Duties of a Citizen] (n.p., Kingdom of Laos, 1960).
50 Thao Nhouy Abhay, *Khamnamkhongkasouangsuksathikan* [Forward of the Ministry of Education], in *Duties of a Citizen*, p. i.
51 *Duties of a Citizen*, p. 71.
52 Ibid.
53 See Christopher Kremmer, *Bamboo Palace: Discovering the Lost Dynasty of Laos* (London: Flamingo, 2003).
54 Ian Baird, 'Secrecy, falsification and information management control: the party and state of the Lao People's Democratic Republic', *Journal of Contemporary Asia*, 48:5 (2018): 739–60.
55 Khamphoui Sisavady, 3 January 2018. Text in author's possession.

CHAPTER ELEVEN

Indonesia: sultans and the state
Jean Gelman Taylor

This volume's title, *Monarchies and Decolonisation in Asia*, appears to suggest a linear progression in the histories of colonies. Yet monarchies existed in Asia prior to colonial rule, and in many places they continued to exist under colonialism. Decolonisation in Indonesia, for instance, has proved to be a rejection of both indigenous and colonial forms of rule. The colony known as the Netherlands East Indies ended up as the Republic of Indonesia in 1945,[1] and yet it is worth noting that the larger, colonial-era political organisations of the 1930s favoured monarchy or ethnic particularity. Parties of secular nationalists who were committed to establishing a republic then had the fewest members.

We should contemplate other paths not taken. The wartime occupiers of the Dutch colony, the Japanese, promoted a different model: a sacred emperor at the pinnacle of government, military executors and a network of organisations mobilising all social classes to contribute resources (oil, rubber, rice, labourers) for Japan's warfare against the West. Java, considered by the Japanese to have the most advanced level of culture in the archipelago, was to become a member of a new transnational community, the Greater East Asia Co-Prosperity Sphere, guided by Japan.

Another model was that of the Islamic state. Islamic states of Indonesia were proclaimed in West Java (1948), in South Sulawesi (1951) and in Aceh (1953). During Indonesia's struggle to prevent the re-establishment of the Netherlands East Indies (1945–49), Islamic paramilitaries fought against troops of the republican National Armed Forces of Indonesia more than they did against the Dutch.

Royal legacies in Indonesia today suggest nostalgia for older traditions. Indonesians still pay deference to people of aristocratic background. They may dress up as royals on their wedding day, honour royal appurtenances such as carriages in museums, or take part in

INDONESIA: SULTANS AND THE STATE

staged festivals featuring descendants of former royal families. But the only serious alternative in Indonesia's modern history to a republican form of government based on popular participation has been Indonesia's military, which backed two presidents who had pretensions to be 'president for life', Sukarno and Suharto.

The first men who proclaimed themselves kings in the Indonesian archipelago early in the Common Era assumed titles and epithets we associate with Hindu and Buddhist states in mainland Asia. Between the twelfth and seventeenth centuries, with the spread of Islam, kings across the Indonesian archipelago were adding to their titles the Islamic designation of 'sultan'. The type of monarchy in polities across the archipelago tells us about conceptions of power and the state, sources of law, and the ruling elite's international orientations and links (Figure 11.1). A new model of rule, that of caliphate, has been espoused in contemporary Indonesia by influential organisations such as (the now banned) Jemaah Islamiyah and Hizbut Tahrir. Historically, caliphs throughout the Islamic world have transformed into hereditary dynastic rulers. Islamic monarchies, such as those of Saudi Arabia and Brunei, continue today.

Figure 11.1 Paku Buwono X of Surakarta in Royal Netherlands Indies Army uniform, c. 1903

It is difficult to gauge popular opinion. Royals who maintained their prerogatives in the Netherlands Indies and the aristocrats who administered colonial rule at district level maintained that the people loved them, and therefore Dutch rule was impossible to implement without their support. In independent Indonesia, opinion polling was banned by Presidents Sukarno and Suharto (in office 1945–65, 1966–98 respectively). If violence is evidence of public opinion on monarchy, we know that Wahhabi-inspired Muslims extirpated the entire Minangkabau royal family in 1815. Sumatrans massacred their sultans and members of royal families after the fall of the Japanese in 1945.

There is a curious paradox in Indonesia's history of monarchy and decolonisation. The Dutch who sailed into archipelago harbours in 1595 had just declared a republic for themselves. Over the years 1568–1648 they fought to rid themselves of Spanish kings and to seal power into the municipal hierarchies of the major merchant cities. These anti-royalists found the Indonesian archipelago full of kings. Throughout a long engagement in the archipelago's affairs, the Dutch preserved cooperative indigenous monarchies, but abolished those principalities whose kings refused to become pensionaries of the colonial state. Under Napoleonic hegemony in Europe, the Netherlands itself again came under the rule of kings. The anti-colonial nationalists, who led Indonesia to independence, pressured most of the archipelago's remaining kings to renounce their inherited prerogatives and enter a republic based on people's sovereignty and elective office. Today the Netherlands retains monarchy while its former colony is a republic.

Indigenous monarchies

Political power, historically, has been polycentric in the Indonesian archipelago. Indonesian communities began converting to Islam perhaps as early as the twelfth century, when that religion was already 700 years old. They became members of a religious culture that was developing folkways, veneration of saints and sites, legends of magical feats by holy men, and belief in the power of amulets. Archipelago kings added the titles of Sultan, Caliph and Defender of the [Muslim] Faithful to their older titles, such as Nail of the Universe. They used royal treasuries now to build mosques. They supported Muslim teachers and holy men, and the copying of Islamic texts. They sponsored students and pilgrims for travel to Mecca and study there. History writing established the founding myths of new harbour states. A wealthy stranger arrives by ship. He performs magical feats that defeat local ascetics and gurus. He marries the king's daughter and succeeds his father-in-law as king. The foreign Muslim man is knit into Indonesian histories.[2]

There was always an orientation to Mecca and Medina in these kingdoms. From the seventeenth century there are documented communities of scholars from widely scattered parts of the archipelago who made lengthy stays in Arabia.[3] They wrote commentaries on the Quran for their home communities, and issued fatwas in response to petitions from their distant kin. Archipelago kings sent envoys to a vaguely perceived 'king of Mecca' requesting permission to assume the title of Sultan. Acehnese power mongers obtained from Mecca a fatwa justifying deposing their female ruler, Sultanah Kamalat Zainatuddin Syah, in 1699.[4] Banten's Sultan Ageng Tirtayasa (r. 1651–82) temporarily rid himself of an inconvenient rival in his son by the pious act of sending him twice on pilgrimage to Mecca.

Sultans and caliphs are understood in Islamic societies as rulers who implement and enforce Islamic law. They are not theologians. The duty of sultan and caliph is to make an observant life possible through the apparatus and power of the state. They channel the state's resources to support Islamic scholars, judges, teachers, preachers and schools. Historically, they enabled and sustained the propagation of Islam and formation of a Muslim society in the territories under their command. In Malay chronicles, sultans are invested with sanctity, supernatural powers and magically charged weapons. Against this there is another record. Across the eighteenth century, for example, there is a history in Aceh of royal rivals and powerful men who deposed reigning sultans through poisonings and assassinations.[5] Rulings from Mecca authorities are still sought and influential in Indonesia. Prior to joining the fighting between Muslims and Christians in the Moluccas, an Islamic jihadist paramilitary sought and received from religious judges in Mecca fatwas endorsing the killing of Christians and broadcast them on 6 April 2000.[6]

The colonial state had sought to bring uniformity to Islamic practice across the archipelago by establishing, in 1883, the Council of Religious Leaders to codify sharia law. Here the Dutch were putting at the disposal of their preferred Islamic influencers the backing and resources of the colonial state. Council members were encouraged and empowered to channel Islamic belief and daily practice in ways beneficial to law and order in the colony, and to endorse potentially controversial public measures, such as mass vaccination programmes. President Suharto pursued a similar policy when he established the Indonesian Islamic Scholars' Council in 1975. His expectation was that the state's favoured Islamic influencers would issue rulings sympathetic to his government's development policies, such as the birth control programmes the state enforced in Indonesia's villages. Here we see colonial state and republican government assuming the role of the Islamic ruler as upholder of (the officially endorsed) Islamic life.

Decolonising

Beginning early in the twentieth century, Indonesians formed numerous self-help, sporting, professional, debating and religious organisations within colonial civil society. These operated alongside Dutch-led groups that supported the arts and social causes such as juvenile welfare and female suffrage for metropole and colony. Some groups (for instance, Ambon Youth) championed regional and ethnic identities. Others identified by religion, for example, the Islamic Union and the Political Association of Javanese Catholics. From the 1920s, political study clubs and associations announced new aspirations in their names and goals. Sukarno's Indonesian Nationalist Party had an archipelago-wide vision: an independent state that would encompass all the islands and communities that had been united within the Dutch colony.[7] These parties came under increasing police surveillance and restriction in the 1930s.

Dutch authorities had their own countervailing social policy, conceived as 'uplift' of the masses from poverty, ignorance and the 'despotism' of their sultans and rajas. This Ethical Policy, formulated at the beginning of the twentieth century, envisaged a long period of colonial tutelage to develop a civic life in which religion was separated from politics. Ultimately, there would emerge an indigenous population Western in outlook and habits, fit for self-governance as a province within a Netherlands Union.

Japan's armed forces brought sudden defeat of colonial defences in 1942 and a complete reorganisation of the Dutch colonial state. Until the Pacific War, the Dutch colony had been administered from Batavia as a single state under civilian rule with a small army and police force, and an emphasis on 'order and stability'. The Japanese dismembered the colony and created three distinct territories, each with its own capital and military or naval commands.[8] In place of one cross-archipelago state linked to Holland there were now three regions sealed off from each other, linked individually through their army and navy commanders to Japan. Evidence of the Dutch was systematically obliterated throughout the archipelago.

The Japanese disbanded all Indonesian political associations that had championed independence. Indonesians were ordered to defer their aspirations for self-rule within the Co-Prosperity Sphere until Japan's war aims had been accomplished. Indigenous political leaders who offered their services to the Japanese military administration on Java were deputed to head the new mass organisations the Japanese established to raise hatred of Western rule and harness local resources and labour for Japan's imperial forces. On Java, the Japanese appointed anti-colonial activists such as Sukarno and Mohammad Hatta to be deputy heads of Putera[9] and of Jawa Hokokai (Java Service Organisation). These organisations drafted Indonesian labourers into a vast, unpaid workforce at home, in Japanese-occupied states on mainland Southeast Asia and in Japan itself. As in any colony, locals made Japan's Indonesia function. Indonesians continued to staff most government offices for the Japanese, some at higher levels than previously under the Dutch colonial administration.

Japanese rule proved a complex problem for Muslim Indonesians. For many, the Japanese ideology of dedication and sacrifice to a sacred emperor in Tokyo conflicted with their world-view that conceived of Mecca as the sacred centre and the Prophet Muhammad as the standard for society's beliefs and behaviour. They resisted pressure from Japanese officers to rid the archipelago of foreign languages, because that meant Arabic, the language of Islam, as well as Dutch and English. They did not welcome the Indonesian-language Quran that the Japanese had commissioned and which was published in 1944.[10] Village religious heads on Java were more enthusiastic in their support for the Japanese. They received trips to Jakarta for month-long training programmes where they endorsed the anti-Dutch, anti-Christian sentiments of their trainers. They welcomed the Japanese decision to form the Army of Allah (Hizbullah) in December 1944.

As victories over Japanese forces were bringing Allied armies closer to the Indonesian archipelago and to Japan itself, Japan's wartime planners accelerated a two-pronged defence strategy in the archipelago. First was the formation and training of indigenous militias. These were to provide the first line of defence, obstructing the anticipated landing of Allied forces, in order to give the Japanese military time to fall back and consolidate. The second tactic was to establish an 'independent' government on Java that would make it impossible for the Dutch to resume administration of their former colony.

In March 1945, Japan's 16th Army Command on Java announced its intention to form the Investigating Committee for Preparatory Work of the Independence of Indonesia.[11] The BPUPKI was to consider and recommend models for an independent state, from which Emperor Hirohito would make his choice. Subsequently, a committee would be established to prepare for the transfer of independence from Japan to an Indonesian administration. The military command named the committee's Japanese and Indonesian members on 29 April. It met in two sessions, 29 May–1 June and 10–17 July 1945.

Islamic state or republic?

During the last thirty years of Dutch colonial rule, Indonesians from a broad range of classes and loyalties – Muslim, Christian, ethnic, nationalist, socialist – had been debating what kind of society should succeed Dutch colonial rule. Now, in conditions of military occupation by Japan and under the supervision of seven Japanese military officers, they had the historic opportunity to review their past, their present and future, to reconcile competing visions, to see if one state really could contain and satisfy the great diversity of peoples, ethnic groups, language communities and religions in the archipelago. Inevitably, the BPUPKI's discussions revolved around two issues that would define the character of the new state: the relationship of government to Islam and the country's territorial reach.

Before setting out the points of contention and eventual compromises, it is worth noting whom Lieutenant General Nagano Yuchiro had selected to debate these large questions. Of necessity, the Indonesian members of the BPUPKI had to be readily available. In view of the dismemberment of the Netherlands Indies and wartime travel restrictions, members could only be drawn from residents of Jakarta, the former Dutch capital and now headquarters of the Japanese military command.[12] Japanese policymakers revised their initial strategy of fostering an Asian Islam and installing an Islamic leadership in Java. Now they sought to influence deliberations by appointing people who saw themselves primarily as nationalists. Those selected were pre-war party activists who had chosen to work for and with the Japanese military occupation. None had been active in the colony's pre-war anti-fascist parties. Such men spent the Japanese occupation in hiding or in gaol.

The Indonesian members came from the privileged classes of the colony. They were medical doctors, lawyers, journalists, educators and party activists. All spoke Dutch. Three of the sixty-two were women. One had obtained her law degree from Leiden University in the Netherlands.[13] The other two female members had held public roles as municipal councillors in the multi-ethnic city administrations set up by the Dutch in Batavia, Semarang and Surabaya. The committee could be said, therefore, to represent the approximately 250,000 indigenous inhabitants of the archipelago who were graduates of Dutch-language schools and followed a Western lifestyle.

Only seven of the committee members were graduates of Islamic colleges. This minority faction of the BPUPKI wanted to give a specifically Islamic character to an independent Indonesia, and could be said to represent rather the millions of Indonesians who identified primarily as Muslim and who had responded to the Islamic parties, such as Sarekat Islam, Nahdlatul Ulama and Muhammadiyah.[14]

In its first session, the Investigating Committee functioned as a forum for debating competing models of governance from a variety of world systems. The Japanese offered their imperial model. In occupied Mongolia and Vietnam they had established sub-emperors. Six of the committee's Indonesian delegates favoured drawing on the royal traditions of Java for a sub-emperor, but they could not agree among themselves which of the royal houses on Java should take the throne.

The majority of the Investigating Committee rejected indigenous royalty as the source of authority, traditions, legitimacy and identity for the new state. They argued that Indonesians of other ethnic groups would never accept a Javanese king as their head. The bulk of discussion centred on what commonality could bind Indonesians from the archipelago's many islands, regions and ethnic groups together. The committee's Islamic group argued that the commonality was Islam. Since most Indonesians adhered to Islam, the new state should be based on its teachings and headed by a president who was Muslim. Only a Muslim president could preside over an Islamic state and oversee the state organs that enforced sharia law. As head of an Islamic state he would appoint religious judges to ensure that all legislation passed by elected assemblies conformed to Islamic principles.

Sukarno's group countered that what united all Indonesians was the common experience of colonial rule. Therefore nationalism, not religion, was the ingredient that would bind all the archipelago's peoples together. The Dutch-educated lawyers in Sukarno's group drew on their European legal training in arguing for separation of religion and state. Supomo maintained that all former colonial subjects should be equal. Indonesia's constitution must, therefore, guarantee freedom of religion for all. The state would be founded on moral values common to all its religions and on devotion to country. Maria Ulfah Santoso proposed a bill of rights that would define and guarantee the liberties of every citizen.

Sukarno argued that citizenship in a nation-state was sufficient protection for everyone. His personal experience in pre-war politics and as head of the Japanese-created mass political party Putera inclined him to conceive of the nation as an organic whole. Politics should not be an arena where competing rights of individuals were defended, but a process of reaching 'consensus'. He said the true Indonesian heritage was not in monarchy, but in the villages of Indonesia, which he imagined as little republics based on mutual cooperation and self-help. He rejected the Islamists' demand that the president be Muslim. The state must be nationalist, not theocratic, and therefore the constitution should stipulate that the president be *asli* (indigenous), meaning, in this context, not of Chinese or Dutch ancestry. In a speech, delivered on 1 June 1945, famous to Indonesians as the *Panca Sila* (Five Pillars [of the State]), Sukarno set out the fundamentals on which all the archipelago's inhabitants should be able to agree. These were: nationalism, humanitarianism, government by consent, social justice and belief in One God.[15]

During the recess in the committee's deliberations a group of nine worked on the draft of a constitution to be presented to the full BPUPKI in the second round of discussions. Members of this working group represented both sides of the debate. Four were leaders of Islamic organisations that supported a state based on Islam. Four of the men identified with the nationalists' cause were Muslim and one was Christian. This group produced a preamble to the constitution that incorporated Sukarno's five broad principles, but acknowledged the peculiar concerns of Muslims in stating that:

> Indonesia's national independence shall be laid down in a Constitution of the State of Indonesia with sovereignty of the people and based on: the belief in the One and Only God, *with the obligation to abide by Islamic law for adherents of Islam* [my italics]; on just and civilised humanity; on the unity of Indonesia; and on democratic rule that is guided by the strength of wisdom resulting from deliberation/representation, so as to realise social justice for all the people of Indonesia.[16]

The clause in the preamble stipulating observance of Islamic law by the Muslim citizens of Indonesia was deliberately opaque. The original Indonesian-language text is: *dengan kewajiban menjalankan syariat Islam bagi pemuluk-pemuluknya*. The clause does not clarify if the Indonesian state, as successor to the archipelago's sultanates, was to flow back into historical channels and assume the role of enabler and enforcer of observant Muslim life. Did the clause instead mean that the government of an independent Indonesia considered obedience to sharia law to be a matter of individual conscience and self-regulation? This ambiguous clause has become known as the Seven Words of the Jakarta Charter.[17]

Numerous objections to the Charter were aired in the second round of discussions. The Islamist group argued that a constitutional guarantee of freedom of religion implied freedom for Muslims to convert to other religions (which is punishable by death under sharia law). Equality of citizenship between Muslims and non-Muslims could result in a non-Muslim taking office as president and interfering in the observance of Islamic law. Furthermore, the Islamic group argued that a state pledged to uphold all religions equally would effectively discriminate against Muslims. Nationalists countered that, without freedom of religion, people would be forced by the state to pray. Non-Muslim citizens would have second-class status in the new country, while many ethnic groups would have to give up their own communal inheritance of traditional beliefs and customs.

To bring debate to a close and present conclusions to the Japanese committee members, Sukarno compromised. He had moved 'Belief in One God' to the position of first principle (from fifth). He now argued that the Muslim majority could use their numbers to vote for legislation that accorded with their convictions after Indonesia had achieved independence. On 12 August the Japanese authorised proclamation of an independent Indonesian state to be made in September that year. They transformed the committee from an investigative body to one authorised to prepare for Japanese-sponsored independence, and appointed Sukarno as its head. They flew Sukarno and Hatta to meet senior officers of the Japanese Southern Command headquarters in Saigon that same day for discussions on the new state.

Outside forces upset this timetable of transition. On 15 August 1945, Japan surrendered to the Allies. Tokyo did not announce its defeat to Japanese forces stationed in the Indonesian archipelago or to members of the Committee now preparing for independence itself. On 16 August a nationalist youth group, better informed than the Preparatory Committee, kidnapped Sukarno and Hatta to compel them to declare independence immediately. They convinced the two that an independent state would be tainted, in the eyes of the Allies, if it were perceived as the gift of Japan. Allied forces should remove the Japanese military from a sovereign country, not from a puppet state. The Allies should find a functioning government, so there could be no question of restoring Indonesia to the Dutch. As a result, on 17 August 1945 in Jakarta, Sukarno proclaimed the Republic of Indonesia. The proclamation made no reference to the grave differences within the committee on the path Indonesia would follow. The text Sukarno read out, in the presence of supporters and Japanese military officers, was:

> We the people of Indonesia hereby declare our independence. Matters concerning the transfer of power, etc., will be attended to in an orderly fashion and as speedily as possible. In the name of the People of Indonesia. Sukarno and Hatta.[18]

On 18 August the Preparatory Committee adopted the constitution minus the Seven Words, appointed Sukarno as president and Hatta as vice president, and transformed itself into the Central National Committee to serve as an interim parliament until elections could be held. In anticipation of the arrival of Allied forces, Hatta had persuaded the Islamic group to consent to dropping the clause 'with the obligation to abide by Islamic law for adherents of Islam'. In these new circumstances, he argued, it was imperative that Indonesian national unity should hold. East Indonesian Christians must be kept within the nation-state, not fearing Muslim rule. And there was another factor. The Indonesian government must present an acceptable, Western face to the Allies. They held the power to accept the new Indonesian state or to sweep it away so Dutch forces could retake administration of the archipelago.

Indonesia, therefore, began as a republic without resolving the status of Islam in the new country. Sukarno's expectation that Muslim concerns would be settled by national elections was not realised. Those elections were not held until 1955, when the Islamic parties received only 25 per cent of the ballots cast. The controversial Seven Words have been reviewed numerous times since in sessions of the Constitutional Assembly and in debates in the People's Representative Assembly.[19] For many Muslim leaders and their followers, resolving the place of Islam in the state is unfinished business that continues to be a source of grievance.

The Central National Committee also addressed the boundaries of the new country that had just come into being. It voted for a state that would incorporate the Malay-Muslim world of Southeast Asia (Indonesia, Brunei, Malaya, and the Muslim regions of Thailand and the Philippines) and leave West New Guinea to the Dutch. It may be noted that Indonesians who today support establishment of a caliphate in Southeast Asia, as a first step towards realisation of a global caliphate, envision it as occupying the same territory that Indonesia's Central National Committee had opted for on 18 August 1945.

Sukarno always maintained that Indonesia was the territory of the former Netherlands Indies. By 1914 the colonial state had reached its greatest extent, stretching from northern Sumatra to West New Guinea. It was the consolidation of an archipelago state accomplished by negotiation, conquest, steamship, rail and radio connections, and by archipelago-wide institutions. Sukarno's consciousness of the colonial state was fostered in his schooldays as a pupil in the colony's Dutch-language school system. His Indonesia was to be, in the words of his campaign slogan, 'From Sabang to Merauke'.[20]

Sultans and the state

Some 340 principalities were incorporated in the colonial state at its apogee. Their rulers were signatories to contracts with the Dutch, recipients of subsidies, acknowledged by the colonial state as first within their principalities. Many of these principalities were located in the outlying fringes of the colony. Rulers, whether sultans, rajas or men using titles such as *panembahan* and *pangeran ratu*,[21] had an ethnic identity with their subjects, an historical identity with their geographical place, and a public identification with the Dutch. The early years of independence were not friendly to what was widely castigated as 'feudalism'. Under pressure from Jakarta, the principalities were dismantled in the late 1950s and early 1960s, and their lands redistributed through the Basic Agrarian Law of 1960.[22]

Only two sultanates survived. These were Surakarta and Yogyakarta, heirs to the ancient Islamic kingdom of Mataram. They were symbols, centres and patrons of Javanese Islamic culture. Surakarta's rulers had sided with the Dutch. The Jakarta government reduced its territory to the royal compound. Yogyakarta's Hamengku Buwono IX (r. 1940–88) chose Sukarno's republicans. He offered his domain as the Republic's capital when Dutch forces took control of Jakarta late in 1945. In acknowledgement, Indonesia's central government recognised the sultanate as an autonomous, self-governing territory under its hereditary sultans within the Republic. Hamengku Buwono IX held important public offices in the new Indonesia. Today the state acquiesces that Yogyakarta's sultan also holds the position of governor of the autonomous territory by hereditary right.

Between 1946 and 1949 the returning Dutch administration had set up 'independent states' within the archipelago based on ethnic 'homelands'. Sukarno's government pressured all these states to dissolve too. By August 1950 Indonesia was a unitary state within the framework of the 1945 constitution. Sukarno's government crushed breakaway movements in the Moluccas (1946) and in Sumatra (1957), and defeated the militaries of the rebel Islamic states. Suharto's armed forces and their associated civilian paramilitaries killed Indonesians identified as communists and destroyed communism as an alternative model for government in 1965–66. Both presidents decreed that all citizens must embrace one of the religions recognised and protected by the state: Islam, Roman Catholic or Protestant Christianity, Hinduism and Buddhism.

Only one breakaway movement temporarily flirted with restoring a sultanate. This was the Free Aceh Movement proclaimed in December 1976 by Hasan di Tiro (1925–2010). In his reading of history, Aceh was still a colonial state because the Javanese, as successors to the Dutch, now colonised Aceh's peoples and resources. The Dutch had abolished Aceh's 400-year-old sultanate in 1903, but di Tiro claimed that its last sultan had passed the mandate to rule to di Tiro's maternal great-grandfather and thereby to himself. He would re-establish Aceh as an independent state whose constitution would be the Quran. The Indonesian government ultimately reached a cessation of hostilities with the Free Aceh Movement in 2005 and withdrew its troops after a decades-long, violent occupation. Aceh remains a special province within the Republic and its administrative bureaucracy, but with Jakarta according jurisdiction over matters involving family, property, banking, public schools, personal behaviours and 'deviant' Islamic teaching to sharia courts of religious judges, and not to sultans.

In the early years of the twenty-first century, some descendants of the archipelago's numerous sultanates have resumed royal titles. They have revived or reinvented the appearance and claims of sultanates within the Republic of Indonesia. These sultanates are mainly a phenomenon of the western and eastern fringes of the archipelago.[23] None challenge the unitary state. The re-emerging of sultans is to be understood, rather, in its Indonesian context. It coincides with the greater administrative autonomy allowed the provinces since the downfall of President Suharto in 1998 and the enactment of Indonesia's Decentralisation Law of 1999.

Revivalism of sultanates is not a response to Islamic movements within Indonesia or globally. Sultans of Landak, Mempawah and Bacan, for example, have not sponsored public proclamations of loyalty to Islamic State and the late Abu Bakar al-Baghdadi. They do not call for the creation of a universal caliphate. Nor are the men who have reclaimed the Islamic title of their forebears assuming, in the narrow context of their historical inheritance, the role of enforcer and implementer of Islamic law. Rather, they present themselves as bearers of their region's history and tradition, of ethnic identity, and preservers of their community's culture. Against 'outsiders' (migrants from other parts of Indonesia or large corporations) they assert guardianship rights to the natural resources of their ancestral territories.

Many of the men resuming royal titles simultaneously serve in Indonesia's provincial governments. Royal titles lend distinction to their efforts in preserving their communities' rituals, textiles and arts. They sponsor festivals in which they and their extended family members parade in royal costume. All these activities have led to their being dubbed 'weekend' sultans.[24]

INDONESIA: SULTANS AND THE STATE

Figure 11.2 President Joko Widodo receives eighty-eight rajas and sultans from across the archipelago at the presidential palace in Bogor, 4 January 2018

The new royals have developed networks with other rajas and sultans across Indonesia under the aegis of the current sultan of Yogyakarta, Hamengku Buwono XII, to promote their interests (Figure 11.2). Jakarta views their activities as stimulating tourism and regional economic development. In anticipation of the Fifth Gathering of Kings and Sultans to be held in Jakarta on 27–28 July 2017, Hari Untoro Drajat of the Ministry of Tourism said:

> We are fortunate to have had so many kingdoms and sultanates in Indonesia that have generated valuable indigenous wisdom and outstanding cultures. These are what we aim to preserve ... Aside from being an authentic identity of the nation, these traditional cultures also play an important role as valuable attractions for tourists from all over the world to visit and observe.[25]

The history of monarchy in the Indonesian archipelago is a history of a polycentric past. Sultanates and rajadoms, large and small, characterise a past of fractured and competing power centres in a vast archipelago. It is a history of disunity. Decolonisation swept away indigenous monarchy, privilege and particularism, as well as foreign rule. Royal legacies today are manifest in pride in Indonesia's unique cultural diversity. The Republic of Indonesia stands for a single state, its borders overlaying the borders of the Netherlands East Indies of 1942. The legacy of colonialism is one state, not many. Indonesia's citizens largely embrace that territorial unity. As heir to the Netherlands East Indies (and not Japan), the central government opts for containment of religious difference and preservation of the nation-state. The majority of Muslim voters in Indonesia's national elections since 1955 have not yet authorised their government to take on the sultans' historic duty of enabling and enforcing Islamic law.

Notes

1 Sukarno declared Indonesia's independence on 17 August 1945. The Dutch formally transferred sovereignty on 27 December 1949 following four years of armed struggle and diplomatic negotiations.
2 Russell Jones, 'Ten conversion myths from Indonesia', in Nehemia Levztion (ed.), *Conversion to Islam* (New York: Holmes and Meier, 1979), pp. 129–58.
3 Azyumardi Azra, *The Origins of Islamic Reformism in Southeast Asia* (Crows Nest, NSW and Honolulu: Allen & Unwin and University of Hawai'i Press, 2004).
4 The fatwa was issued by Kadhi Maliku'l Adil. Sher Banu A. Latif Khan, 'Rule behind the Silk Curtain: the Sultanahs of Aceh 1641–1699', PhD dissertation, University of London, 2009, p. 14.
5 Lee Kam Hing's list of sultans in eighteenth-century Aceh shows that some occupied the throne for a few days only. Appendix, *The Sultanate of Aceh; Relations with the British 1760–1824* (Kuala Lumpur: Oxford University Press, 1995).
6 Nico J.G. Kaptein, 'The voice of the ulama: fatwas and religious authority in Indonesia', *Archives de sciences sociales des religions*, 125 (January–March 2004), 126.
7 Chinese Indonesians also founded self-help societies. In 1932, those promoting integration established the Party of Chinese Indonesians (Partai Tionghoa Indonesia).
8 Sumatra was under Japan's Twenty-Fifth Army, Java under the Sixteenth; Kalimantan, Sulawesi and the eastern islands were under command of the Navy. Early Japanese plans had envisaged joining Sumatra with Singapore to form a new state, Syonan-to, 'Light of the South'. The areas under naval command were to remain permanent possessions of Japan.
9 Putera was the acronym for Putera Tenaga Rakyat (Centre of People Power).
10 Some Qurans had been published with interlinear translation in Indonesian. The objection to this 1944 Quran was that the text was in Indonesian alone.
11 It was known by the initials of its Indonesian name, BPUPKI (Badan Penyelidik Usaha Persiapan Kemerdekaan Indonesia).
12 In changing the city's name from Batavia to Jakarta, the Japanese revived memory of the sultanate of Jayakerta, conquered by Dutch forces in 1619.
13 She was Maria Ulfah Santoso. By the end of Dutch colonial rule some 350 Indonesians had earned degrees at Dutch universities.
14 The 1930 Census recorded the population of the Netherlands Indies as 60.7 million. Indonesia's population today is 268 million. On pre-1940 secular and religious organisations, see M. C. Ricklefs, *A History of Modern Indonesia since c. 1200* (Basingstoke: Palgrave Macmillan, 2008, 4th edn), Part IV.
15 *Panca Sila* alluded to Indonesia's complex heritage. The words were Sanskrit, while the five principles paralleled the five pillars of Islamic belief. Under President Suharto *Panca Sila* was transformed from motherhood statements into the state's ideology through complex elaboration, training programmes, and compulsory study in schools, universities and public agencies. In 1983 Suharto declared that all organisations in Indonesia, secular and religious, must adopt *Panca Sila* as their sole ideological foundation.
16 An English translation of Sukarno's *Panca Sila* speech is in Herbert Feith and Lance Castles (eds), *Indonesian Political Thinking* (Ithaca, NY: Cornell University Press, 1970), pp. 40–9.
17 R. E. Elson, 'Another look at the Jakarta Charter Controversy of 1945', *Indonesia*, 88 (October 2009), 105–30.
18 The handwritten draft is kept in Indonesia's National Monument in Independence Square in Jakarta. It may be viewed on many websites, including https://spiceis landsblog.com/2017/08/17/the-indonesian-proclamation-of-independence/.
19 Ridho al-Hamdi, 'The Jakarta Charter in post-Soeharto Indonesia: political thoughts of the elites in Muhammadiyah', *Jurnal Masyarakat Indonesia*, 41 (2015), 43–56.

20 Sabang lies off the northern tip of Sumatra. Merauke was the Dutch administrative town situated at the border with East Papua. Indonesia's resolve to retain the western province of New Guinea within the state is knit into the history of its movement for independence as a nationalist, rather than an Islamic, state.
21 *Panembahan* literally means 'one who is worshipped'. *Pangeran* means 'prince'.
22 Articles 1 and 2 of the Basic Agrarian Law state that the government controls Indonesia's earth, water and airspace and their natural resources on behalf of the nation, and determines legal relationships between people and resources for the nation's prosperity.
23 See Table 7.1, 'Recently revived principalities in Indonesia', in Gerry van Klinken, 'Return of the sultans: the communitarian turn in local politics', in Jamie S. Davidson and David Henley (eds), *The Revival of Tradition in Indonesian Politics* (New York: Routledge, 2007), pp. 149–69.
24 Van Klinken, 'Return of the sultans', p. 149.
25 See www.indonesia.travel/au/en/event-festivals/the-5th-gathering-of-kings-and-sultans-in-the-indonesian-archipelago-held-in-jakarta, with accompanying photographs from the 2016 gathering.

CHAPTER TWELVE

Defending the Sultanate's territory: Yogyakarta during the Indonesian decolonisation, 1942–50

Bayu Dardias Kurniadi

This chapter discusses the only surviving monarchy in Indonesia during the 1942–50 period of decolonisation. It explains how the Yogyakarta[1] Sultanate survived by consolidating authority over its traditional land through the formation of a Special Region in the Republic of Indonesia in 1950, while other sultanates failed to resist anti-monarchy movements that led to their overthrow. It discusses two crucial periods: the Japanese occupation (1942–45) and the revolutionary period (1945–50). During these periods, almost all traditional dynastic houses were targeted by anti-monarchy movements as they were seen by educated urban Indonesians as 'overprivileged servants of the colonial regime'[2] who 'had little sympathy for the Republic, given the intensely anti-aristocratic views of the radical movement'.[3] In many parts of Indonesia, sultans and rajas were kidnapped, exiled or murdered, and their palaces looted and burned; other monarchies were simply disestablished.[4] In eastern Sumatra, for instance, out of thirty-four native states, only twenty-five survived by the early 1950s, and within Indonesia as a whole all but Yogyakarta had perished by 1959.

Unlike monarchies in most other Southeast Asian countries, where a single ruler controlled most of the area that later became a nation-state, the East Indies archipelago was marked by hundreds of small, disintegrated and institutionally low-level sultanates or kingships, which some scholars refers to as 'aristocracies'. The Dutch conquered and imposed agreements on these monarchies, requiring them to accept Dutch sovereignty. In many cases, they instituted a system of indirect rule under which sultans and rajas retained some of their privileges within the colonial structure. In many regions of the East Indies, the leaders of royal houses maintained their status as divine rulers to enhance their legitimacy and encourage docility among subjects, as is revealed in the royal titles. For instance, the Yogyakarta sultan bears the title of *Hamengkubuwono senopati in ngaloga sayidin panatagama Kalifatullah*, meaning 'He who holds the universe in his lap, leader in the battlefield, leader of the religion, representative of Allah on the earth'.

In the late 1930s, the Dutch had offered long contractual agreements to only 14 or 16 of the 282 principalities in the archipelago, including four principalities in Java – Kasultanan (Yogyakarta), Kasunanan (Surakarta), Pakualaman and Mangkunegaran – that institutionalised these monarchies.[5] The Sultanate of Yogyakarta and the Kasunanan of Surakarta were the most institutionalised of all, and the Dutch placed two Residents to oversee Yogyakarta and Surakarta. In 1942, the Yogyakarta region consisted of two ruling dynasties: the major Sultanate of Yogyakarta (led by Sultan Hamengku Buwono IX) and the minor Pakualaman Principality (led by Pakualam VIII). The palace compound of the Yogyakarta sultan encompassed 140 hectares, with thirty-nine buildings divided into seven sections; 10,000 royal servants worked daily for the sultan. The territory of the sultanate comprised around 3,000 square kilometres, with a population of approximately two million people. The Pakualaman Principality, which had previously been part of the Yogyakarta Sultanate and was completely surrounded by it, had a small palace and controlled around 180 square kilometres.

At the end of the colonial period, the Sultan of Yogyakarta was Hamengku Buwono IX (Figure 12.1). The many scholars who have written about Sultan Hamengku Buwono IX's role during decolonisation and the struggle for Indonesian independence can be placed in three main groups. The first consider Yogyakarta as the main battleground against the Dutch return to Indonesia following the Second World War, especially when Yogyakarta became the temporary capital of Indonesia.[6] Yogyakarta gave refuge to republican leaders and, when Jakarta was hostile towards them, the sultan offered his territory to host and finance the republic that had been declared in 1945. Only with the support of the Yogyakarta population was the transfer of authority from the Dutch colonial administrators to the Indonesian government finally achieved in 1949. The second group of historians focuses on the personal heroism of the sultan, his democratic role during decolonisation and his firm stance in supporting the fledgling republic.[7] The sultan acted decisively in support of the republic and refused a Dutch offer that would have made him ruler of all of the large island of Java.[8] Rather, he stood shoulder to shoulder with the nationalists in challenging the return of the Dutch after 1945. The third group compares the Yogyakarta sultanate to the neighbouring and then more powerful Surakarta royal houses (Kasunanan Surakarta and Mangkunegaran Principality; the latter – in a position similar to that of Pakualaman

Figure 12.1 Sultan Hamengku Buwono IX of Yogyakarta

and Yogyakarta – is surrounded by Surakarta). Even though both the Yogyakarta region and the Surakarta region received special status in the new republic in 1945, Surakarta lost that position in 1946, mostly because of its leaders' lack of support for the republicans.[9]

Building on the work of previous scholars, in this chapter I offer a different approach to understanding Sultan Hamengku Buwono IX's role during the Indonesian struggle for independence. I argue, first, that the sultan's priority was to defend his traditional territory and ultimately his ascribed status as sultan and political status as governor. The ultimate goal of the sultan's eclectic political movement was to safeguard his territory through the creation of a 'Special Region' within the republic, where he retained executive leadership in the newly formed province. Moreover, from 1942, both royal leaders, Sultan Hamengku Buwono IX and Pakualam VIII, cooperated to face the Japanese occupation. Second, the early period of independence was marked by the transition from traditional to modern administrative leaders. During this period, the survival of Yogyakarta's monarchies lay in the sultan's brave decision to support the new republic and to adopt progressive changes in his sultanate. These decisions further increased his traditional legitimacy and, therefore, Yogyakarta survived the anti-monarchy and leftist movement[10] which sought to end the rule of the royal dynasties. Third, the Sultan of Yogyakarta displayed a combination of traditional charisma and administrative and political skills that enabled him to appear as a national leader.

This chapter is structured chronologically, beginning with the inauguration of the new Sultan of Yogyakarta in 1939. While recognising the central role of the sultan, I explain the strategies used by the leaders of the Yogyakarta dynasties to defend their land, including moving the Indonesian capital from Jakarta to Yogyakarta from 1946 to 1949. The chapter then explores how the national positions held by the Sultan of Yogyakarta as Minister of Defence and as an Indonesian representative during the transfer of authority in 1949 increased his political bargaining power in defending the territory, leading to the creation of the Yogyakarta Special Region as a province, with Sultan Hamengku Buwono IX appointed as governor and Pakualam VIII as vice-governor for life in 1950. The chapter concludes with the successful formation of the Yogyakarta Special Region amid the general disestablishment of sultans and rajas in Indonesian local politics during the 1950s.

The Japanese occupation, 1942–45

Japanese forces occupied the Netherlands East Indies, displacing the Dutch, from 1942 to 1945. The Sultan of Yogyakarta and the ruler of

Pakualaman used the Japanese occupation of Indonesia to strengthen their legitimacy by implementing reforms that would prove useful during the formation of the Yogyakarta Special Region. First, Sultan Hamengku Buwono IX of Yogyakarta and Pakualam VIII sacrificed their traditional rivalry by working together on various projects. The development of the Mataram Canal (*Selokan Mataram*) not only prevented the out-migration of forced labourers (*romusha*), but also increased rice productivity in Yogyakarta. Second, the sultan initiated administrative and bureaucratic reform by simplifying the chain of command. Third, he combined traditional and administrative authority by abolishing the position of grand vizier (*pepatih dalem*). Indeed, Frank Dhont argues that the ability of Yogyakarta's principalities to survive as a Special Region was rooted in the socio-political capital the rulers invested during the Japanese occupation.[11]

Prince Dorojatun, the future sultan, had been living with a Dutch family in the Netherlands since the age of five, with the nickname *Hengkie*. He attended Dutch schools and was studying for a Bachelor of Indonesian Law and Political Study at Leiden University when his father asked him to return to Java following the outbreak of the Second World War. On 18 October 1939, in Batavia (now Jakarta), the ailing Sultan Hamengku Buwono VIII gave Prince Dorojatun the ceremonial Crown Prince's dagger *Keris Joko Piturun* as a sign that the monarch had chosen his successor. Sultan Hamengku Buwono VIII passed away shortly after he returned to Yogyakarta. The following year, aged twenty-eight, Dorojatun became Sultan Hamengku Buwono IX of Yogyakarta after signing a contractual agreement with the Dutch. The status of the Yogyakarta Sultanate was indirectly controlled by the colonial authorities, with the provision that the son of his official wife would have precedence over any son of minor wives in succession to the throne.[12] However, the contract soon became worthless as the Japanese advanced rapidly through Southeast Asia. After the Japanese conquered Singapore in February 1942, the Dutch asked the four Javanese rulers in Yogyakarta and Surakarta to 'escape' to Batavia, then withdraw to Australia. The young Sultan of Yogyakarta soon showed his independence by rejecting the offer. This was a rare case of refusal to comply, as most royal houses sided with the Dutch.

When the Japanese invaded, 278 traditional dynasties remained in the East Indies.[13] The Japanese divided the Netherlands East Indies into three regions, placed Java under the control of the 16th Army on 7 March 1942, and seeded the embryo for its Special Region status. The Japanese continued the Dutch administrative system in Java. Batavia and its surrounding area became a special municipality (*Tokubetu Si*), and the four principalities in Yogyakarta and Surakarta were divided into two governorships, or special territories (*Kooti Zimukyoku*), with their leaders summoned to Batavia to swear an oath of loyalty to Japan on 8 August 1942. The head of the *Tokubetu Si* and *Kooti Zimukyoku* were responsible directly to the *Gunseiken*, the highest administrative official in Java. As noted by Muhammed Abdul Aziz, the position of traditional rulers underwent significant changes under the Japanese administration as they fell directly under the military command.[14] In both Yogyakarta and Surakarta, the Japanese established a governorship: *Djokjakarta Gunseibu* for the Kasultanan (the Yogyakarta sultanate) and Pakualaman, and *Surakarta Gunseibu* for the Kasunanan (the Surakarta sultanate) and Mangkunegaran. This provided continuing recognition of what had been the four *Vostenlanden* (or 'princely lands') under the Dutch. Among the four Javanese rulers, the Sunan of Surakarta[15] acted as *primus inter pares*. These forced administrative arrangements later led to the creation of the Special Region of Yogyakarta and the Special Region of Surakarta[16] during the revolutionary period, during which time the rulers maintained their traditional power. As such, the Japanese occupation did not disturb the traditional authority of the rulers in controlling land, but benefited them through the establishment of sultanates as special regions.

Geographical factors helped ensure stronger cooperation between the rulers of Yogyakarta compared with their Surakarta counterparts. Pakualaman controlled around six per cent of the land within Yogyakarta, and Pakualam, despite being the older of the two men, served as deputy to the sultan. By contrast, the Mangkunegaran principality covered a larger area – 80 per cent of the total area of Surakarta – and had its own militia. Here the Mangkunegara refused to become a deputy of the Sunan, and the two leaders had a competitive relationship.[17] Kasultanan thus dominated Yogyakarta politics, while the Kasunanan and the Mangkunegaran had relatively equal power in territorial control. Dhont argues that 'the two men managed to get along, and this relationship served them well and into the era of Indonesian independence, where they maintained the top positions in the *Daerah Istimewa Yogyakarta* (Special Administrative Region of Yogyakarta)'.[18]

The cooperation between the Kasultanan and the Pakualaman can be seen in the Mataram Canal project, an implementation of the Japanese policy of prioritising food production for self-sufficiency. The Japanese saw Indonesia as 'an indispensable source of raw materials',[19] and required that 70 per cent of each crop be delivered to the Japanese military administration.[20] Sugarcane was soon replaced by rice and other food crops,[21] and the sultan argued that the only way to support the war effort was to build a canal that could optimise rice production. Even though it is difficult to obtain accurate rice production data from Yogyakarta for that period, it is interesting to look at the official Japanese statistics, which show a striking contrast in rice production between Yogyakarta and Surakarta despite their relatively similar area and population. According to the rice delivery targets for 1943, for example, Yogyakarta was only expected to deliver 12,619 tonnes of rice, less than half that of Surakarta (30,521 tonnes).[22] Thus, given that the sugar production data indicated Yogyakarta and Surakarta had similar production levels, data on rice production during the Japanese occupation might have been fabricated by Yogyakarta officials in order for rice not to be taken by the Japanese but to be kept to feed the Yogyakarta populace.

Following the sultan's suggestion, then, the major project of building the 31.2-kilometre Mataram Canal (20 kilometres in the Kasultanan territory and 12 in Pakualaman territory) was initiated. Between July 1944 and July 1945, it connected the Progo River in the west and the Opak River in the east. The project cost ƒ. 1.2 million, with ƒ. 1 million covered by the Japanese administration. Ten Japanese engineers worked on the project, which required around 358,000 workers, and was designed to prevent floods and droughts and provide irrigation for 13,000 hectares of land.[23] Averaging between 26 and 32 metres in width, the canal was crossed by thirty small bridges. A high-level sultanate official[24] claimed the Mataram Canal was the Sultan of Yogyakarta's initiative to prevent local residents from becoming *romusha* elsewhere and to reduce unemployment (which had been exacerbated by the decline of the sugar industry). Many *romusha* sent outside Java received harsh treatment, and only a few returned alive after the war ended.[25] By fabricating figures for rice production but also increasing rice productivity through the canal and preventing the recruitment of *romusha*, the sultan buttressed his legitimacy among his subjects.

A second initiative of the sultan was a series of bureaucratic and administrative reforms intended to reduce the bureaucracy and to promote modern methods of recruitment to the public service. In 1944, the sultan established a new office (*Kyokykyoku*) under his leadership to recruit persons with administrative skills, reduce layers of bureaucracy and establish more efficient government of the people of Yogyakarta. Then, on 14 July 1945, he dismissed the hereditary grand vizier, who had acted as prime minister. Soon afterwards, the sultan took over all of the grand vizier's political and administrative powers, thereby combining traditional and administrative authority as both the 'head of state' and 'head of government'. Combining power was a risky political calculation. As Benedict Anderson has argued, the Javanese sultan was perceived as divine, and thus the grand vizier acted as an intermediary actor who prevented direct contact between the sultan and his subjects, and the change was perceived as potentially reducing his legitimacy.[26] However, the sultan soon proved himself very talented in combining traditional and modern administrative authority.

Following on from these changes, the sultan closed the royal palace to Japanese officials by asking them to meet him in his new office (which was previously the grand vizier's office), which was simpler than meeting in the highly ceremonial palace setting. The sultan's office increased connections between the ruler and the people of Yogyakarta.[27] The new office also gave the sultan access to the republican cause through the progressive Indonesian National Committee of Yogyakarta (KNID-Yogyakarta), the embryo of the local government body which was to replace the Japanese Principalities Advisory Council after the war.

However, as independence approached, there was a preference among the nationalists for a republic rather than monarchy. During the first meeting of the Investigating Committee for Preparatory Work for Indonesian Independence (*Badan Penyelidik Usaha-usaha Persiapan Kemerdekaan Indonesia* – BPUPKI)[28] on 28 May 1945, the key issue concerned the formation of a future state as either a monarchy or a republic. A small group of monarchists, including two of the sultan's brothers (Prince Puruboyo and Prince Bintoro), were unable to resist the demands of the republicans. One reason was that 'no single ruler had wide recognition and acceptance' as a potential future monarch for the country.[29] However, others argued that the most important aspect of state formation was to lead the people into prosperity. Soepomo, a noted nationalist leader, for instance, argued at a discussion on 29 May 1945 that the most important point was the capacity of the head of state to lead all the people, regardless of whether the state was a republic or monarchy.[30] In the final vote on the issue, fifty-five members favoured the republican model, while only six supported a monarchy. This first blow to royal rule challenged the existence of the dynasties. It was clear that the royal houses had lost the privileges they had enjoyed during the colonial era and that the only way to defend the sultanates and other princely states was for the rulers to engage in national politics and demand special status for their regions, which would allow them to retain some of their traditional authority.

The struggle for Special Region status during the revolutionary period, 1945–49

After achieving administrative and traditional legitimacy during the Japanese occupation, the Sultan of Yogyakarta had the necessary clout to demand special status for his territory and direct responsibility to the president of an independent Indonesia. It was nevertheless clear that the republicans were apprehensive about a monarchy. Therefore, the best strategy to maintain control over his domain was to ensure that Yogyakarta obtained a special status within the Indonesian republic. The pressure of the republicans, leftists and anti-monarchy movement left the sultan no option other than to participate in national politics. The sultan showed his strong republican stance by offering Yogyakarta as the de facto capital of the nascent Indonesia. By doing so, he was becoming a national leader without leaving his people in Yogyakarta. This effort eventually resulted in the formation of the Yogyakarta Special Region.

The nationalist leaders Sukarno and Mohammad Hatta proclaimed Indonesian independence on 17 August 1945, two days after the Japanese surrendered to the Allies. The sultan decided to associate himself with the revolutionary youth as this would enable him to be included within the republican movement. The youth were the main actors in the anti-monarchy movements in almost all parts of Indonesia, including Jakarta,[31] northern Java,[32] eastern Sumatra[33] and eastern Kalimantan.[34] The sultan received youth support, first from a group calling itself 'We are the Sultanate's Youth' (Pemuda Kita Kesultanan – PEKIK)[35] on 27 September. He had earlier gathered the representatives of the youth movements in his office on 19 August, an opportunity to appraise and control the youth movements, and to confirm his legitimacy as the leader of Yogyakarta. He told the gathering:

> We have been occupied by other nations for centuries. We were repressed all that time, and now we are free. Ecstatic feelings have come to the surface. It is this ecstasy that we have to take control of. Let it soar, let it flare up. But don't let it harm anything unnecessarily. History has shown that whenever a huge and sudden change like this happens, young people always come to the fore. Therefore, I ask you to safeguard the community, in kampongs [villages], companies, stores, and others. Let there be no riots. If something happens, report to me. My deputy in liaison with you is Pangeran [Prince] Bintoro.[36]

Yogyakarta *Kooti* and Surakarta *Kooti* (the area of the four Javanese traditional authorities), however, failed to be established as part of Indonesia's regions in August 1945. When the first eight provinces (three in Java) were determined during the Indonesian Independence Preparation Committee (Panitia Persiapan Kemerdekaan Indonesia – PPKI) meeting on 19 August, the issue of *Kooti*, or special territories, was postponed, and they remained with their 'de facto' status. As such, the four Javanese royal houses were not part of the

Central Java Province. During discussions, Prince Puruboyo, the representative of Yogyakarta *Kooti*, asked for 100 per cent *zelfstandigheid* (independence/autonomy). The PPKI's leader, Sukarno, refused, because this would create a state within a state and violate the first article of the 1945 constitution. Prince Puruboyo replied that independent status would be temporary, lasting only until the government was settled. Oto Iskandardinata, a representative from West Java, proposed a middle road, giving the *Kooti* the status of special regions, to be regulated later by Presidential Decree. Prince Suryohamijoyo from Kasunanan proposed that, for the future of Surakarta, there should be two Residents as official representatives of the central government in Surakarta, dealing with Kasunanan and Mangkunegaran. These Residents should be of equal status to the governor of Central Java, as in colonial times. The discussion of the issue, however, was ended by Sukarno, and all members decided to postpone consideration of the *Kooti* problem, though it was agreed that the *Kooti* would not be part of the three provinces in Java.[37]

Postponing a resolution of the status of the *Kooti* reduced the dynasties' political space for participation in the newly established government and created uncertainty as the royal houses were not regulated in new legislation, Law No. 1/1945, on Local Government. Without a governing instrument the traditional authorities were relics of the past in a fast-changing political structure. In short, the monarchies received a double blow, having failed at the national level during the formation of the state, and at the provincial level of government, in the formation of the temporary governing body, the Indonesian National Committee (KNI).

The KNI was formed on 22 August, and the nationalists established its Yogyakarta chapter, KNID-Yogyakarta,[38] in the early weeks of independence, without prior consultation with the sultan. KNID-Yogyakarta assumed executive, legislative and judicative powers, 'to serve as the leading body, and further, to guide the people in the revolution and to defend the newly proclaimed national independence'.[39] This council had eighty-seven members representing people of a wide variety of backgrounds in Yogyakarta, and was led by a republican, Mohammad Saleh. Among those KNID-Yogyakarta members, only twelve have names reflecting high royalty status, with the sultan's brother, Prince Puruboyo, sitting on the steering committee. (In Surakarta, meanwhile, political developments eventually placed the Kasunanan and Mangkunegara under the administration of the Governor of Central Java.)[40]

These rapid political developments made the Sultan of Yogyakarta (supported by Pakualam) realise that the only way to survive in such a tumultuous period was to reclaim their domains within the republic through the status of a Special Region. To do so, the sultan combined his traditional charisma with administrative skills to maintain his leadership of Yogyakarta. On 6 September 1945, two officials from the central government in Jakarta handed over an Establishing Charter, dated 19 August, to four rulers of royal houses in Java, 'confirming the four rulers in their positions, with the understanding that they would devote all their energies to the service of the republic'.[41] On 1 September, both rulers of Surakarta acknowledged the independence of Indonesia and became part of the republic, with the proviso that they be installed as the governing powers of their territories directly responsible to the Indonesian President.

The Sultan of Yogyakarta and Pakualam acted similarly by sending a telegram to Jakarta on 6 September, containing a decree of the previous day asserting that they were part of the Indonesian Republic, with the proviso that they retained all powers and were directly responsible to the Indonesian President. The verbatim content of the four statements showed some coordination among the four dynasties. The agreements presented advantages to all parties. The republic needed allies to support its declaration of independence. Meanwhile, the traditional rulers were facing pressure from leftist uprisings, as well as nationalist and anti-monarchy movements. Siding with the republic was one step towards protecting their traditional authority and territory. On 12 October, the sultan received the support of the Mataram People's Army (Tentara Rakyat Mataram – TRM).[42] The sultan then closely intervened in the 'Yogyakarta Government' by taking over the leadership of KNID-Yogyakarta. The *Lasjkar Rakyat* (People's Militia) was formed by the sultan, Pakualam and the KNID-Yogyakarta on 26 October 1945. This ordinance establishing the militia, issued by both traditional and republican leaders, represented a sign that traditional authority was blended with modern administration, a situation hardly found in other areas of Indonesia, including Surakarta. Anderson has furthermore described *Lasjkar Rakyat* as being 'tightly linked with, indeed form[ing] a completely loyal appendage of, the administrative apparatus of the Sultanate'.[43] On 29 October, the KNID-Yogyakarta working committee was formed, its establishment once again announced by the sultan, Pakualam and Muhammad Saleh. Having received firm militia support and becoming an inseparable part of KNID-Yogyakarta, on the next day the sultan and Pakualam issued a joint statement regarding local power during the inauguration of the KNID-Yogyakarta working committee. He declared that 'all powers which were held by the former colonial regimes, in the Dutch time exercised by the Governor and his staff, in the Japanese time by the Japanese Military Government and its staff, have been wrested by the people and handed over to me'.[44] Thus, two and a half months after independence, the sultan had gained firm control over his domain in Yogyakarta as Head of the Special Region of Yogyakarta.

To firmly secure Yogyakarta's political power, the sultan needed to be involved in national politics, where he had not yet ventured. A Vice-Presidential Decree of 3 November regarding the formation of political parties meant the unelected KNID was seen as unrepresentative and unreflective of social and political structures. In the event, KNID's authority could be overturned based on election results. The sultan's involvement in KNID-Yogyakarta was thus insignificant in securing his domain and special administrative status in the near future. Sudden political changes at the national level left the sultan's aim of special status uncertain, especially after several leftist parties began to campaign and received support in Yogyakarta. On 1 November 1945, for instance, Sutan Syahrir declared the establishment of the Indonesian Socialist Party (Partai Sosialis Indonesia – PARSI) in Yogyakarta. Its initial congress, held on 12 November, saw attendees from fifty-one regions and thirty-four bodies as well as 750 observers. On 19 November, the Socialist People's Party (Partai Rakyat Sosialis – PARAS) was set up in Cirebon, and was clearly intended to oppose *ningrat* (royals) and feudal mentalities.[45] Therefore, the only way for the sultan to maintain a special status for his domain was through participation in national politics.

Controlling Yogyakarta militarily was an important step towards increasing the sultan's bargaining position and his involvement in national politics. Moreover, in a meeting held on 12 November in Yogyakarta, the Indonesian army and division commanders chose the Sultan of Yogyakarta as the Minister of Defence, and Sudirman (who was not from Yogyakarta) as the Army commander. However, in Jakarta the newly inaugurated Prime Minister, Sutan Syahrir, immediately appointed Amir Syarifuddin as Minister of Defence and Urip Sumohardjo as Army Commander, unaware of the local political situation. He then appointed the Sultan of Yogyakarta as Minister of State, with the Coordinating Function for Security. After six weeks of deadlock, both Sudirman and Syarifuddin finally agreed to recognise each other's positions.[46] In addition, both the sultan and the Sunan of Surakarta received the honorary rank of general in recognition of their traditional status.[47] Thus, during the early months after Indonesia proclaimed its independence, the sultan made firm steps towards becoming a national leader through military positions.

The sultan established further links with national leaders, including Sukarno, whom he had met briefly during the Japanese occupation, and he made Yogyakarta a centre for many nationalist groups. These moves had great significance both for the sultan and for the republic, especially after the Allied Forces for the Netherlands East Indies arrived in East Java, West Java and Sumatra on 29 September, and in Yogyakarta on 21 October. The sultan soon became Sukarno's close confidant. The new republic faced a critical situation when the Dutch advanced to Jakarta and almost assassinated Prime Minister Sutan Syahrir on 26 December 1945. On 2 January 1946, the sultan, Pakualam, and KNID-Yogyakarta offered Yogyakarta as the Indonesian capital. Two days later, Yogyakarta became the de facto capital, a situation that lasted until the transfer of authority when the Netherlands officially recognised Indonesian independence in 1949.

With Yogyakarta as the de facto capital, the sultan benefited greatly in terms of his political aspirations. First, the sultan had become a vital part of the struggle for independence, especially after the Dutch exiled Sukarno and other leaders. Second, at this critical moment, he became a national leader without needing to leave his palace and subjects in Yogyakarta. Third, he was afforded access to the national stage and was able to show his leadership and administrative skills, despite being a relative newcomer compared with other leaders (who had been involved in the nationalist movement since the 1920s).

During the period 1946–49, the sultan was one of the few republican leaders who was always in Yogyakarta. Following the Second Dutch Military Action in 1948, President Sukarno, Vice-President Hatta and other prominent leaders were captured in Yogyakarta and exiled to Sumatra and Bangka on 22 December. The Indonesian temporary government was established in Sumatra, and the Indonesian army began guerrilla warfare around Yogyakarta under Sudirman's leadership (with strong underground support from the sultan). The sultan also masterminded the 'General Attack' by nationalists on 1 March 1949, which reclaimed Yogyakarta for six hours before the Dutch restored their military control. He refused the Dutch offer to collaborate and stood firmly by his republican principles, using his status as sultan in the service of the republic.[48] On 27 December 1949, the sultan became an Indonesian representative for the transfer of sovereignty from the last High Commissioner of the Crown of the Netherlands East Indies, Antonius Lovink, in Jakarta.

The sultan's strategy bore fruit when regulations concerning Yogyakarta's status as the Indonesian capital appeared necessary. On 7 June 1947, Sukarno issued Law No. 17/1947 concerning the establishment of the City (Haminte) of Yogyakarta within the *'Daerah Istimewa Yogyakarta'* (Yogyakarta Special Region), the first mention of a new status by the Indonesian government in law. The law stipulated that land authority remained with the sultan, while the central government directly controlled other matters. The formation of the Province Yogyakarta Special Region (of which the City of Yogyakarta was a part) was finalised in 1950 with the detailing of the privileges of its rulers. First, Sultan Hamengku Buwono IX and Pakualam VIII became Governor and Vice-Governor for life. Second, the Sultan of Yogyakarta as Governor held authority and control over his traditional land. Therefore, the complex transformation from the Dutch colonial government to the government of the independent Republic of Indonesia did not have a significant impact on power relations in Yogyakarta.

In contrast, the inexperienced leaders of Surakarta's two principalities were unable to survive in the republic. First, the Surakarta rulers did not have adequate time to prepare for such tumultuous political manoeuvres as took place. Sultan Hamengku Buwono IX ruled from 1939, and Pakualam VIII from 1937; as such, they respectively had six and eight years of experience. In contrast, after Sunan Pakubuwono XI of Surakarta reigned for six years (26 April 1939 to 1 June 1945), he was succeeded by his inexperienced eldest son, Sunan Pakubuwono XII, then aged twenty, only two months before the proclamation of Indonesian independence. Second, neither ruler of Surakarta had sufficient educational experience and maturity to press their claims successfully. Compared with Hamengku Buwono IX, who had received a Dutch education from his early childhood, Sunan Pakubuwono XII only left his school in Bandung after the beginning of the Pacific War. Similarly, Mangkunegoro VIII, of Mangkunegaran, began his rule in 1944, at the age of nineteen. Of the four rulers at the time of independence, Pakualam VIII was the oldest (35 years old), followed by Hamengku Buwono IX (33 years old); both Mangkunegoro VIII and Sunan Pakubuwono XII were 20 years old. Therefore, even though both Surakarta and Yogyakarta received the status of Special Region in 1946, they had different capacities to maintain that status during the subsequent political transformations. Surakarta's special status was postponed in 1946, and eventually abolished in 1950 when its territory was integrated into the Central Java Province.

Conclusion

This chapter has discussed the survival of the Yogyakarta Sultanate during the period of decolonisation from 1941 to 1949 when the Japanese occupied Java and then after the Dutch returned to Indonesia. That survival can be credited to Sultan Hamengku Buwono IX's persistent efforts to maintain control over his traditional territory and rights, which he successfully achieved through the formation of the Special Region of Yogyakarta. During the Japanese occupation, Sultan Hamengku Buwono IX had shown that he was both a charismatic traditional leader and an efficient administrator. The Japanese occupation had created an environment for a modern dynasty and figure such as the Sultan of Yogyakarta. His reform of traditional structures of administration increased his legitimacy among the residents of Yogyakarta. The willingness of Pakualam to become his deputy strengthened both rulers' potential to lead the Special Region. In later years, the sultan transformed from being a local monarch to emerge as a national political actor, and achieved the granting to Yogyakarta of a special status within the republic.

During the period of decolonisation, Hamengku Buwono IX never lost control over the Yogyakarta Sultanate. He smoothly associated his territory with the nationalist cause, not only because of his firm republican stand but also because of his combination of personal charisma and administrative capabilities, undertaking reforms from within the structure of the sultanate. The strategy of establishing Yogyakarta as the capital of the republic significantly raised the sultan's profile in national politics. Only a year after transfer of authority, Yogyakarta Province received the status of Special Region. This proved not to be the case in Surakarta, and thus the Sultan of Yogyakarta – now with the position of hereditary governor of Yogyakarta as well as his traditional position – and Pakualam remain the only official recognised royal figures in present-day Indonesia. Since 2012, a new arrangement for the Yogyakarta Special Region has been enacted making the sultan and Pakualam hereditary governor and vice-governor, and confirming traditional land rights and the budgetary, cultural and bureaucratic structures of their states.

Notes

1 Yogyakarta was spelled Djokjakarta and Jogjakarta. The sultanate, and its ruler, were the 'Kasultanan' in Javanese.
2 Anthony J. S. Reid, *The Indonesian National Revolution 1945–1950* (Harlow: Longman, 1974), p. 4.
3 Michael van Langenberg, 'East Sumatra: accommodating an Indonesian nation within a Sumatran residency', in Audrey R. Kahin (ed.), *Regional Dynamics of the Indonesian Revolution: Unity from Diversity* (Honolulu: University of Hawai'i Press, 1985), pp. 113–43.
4 See, for instance, Anthony J. S. Reid, *The Blood of the People: Revolution and the End of Traditional Rule in Northern Sumatra* (Oxford: Oxford University Press, 1979).
5 In the strong and institutionalised states, relations between the Dutch and the hereditary ruler were agreed upon the ruler's coronation coronation, which covered succession to the throne, the ruler's salary and land rights. See Robert Cribb and

Colin Brown, *Modern Indonesia: A History Since 1945* (London: Longman, 1995), p. 6, and John Monfries, *A Prince in a Republic: The Life of Sultan Hamengku Buwono IX of Yogyakarta* (Singapore: Institute of Southeast Asian Studies, 2015), p. 69.
6 Reid, *The Indonesian National Revolution*; Benedict Anderson, *Java in a Time of Revolution, Occupation and Resistance, 1944–1946* (Ithaca, NY: Cornell University Press, 1972); Kahin, *Regional Dynamics of the Indonesian Revolution*; George McTurnan Kahin, *Nationalism and Revolution in Indonesia* (Ithaca, NY: Cornell University Press, 1952).
7 Atmakusumah, *Takhta untuk Rakyat: Celah-Celah Kehidupan Sultan Hamengku Buwono IX* [The Crown for the People: The Life of Sultan Hamengku Buwono IX] (Jakarta: Gramedia Pustaka Utama, 2011); John Monfries, 'The Sultan and the revolution', *Bijdragen tot de taal-, land- en volkenkunde*, 164:2 (2008), 269–97; Monfries, *A Prince in a Republic*; Selo Soemardjan, *Social Changes in Yogyakarta* (Ithaca, NY: Cornell University Press, 1962).
8 M. C. Ricklefs, *A History of Modern Indonesia c. 1300 to the Present* (Redwood City, CA: Stanford University Press, 1981), p. 219.
9 Peter Carey, 'Yogyakarta: from sultanate to revolutionary capital of Indonesia. The politics of cultural survival', *Indonesia Circle: School of Oriental and African Studies. Newsletter*, 14:39 (1986), 19–29.
10 The leftist movement included those who promoted communist and socialist agendas.
11 Frank Dhont, 'Outlasting colonialism: socio-political change in the Javanese principalities under the Japanese occupation of Indonesia during World War II', PhD dissertation, Yale University, 2012.
12 Monfries, *A Prince in a Republic*, p. 77.
13 Usep Ranawidjaya, *Swapraja Sekarang dan Dihari Kemudian* [Swapraja the Present and the Future] (Jakarta: Djambatan, 1955).
14 Muhammed Abdul Aziz, *Japan's Colonialism and Indonesia* (The Hague: Martinus Nijhoff, 1955), pp. 153–7.
15 The leader of Kasunanan Surakarta was called Sunan, with a traditional role similar to that of a sultan.
16 The word '*daerah istimewa*' or Special Region was used first by the Japanese Army Commander in Java in August 1942: 'in Surakarta and Jogjakarta special rules regarding the administration were effective since the former times. Hence the Japanese Military Administration has decided to maintain those *daerah istimewa* forever'. Soemardjan, *Social Changes in Yogyakarta*, pp. 62, 153, 156, 199.
17 Dhont, 'Outlasting colonialism', p. 257.
18 *Ibid.*, p. 268.
19 László Sluimers, 'The Japanese military and Indonesian independence', *Journal of Southeast Asian Studies*, 27:1 (1996), 19–36.
20 Soemardjan, *Social Changes in Yogyakarta*, p. 46.
21 Anderson, *Java in a Time of Revolution*, p. 351.
22 Shigeru Sato, *War, Nationalism and Peasants: Java under the Japanese Occupation 1942–1945* (London: M. E. Sharpe, 1994), pp. 117–29.
23 Dhont, 'Outlasting colonialism', p. 294.
24 Confidential interview on 13 February 2015 in the Kraton Yogyakarta.
25 Shigeru Sato, 'Forced labour mobilization in Java during the Second World War', *Slavery & Abolition*, 24:2 (2003), 97–110.
26 Benedict Anderson, 'The idea of power in Javanese culture', in Claire Holt (ed.), *Culture and Politics in Indonesia* (Ithaca, NY: Cornell University Press: 1972), pp. 1–70.
27 Dhont, 'Outlasting colonialism', p. 266.
28 BPUPKI was created by the Japanese occupation following Prime Minister Kuniaki Koiso's promise of eventual independence for the country. The committee met in Jakarta (28 May to 1 June 1945) and provided the forum for Sukarno's speech outlining the Indonesian ideology of *Panca Sila*. In its second session (10–17 July 1945),

BPUPKI drafted the Indonesian constitution. Robert Cribb and Audrey Kahin, *Historical Dictionary of Indonesia*, 2nd edn (Lanham, MD: Scarecrow Press, 2004), p. 36.
29 Monfries, *A Prince in a Republic*, p. 117.
30 State Secretariat, *Risalah sidang BPUPKI dan PPKI: 29 Mei 1945–19 Agustus 1945* [Minutes of BPUPKI and PPKI meetings: 29 May 1945–19 August 1945] (Jakarta: Sekretariat Negara, 1992), pp. 34–5.
31 Robert Cribb, *Gangsters and the Revolutionaries: The Jakarta People's Militia and the Indonesian Revolution 1945–1949* (Honolulu: University of Hawai'i Press, 1991).
32 Anton Lucas, 'The Tiga Daerah affair: social revolution or rebellion?', in Kahin (ed.), *Regional Dynamics of the Indonesian Revolution*, pp. 23–53.
33 Langenberg, 'East Sumatra', pp. 120–3.
34 Burhan Djabier Magenda, *East Kalimantan: The Decline of Commercial Aristocracy* (Jakarta/Kuala Lumpur: Equinox, 2010).
35 The young courtiers of the sultanate established PEKIK in late August 1945. It claimed 400 members and was led by Prince KRT Probosuprojo.
36 Suhartono W. Pranoto, *Yogyakarta, the Capital of the Republic of Indonesia 1946–1949* (Yogyakarta: Kanisius, 2002), p. 29.
37 State Secretariat, *Risalah Sidang BPUPKI dan PPKI*, pp. 348–50.
38 Komite Nasional Indonesia Daerah (KNID) was a local committee established at every level of government after the establishment of the KNI. KNID worked in the absence of direction from KNI. Cribb and Kahin, *Historical Dictionary*, p. 219.
39 Soemardjan, *Social Changes in Yogyakarta*, p. 62.
40 T. B. Simatupang, *Report from Banaran: Experiences during the People's War* (Ithaca, NY: Cornell University, 1972), p. 67.
41 Anderson, *Java in a Time of Revolution*, p. 115.
42 Pranoto, *Yogyakarta, the Capital*, p. 52.
43 Anderson, *Java in a Time of Revolution*, p. 268.
44 Soemardjan, *Social Changes in Yogyakarta*, p. 64.
45 Anderson, *Java in a Time of Revolution*, p. 202.
46 Cribb, *Gangsters and the Revolutionaries*, pp. 118–19.
47 During the Dutch colonial period, the sultan was part of the Dutch military with the rank of major-general. See Kraton-Yogyakarta, *Kraton Jogja: The History and Cultural Heritage* (Yogyakarta: Karaton Ngayogyakarta Hadiningrat, 2002), p. 39. The granting of the honorary rank of general to Sultan Hamengku Buwono IX was finalised in 1950 through Presidential Decree No. 14/1950.
48 Hedi Shri Ahimsa Putra, 'Remembering, misremembering and forgetting: the struggle over "Serangan Oemoem 1 Maret 1949" in Yogyakarta, Indonesia', *Asian Journal of Social Science*, 29:3 (2001), 471–94.

CHAPTER THIRTEEN

The uses of monarchy in late-colonial Hong Kong, 1967–97
Mark Hampton

Hong Kong occupies a famously unusual place within the British decolonisation narrative. As John Darwin noted in an essay published at the time of the handover to China in 1997, Hong Kong lacked a substantial indigenous nationalist movement clamouring for Britain's exodus, and nor did the colonial government suffer a breakdown in collaboration with local elites. Independence was never a plausible goal for the territory, and accordingly, following Governor Mark Young's aborted efforts to introduce democratic constitutional reforms in 1946, the colonial authorities did not broach the question of self-government until the 1990s, when the end of British rule was imminent.[1] Until the 1960s, most people living in Hong Kong were immigrants or sojourners, and such nationalist aspirations as existed were generally aimed externally; for instance, against the Qing or Japanese. Even after the emergence of a pronounced local 'Hongkonger' identity, Britain's diplomats rarely saw Hong Kong in its own terms, but rather (in Darwin's phrase) as 'one square on the larger chessboard of Anglo-Chinese relations'.[2] Accordingly, the 1997 change of sovereignty was treated as a negotiation between two sovereign countries, the United Kingdom and the People's Republic of China (PRC). This chapter explores the uses of monarchy in the last thirty years of British rule, 1967–97, years in which the colonial government sought to rebuild legitimacy following a major crisis, grappled with uncertainty about continued rule, and ultimately prepared to transfer sovereignty to the PRC.

Origins

Hong Kong's atypical decolonisation process grew naturally out of the colony's origins. Hong Kong island became a British possession in 1842 in the wake of the 'First Opium War' through the decision of the naval commander, Charles Elliot – a decision that led to Elliot's dismissal from his post. Foreign Secretary Viscount Palmerston, deriding the colony as a 'barren island with hardly a house upon it', chastised Elliot for not having taken a more suitable prize. The British added the tip of Kowloon Peninsula, just across the harbour from Hong Kong island, in 1860, following the Arrow War (the 'Second Opium War'). Largely in order to improve the colony's defensibility, the British negotiated a 99-year lease of a large rural hinterland in 1898, calling it the New Territories. Although this lease added a territory twelve times larger than the existing colony, the expanded colony remained of less interest to Britain in its own right than as a secure outpost from which to trade with China. As a result, nineteenth-century colonial authorities, with some exceptions, showed little interest in the needs of the local population, much of which comprised sojourners.[3] After the Second World War the infrastructures of the ceded and leased territories became increasingly integrated so that, by the 1970s, any hope of keeping control of Hong Kong island and Kowloon would depend upon renewing the New Territories lease.

The chronology of Hong Kong's formal decolonisation process is also distinct. Hong Kong remained a crown colony until 1997, well after Britain had relinquished other imperial territories of any size or importance. More importantly, the main period of British decolonisation, the late 1940s to the late 1960s, was precisely the decades in which Hong Kong began its modernisation. Prior to the Second World War, Hong Kong was, as Robert Bickers terms it, a 'backwater', much less significant to British concerns than Shanghai.[4] Its inter-war population peaked at well under two million; and while this declined to about 600,000 at the end of the war, it had reached two million by 1951 and was nearing four million by 1971. This population explosion was stimulated firstly by the Chinese Civil War (1945–49) and then the subsequent victory by the Communist Party, which created a refugee crisis in the early 1950s. Yet it also resulted from a healthy birth rate; in both 1961 and 1971 nearly half of the colony's population was under 20 years of age.[5] The rapid population growth prompted a purportedly 'laissez-faire' government to adopt an extensive public housing programme, followed by building New Towns – planned urban communities within the mostly rural New Territories, including housing as well as employment opportunities, amenities and government offices – starting in the late 1950s. Moreover, with British business shut out of mainland China after 1949, and given the usefulness of Hong Kong's Cold War role as a 'window on China' and a 'West Berlin of the East', the colony's strategic importance to both Britain and the United States remained considerable.[6] Provocatively, Darwin argues that Britain had effectively 'decolonized' Hong Kong by 1952: it was now an informal empire masquerading as a formal one insofar as the nominal sovereign had effectively yielded to the PRC the right to prescribe the local constitutional order. Chi-kwan Mark articulates a different chronology, but also argues that by 1968, three full decades before the 'Handover', Britain had mentally decolonised Hong Kong, citing a recognition of 'lack of means' and 'loss of will' to maintain control of the colony.[7] Yet notwithstanding these important shifts, the colonial government not only remained formally in charge, but actively managed Hong Kong's development throughout this period of general decolonisation, and beyond.

Monarchy

If Hong Kong's decolonisation process is atypical, then it should not surprise us that Britain's monarchy played a very different role in this process than in many other colonies. Philip Murphy has shown that the monarchy exercised an influence over the transition between Empire and Commonwealth, an influence that Whitehall was happy to use on occasion, but which also could create complications, for example when Commonwealth dictators behaved badly or when former colonies were determined to become republics. To avoid such embarrassments, travel by the sovereign was carefully planned to avoid any inadvertent displays of support for anti-monarchical regimes. While Queen Elizabeth II saw the Commonwealth as an opportunity to give the crown a new and important role beyond Britain, the development of this institution also recognised the reality that some former British colonies did not want the Queen to remain their head of state. For those who retained the Queen as head of state, a theory of an indivisible monarchy with separate jurisdictions, articulated by King George VI during the inter-war period, gave way to an understanding that the British monarch was head of state of each independent nation separately. Indeed, even before the Second World War this point had been pressed by the Dominions, above all Canada.[8]

By comparison, the monarchy's role in late-colonial and post-colonial Hong Kong was relatively straightforward. As a crown colony, Hong Kong's relationship to the crown was formally defined: although, in practice, the Governor consulted closely with commercial and financial elites in the territory, in principle he exercised untrammelled power on behalf of the crown.[9] Nor would there be any thorny questions about the monarch's role after the change of sovereignty, of the sort described by Murphy; if independence was not on the cards, because Hong Kong would one day return to China, neither was Commonwealth membership, and any affective hold over Hong Kong people the royal family might continue to enjoy would be entirely unofficial.

Prior to 1967, the colonial government did not systematically use the monarchy as a legitimisation tool, partly because it took a fairly casual attitude towards public relations more broadly. To be sure, royal iconography was present, for example on coins, stamps and statues, or through royal patronage of social clubs and learned societies – the Royal Hong Kong Jockey Club perhaps the most famous example. Jan Morris has stated that the 'monarchical status' of Hong Kong, 'like that of old China, [hung] like a thin miasma over its affairs'.[10] Yet the monarchy was not systematically used to cement an imperial identity or Hong Kong 'national' identity, as in the case of the white settler colonies; more commonly it was employed as a bald statement of sovereignty.[11] Adam Gilbert has noted, for example, that the 1948 Hong Kong stamp commemorating the twenty-fifth wedding anniversary of King George VI and Queen Elizabeth lacked any 'prominent Chinese symbolism'; it was part of a series designed for all British overseas territories, with only the territories' names being different, and the colonial governments had no input into their design. The stamp commemorating the coronation of Queen Elizabeth II did not even render the name 'Hong Kong' in Chinese, so that only English readers would be able to identify the stamp's origins. As Gilbert argues, 'not only was this stamp a celebration of a British institution, it was created primarily for a British (and English-speaking) audience'.[12] In a period in which more than half of the population had been born in mainland China and barely one per cent spoke English as their usual language, this decision marked a lack of interest in using the monarchy as a tool for either cultural integration or inculcating affective Britishness.[13]

During the final three decades of British administration, the colonial government sporadically attempted to make use of monarchy, to an extent it had never done before, in order to build popular support for its rule. The remainder of this chapter will examine a proposed royal visit that did not happen, and two that did, in order to understand how their use (or intended use) reflected the situation of the colonial government at different stages in the process of decolonisation. These short case studies will necessarily be suggestive rather than comprehensive, not only for the sake of brevity but also because of archival limitations.[14] Nonetheless, they show that as the Hong Kong government became interested in public relations, it saw the monarchy as a potential tool for building its legitimacy. They also show, not surprisingly, that officials in Hong Kong did not always share the same perspectives as those in London – or indeed the local population.

The royal visit that never was

Between late 1964 and late 1968, the colonial government in Hong Kong tried unsuccessfully to arrange a royal visit from London. Initially, in December 1964 Governor David Trench had asked the Colonial Office for an appearance from Queen Elizabeth II, as part of a future trip that would possibly include Malaysia and Thailand. According to Trench's September 1966 recollection, it 'was thought there might be some dangers in the proposal, which would have to be carefully assessed'; in context, he meant the possible reaction of the PRC government. This vague summary of the reason plans had not moved forward came in the context of another gambit, a late 1968 visit timed to coincide with the opening of a major infrastructure project, the Plover Cove Water Supply Scheme. According to Trench, such a visit would avoid the dangers of a more general visit that 'might be objected to by the Chinese as a gratuitous display of sovereignty'. Instead, a visit to the opening of such a major project that was 'clearly designed for the benefit of the people of Hong Kong and without any international political overtones' would be much less likely to provoke a PRC reaction, particularly since Hong Kong and the Chinese government had previously cooperated concerning water supply issues. Moreover, a recent visit by Princess Margaret (in March 1966) had not antagonised Beijing. Trench acknowledged that 'some dangers will remain, and Chinese attitudes can certainly never be predicted with entire confidence so far ahead'. He emphasised that such a visit would help improve Hong Kong people's attitudes towards the United Kingdom – 'feelings which are not as warm as they might be at the present time'.[15]

Trench's September 1966 request constituted an attempt to harness the mystique of the monarchy in order to enhance the legitimacy of the Hong Kong government at a moment of weakened prestige following the Star Ferry Riots of early April. The riots had been triggered by an announced increase in the prices of first-class tickets on the ferry between Hong Kong island and Kowloon, at a time when no cross-harbour tunnels had yet been built. The riots seem to have reflected a fear that, if the fare increases were approved, then others would follow. They also signalled that a largely Hong Kong-born youth population, particularly in a decade of rapid economic growth and inflation, expected greater provision of public services than had a previous generation, mostly comprising a transient population.[16] The riots had been quickly contained, but nonetheless alerted the colonial government that the relationship with its subjects had become chilly, particularly given the involvement of young people in the demonstrations. Trench's request and its reception in London also remind us that the colonial government and Whitehall did not always share the same perspectives or concerns. W. S. Carter, the Head of the Hong Kong and West Indies 'C' Department within the Commonwealth Office, wrote confidentially in late February 1967 to Sir Edwin Bolland, Head of the Foreign Office's Far East Department, that Trench's arguments the previous September did not merit a reversal of London's previous rejection of a visit, and that the risks had only grown since that date. He also questioned Trench's claim that the water supply system would not be seen as political, particularly since it raised the prospect of Hong Kong's water independence from China.[17] Yet, after Bolland replied that the Foreign Office was still considering Trench's proposal of a visit by the Queen in conjunction with the Plover Cove opening, Carter guardedly stated that he felt, 'rather more by instinct than anything else, that a really adverse Chinese reaction is unlikely'. Instead, Beijing was more likely to 'make an entry on their private balance sheet' than react publicly.[18] The British chargé d'affaires in Beijing, Donald Hopson, likewise regarded the risks as low. Yet caution continued to predominate, particularly in a rough period in Sino-British relations during the early stages of the Cultural Revolution. The Royal Visits Committee, the Foreign Office committee charged with setting the royal family's travel schedule, noted at its April meeting that it had been 'reluctant' not to recommend a visit by the Queen; a reigning monarch had never visited the colony, and Hong Kong was, by the mid-1960s, 'by far the biggest of our remaining colonies' both by population and economic importance. Nonetheless, members concluded that the risks were too great.[19] On 26 April, Sir Saville Garner, the Permanent Secretary for Commonwealth Relations, informed Trench that although the risks seemed low, they were still too great to allow the visit.[20]

Even before Whitehall's final decision on a visit by the Queen, the Hong Kong and British governments explored other possibilities. Trench suggested Prince Charles as a visitor, but as he would shortly begin his studies at Cambridge, he would not be available.[21] Instead, Prince Philip, the Duke of Edinburgh, became the likely candidate; he had visited Hong Kong before, without incident, in 1959, and in 1964 the Foreign Office had raised no objection to a future visit.[22] In early March 1967, the Commonwealth Policy and Planning Department discussed the possibility of postponing a South East Asian trip that was tentatively planned for March 1968 until later in the year, but found logistical difficulties in doing so given the Duke's other travel commitments.[23] Nonetheless, in its April notes for the Royal Visits Committee, mentioned above, it still held out this possibility.[24]

Scheduling difficulties already noted, the matter became trickier still with the riots beginning in May 1967. Like the Star Ferry riots, these riots were fuelled by social discontent among the youth; unlike the 1966 riots, however, the 1967 ones were organised by leftists inspired by the Cultural Revolution in mainland China. They became, as Ray Yep and Robert Bickers put it, a 'major anti-colonial movement'. Ultimately leading to 51 deaths, 4,500 arrests, 'and a campaign of bombings which threatened to destabilize the colony', the riots seriously complicated Sino-British relations, and briefly raised the spectre of an early change of sovereignty. Only by introducing repressive emergency measures, and only with the tacit acquiescence of the PRC, did the colonial government eventually bring the situation under control.[25] In this context, during the second half of 1967 and well into 1968 Beijing's potential reaction became an even more prominent concern than before. Moreover, although not discussed in the memoranda concerning the proposed visit, the diplomatic crisis surrounding the detention of British journalist Anthony Grey by the PRC government, beginning in July 1967, surely factored into the Foreign Office's thinking.[26] By November, it had ruled out a visit by the Duke, citing both his existing commitments and the fear that, given present tensions between Britain and China, he was too close to the throne.[27] Further attempts to identify an alternative member of the royal family who could attend came to nought. The Royal Visits Committee noted in March 1968 that during the riots the Hong Kong public had shown loyalty and support to the Governor and his administration, and argued that continued support depended upon the 'maintenance of public confidence in our intentions towards and support for the Colony'. To this end, a royal visit could be a major boon. Even so, in the current context, the danger was that pursuing it could backfire. Given logistics, such a visit would become public knowledge well in advance, and if a hostile Chinese reaction forced a subsequent cancellation, the cancellation would 'underline our impotence in the face of Chinese pressure and the Colony's dependence on China's good will'. The possibility of Beijing-inspired local agitation was also noted.[28] By May 1968, following further consultation with Governor Trench, the idea was abandoned.[29] In January 1969, Plover Cove was officially opened with Governor Trench himself presiding instead of either the Queen or the Duke.

Where the 1968 proposed royal visit, despite the Governor's pleas, fell victim to Whitehall's caution concerning China's reaction and the consequences for British diplomacy and royal prestige, following improvements in Sino-British relations the royal couple made two visits to Hong Kong, in 1975 and 1986. Both visits were widely reported in the Hong Kong press, and local coverage was closely monitored by the Government Information Services. The two visits received different framings and different press receptions, each reflective of their particular moments in the decolonisation process.

The 1975 royal visit

In the aftermath of the 1967–68 riots, the Hong Kong government engaged in a period of major reform and rebranding. The government addressed bureaucratic corruption, ultimately establishing the Independent Commission Against Corruption. It accelerated the 'sinicisation' and localisation of the civil service, increasing the numbers of Hong Kong people in the ranks. It expanded public housing and introduced modest social welfare programmes. Although these reforms began on Governor Trench's watch, they accelerated under his successor, Murray MacLehose, who in 1971 was the first governor from a diplomatic rather than a colonial administrative background. To a large extent these reforms derived from pressure from London, and 'a sudden leap in the scope and pace of the reforms' occurred after 1976 that went well beyond Governor MacLehose's intentions.[30] Yet throughout the decade, and especially in the immediate aftermath of the 1967–68 riots, the Hong Kong government operated from the premise that the major problem was that a communication 'gap' had opened between the government and people; the problems were less ones of substance than of image. To this end, anachronistic titles were changed: the Secretary for Chinese Affairs became the Secretary for Home Affairs in 1969, and the Colonial Secretary became the Chief Secretary in 1976. The government established an ombudsman to receive complaints, and the Government Information Services made more coordinated efforts to sell the idea that the government was responsive to public needs. As critics, including Urban Council member Elsie Elliott, alleged, the government chose public relations rather than democratic reform.[31]

A key example of rebranding included the renaming of the Hong Kong Police as the Royal Hong Kong Police in April 1969 – a move recognising both the force's loyalty and effectiveness in paramilitary tactics during the earlier riots, and widespread public recognition of its 'heroic' status in restoring order. As Georgina Sinclair has noted, the riots helped the police to win public support, and the 'royal' honorific contributed to the police force's efforts to transform its colonial image into a 'civil style of policing'.[32] Yet while ostensibly honouring the police, the renaming effectively tied the monarchy – and hence the governor who represented it – to the only widely popular arm of the colonial state.

This was the context in which Queen Elizabeth II and Prince Philip visited Hong Kong in 1975. As Governor Trench had in 1966–67,

Governor MacLehose in 1974 pushed for a royal visit. Once again, the Governor's request would be weighed against the wider concerns of the diplomats (since 1968 overseen by the merged Foreign and Commonwealth Office, FCO) and the crown, including the Queen's travel schedule. In May 1974, A. C. Stuart, Head of the FCO's Hong Kong and Indian Ocean Department, having discussed the matter with MacLehose, proposed that the Queen add a Hong Kong visit to an already announced May 1975 state visit to Japan. At the same time, although preparations for the visit would take several months, MacLehose hoped to delay the announcement until the autumn, out of caution against a backlash from China. He advised Stuart in late May to push for a commitment to the visit the following year, so that a 'small and secure group' could begin preparations, while postponing the announcement until later in the year.[33] The ensuing discussion over the next several months included such mundane details as how to fit the visit between already scheduled visits to Jamaica and Japan, where the Queen should break up the long journey between Jamaica and Hong Kong (Wake Island or Guam?), the unavailability of the royal yacht *Britannia* for the Asian leg, and the exact timing of the arrival in Japan (which would affect the timing of the departure from Hong Kong). The FCO and the colonial government continued to negotiate the timing of the announcement.[34] More relevant to the Governor's aims for the visit, MacLehose proposed a special commemorative postage stamp that would include the Queen and Prince Philip and the Hong Kong Coat of Arms. The colonial government debated the merits of a fireworks display – appropriately majestic, but at the same time something that could raise the question of reversing the Hong Kong fireworks ban in force since 1967; in an economic recession, fireworks could also be criticised as extravagant.[35] For its part, the British government's Central Office of Information liaised with its Hong Kong counterpart, the Government Information Services (GIS), in order to provide appropriate materials for explaining the monarchy to Hong Kong people, asking the GIS for input as to the 'level of readership to be catered for', including, for example, the degree of understanding the people had of how the monarchy worked. The London office indicated that it could not provide Chinese-language materials, but would rely on the Hong Kong government to arrange translations.[36]

Yet notwithstanding the efforts made by the colonial and British governments, the local Chinese-language press reflected the political stances that respective papers took more generally. The *Tin Tin Daily News*, a largely pro-Beijing paper, in October 1974 greeted news of the proposed visit critically; while it acknowledged that Hong Kong people would welcome the visit, it attributed this predicted response merely to the fact that no British monarch had ever come to the territory previously. Overall, it viewed the visit's likely outcome as counter-productive, as it would only serve to highlight and aggravate the problem of Hong Kong's anomalous position, a topic that neither the British, colonial, nor PRC governments wished to address. Although the newspaper did not elaborate, in context it clearly referred to the discrepancy between the New Territories' colonial status, the lease whose coming expiration had not been addressed, and the Chinese government's persistent refusal to recognise the nineteenth-century cession of Hong Kong island or Kowloon to Britain, combined with Beijing's current unpreparedness to press the issue. Above all, the paper editorialised, it would 'be naïve to assume the sense of belonging could be enhanced after the Queen's visit'.[37] On the other hand, the pro-British and pro-Taiwanese *Sing Tao Jih Pao*, a few weeks later, took a friendlier line, citing the forthcoming visit as evidence that Britain valued Hong Kong's importance. It emphasised the complementary nature of Hong Kong and British cultures, both of which favoured peace, keeping promises, and democracy and freedom.[38]

Following the announcement of the tentative programme for the May visit, the Chinese press, in the words of the Government Information Service's internal report, 'reacted enthusiastically with 7 editorials'. As the GIS's own summary of the editorials reveals, however, this enthusiasm did not imply an uncritical attitude towards the upcoming visit. It noted that both the *Nam Wah Man Po* and the *Express* cautioned against extravagant spending on the visit in light of current economic and budgetary difficulties. The *Tin Tin Daily News* offered the somewhat backhanded hope that the Queen's visit would bring a 'temporary prosperity which in turn will lift us out of the slump'. Other papers welcomed the proposed fireworks display, though some noted the legal difficulty given that the Hong Kong government had banned fireworks since the riots in 1967. The *New Life Evening Post* argued for 'lifting the ban on a restricted basis for special occasions'. The *Sing Tao Jih Pao* argued that unless the Hong Kong government formally lifted the ban ahead of the visit, it would give rise to suspicion that it enforced the law unequally. In addition, it advocated that the fireworks should be of Chinese rather than British origin.[39]

The forthcoming visit did not remain a constant focus for the press during the next few months, but in late April a planned boycott by student groups prompted several newspapers to address both the boycott and the visit itself. The *Kung Sheung Daily News*, while critical of the proposed boycott, took the occasion to criticise the expense as well as the Queen's itinerary, which included stops at a public housing estate (Figure 13.1), the Hung Hom Railway Terminal

Figure 13.1 The Queen pauses to talk to some of the thousands of people who greeted her at a Kowloon housing estate, May 1975

and a container terminal. Focusing on such evidence of Hong Kong's modernisation and growth, the paper worried, might give the Queen a false picture of Hong Kong's prosperity, thus undermining efforts to obtain trade benefits from the European Economic Community or to reduce Hong Kong's defence contribution. The *Hong Kong Times*, by contrast, saw value in the exhibition entitled 'Progress in Hong Kong', noting that the territory's youth, oblivious to the 'breathtaking' and 'miraculous' development over the past two decades, focused excessively on its remaining problems. The *Tin Tin Yat Po* saw another side to these accomplishments: following two decades of 'rapid progress', Hong Kong's 'economic and political value' to Britain was greater than it had ever been; hence, the Queen's visit reflected that Britain needed Hong Kong every bit as much as China did.[40]

In early May, the royal visit attracted eighteen editorials in Hong Kong's Chinese-language press. The press continued to focus on some of the same themes as previously, but also distinguished carefully between the Hong Kong government and the Queen, often holding out hope that the Queen could help correct some deficiencies of the former. For example, the *Kung Sheung Daily News* hoped that the visit would have alerted the Queen to Hong Kong's fiscal and economic problems, leading her to help reduce the colony's contribution to the cost of its defence, while the *Kung Sheung Daily News*, *Tin Fung Yat Po* and *Wah Kiu Yat Po* hoped that the Queen's better understanding of Hong Kong crime and the feelings of the local population would lead to the reinstatement of capital punishment. Other newspapers noted the increase in the number of organisations that petitioned the government during the Queen's visit, an indication that the public remained dissatisfied with the government's performance despite the post-1967 reforms. At the same time, the *Nam Wah Han Pao* ridiculed the claim by university students that the Queen's visit constituted an attempt to reassert British sovereignty over Hong Kong, arguing that British sovereignty was not in question whether or not a visit took place.[41]

The 1986 royal visit

The 1986 royal visit occurred in a very different context to the one in 1975. During his 1979 visit to China, Governor MacLehose had raised the question of the New Territories' lease, due to expire in 1997; it quickly became clear that China did not intend to renew the lease, thus forcing the reversion of Hong Kong Island and Kowloon to Chinese sovereignty, given the infrastructural integration of the Colony. Between 1982 and 1984 British and Chinese authorities negotiated the terms, without direct representation for Hong Kong's people, and at the end of 1984 signed the Sino-British Joint Declaration confirming the 'Handover' at the end of June 1997. In this context, the 1986 royal visit was not concerned with supporting the legitimacy of the colonial government, as the 1975 visit had been, but constituted an early contribution to what became a sustained programme of legacy building.

In his post-visit report to the Secretary of State for Foreign and Commonwealth Affairs, Governor Edward Youde contrasted the contexts of the two visits, creating for Whitehall's consumption a story of Hong Kong's modernisation. In 1975, Youde argued, Hong Kong had been 'very much a British Colonial territory', with minimal cross-border dealings; in 1986, Hong Kong was a major international city that maintained 'increasingly close relations' with the PRC. The report noted in passing the impending change of sovereignty, giving greater emphasis to Hong Kong's economic transformation and the 'development of public participation in administration of the territory'. In contrast to 1975, when Hong Kong was only beginning to escape from the shadow of the 1967–68 riots and the global oil shock of 1973, eleven years later, despite lingering 'anxieties' and 'vulnerabilities', Hong Kong had 'not only survived its earlier problems', but had 'become a major international city' that had 'demonstrated a remarkable ability to survive economic and political uncertainties'. The report reveals that not only could the royal visit communicate a message to Britain's (now very obviously temporary) colonial subjects, but to the British themselves, concerning Britain's achievement in Hong Kong: Youde emphasised not only the effect of the royal itinerary on the Hong Kong people, but on the Queen and Prince Philip themselves. A visit to the Hong Kong and Shanghai Bank's 'highly acclaimed building' had afforded a panoramic 35th-floor view of 'some of the impressive physical development of Hong Kong, much of which had taken place since their previous visit'. The royal couple visited, as well, Hong Kong Polytechnic and Sha Tin New Town – the latter in 1975 had only begun its development and transformation from a 'large fishing village', but now, in 1986, it was a 'large conurbation of high-rise housing'.[42]

Yet the visit was not only for the benefit of Queen Elizabeth II and Prince Philip, but for the Hong Kong population, and Youde emphasised the visit's success in demonstrating the 'continuing commitment of the United Kingdom to Hong Kong and its confidence in the future of the territory'. This success was particularly important given Hong Kong's new position, one that Youde called an 'inherent paradox': a 'British Dependent Territory with a population of 98% Chinese, an international city with more American residents than British, and a territory now in transition to its new status under Chinese sovereignty'.[43] Local press coverage was mostly favourable, with even the pro-Beijing leftist *Wen Wei Po* noting that the dances in the 'Youth Spectacular' revealed Hong Kong's cultural hybridity. To a large extent, press coverage reflected the colonial government's desired message. Indeed, the assessment by the pro-Taipei rightist *Sing Tao Jih Pao*, that the public was 'a bit distant' towards the Queen following the Joint Declaration, and that some of the 'pragmatists' thought that the government had wasted public money on the visit, was one of the few negative accounts.[44]

Much more typically, the *Express* attributed the warm public reception for the Queen to her lack of 'substantial government responsibility', as a consequence of which she symbolised 'peace, luck, stability, kindness and friendliness', but also to Britain's role in developing Hong Kong into the 'Pearl of the Orient' during its period of rule. *Ming Pao* similarly attributed the public reception to the Queen's representation of British national policy, including the protection of 'democracy, freedom, human rights, and world peace'. The *Hong Kong Daily News* described a speech by the Queen in which she affirmed that maintaining current political and economic systems as well as traditions and lifestyles were 'very important to Hong Kong citizens', and echoed Governor Youde's line that the Queen's visit demonstrated that the British had not abandoned Hong Kong, and that the future was promising.[45]

The colonial government had intended the 1975 royal visit to help build legitimacy for a sovereign but fragile government during an uneasy period of reform following the riots of 1966 and 1967–68. These intentions belong to the wider context of a government seeking to build popular attachment to a 'Hongkonger' identity. A sampling of press opinion suggests mixed results. By contrast, the 1986 royal visit came shortly after Britain's impending surrender of Hong Kong had been agreed, and while the Basic Law – Hong Kong's post-1997 'mini-constitution' – was being negotiated. In this context, the colonial government was less interested in using the visit to build legitimacy than to help craft a legacy of Britain's accomplishments in Hong Kong, one that included modernisation and good government. It also sought to demonstrate continued British commitment to Hong Kong notwithstanding the 'Handover'. Broadly speaking, the local press proved more receptive to the government's framing than it had in 1975.

1997

The Queen did not visit Hong Kong again, neither in the remainder of the colonial era nor in the two decades since the 'Handover'. In keeping with custom established when other British colonies gained independence, the Queen was not present for the change of sovereignty; Prince Charles delivered her speech. The 1997 speech echoed many of the 'legacy-building' themes articulated during the 1986 visit, but in a more anxious context. Following the 1989 Tiananmen Square protests and their bloody suppression, the imminent departure of the British, combined with a refusal to allow widespread right of abode in the United Kingdom for their Chinese subjects, Britain faced accusations of abandoning the Hong Kong people to a tyranny.[46] In response, in 1992 the government chose Chris Patten as the last governor of Hong Kong, the first who came neither from the Colonial Office (as had most) nor the Foreign Office – the political task at hand required a seasoned politician. Patten, one of the Conservative Party heavyweights, was fortuitously available. Had the Conservative Party, as widely expected, lost the 1992 election, Labour would never have appointed him. Yet having masterminded the Conservative Party's electoral victory, which should have meant a cabinet position for him, he surprisingly lost his own seat. As a result, the last governor was a front-ranking British politician. During his five years in office, Patten introduced sweeping democratic reforms that not only had never been introduced while it appeared Britain could continue to rule, but which also stood almost no chance of surviving the change of sovereignty. What they did accomplish, however, was to let Britain claim to have introduced representative government to Hong Kong.[47] The Queen's 'Handover' speech celebrated the British legacy: the thriving modern economy that Britain's Chinese subjects had built during the colonial period, the preservation of Hong Kong's way of life and, if not quite independence, 'autonomy', that the departing colonial power had negotiated, and the 'unwavering support' that Britain would continue to give to its former colony.[48]

Legacies

Beginning in the 1960s, when the Hong Kong government became more deliberate than previously in selling itself to its subjects through public relations, it saw the monarchy as one of the symbols that could be used in building popular legitimacy. As a result, it pressed for a visit from Queen Elizabeth II. In the 1960s and 1970s, this process was driven by the Hong Kong government. Once it was satisfied that the risks of embarrassment to the monarchy or of a diplomatic incident were sufficiently low, the FCO agreed, and the 1975 visit served as a key moment in a major rebranding exercise by the Hong Kong government in its efforts to rebuild or strengthen fragile legitimacy following the 1967 crisis. This visit occurred during a period in which a distinct 'Hongkonger' identity was emerging, Sino-British relations had improved markedly, and British and Hong Kong officials were guardedly optimistic concerning Britain's future in the colony. Once it became clear, by the mid-1980s, that a change of sovereignty was imminent, initiative passed more clearly to the FCO. Rather than working to build legitimacy for continued British rule, public relations efforts aimed at cementing Britain's legacy as a successful colonial power that had built a great modern international city and would withdraw but leave a free and prosperous population. In these efforts, the monarchy played its role.

Acknowledgements

The work described in this chapter was substantially supported by a grant from the Research Grants Council of the Hong Kong Special Administrative Region, China (Project No. LU13601415). In addition, I am grateful to Miss Ronnie Yim for research assistance and translation of all the Chinese newspaper sources cited directly, and to Dr James Fellows for sharing research material.

Notes

1. John Darwin, 'Hong Kong in British decolonisation', in Judith M. Brown and Rosemary Foot (eds), *Hong Kong's Transitions, 1842–1997* (Basingstoke: Macmillan, 1997), pp. 16–32.
2. Darwin, 'Hong Kong in British decolonisation', p. 22.
3. Jon Bursey, *Captain Elliot and the Founding of Hong Kong: Pearl of the Orient* (Barnsley: Pen & Sword Books, 2018); Christopher Munn, *Anglo-China: Chinese People and British Rule in Hong Kong, 1841–1880* (London: Routledge, 2013); John Carroll, *Edge of Empires: Chinese Elites and British Colonials in Hong Kong* (Cambridge, MA: Harvard University Press, 2005).
4. Robert Bickers, 'The colony's shifting position in the British informal empire in China', in Brown and Foot, *Hong Kong's Transitions*, pp. 39–40.
5. *Hong Kong Statistics, 1947–1967* (Hong Kong: Census and Statistics Department, 1969), pp. 13, 17; *Hong Kong Annual Digest of Statistics* (Hong Kong: Census and Statistics Department, 1978), pp. 23, 29.
6. David Clayton, *Imperialism Revisited: Political and Economic Relations Between Britain and China, 1950–54* (Basingstoke: Macmillan, 1997); James Fellows, 'The rhetoric of trade and decolonisation in Hong Kong, 1945–1984', PhD dissertation, Lingnan University, 2016.
7. Darwin, 'Hong Kong in British decolonisation', pp. 20, 30; Chi-kwan Mark, 'Lack of means or loss of will? The United Kingdom and the decolonization of Hong Kong, 1957–1967', *The International History Review*, 31 (March 2009), 45–71.
8. Philip Murphy, *Monarchy and the End of Empire: The House of Windsor, the British Government, and the Post-war Commonwealth* (Oxford: Oxford University Press, 2013), pp. 13, 22, 31, 71–8, 83, 90.
9. Mark Hampton, *Hong Kong and British Culture, 1945–97* (Manchester: Manchester University Press, 2016), pp. 134–6.
10. Jan Morris, *Hong Kong: Epilogue to an Empire* (New York: Vintage, 1997), p. 203.
11. For an overview of the uses of monarchy in the context of royal tours, see Robert Aldrich and Cindy McCreery, 'Empire tours: royal travel between colonies and metropoles', in Robert Aldrich and Cindy McCreery, *Royals on Tour: Politics, Pageantry and Colonialism* (Manchester: Manchester University Press, 2018), pp. 1–22.
12. Adam Gilbert, 'Post-imperialism: the postage stamps and postal history of Hong Kong, 1842–1997', PhD dissertation, Sheffield Hallam University, 2018, pp. 48–9.
13. This is consistent with a prevailing lack of interest among colonial authorities in cultivating an affective British identity among their Chinese subjects. See Hampton, *Hong Kong and British Culture*, ch. 6.
14. See Murphy, *Monarchy*, pp. xi to xii for a broader discussion of the limitations of the archival record concerning the monarchy.
15. The National Archives, London (hereafter TNA), FCO 40/136, David Trench to Sir Saville Garner (copy), 6 September 1966; attached to David Trench to W. S. Carter, 13 February 1967. The September letter went missing, and a copy had to be resent by telegram for consideration; see TNA FCO 40/136, W. S. Carter to Sir Arthur Galsworthy, 10 February 1967.
16. John Carroll, *A Concise History of Hong Kong* (Lanham, MD: Rowman & Littlefield, 2007), pp. 149–50.
17. TNA FCO 40/136, W. S. Carter to E. Bolland, 22 February 1967.
18. TNA FCO 40/136, E. Bolland to W. S. Carter, 8 March 1967; TNA FCO 40/136, W. S. Carter to E. Bolland, 29 March 1967.
19. TNA FCO 40/136, 'Royal Visits Committee: Visit by H.M. The Queen to Hong Kong', 7 April 1967.
20. TNA FCO 40/136, Sir Saville Garner to Sir David Trench, 26 April 1967.
21. TNA FCO 40/136, Sir Saville Garner to Sir David Trench, 26 April 1967.

22 TNA FCO 40/136, 'Royal Visits Committee: Visit by H.M. The Queen to Hong Kong', 7 April 1967.
23 TNA FCO 40/136, Undated meeting minutes, attached to E. Bolland to W. S. Carter, 8 March 1967.
24 TNA FCO 40/136, Commonwealth Policy and Planning Committee, 'Royal Visits Committee: Note for Special Meeting on 7 April 1967'.
25 Ray Yep and Robert Bickers, 'Studying the 1967 riots: an overdue project', in Robert Bickers and Ray Yep (eds), *May Days in Hong Kong: Emergency and Riot in 1967* (Hong Kong: Hong Kong University Press, 2009), p. 1. See also Gary K. W. Cheung, *Hong Kong's Watershed: The 1967 Riots* (Hong Kong: Hong Kong University Press, 2009).
26 James Fellows, 'Colonial autonomy and Cold War diplomacy: Hong Kong and the case of Anthony Grey, 1967-9', *Historical Research*, 89 (2016), 567-87.
27 TNA FCO 40/136, H. P. Hall to Sir David Trench, 8 November 1967.
28 TNA FCO 40/136, 'Royal Visits Committee: Visit by a member of the Royal Family to Hong Kong', 13 March 1968.
29 TNA FCO 40/136, Morrice James to Sir Michael Adeane, 29 May 1968.
30 Ray Yep and Tai Lok Lui, 'Revisiting the golden era of MacLehose and the dynamics of social reforms', in Ray Yep (ed.), *Negotiating Autonomy in Greater China: Hong Kong and its Sovereign Before and After 1997* (Copenhagen: NIAS Press, 2013), pp. 110-41.
31 Hampton, *Hong Kong and British Culture*, pp. 138-49.
32 Georgina Sinclair, *At the End of the Line: Colonial Policing and the Imperial Endgame 1945-80* (Manchester: Manchester University Press, 2006), p. 182; Kevin Sinclair, *Asia's Finest: An Illustrated Account of the Royal Hong Kong Police* (Hong Kong: Unicorn Books, 1983), pp. 8-9.
33 TNA FCO 40/582, A. C. Stuart to Collins, 21 May 1974; TNA FCO 40/582, MacLehose to Stuart, 23 May 1974.
34 TNA FCO 40/582, Callaghan to Routine Hong Kong, 22 July 1974; TNA FCO 40/582, JNO Curle to Routine Tokyo, 10 May 1974 (Repeated to Governor Hong Kong); TNA FCO 40/582 Callaghan to Priority Hong Kong, 17 October 1974; TNA FCO 40/582 A. C. Stuart to Mr Wale and Sir D. Watson, 9 October 1974.
35 TNA FCO 40/582, Memorandum for Executive Council, Royal Visit Firework Display, 5 December 1974; TNA FCO 40/582, B. J. Baxter to William Heseltine, 11 November 1974.
36 FCO 40/582, K. W. Sutton to David Ford, 30 October 1974; FCO 40/582, Royal Visits Overseas: Checklist for Publicity, 28 October 1974.
37 Editorial, *Tin Tin Daily News*, 3 October 1974. Hong Kong Public Records Office [hereafter HKPRO], Hong Kong Records Series [hereafter HKRS] 70-8-5222.
38 Editorial: 'Queen will visit Hong Kong Next Year', *Sing Tao Jih Pao*, 23 October 1974. HKPRO HKRS 70-8-5222.
39 Press Review No. 318, 10.2.75-18.2.75, 'Royal Visit', HKPRO HKRS 70-8-5222.
40 Press Review No. 328, 23.4.75-30.4.75, 'The Royal Visit', HKPRO HKRS 70-8-5222.
41 Press Review No. 329, 20.4.75-8.5.75, 'The Royal Visit', HKPRO HKRS 70-8-5222. See also 'Elizabeth's Visit Stirs Hong Kong', *The New York Times*, 8 May 1975, p. 1.
42 TNA FO 972/160, Foreign Policy Document No. 158, 'Royal Visit to Hong Kong, 1986'.
43 TNA FO 972/160, Foreign Policy Document No. 158, 'Royal Visit to Hong Kong, 1986'.
44 'Youth Spectacular – a melting pot of HK culture', *Wen Wei Po*, 26 October 1986, HKRS 312-1-27; 'Queen's visit creates a trend', *Sing Tao Jih Pao*, 23 October 1986, HKRS 312-1-26. The *Tin Tin Daily News*, by contrast, explicitly denied that Hong Kong people minded the expense of the Queen's visit; 'Hong Kong people have no complaint about money spent on the reception of the Queen', *Tin Tin Daily News*, 24 October 1986, HKRS 312-1-27.

45 'Welcome Queen's visit to Hong Kong', *Express*, 21 October 1986, HKRS 312–1–26; 'Why was the Queen so popular?', *Ming Pao*, 21 October 1986, HKRS 312–1–26; 'Editorial: the Queen is deeply impressed by HK', *Hong Kong Daily News*, 22 October 1986, HKRS 312–1–26. See also 'Letter to the editor: the royal visit has enhanced people's confidence toward the territory's future', *Ming Pao Evening News*, 5 November 1986, HKRS 312–1–26.
46 See, for instance, William McGurn, *Perfidious Albion: The Abandonment of Hong Kong* (Washington, DC: Ethics and Public Policy Center, 1992).
47 Hampton, *Hong Kong and British Culture*, pp. 153–6.
48 'Words of a prince and a president: continuity, change, and assurances', *The New York Times*, 1 July 1997.

CHAPTER FOURTEEN

From absolute monarch to 'symbol emperor': decolonisation and the Japanese emperor after 1945

Elise K. Tipton

Defeat in 1945 brought an end to the Japanese empire and occupation by foreign powers for the first time in Japanese history.[1] Considering that Japan was the only non-Western country to possess colonies rather than being a colony itself, 'de-imperialisation' might be a more appropriate term than 'decolonisation' to describe Japanese developments after the Second World War.[2] Japan not only lost the territories throughout Southeast Asia that it had occupied during the late 1930s and early 1940s, but also colonies gained as spoils of war in the 1890s and early twentieth century.[3] Japan had obtained Formosa/Taiwan and the Pescadores Islands after defeating China in 1895, then Korea as a protectorate and the southern half of Sakhalin/Karafuto after the Russo-Japanese War (1904–5). It formally annexed Korea in 1910. Micronesia had become a Japanese trust territory in the peace settlement following the First World War. With defeat, Japan also lost its privileges in the collective informal empire in China and its de facto control over the puppet state of Manchukuo, which had been established after Japan invaded Manchuria in 1931. Moreover, the United States took over Okinawa, which had been incorporated into Japan as a prefecture in 1879, and the Soviet Union occupied the Kuril Islands north of Hokkaido.[4]

But in addition to reducing Japanese territories to its four main islands, ending its ambitions to become a colonial power again or even to use force as a means for settling disputes with another nation, the American-dominated Occupation made radical reforms of democratisation throughout politics and society. Because the emperor stood at the apex of the political system that had driven Japanese imperialist expansion, transformation of the Japanese monarchy emerged as the core of these reforms. However, just how it would be transformed was not at all clear as the Occupation began. Debates among the Allies and Japanese leaders raged over the future of both Hirohito the person and the institution of the emperor. Ultimately, a new constitution transformed the emperor from an absolute monarch into a 'symbol emperor', and although imposed by the Occupation, the transformation became widely supported and completed in the decade after the Occupation ended in 1952. However, because Hirohito remained on the throne until his death in 1989, the issue of his war responsibility recurred at home and abroad, and both the far right and left vigorously expressed critical, though different, views of the role and treatment of the imperial family even as younger generations became indifferent to the imperial house. Moreover, the relation between the symbol emperor and Japanese democracy remains a controversial element at the centre of political and intellectual debates even in the twenty-first century.[5]

The difficulties of separating the man from the institution meant that Hirohito's death and funeral and Akihito's accession to the throne in 1989 occasioned an 'emperor phenomenon' in the media and among intellectuals, political activists and politicians. Controversies arose over the ostensible separation between private and public ceremonies because constitutional changes separated religion (Shinto) and the state, where previously under the Meiji Constitution of 1889 the emperor ruled as an absolute monarch, being the descendant of the Sun Goddess Amaterasu. Consequently, certain Shinto rites were conducted behind a curtain as 'private' ceremonies, but once the curtain was opened, the funeral procession became a 'public' ceremony funded by the government and broadcast by all television channels. Media coverage emphasised the great age of the imperial household's rites, lending support to some leftists' claims that the 'emperor phenomenon' would lead to a resurgence of a pre-war and wartime type of 'emperor system' (*tennōsei*).[6] At the same time, a historian of the Japanese monarchy, Takashi Fujitani, argues that there was little likelihood of such a resurgence because the television medium itself distanced the emperor from viewers and the media's reference to the new emperor system as the '*akarui tennōsei*' ('bright and cheerful emperor system') had transformed the imperial family into simply another commodity 'to be consumed' in Japan's affluent post-war society.[7]

There were also controversies over the representatives of foreign countries. On the one hand, representation from 164 countries and twenty-eight international organisations, including fifty-five heads of state (notably, US President George Bush Snr and President François Mitterrand of France), recognised Japan's re-entry into international politics, its close ties with the United States and its economic power as the world's second largest economy by the 1980s. On the other hand, debate in Great Britain, Australia, the Netherlands, New Zealand,

China, Korea and Singapore over who to send reflected continued hostility to Hirohito, who was held responsible for sufferings during the Second World War. The British tabloid newspaper *The Sun* exemplified the hate in an article headlined 'No Tears for Evil Lord of Japan': 'Hirohito died unpunished for his part in some of the most heinous crimes ever inflicted on mankind.'[8] In the end, Queen Elizabeth II sent her husband Prince Philip to represent Great Britain.

These controversies over Hirohito's funeral both at home and overseas derived from the lack of resolution regarding Hirohito's war responsibility and from his retention on the throne after 1945. Just as the legacy of Japan's empire continues to shape political relations in East and Southeast Asia today,[9] royal legacies resonate through Japanese politics and culture in spite of radical constitutional changes. To understand these contradictions, we need to go back to debates over surrender and Occupation policies and to trace steps in the transformation of the emperor into a 'symbol emperor'.

Debates over surrender and occupation policies

Debates over surrender and planning for post-war policies in both Japan and the United States during 1944 and 1945 reveal the crucial importance attached to the future of the emperor, which in turn would affect the future of not only Japan, but also Asia and the world more broadly. In *Son of Heaven: The Problem of the Mikado* the author and journalist Willard Price expressed a view of surrender that was widely held at the time: 'It is a striking fact that whenever intelligent conversation turns to the issue of what-to-do-with-Japan it usually narrows at once to what-to-do-with-the-emperor.'[10] Moreover, Price went on to warn that 'what happens in Japan may set the pattern for that Asia, and thus for the world ... It is a mistake to think that we shall never have to worry about Japan after we sheer away her conquered territories and shut her up in her own tight islands.'[11]

During the last year of the war advocates of surrender in Japan argued with diehard military leaders, but even surrender advocates wanted a guarantee from the Allies that the emperor would remain in the post-war order. The Potsdam Declaration, released after the meeting of American President Harry Truman, British Prime Minister Winston Churchill and Nationalist China leader Chiang Kai-shek on 26 July 1945, demanded unconditional surrender or the alternative of 'prompt and utter destruction'. Nevertheless, it left ambiguous the form of a future government, notably the status of the emperor. Historians are divided over Hirohito's role in delaying the decision to surrender.[12] The division generally correlates with historians' views of Hirohito's role in political decision-making, in particular as commander-in-chief of the armed forces, since he became emperor in 1926. Critics such as Herbert Bix and David Bergamini argue that Hirohito played a highly active role in supporting the actions carried out in his name from the beginning of the war to its end. While Bix does not agree with Bergamini that the emperor prolonged the war to satisfy a love of war or malicious intentions, he blames Hirohito for not acting decisively to sue for peace when defeat appeared inevitable by the early months of 1945.[13]

Rejecting Bergamini's view of Hirohito, Irokawa Daikichi instead describes the emperor as a 'complex person' who, unlike his grandfather, the very decisive Meiji emperor, 'castigated but did not punish the militarists for their arbitrary actions and as a result, some of the top military officials did not take him seriously. In the end, the emperor was dragged along by the military'.[14] Other historians, such as Hata Ikuhiko, point out that although the emperor had sometimes delayed approval or suggested modifications to plans submitted to him by army and navy leaders, military authorities often disregarded his wishes. Regarding the ending of the war, Hata concludes that the emperor shifted the direction of Japanese policy towards seeking an end to the war at the Imperial Conference of 22 June.[15] Then in August, facing a deadlock among civilian and military leaders in response to the Potsdam ultimatum and after the atomic bombings and entry of the Soviet Union into the war, Hirohito made a rare intervention with the 'sacred decision' to surrender. The fact that the emperor made an unprecedented radio broadcast announcing the decision reveals the importance of his role.[16] According to Irokawa, 'the situation had become so desperate that no other way out was available'.[17] Even then, as Stephen Large points out, it is significant that 'it took two imperial interventions to end the war'.[18] Differences aside regarding Hirohito's role in ending the war, historians all emphasise that the fate of the imperial institution, the embodiment of Japan's national polity or *kokutai*, was crucial in the debates surrounding the decision to surrender.

Meanwhile, in the United States, planning for post-war political change in Japan had begun unusually early in the war (in contrast to the First World War) and was systematically organised. In a major Japanese–American collaborative study of the Occupation, co-editor Robert Ward echoed Price's view forty years later when he noted that 'no political issue concerning the post-war treatment of Japan received more attention or proved more controversial than the question of what was to be done about the emperor. ... [Treatment of the emperor] was almost a shorthand symbol for the more general problem of the democratization of Japan'.[19] Views ranged widely: at one end a belief that only abolition of the monarchy could ensure a durable liberalisation of Japanese politics, and at the opposite end a conviction that the United States could only hope to democratise Japan by working through the emperor. However, Ward highlights the fact that 'all shared the traditional Japanese view that at the heart of the Japanese political system lay the imperial institution'.[20]

The first formal State Department paper in May 1943 on the 'Status of the Japanese Emperor' set out arguments both for and against his retention. Although it did not express a policy preference, the arguments for retaining the monarchy received more extensive discussion, and the vast majority of Japan experts among the planners supported its continuation. These so-called 'Japan hands', such as former ambassador to Japan Joseph Grew, recommended the emperor's retention as the main stabilising factor for ending the war and establishing democracy. However, from this early date it was also clear that senior State Department officials, including Secretary of State Cordell Hull and assistant secretary Dean Acheson, were opposed, for they regarded the imperial institution as the root of militarism and concluded therefore that it should be abolished. Controversy among State Department planners continued and after the surrender was complicated by the issue of whether or not to put Hirohito on trial as a war criminal.[21]

At the beginning of the Occupation, the Soviet Union, Australia and other Allied nations called for severe treatment of the emperor along with Japanese government officials.[22] Similarly, in Japan, communists called for Hirohito's arrest as a war criminal as well as abolition of the imperial institution. However, in Washington, DC, General Bonner Fellers and other important Occupation figures supported maintenance of Hirohito and the monarchy. British leaders as well as Fellers regarded this as a necessary bulwark against communism. British leaders also wanted to restore and protect the Greek monarchy during the post-war civil war.[23]

In the end, General Douglas MacArthur, Supreme Commander of the Allied Powers (SCAP) with virtually unrestricted authority over the Occupation, came to the decision that retaining Hirohito as well as the imperial institution would ensure demilitarisation and implementation of Occupation policies without major resistance from the Japanese. This was foreshowed by not requiring Hirohito or any representative of the Imperial Household Ministry to participate in the signing of the surrender documents.[24] After his first meeting with Hirohito on 27 September, MacArthur declared that he would protect the emperor's position as a means of ensuring that the Occupation proceeded smoothly. In a post-Occupation statement MacArthur emphasised his belief that 'vicious efforts to destroy the person of the Emperor and thereby abolish the system became one of the most dangerous menaces that threatened the successful rehabilitation of the nation'.[25]

The photograph of this first of eleven meetings (Figure 14.1), all held at MacArthur's headquarters, became an icon of the Occupation as it symbolised the emperor's and Japan's subordination to SCAP, often referred to as the new 'emperor' of Japan. Japanese government officials tried to ban the photograph's publication for they were appalled at the humiliating contrast between the relaxed MacArthur, casually dressed in khaki without any medals, and the smaller and stiff Hirohito in formal morning coat. Details remained secret, but according to the Japanese interpreter's notes, various observers and MacArthur's own memoirs, MacArthur initially received the emperor coldly in his office. Yet by the end of the meeting MacArthur relaxed his expression, changed his attitude towards the emperor and even saw the emperor off at the entrance.[26] Perhaps MacArthur's favourable impression of the emperor reinforced his decision to keep Hirohito on the throne.

Figure 14.1 Emperor Hirohito visiting General Douglas MacArthur, 27 September 1945

From 'manifest deity' to peace-loving 'human'

Nevertheless, Hirohito's fate as well as that of the imperial institution remained in doubt until a new constitution was written in 1946. Debates and speculation in all circles arose over his possible abdication and trial as a war criminal.[27] While Hirohito himself offered to abdicate, many conservative Japanese leaders feared that abdicating would make Hirohito more vulnerable to being charged with war crimes. To prevent this, Japanese officials, supported by SCAP GHQ, made concerted efforts to turn him into a peace-loving emperor who had been forced to support war by the militarists.[28] The transformation into a 'symbol emperor' began with his appearance in civilian clothes, in contrast to all his wartime presentations in military uniform. His 20 November 1945 visit to Yasukuni Shrine, which was dedicated to war dead and would later hold the remains of Class A war criminals, was the last time that he wore a military uniform.[29]

More dramatic was Hirohito's New Year's Day rescript in January 1946 declaring that he was not an *akitsumikami* or 'manifest deity'. This is a more esoteric word than the term 'divine' that was used in the official English translation,[30] but writers of the Japanese version had gone through many revisions to avoid an unequivocal repudiation of his alleged descent from the gods. The declaration also came in the middle of the rescript, putting the emphasis on the initial extended reference to the liberal and peace-loving ideals of the Meiji Charter Oath of 1868 and thus drawing a line of continuity with the strong personality and modernising image of the Meiji emperor (who reigned from 1868 to 1912). In any case, this so-called 'renunciation of divinity' or 'declaration of humanity' received extravagant praise from MacArthur and the desired positive response in the American media.[31]

To support this image of the emperor as 'human', GHQ collaborated with the Japanese government to bring the emperor 'down from the clouds' by sending Hirohito on tours of the country to mingle with the people, preceded and protected by American soldiers and military police. Occupation officials supporting the tours also hoped that seeing the emperor would bolster the Japanese people's mood in the dire economic conditions of imminent famine and flourishing black markets.[32] In addition, Hirohito's tours could remind people of his grandfather's tours in the 1870s and 1880s that had helped to legitimise the new Meiji government and its radical reforms. The tours began in February 1946 and ended in August 1954 after he had visited farms, coal mines, factories, schools and numerous other places in all prefectures except Okinawa (under American rule until reversion to Japan in 1971). They proved immensely successful, so popular in fact that the tours were temporarily suspended in early 1948. This was because some Occupation officials thought that rather than democratising the monarchy, they were promoting the old idolatry, while the Soviet Union, China and Australia argued that the people's admiration generated by the tours was becoming an obstacle to prosecution of war criminals.[33]

Hirohito himself can be credited for much of the tours' success, but for different reasons from his grandfather's. Unlike the vigorous Meiji emperor, who represented a masculine father figure, Hirohito was reserved in personality. Unused to contact with ordinary Japanese, his awkwardness and inability to carry on conversations actually worked to convey his humanity and even attract the sympathy of the thousands of people who crowded to see him. He became known as the '*Ah, sō* [Oh, is that so?]' emperor for his characteristic innocuous response to comments, a jibe, though gentle, that would have been unheard of in previous times. Some foreign journalists castigated him for his ordinary physical appearance, ill-fitting suits, lack of coordination and obvious discomfort being in public. Others from the Japanese left were more direct in their vitriol. For example, the cover of the April 1950 issue of the journal *Shinsho* pictured Hirohito doffing his hat on a ground of skulls. Nevertheless, large crowds cheered '*banzai*', and local governments spent substantial sums as they vied for his visits and cleaned up places where he would visit, leading left-wing cartoonists to call the emperor 'the Broom', and depict him with bristles for a head to lampoon him for precipitating the clean-ups by local authorities.[34] The Occupation officials responsible for suspending the tours were on the right track in that the tours began the making of the emperor into a media celebrity.

Meanwhile, the emperor took other opportunities for engagement with ordinary Japanese when volunteers were invited into the palace grounds to help clear out rubble and weeds. Opening the palace grounds to the public was unprecedented and a huge privilege. When Hirohito learned of their efforts, he arranged to meet them and contacted the empress to encourage her to thank them too. These 'sweeping brigades' from northeastern Honshu would continue for more than forty years, involving almost one million participants. In return, the emperor, empress and crown prince greeted and thanked them; then the volunteers received a tour of the inner palace and gifts of cigarettes and two cakes imprinted with the imperial crest.[35]

The 1947 Constitution and creation of the symbol emperor

While such encounters with ordinary Japanese helped to humanise while also popularising the emperor in early 1946, more momentous steps were being taken towards a radical transformation of his role in the post-war political system. In February, a Japanese government committee presented its draft of a revised constitution, but since it consisted of merely cosmetic changes to the Meiji constitution, MacArthur summarily rejected it and ordered a small Government Section group headed by General Courtney Whitney to come up with an acceptable draft in one week's time. According to Whitney, pressure for completion in such a short time came from the impending meeting of the Far Eastern Commission that included Allied countries hostile to the emperor and imperial institution and possessed of veto powers over MacArthur's directives on constitutional reform.[36]

In addition to Whitney, only four of the twenty-four Government Section group were lawyers and none except Colonel Charles Kades had expertise in constitutional law. Only three had substantial knowledge of or experience in Japan: China historian Cyrus Peake, journalist Harry Emerson Wildes, and twenty-two-year-old Beate Sirota, who had lived in Japan until going to college in the United States. Politically, their views ranged from conservative Republican to New Deal Democrat, notably Kades, the real leader of the steering committee, but in general an idealistic spirit overcame political differences. MacArthur had given Whitney three principles to be included in the new constitution: the first related to retention of the emperor; the second, abolition of war as a sovereign right of the nation; and the third, abolition of the feudal system and the peerage system.[37] However, Kades's team interpreted and redefined the principles in a most liberal manner. Notably, the two young officers responsible for the section on the emperor ignored MacArthur's first principle, 'Emperor is at the head of state', when describing him as the 'symbol' of the state and of the unity of the people.[38] Gathering together many foreign constitutions, the committee eventually formulated a parliamentary system roughly on the British model, but also incorporating a broad range of civil liberties and human rights.

Government Section's draft stunned the Japanese officials when it was presented to them, for it was in some ways even more progressive than the American constitution.[39] When presenting the draft to Foreign Minister Yoshida Shigeru and Minister of State Matsumoto Jōji, Whitney stressed the need to adopt the SCAP draft in order to save the emperor from trial as a war criminal. Although perhaps intended as advice, Matsumoto interpreted it as a threat.[40] Again, this exemplifies the importance of the emperor's future in the minds of Japanese government leaders in persuading them to implement Occupation reforms.

Regarding the monarchy, Article 1 stated that 'the Emperor is a symbol of the state and of the unity of the people, deriving his position from the will of the people with whom resides sovereign power'. This contrasts sharply with the opening of the 1889 Meiji Constitution that declared the emperor in 'a line unbroken for ages eternal' as 'sacred and inviolable', 'the head of the Empire, combining in Himself the rights of sovereignty ... [and] the supreme command of the Army and Navy'.[41] The emperor thus lost all his imperial prerogatives (notably as commander-in-chief of the armed forces), reducing his role to ceremonial functions and governed by the Diet and Cabinet. Among other legislative changes, *lèse-majesté* was no longer a crime. The Imperial Household Minister, who 'advised and assisted' the emperor autonomously from the pre-1945 Cabinet, now became the Director of the Imperial Household Agency under the Prime Minister's Office. In addition, while remaining dynastic and roughly based on the British model, the imperial family was reduced to the nuclear family as all collateral lines in addition to the aristocracy were abolished. Moreover, in contrast to the British royal family, the Japanese imperial family lost all its properties and other assets.

Besides this radical change in the position of the emperor, the other essential provision of the new constitution from SCAP's point of view was the renunciation of war in Article 9. This unique constitutional clause reads as follows: 'War as sovereign right of the nation is abolished. The threat or use of force is forever renounced as a means for settling disputes with any other nation.' It further denied Japan rights of belligerency or maintenance of armed forces.[42] Theodore McNelly goes so far as to argue that the inclusion of the ban on war and arms was aimed at preservation of the monarchy, for it removed objection to perpetuation of the imperial institution among certain Allies by making the emperor the symbol of a pacifist state rather than commander-in-chief of the military and aggressive imperialism.[43]

However, although radically reduced in many ways, the emperor's position in politics remained ill defined, for the question of whether he was the head of state was not declared. Confusion and debates among Japanese academics also arose over the word 'symbol', its vagueness as a term in the Japanese language and this first-time use in Japanese law.[44] Scholars at the time of the new constitution and since have even debated the historic nature of the reform. Some scholars contend that this post-war 'symbol emperor' is a return to the pre-modern imperial tradition when few emperors actually ruled.[45] Others such as Kenneth Ruoff argue that rather than being traditional, the monarchy 'has been profoundly shaped by the Occupation-era constitution and fifty years of societal evolution', so that it has become 'thoroughly embedded in Japan's postwar culture of democracy'.[46]

DECOLONISATION AND THE JAPANESE EMPEROR AFTER 1945

The making of the symbol emperor during the 1950s and after

Considering the vagueness of the word 'symbol' and debate among both scholars and politicians regarding the post-war role of the emperor, it should not be surprising that the symbol monarchy only gradually gained legitimacy and widespread acceptance during the decade of the 1950s, and even after that it continued to evolve. Conservative governments, the media and Japan's 'economic miracle' during the late 1950s contributed greatly to its acceptance, culminating in Crown Prince Akihito's celebrated marriage to a commoner, Shōda Michiko, in 1959.[47] Although the daughter of a wealthy, well-connected businessman, Shōda was the first commoner to marry into the imperial family, thus exemplifying the values of the new Japan – democracy, equality and marriage for love. Consumer industries and the new television industry took advantage of the event to create a 'Michi boom'. Nearly two million television sets were sold by 1958 to watch the wedding procession in a British-style horse-drawn carriage (as opposed to a palanquin), which linked trappings of a traditional Western monarch with the modern love match.

An influential essay by Hōsei University professor Matsushita Keiichi claimed in the respected journal *Chūō kōron* that the 'wedding boom' marked the final nail in the coffin of the pre-war emperor system, not a sign of its revival. He argued that the transformation of the Crown Prince from a living god to a media star and the younger generation's overwhelmingly positive response to the marriage indicated the 'postwarness' of the monarchy, its becoming 'the emperor system of the masses'. Not all agreed, including representatives of both the left and right. Leftist Inoue Kiyoshi in a reply essay questioned the autonomy of the mass media and the institutionalisation of popular sovereignty, while conservatives both denied that the monarchy had changed and criticised the media, especially the popular weekly magazines, for undermining the dignity of the imperial family.[48]

Certainly, regular and extensive attention in the mass media was significant during the 1960s in presenting the imperial family as the model Japanese family. Magazines treated its members as 'stars', but in 'extremely polite, yet warm and affectionate' language.[49] They depicted imperial family members as modern personalities with idealised middle-class respectability, which was significant in the decade of the so-called economic miracle, when the vast majority of Japanese achieved their aspirations for middle-class status. The imperial family remained esteemed, but was no longer surrounded by awe. Newspaper editor Kawai Kazuo concluded in 1960 that 'however glamorous ... it is hardly likely that his [Hirohito's] people will ever regard him – or that he will ever regard himself – as a mysterious presence behind the clouds of a Japanese Olympus'.[50]

Regarding Hirohito, a self-imposed 'chrysanthemum curtain/taboo' led the media to avoid discussing his pre-war decisions and war responsibility, and instead to focus on his role in ending the war and his peaceful post-war life as a family man and marine biologist. The popular weekly *Shūkan sankei* provides an excellent example of such efforts to link Hirohito with Japan's modern, peaceful democracy:

> Surely, His Majesty is a star. But he is also a human being. With all our strength we must not allow His Majesty to be shoved back up above the clouds as he was in the past. At the edge of the willowed imperial moat His Majesty walks hand in hand with his grandson. At his side, two, three body guards. Passersby greet His Majesty. This might be quite far from [today's] reality, but does not precisely this kind of tranquil, peaceful scene befit the symbol of Japan?[51]

Royal legacies

Mindful of the fundamental change in its status and the values of the new Japan, the imperial family and Imperial Household Agency cooperated in this remaking of the emperor into a 'people's emperor' or 'emperor of the masses'. But although the symbol emperor matured under Hirohito, it was still constrained as long as he lived. Crown Prince Akihito, not Hirohito, was sent as Japan's representative to Queen Elizabeth II's coronation in 1953 because war hostilities remained too fresh in the memories of the British people. When Hirohito embarked on a European tour in 1971 and visited the United States in 1975, the issue of his war responsibility reignited. Besides leftist opposition at home, protests in London marred Hirohito's fond memories of his 1921 tour to Europe as crown prince and Queen Elizabeth's restoration of British honours previously awarded to Hirohito that had been rescinded during the war.[52] Demonstrators in Belgium, the Netherlands and Germany were even more hostile. Dismayed by this failure of imperial diplomacy, Japanese government officials hesitated to send Hirohito to the United States, although Presidents Richard Nixon and Gerald Ford had extended invitations. When he did go, however, it proved successful. President Ford made no reference to the war in his banquet toast, and Hirohito referred to 'that most unfortunate war, which I deeply deplore' while thanking the United States for assisting post-war reconstruction. While curious about this mysterious foreign emperor, what most Americans saw was merely an elderly man enjoying a football game, riding a farm tractor and posing with Mickey Mouse at Disneyland.[53]

DECOLONISATION AND THE JAPANESE EMPEROR AFTER 1945

Hirohito's successor Emperor Akihito made great efforts to put the war in the past through many international tours and apologies to individuals and countries that had suffered from Japanese aggression. In 2001 he made a public reference to his ancestor being a Korean queen, which had long been known in academic circles, but not acknowledged in Japanese textbooks or the media. After 2015, in the yearly commemoration speeches marking the end of the war Akihito expressed his 'deep remorse' over the deaths caused by the war.[54] However, he never visited the former colonies of Korea or Taiwan. In addition, war issues related to 'comfort women' and 'forced labour' continue to cause friction between South Korea and Japan, and in February 2019 the speaker of the South Korean National Assembly, Moon Hee-Sang, involved the emperor by demanding an apology to the 'comfort women' from both Emperor Akihito and the Japanese prime minister.[55]

At home, Akihito and the empress tried to narrow the distance between themselves and the people, notably during visits after natural disasters. To a great extent they succeeded, though often to the disgust of right-wing organisations. In August 2016 Akihito released an unprecedented video expressing his desire to abdicate. Of note was the explanation of his conception of his role 'as symbol of the State and the unity of the people' as 'being with the people'. Because of this, he rejected the possibility of 'perpetually reducing the Emperor's acts in matters of state and his duties as the symbol of the State' as he aged.[56] In other words, he did not believe that the emperor could fulfil his duties as symbol of the state by simply existing out of contact with the people. His successor, then Crown Prince Naruhito, declared his intention to carry on this legacy of 'always being beside the Japanese citizens'.[57]

Even though Akihito explicitly referred to his lack of powers related to government, and even as both the right and left accepted the symbol emperor by the 1990s when Akihito ascended the throne, certain continuities or royal legacies exist. To begin with, Hirohito, Akihito and Naruhito are called 'emperor', not 'king', even though Japan has no empire, and despite Article 9, succession rites pass on the imperial regalia that include a sacred sword. In addition, the emperor is still male, despite the inclusion of a gender equality clause in the constitution.[58] He is treated as a head of state, which leftists regard as unconstitutional (though the matter is unclear in the constitution), and although removed from political decision-making, Hirohito, Akihito and Naruhito have continued to receive ministerial briefings.

Furthermore, the conservative Liberal Democratic Party governments that have monopolised power since the 1950s have consistently tried to use imperial prestige to further their policy agendas, but with the notable exception of blunting the impact of Akihito's war apologies. Promoting the emperor as Japan's cultural leader, they re-established Foundation Day in 1966, though without the pre-war association with the mythical founder Emperor Jimmu. Then, in 1979, the government enacted the Reign Name Law for year dates, a symbol of Japanese cultural distinctiveness.[59] Accordingly, the year of Hirohito's death (1989) was Shōwa 64 and Heisei 1 the first year of Akihito's reign. The reign name for Emperor Naruhito, who ascended the throne on 1 May 2019, is *Reiwa*, meaning 'good fortune and peace'. Significantly, this is the first time that the *rei* kanji was chosen from Japanese rather than Chinese literature.

Resistant to fundamental change, the government enacted a special 'one time only' law to enable Akihito's abdication while he is still alive. As was the case with Akihito's accession, it used state funds to pay for Shinto enthronement rituals. Again, some opposed this as violating the constitution's separation of religion and the state. Sensationally, this time critics included Akihito's younger son Prince Akishino, who would become second in line to the throne and whose son is third. Akishino publicly stated that costs should be covered by the imperial family's private, not public, activities expense fund.[60]

Conservative governments have thus kept the monarchy important in Japanese society and culture, but not without controversy. Consequently, and by way of conclusion, this has in no way undermined the constitution and its fundamental transformation of the emperor from absolute monarch to symbol emperor.

Notes

1. I have used Japanese name order of surname first, except where the author has published in English and uses Western name order.
2. 'Deimperialization' is used in a 2016 book title: Barak Kushner and Sherzod Muminov (eds), *The Dismantling of Japan's Empire in East Asia: Deimperialization, Postwar Legitimation and Imperial Afterlife* (Milton Park and New York: Routledge, 2016).
3. For a summary treatment of Japanese imperialism, see Elise K. Tipton, 'Japan: the Meiji Restoration (1868–1945)', in Jim Masselos (ed.), *The Great Empires of Asia* (London: Thames & Hudson, 2010). For a specialist treatment, see Ramon Myers and Mark Peattie (eds), *The Japanese Colonial Empire, 1895–1945* (Princeton, NJ: Princeton University Press, 1984).
4. The Soviet Union did not sign a peace treaty with Japan, and the Kuril Islands remain a matter of dispute between Russia and Japan up to the present.
5. See R. Kersten, 'Revisionism, reaction and the "symbol emperor" in post-war Japan', *Japan Forum*, 15:1 (2003), 15–31.
6. Takashi Fujitani, 'Electronic pageantry and Japan's "symbolic emperor"', *Journal of Asian Studies*, 51:4 (November 1992), 828.
7. Ibid., p. 847. Taking a broader sweep, Fujitani's book, *Splendid Monarchy: Power and Pageantry in Modern Japan* (Berkeley: University of California Press, 1996), provides an excellent description and analysis of how the imperial institution became central to modern Japanese politics and society.

8 Quoted in Toshiaki Kawahara, *Hirohito and His Times: A Japanese Perspective* (Tokyo and New York: Kodansha International, 1990), p. 5.
9 On the messy dismantling of Japan's empire and the empire's legacy, see Kushner and Muminov, *Dismantling of Japan's Empire*.
10 Willard Price, *Son of Heaven: The Problem of the Mikado* (London and Toronto: William Heinemann, 1945), p. 1.
11 Ibid., p. 2.
12 For differing views of five scholars from the United States, Japan and Britain about the impact of the atomic bombs and Soviet entry to the war on the decision to surrender and about Emperor Hirohito's role, see Tsuyoshi Hasegawa (ed.), *The End of the Pacific War: Reappraisals* (Stanford, CA: Stanford University Press, 2007).
13 Herbert Bix, *Hirohito and the Making of Modern Japan* (New York: HarperCollins, 2000), pp. 519–25; David Bergamini, *Japan's Imperial Conspiracy* (London and Toronto: Heinemann, 1971).
14 Irokawa Daikichi, *The Age of Hirohito: In Search of Modern Japan* (New York: Free Press, 1995), p. 93.
15 Ikuhito Hata, *Hirohito: The Shōwa Emperor in War and Peace* (Folkestone: Global Oriental, 2007), pp. 48, 58.
16 Kawai Kazuo, *Japan's American Interlude* (Chicago: University of Chicago Press, 1960), p. 79.
17 Irokawa, *Age of Hirohito*, p. 93; Hata, *Hirohito*, pp. 63–4.
18 Stephen Large, *Emperor Hirohito and Shōwa Japan: A Political Biography* (London and New York: Routledge, 1992), p. 125. Large emphasises the deadlock in the council as the stimulus for the departure from political neutrality that the emperor had followed consistently in the past (p. 126).
19 Robert E. Ward, 'Presurrender planning: treatment of the Emperor and constitutional changes', in Robert Ward and Sakamoto Yoshikazu (eds), *Democratizing Japan: The Allied Occupation* (Honolulu: University of Hawai'i Press, 1987), p. 3.
20 Ibid.
21 Ibid., pp. 4–5; Futoshi Shibayama and Ayako Kusunoki, 'The Pacific War and the occupation of Japan, 1941–52', in Iokibe Makoto (ed.), *The History of US–Japan Relations: From Perry to the Present*, trans. Tosh Minohara (Singapore: Palgrave Macmillan, 2017), pp. 107–9; David Titus, 'The making of the "symbol emperor system" in postwar Japan', *Modern Asian Studies*, 14:4 (1980), 530.
22 Shibayama and Kusunoki, 'Pacific War', p. 116; Kiyoko Takeda, *The Dual Image of the Japanese Emperor* (Basingstoke: Macmillan Education, 1988), foreword by Ian Nish, p. xiv.
23 Kenneth Ruoff, *The People's Emperor: Democracy and the Japanese Monarchy, 1945–1995* (Cambridge, MA and London: Harvard University Asia Center, 2001), p. 16. On policies of Allied powers, see Yuma Totani, *Tokyo War Crimes Trial: Pursuit of Justice in the Wake of World War II* (Cambridge, MA: Harvard University Asia Center, 2008), ch. 2.
24 John Dower, *Embracing Defeat: Japan in the Aftermath of World War II* (London and New York: Penguin, 1999), p. 41.
25 Ibid., p. 611, n. 41.
26 For descriptions of the visit, see Kawahara, *Hirohito and His Times*, pp. 143–8; Dower, *Embracing Defeat*, pp. 293–7; Peter Mauch, 'Hirohito and General Douglas MacArthur: the first meeting as documented by *Shōwa tennō jitsuroku*', *Diplomacy & Statecraft*, 28:4 (2017), 585–600. Mauch focuses on the question of whether Hirohito offered to take responsibility for the war. Regarding the first and other visits, see also Hata, *Hirohito*, pp. 186–7, 190–1. Hata highlights the dearth of reliable sources that would reveal the emperor's political role during the Occupation. Documents on the American side are kept in the National Archives in Washington, DC, but documents on the Japanese side, notably summaries of the meetings between Hirohito and MacArthur where Foreign Ministry officials served as interpreters, remain tightly classified (pp. xxiv–xxv).

27 Until lead American prosecutor Joseph Keenan announced in June 1946 that Hirohito would not be prosecuted. Totani, *Tokyo War Crimes Trial*, p. 215.
28 Herbert Bix, 'Inventing the "symbol monarchy" in Japan, 1945–52', *Journal of Japanese Studies*, 21:2 (Summer 1995), 323.
29 Ben-Ami Shillony, *Enigma of the Emperors: Sacred Subservience in Japanese History* (Folkstone, Kent: Global Oriental, 2005), p. 221.
30 See Kawai on Japanese people's sense of 'divine' as spiritual rather than the Western concept of god. Kawai, *Japan's American Interlude*, ch. 5.
31 Dower, *Embracing Defeat*, pp. 313–14; Bix, 'Inventing the "symbol monarchy"', pp. 329–31.
32 Irokawa, *Age of Hirohito*, p. 102.
33 Bix, *Hirohito and the Making of Modern Japan*, pp. 630–1.
34 For descriptions of the tours, see Dower, *Embracing Defeat*, pp. 330–8; Irokawa, *Age of Hirohito*, pp. 101–7; Kawai, *Japan's American Interlude*, pp. 85–7.
35 Kawahara, *Hirohito and His Times*, pp. 155–6.
36 Dower, *Embracing Defeat*, p. 363.
37 *Ibid.*, pp. 360–1.
38 *Ibid.*, pp. 364–9.
39 For a description of the constitution writing process, see Dower, *Embracing Defeat*, ch. 12 and note 3 on pp. 608–9; *The Pacific Century*, PBS documentary series, 1992, Episode 5, 'Reinventing Japan', includes interviews with members of the Government Section constitutional committee; Theodore H. McNelly, '"Induced revolution": the policy and process of constitutional reform in occupied Japan', in Ward and Sakamoto, *Democratizing Japan*, pp. 76–106.
40 McNelly, '"Induced revolution"', p. 82.
41 For a comparison of Chapter 1 of the two constitutions, see Ruoff, *The People's Emperor*, p. 1. Kawai highlights the unprecedented idea of popular sovereignty as a fundamental change in the national polity not only in political theory, but its embeddedness in Japanese social organisation. Kawai, *Japan's American Interlude*, pp. 57–8.
42 The clause left vague the possibility of rearmament for self-defence, hence the naming of Japan's armed forces the 'Self-Defense Force'. But the ambiguity introduced controversy over the SDF's role and constitutionality in subsequent decades up to the present.
43 McNelly, '"Induced revolution"', p. 102. Kimijima Akihito similarly sees Article 9 as separating the emperor from militarism and integrating him into the post-war 'Pax Americana' in 'Peace in East Asia and the Japanese Constitution: a reexamination 60 years after its making', *Ritsumeikan Kokusai Kenkyū Bulletin*, 21–3 (March 2009), 170.
44 On the vagueness of the word 'symbol', see Nakamura Masanori, *The Japanese Monarchy: Ambassador Joseph Grew and the Making of the 'Symbol Emperor System', 1931–1991* (Armonk, NY and London: M. E. Sharpe, 1992), Preface by Herbert Bix, ch. 9, Appendix 1. For a summary of academic debates, see Titus, 'Making of the "symbol emperor system"', pp. 547–9.
45 Among Western scholars, see Shillony, *Enigma of the Emperors*, p. 225.
46 Ruoff, *The People's Emperor*, p. 3.
47 In September 2018 the couple nostalgically repaid a visit to the tennis court at the elite Karuizawa tennis club where they famously met in 1957, the last visit as emperor and empress before the emperor abdicated in April 2019. *Japan Times Online*, 24 September 2018 (accessed 24 September 2018).
48 Ruoff, *The People's Emperor*, pp. 231–8. On the diversity of popular attitudes to the emperor by 1960, see Kawai, *Japan's American Interlude*, pp. 88–90.
49 Titus, 'Making of the "symbol emperor system"', pp. 556–63.
50 Kawai, *Japan's American Interlude*, p. 88.
51 Translation quoted in Titus, 'Making of the "symbol emperor system"', pp. 563–4.
52 On Hirohito's 1921 European tour as crown prince, see Elise K. Tipton, 'Royal symbolism: Crown Prince Hirohito's tour to Europe in 1921', in Robert Aldrich

and Cindy McCreery (eds), *Royals on Tour: Politics, Pageantry and Colonialism* (Manchester: Manchester University Press, 2018), pp. 191–210.
53 Kawahara, *Hirohito and His Times*, pp. 193–9; Large, *Emperor Hirohito*, pp. 182–90.
54 'Emperor repeats phrase "deep remorse" in his last official war-end anniversary speech', *Japan Times Online*, 15 August 2018 (accessed 15 August 2018).
55 'Upping the ante in "comfort women" row, South Korea speaker brands Japan a "brazen thief"', *Japan Times Online*, 18 February 2019 (accessed 19 February 2019).
56 'Text of Emperor Akihito's unprecedented video message', *Japan Times Online*, 8 August 2016 (accessed 9 August 2016).
57 'Crown Prince ready to honor legacy in new role as next emperor', *Japan Times Online*, 23 February 2019 (accessed 23 Feb. 2019).
58 Liberal Democratic Party governments have shelved or rejected attempts to revise the Imperial Household Agency law restricting succession to the male line that dates to the Meiji period and most recently to discuss allowing women to remain in the imperial family if they marry a commoner, prompted by Princess Ayako's marriage to Moriya Kei in 2018. See, for example, 'Japanese Princess Ayako gives up royal status to marry commoner', *Reuters*, 29 October 2018 (accessed 21 November 2018). On past and future succession issues, see Ben-Ami Shillony, 'The Japanese imperial institution: crisis and continuity', The Suntory Centre, London School of Economics and Political Science Discussion paper, No. IS/06/512 (November 2006), pp. 1–17, https://www.researchgate.net/publication/4809028 (accessed 6 October 2016).
59 Ruoff, *The People's Emperor*, ch. 5.
60 'State sticks to stance on funding Imperial ritual despite Prince Akishino's misgivings', *Japan Times Online*, 30 November 2018. (accessed 30 November 2018); 'Japanese Prince insists Royal family pays for succession ceremony, not taxpayers', ABC News, 1 December 2018, https://www.abc.net.au/news/2018-12-01/japanese-prince-wants-royals-to-pay-for-succession-ceremony/10573894 (accessed 19 December 2018).

CHAPTER FIFTEEN

Dramatising Siamese independence: Thai post-colonial perspectives on kingship
Irene Stengs

In Thailand, no other TV soap series has been as popular as the historical love story *Bupphesanniwat* ('Love Destiny'), aired twice a week from 21 February to 11 April 2018.[1] Combining elements of romance, historical drama, ghost story and comedy, the series – situated in the seventeenth-century Ayutthaya of Siam[2] – became a cultural phenomenon. Its main protagonists instantly acquired the status of national celebrities, participating in high society events, advertisements and talk shows.[3] The series gave a boost to 'nobility style traditional' Thai outfits and hairdos, especially in festive, leisure and ceremonial settings.[4] In many respects, *Bupphesanniwat* seamlessly connected with the first 'Love and Warmth at Winter's End' (*un ai rak khlay na nao*) festival (8 February–11 March 2018) at the Royal Plaza in Bangkok, an initiative of Thailand's present monarch, King Vajiralongkorn (Rama X, r. 2016–). Reflecting the 'long standing bond between the monarchy and the Thai people' and 'the magnificence of Thai arts, culture, and traditions', the event entailed exhibitions dedicated to the achievements of King Chulalongkorn (Rama V, r. 1865–1910) and King Bhumibol (Rama IX, r. 1946–2016), with food stalls selling traditional Thai food, while encouraging visitors to 'dress in traditional Thai period costume from the golden reign of King Rama V the Great, or wear Thai textiles or polite attire of this bygone era'.[5]

Bupphesanniwat and the Winter Festival reflect and further stimulate a wider interest in popular history and archaeology, which is primarily geared towards the deeds and heroism of kings and royal rulers of the former kingdoms of Siam, today's Thailand. A central strand in this royalist historiography is the recurring struggle for the nation's independence, safeguarded time and again by the bravery and wisdom of its kings and an occasional queen. The most important element in this narrative is that Thailand is the only country in Southeast Asia never to have been colonised. The monarchy receives all credit for this extraordinary achievement. The authoritative voice of this narrative, as Tamara Loos puts it, forces 'every serious historian of Siam or modern Thailand to come to terms with this question by elucidating, assessing, and qualifying Siam's sovereignty in an era of globalization'.[6]

In a chapter on the genealogies of historical writing in Siam/Thailand, Thongchai Winichakul shows how the foundation for such an interpretation of Siam's sovereignty was laid by Prince Damrong Rajanuphab (1862–1943), the 'Father of Thai History', in a book titled *Thai rop phama* ('The Thai fought the Burmese', 1917).[7] As the title suggests, the book was not about Western imperialism or aggression but about the Siamese battles against the Burmese, Siam's arch-enemy. 'Rewriting and repackaging' the royal chronicles of Ayutthaya (*phongsawadan*), originally recordings of wars between kings, Damrong presented the latter as a sequence of wars between nations (*chat*).[8] In this perspective, the Burmese appear as colonialist aggressors, attacking an 'ever-peaceful Siam'.[9] Even the two times Siam was defeated, a new royal hero rose to fight the Burmese and restore the kingdom's independence. The defining moments in this historiography are the victories of King Naresuan (1560–1605) in 1590, and King Taksin (1734–82) in 1767. The latter would be dethroned in 1782 by General Chakri, founder of the house of Chakri (Rama I, r. 1782–1809), Thailand's current dynasty. Altogether, *Thai rop phama* presents 228 years of struggle between Siam and Burma, attributing the heroism to royal men, with two exceptions: the sixteenth-century Ayutthaya Queen Suriyothai (1511–48) and the guerrilla resistance of eighteenth-century peasant warriors in a village named Bang Rajan.

Significantly, although Damrong wrote this anti-colonial royalist history in the wake of European colonial expansion, he does not refer to the Siamese experiences of colonial threats, the so-called Pak Nam crisis (1893), in particular. In July of that year, French gunboats blocked the Chao Phraya river, holding the king's palace in Bangkok at gunpoint. The French objective was to take control over the eastern side of the Mekong river – present-day Laos – until then a region that, from Siamese perspective, was Siamese territory. There was no way that the Siamese could resist the French. The humiliation had a traumatic impact on the monarch, King Chulalongkorn, and the Siamese elite. Damrong's new history offered the royal elite the comfort and confidence to come to terms with the trauma, reassuring them that Siam would survive just as in Ayutthaya times. Thai historiography, therefore, in the words of Thongchai, 'is an allegory of colonial power. The entire narrative of Thai wars against Burma is allegorical. Modern Thai historiography is to a large extent an allegory'.[10] With Damrong's work, 'independence' became a quintessential Siamese/Thai quality, and a trope that still dominates the royalist nationalism of Thai politics and historiography of today.

Taking the success of the *Bupphesanniwat* series as its point of departure, this chapter will address how the veneration for the monarchy is built on a specific narrative of Siam's post-colonial history, a narrative that originated earlier with the work of Damrong during the reign of King Chulalongkorn, but that has been given further substantiation time and again in literature, theatre plays, documentaries and films right up to the present time. Considering the significance of these works, my approach is not historical. Instead, I will highlight how Thainess or 'being Thai' (*khwam pen thai*) implies 'being independent', and finds expression in a religiously informed popular culture, with, as its central focus, veneration for the monarchy.

An archaeologist in love

Based on a popular novel with the same title, *Bupphesanniwat* is situated in the reign of King Narai of Ayutthaya (r. 1656–88). The love story unfolds against the background of a growing influence of foreigners – the French in particular – on the kingdom's political and economic affairs. Ketsuran, a twenty-first-century student of archaeology, dies in a car crash on her way home from a study trip to one of the temple ruins of Ayutthaya. Karma makes the kind-hearted Ketsuran awaken in the body of Karaket, the daughter of the ruler of the city of Phitsanulok, who during her life had been a haughty, wicked and violent person. As a consequence of their karmatic connection, Ketsuran is to marry Karaket's betrothed, an official at the court of King Narai.

Although *Bupphesanniwat* mainly relates the complicated development of the romance, the series also reserves a central role for Constantine Phaulkon, a Greek adventurer, who succeeded in becoming a powerful minister towards the end of Narai's reign.[11] Phaulkon, bold, witty, smart and linguistically gifted, was appointed supervisor of the Siamese godown (entrepôt) one year after his arrival in Siam, in 1678. Narai was distrustful of foreigners, but developed a preference for and keen interest in the French, their court culture and their astronomy, clockworks and works of arts. This favouritism was encouraged by Phaulkon, who needed French support for his personal purposes. For the French, the primary aim was to convert the king and the Siamese population to Catholicism, an objective that Phaulkon – as a mediator and interpreter – was able to hide from the king. Narai was not much inclined to listen to the warnings of his Siamese ministers and advisers. *Bupphesanniwat* shows how the main characters share their worries about the potentially bad influences of Phaulkon on the king and the possible consequences for the kingdom (*phaendin*).[12] Early in 1688, when Narai had fallen seriously ill, Ok-phra Phetracha, the king's foster-brother, staged a *coup d'état* to put a halt to this situation, and had Phaulkon executed. In line with the Thai historiography outlined above, *Bupphesanniwat* connects with the patriotic quality of 'being Thai', the combination of being united as a people with love for the king, and in dedication towards the kingdom's independence. The nationalist narrative also translates into a strong accentuation of Thailand/Siam's culture and values.

Clearly, the series has a significant educational dimension. First, there is ample attention to the etiquette and tasks of women.[13] This implies proper – modest and self-controlled – bodily conduct and speech, consisting of a dedicated and pious Buddhism focused on merit making, and proficiency in the crafts of flower decoration and fruit carving as well as the preparation of sophisticated traditional dishes, sweets in particular. The series regularly shows close-ups of the finished products or has its main female characters reciting recipes. For Ketsuran, this implies being subjected to a strict new bodily and behavioural regime, to which she, in the end, more or less submits.

Second, through the eyes of the knowledgeable Ketsuran, the series narrates the story of the greatness and treasures of the Kingdom of Ayutthaya. The viewer follows Ketsuran's excursions – all by boat, at the time the major means of transport – to the city, and her delight and enthusiasm when finding in full glory the temples, palaces and fortresses she knows so well from her study. When passing Fortress Phet, for instance, a very excited Ketsuran says to herself: 'Fortress Phet, such a blessing to see ... It is very beautiful and majestic. No wonder it is the entrance to Ayutthaya'.

Third, the series teaches the viewers about the reign of King Narai, which simultaneously offers an opportunity to demonstrate the accuracy of the twenty-first-century Thai history curriculum. A central episode (11/1) in this respect is the audience of the French ambassador with Narai on 18 October 1685 (Figure 15.1). The event, which Ketsuran is not allowed to attend, evokes an elaborate flashback to her classes. In the flashback we see her professor lecturing and showing a PowerPoint presentation with contemporary engravings. The image capturing this historical moment is that of the ambassador handing over the letter of the Sun King Louis XIV to King Narai.[14] The story behind the image is that the ambassador refused to accept Siamese court protocol of prostrating himself before the king, which would not have allowed him to hand the letter directly to the king. To solve the situation, protocol was changed for the occasion, and the ambassador was allowed to hand over the letter while standing, raising a

Figure 15.1 This famous, undated engraving by Jean-Baptiste Nolin depicts the audience of the French ambassador with King Narai on 18 October 1685

golden tray with the letter upwards to the king, who was seated on his throne in a much higher balcony. To show his displeasure with the situation, the ambassador did not raise the tray high enough, obliging the king to lean out from his balcony to reach for the letter.

For the viewer, the engraving of the scene blurs into the 'real event', a precise re-enactment of the scene of Narai reaching out. Relevant for the argument here is that Ketsuran, who through her study knows both the image and its political context, now is able to find out whether what she has learned is correct. Her informed questioning of her betrothed and his father, who had both attended the ceremony, confirms everything she knows, leading her to exclaim in excitement that 'history is not wrong' and 'it is the truth' (*pen khwam jing*). The didactic elements of *Bupphesanniwat*, albeit wrapped up in humour and appealing aesthetics, are not to be regarded as mere entertainment, but as an inherent dimension of a cultural politics geared at promoting Thai moral values and culture, with a pivotal role for love for the king/monarchy and national unity.[15]

The colonial rule of an absolute monarchy

In today's politics, history curricula and popular culture, Thailand's cultural, religious and political independence has remained a major topic of pride and a reason for concern. In line with Damrong's historiography, the successes of the past continue to serve as a source of inspiration and encouragement in the present, including the relevance of the claim of Siam/Thailand as an ever-independent kingdom. Here, a deep gap separates the popular persistence of this royalist-nationalist narrative from the excellent critical scholarly work that has been done on the subject since the mid-twentieth century.

For Siam, the period of high imperialism coincided with the Fourth and Fifth Reigns (King Mongkut or Rama IV, r. 1851–68, and King Chulalongkorn). As demonstrated by Thongchai, the dominant vision of this period in both Thai and English historical studies follows another narrative authored by Damrong: that of the Chakri Reformation.[16] As Minister of the Interior from 1892 to 1915, Damrong was the intellectual architect of the kingdom's administrative reforms, which were mainly implemented during the Fifth Reign. According to the prince's personal recollections, 'Chulalongkorn reminded Damrong of foreign threats to Siam at the time and thus encouraged him to undertake the reform. If Siam did not quickly tidy up its provincial administration but carelessly left it in such a mess, the country would be in danger. Siam might lose its independence'.[17] The substance of the reforms was the centralisation of control by the Bangkok administration over such areas as finance, justice and education by gradually displacing the local autonomy of tributaries and provinces. In fact, the Bangkok rulers largely implemented the style of governing of neighbouring colonial regimes, which made the centre actually a colonising power.

Colonialism as an external pressure and as a regime model offered the kingdom an opportunity to consolidate itself as an integrated nation-state. Time and again, and from various perspectives, a wide range of scholars have shown how a binary framework of colonised/coloniser falls short for addressing the ambiguities and contradictions of the Siamese colonial experience.[18] Instead, notions of Siam/Thailand as semi-colonial and crypto-colonial have been employed, thus positioning the debate in post-colonial theory.

However, in the standard view on the Siamese history of the late nineteenth century, the Chakri Reformation was the necessary, modernising 'revolution' that made it possible for the country to overcome foreign threats. Siam appears as a victim, suffering the loss of territories to the French and British colonial powers, yet – thanks to the smart policies and diplomatic skills of its monarchs – victorious in the maintenance of its independence. The expansionist desires behind the reform are conspicuously absent from this perspective, as are the opportunities the reform offered to centralise state power in the hands of the royal family and a few affiliated families. No Siamese king ever had such absolute power as Chulalongkorn. Yet, this dimension plays no role in the general veneration for this king. Chulalongkorn is remembered as the king who, thanks to his diplomatic skills and determination to bring progress and modernity, saved Thailand from becoming a colony.[19]

Of immediate relevance for the topic of concern here is that, unlike in many directly colonised states, in Thailand it is not 'the people' but the royal rulers who are the heroes of national independence. Against this background, criticising the monarchy is tantamount to a lack of patriotism, and even regarded as un-Thai. Although the royalist version of the Siamese colonial experiences has been thoroughly deconstructed, contextualised and reinterpreted, the critical scholarly perspective informing these studies will inevitably remain largely confined to academic contexts.[20] The exalted veneration for the monarchy generates a continuous production of royalist-nationalist inclined popular culture, a situation reinforced by a severe *lèse-majesté* legislation that precludes even the slightest criticism of anything royal. This sensitivity concerns both kings from the past and the present-day monarchy.[21]

Martial morals

The origins of the Thai morals and values articulated in historical dramas such as *Bupphesanniwat* can be traced back to the official nationalist doctrine developed by King Vajiravudh (Rama VI,

r. 1910–25). Central to Vajiravudh's nationalism are the three concepts of Nation, Religion and King, the interrelationship of which, in the words of Scot Barmé was:

> [B]ased on a simple form of logical argument with the emphasis, naturally enough, focusing on the centrality and necessity of the monarchy. On the one hand the king was identified as the embodiment of the nation (as the people's "representative"), and also as "chief warrior", whose task it was to defend "Thainess" or independence, and Buddhism, the moral basis of the nation.[22]

Of particular relevance were King Naresuan and King Taksin, since, for Vajiravudh, these kings 'embodied the royal ideal by leading the Thais to victory against the Burmese and maintaining Siam's national independence'.[23]

Barmé's study of the political significance of the prolific playwright Luang Wichit Wathakan (1898–1962) shows the importance of Wichit in popularising the above themes. From the 1930s onwards, Wichit's writings, speeches and historical-musical dramas reached a rapidly growing audience through newspapers and the national radio broadcast system. Connecting with the ideological themes earlier set out by Damrong and Vajiravudh, Wichit had a clear opinion on the relationship between 'being civilised' and 'independence':

> [T]he result of our civilization is to be seen in the fact that we have twice lost our country to the Burmese and then regained it within the space of two or three years. It appears that there is no other country in the world which has lost and regained its freedom two times. We still have our independence while our neighbours do not ... and we have the respect of other countries. If that's not civilization, what is?[24]

The struggle for independence is the central topic of most of Wichit's historical melodramas, as, for instance, the play 'King Naresuan Declares Independence' (*Somdet phra naresuan phrakat issaraphap*, 1934) illustrates. The opening sentences of the play, a conversation between Naresuan and a Siamese nobleman, demonstrate the dramatic force attributed to the meaning of independence: 'We must recover our independence. Independence is the heart of our life. For any *prathet* [country] without independence, people of that *prathet* are not human'[25] (Figure 15.2).

Like Vajiravudh, Wichit appreciated Naresuan and Taksin because of their martial qualities, a quality that he attributed to the Thais, a 'martial race' in general, 'portraying them as natural fighters who had always been willing to sacrifice themselves in order to maintain their independence, that is, their Thainess'. Being entirely devoted to the power and glory of the Thai state, Wichit's work lent itself very well

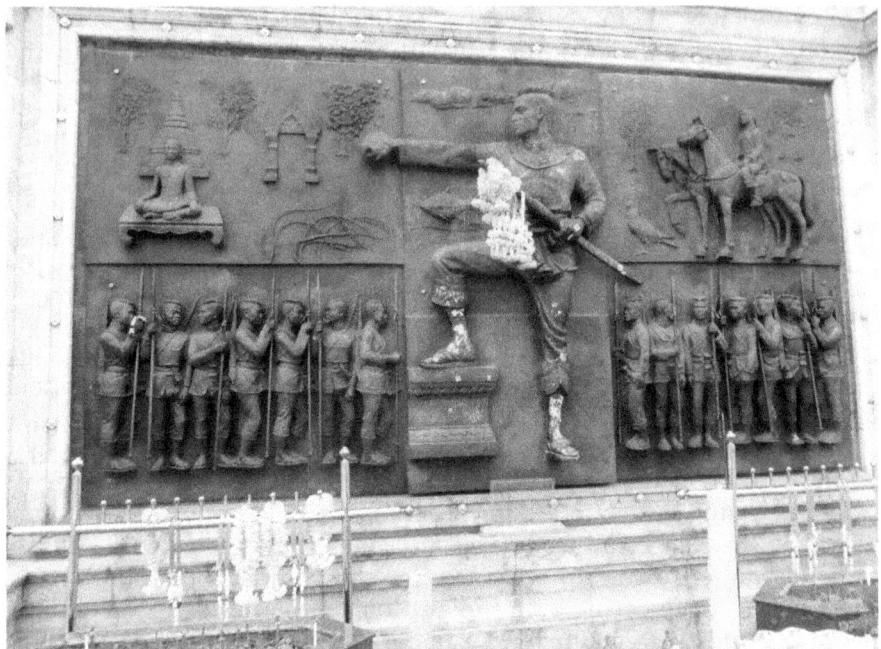

Figure 15.2 Panel of the King Naresuan the Great Monument in Ayutthaya, depicting King Naresuan's declaration of independence

to propaganda. The playwright's enthusiasm for martial qualities made his productions popular among the military in particular. Much of his work became compulsory study material, not only for army cadets but also in the national school system.[26]

The appropriation of art and popular culture for educational and political purposes is, of course, nothing particularly Thai, nor confined to the 1930s, a period of major political transitions, most importantly the *coup d'état* of 1932 that replaced the absolute monarchy by a constitutional monarchy. Entering into the circumstances and events that led to this political watershed, a subject that has been dealt with extensively by Chaiyan Rajchagool and other scholars,[27] would lead too far from the central aim of this chapter: understanding the compelling force of the notion of independence in the construction of Thainess, and the continuing relevance of the monarchy in achieving it. As Jory, following Thongchai, puts it:

> It was ironically the monarchy's enemies, the promotors of the 1932 coup, who ensured the victory of this genre over all others by its dissemination in barely altered form to the Thai population through the

compulsory education system and state media. The outcome has been a greater dominance of royalist-nationalist historiography than could have been imagined in the era of the Absolutist Monarchy.[28]

Indeed, a succession of regimes – military as well as democratic – has employed Damrong's historiography to legitimise their rule, projecting their own imaginations on what an independent and modern Thailand would entail. What is remarkable, however, is the persuasive power this royalist anti-colonial narrative continues to exert, albeit in fluctuating intensity, on the cultural politics of the late twentieth and twenty-first century. A first explanation, I suggest, may be the important role that portraits, statues and monuments – royal monuments in particular – play as material mediators in the domains of popular religiosity, nationalism and entertainment. Monuments, in other words, may appear as dramatic performers of the struggle for independence in present-day Thai society.

Moving monuments

In Thailand, public worshipping at royal monuments – this 'monument-scape', including a few heroine queen warriors – is a widespread daily practice, demonstrating time and again the religious significance of these objects. These practices are rooted in the belief that the spirit (*winyan*) of the person depicted – or part of his or her essence – resides in the portrait. Whether that portrait is a mass-produced copy of a photograph or an original piece of art (like a statue) is irrelevant. As Thai royalty is believed to be sacred, so are their portraits. Through their portraits deceased kings continue their protective presence in today's mundane world. It is against this background that we may understand the ubiquitous presence of royal portraits in present-day Thai society.[29]

This section highlights a particular selection of the Thai monument-scape, namely that where the struggle for the nation's independence is most central. My selection is further motivated by these monuments' role in a sequence of so-called period films (*nang yon yok*), all produced early this century: *The Legend of the Village Warriors of Bang Rajan* (2000), *The Legend of Queen Suriyothai* (2003) and *The Legend of King Naresuan* (2007). Altogether, the *Naresuan* cycle comprises six parts, with the final episode released in 2015.[30] The main topic of these blockbuster movies is the heroism of the Thai and the willingness to sacrifice oneself in the struggle to safeguard the nation's independence. The films have received ample scholarly attention.[31] Their production and successes are generally connected with persistent anxieties about Thai culture and sovereignty being under threat in a rapidly globalising world. Of particular relevance here are the economic crisis of 1997 and the perception of the ensuing IMF programme as a neo-colonial, Western imperative. Although these circumstances definitively impacted on nationalist sentiments of the time, they cannot fully account for the continuous reproduction of the royalist-nationalist discourse, in whatever cultural form. Therefore, I want to turn our attention to the potential of sculptures and statues to move people: many Thais are emotionally involved with their monuments. This is one reason why we may speak of 'moving monuments'. Second, as will become apparent, in the movies the monuments literally move. Third, the movies can be regarded as monuments in their own right, unlike the bronze sculptures that informed their imagery, moving by nature.

King Naresuan's victory

The first monuments I seek to address are the ones established for Naresuan, a monarch of truly monumental presence. His adventurous life story started with the fall of Ayutthaya in 1569. Prince Naresuan, at the time nine years old, was then taken hostage by the king of Burma (Hongsawadi, today's Pegu) to enforce upon Ayutthaya a position of vassal state of Burma. After six years Naresuan was able to return to Siam to become the governor of the northern provinces and eventually (in 1590) king of the entire Kingdom of Siam.

Five crucial moments in Damrong's historiography continue to appeal to the Thai imagination. The first is a cockfight between the roosters of Prince Naresuan and the Burmese crown prince, lost by the latter, during the time Naresuan was still kept hostage at the Burmese court (Figures 15.3 and 15.4). Reputedly, the following conversation took place. The angry crown prince declared: 'The cock of the prisoner of war is really a good fighter', whereupon Naresuan answered: 'This cock can fight not only for a bet of money, but also for the stake of the country'.[32] For today's interpretation of the very existence of Thailand as an independent nation-state, this conversation has been crucial, as it made Prince Naresuan aware of the then subordinate position of the Siamese. The second key moment is King Naresuan's declaration of independence (*prakat issaraphap*) in 1584. The declaration was ritually performed by pouring 'water on the earth from a golden goblet'.[33] The third is Naresuan's gunshot across the Satong river, also in 1584, that killed the Burmese commander.[34] The significance of this gunshot – beyond demonstrating the superiority of the shooter – is connected to Naresuan's initiative of freeing captured 'Siamese' peasants from their 'Burmese' oppressors, and leading them back to their 'home country'.[35] Fourth, there is the water of allegiance

Figure 15.3 Panel of King Naresuan the Great Monument in Ayutthaya depicting the cockfight between the roosters of Prince Naresuan and the Burmese crown prince

Figure 15.4 Roosters offered by worshippers of King Naresuan at the King Naresuan the Great Monument in Ayutthaya

drinking ceremony, again in 1584, to unite the Siamese people with 'military and civil officers as well as the common people ... to swear to fight against the enemy and redeem Siam to become an independent country'.[36] Fifth, and finally, there is the decisive battle with the Burmese on 25 January 1592, in the province of Suphanburi. As the story goes, this final battle took the form of a duel on elephants between – by now – *King* Naresuan and the same Burmese crown prince who dared to humiliate the king after the cockfight. As a commemoration of his victory, Naresuan erected a stupa (*don chedi*) on the spot where he defeated the Burmese prince. Some years before the publication of *Thai rop phama*, Damrong had started a search for the remains of the stupa. He finally identified ruins in Suphanburi discovered in 1913 as the victorious stupa of King Naresuan.

Reproduced in numerus mediums – statues, posters, stamps, banknotes, as well as the Naresuan movies – the cockfight, the elephant combat and the scene of the declaration of independence, depicting a seated, fierce Naresuan pouring water from the goblet in front of nobles and army commanders, have become established images, known virtually everywhere in Thai society (Figure 15.5). Yet, the most

THAI POST-COLONIAL PERSPECTIVES ON KINGSHIP

Figure 15.5 Statue of King Naresuan mounted on a war elephant in Suphanburi province on Royal Thai Army Day 1991; this was reputedly the location where the king fought his victorious battle against the Burmese crown prince on 25 January 1592

important monuments are to be found in the towns where he reputedly lived or won battles. Such statues can either be erected by (local) authorities on public locations, such as squares or amidst sixteenth-century ruins, or statues erected in temples. Regarded as the fiercest of the royal defenders of independence, the subsequent military regimes after the Second World War adopted Naresuan as their patron saint, and many Naresuan statues decorate army compounds. In 1952, the date of 25 January – reputedly the day of the victorious elephant duel – was officially declared Royal Thai Army Day.[37] Seven years later, on 25 January 1959, King Bhumibol officially inaugurated a dual monument in Suphanburi: a combination of the restored Naresuan stupa with a huge statue, depicting the fighting Naresuan on elephant back, right at the moment he delivers the deadly blow. Two other figures accompany the king: the elephant driver taking care of the king's weaponry, seated on the back in the middle; and an extra mahout at the elephant's rear. The intensified military interest in the historical warrior at the time has to be situated in the context of the increasing militarisation of Thai society, as a consequence of Cold War and anti-communist policies. Yet, although this threat has virtually disappeared, the number of Naresuan statues and monuments has only increased over the last decades. Widely worshipped, virtually all Naresuan monuments receive increasing quantities of brightly painted plaster roosters, placed in tribute by venerators of the king.

Queen Suriyothai's sacrifice

In 1548, a Burmese army invaded the Kingdom of Ayutthaya and besieged the capital. As the story goes, Queen Suriyothai, disguised as a (high-ranking) soldier (*uparat*), mounted on a war elephant, followed her husband King Maha Chakkraphat (r. 1548–69) into war. At a certain moment, the queen sees how her husband is about to lose a duel on elephants with the Burmese viceroy. To safe her husband's life, she forces herself in between the viceroy and the king. In the attempt, she is killed by the viceroy. On that day, the battle remained undecided, but some time later the king was able to force the Burmese to withdraw and to save Ayutthaya. Her deed of ultimate courage and self-sacrifice for her husband and the nation makes Suriyothai one of the foremost heroines of present-day Thai historiography. In Ayutthaya, Damrong discovered the stupa (*chedi*) with the queen's ashes.

Although, thanks to Damrong, the story of Suriyothai has been included in school history books from the early twentieth century onwards, only in 1995 was a monument dedicated to the queen unveiled. The decision to erect a monument was taken earlier, in 1980, but it had taken the artist almost fifteen years to complete the statue. The monument stands on the Makamyong plain in Ayutthaya, the location where the historical battle is supposed to have taken place. The monument was unveiled on 12 August, the birthday of the then Queen Sirikit (1932–), and the day is, therefore, also Thailand's Mothers' Day. This day was chosen because it had been the queen who took the initiative for the monument.

The monument resembles the Naresuan statue, again depicting three figures on the back of a war elephant: two mahouts and a hero(ine). Seated on the elephant's neck, Suriyothai is captured just before the deadly blow of the Burmese viceroy that will put an end to her life. Reputedly, the historical queen's features resemble those of Sirikit, an expression of the now queen mother's personal commitment to Suriyothai. The monument also differs from that of Naresuan. Where the Naresuan monument is a solitary sculpture, the Suriyothai monument is surrounded by several other figures. Four soldiers on foot accompany the queen. After the unveiling, rumours circulated that these warriors had been moulded after four military leaders involved in the *coup d'état* of 1991. In addition, the scene comprises several other groups of statues, such as a group of Burmese war elephants and a group of mourning commoners (of all ages and descent), their gaze directed at the queen, who is about to die.[38]

Sirikit's interest in Suriyothai has been instrumental in the making of the movie *The Legend of Queen Suriyothai*. It is common knowledge that Sirikit strongly identifies with her historical predecessor.[39] Statements on the topic by people close to the queen have regularly appeared in the newspapers. Rumour (which does not appear in the press in Thailand) has it that the queen regards herself as a reincarnation of the warrior queen. We have to understand the interest of Sirikit in promoting the story of Suriyothai in this context. In 1999, Sirikit approached one of Thailand's most established film directors, M. C. Chatrichalerm Yukol (Than Mui), himself of royal lineage, to make a movie about the life of Suriyothai. Her motivation for the initiative was explained by one of her ladies-in-waiting: 'Her Majesty is very impressed with Queen Suriyothai's sacrifice and would love to introduce Suriyothai's name and story to the world.'[40] (Figure 15.6).

The highpoints of the movie, the largest Thai production ever, are, of course, the dramatic moments at which the queen decides to join her husband in the defence of Ayutthaya, and the final moment in the battle, with the queen showing no fear at intervening against the Burmese viceroy. In the shots of the queen on the war elephant, the viewer recognises the image of the monument. The whole scene of the queen's death – her falling from the elephant, her blood on

Figure 15.6 Image of Queen Suriyothai from the film *The Legend of Queen Suriyothai's Sacrifice* as reproduced on a can of Singha beer

Thailand's soil – is shown in slow motion. Then, the viewer recognises another image from the monument, the kneeling commoners, this time soldiers on the battlefield, paying tribute.

The image of Suriyothai on a war elephant links her heroism to that of Naresuan. However, as Amporn (following Thongchai) argues, her role rather embodies that of the 'ideal wife': her sacrifice is an act of devotion to her husband, and that saves the country from the Burmese.[41] Although Suriyothai is depicted as a strong, intelligent and brave woman, devotion to husband and nation remain the prevailing moral standard for women. Such traditionalism, in fact, also permeates

THAI POST-COLONIAL PERSPECTIVES ON KINGSHIP

Bupphesanniwat: in the end, Ketsuran's independent and modern mind is remoulded into obedience and devotion to husband and family.

Bang Rajan's bravery

Bang Rajan, a village in Sing Buri province, is part of the narrative of the 1767 Burmese invasion and the fall of Ayutthaya, the place where part of the Burmese army is met by courageous Siamese peasant guerrilla resistance. In Damrong's historiography, the central heroes appear as individuals, with names and their own specific characters. It takes the Burmese soldiers, far better equipped and trained than the Siamese, eight attacks to overpower these unexpected enemies. In the end, all the villagers – men, women and children – are killed by the Burmese. In this epic, perseverance, bravery and self-sacrifice appear as genuine Siamese qualities, also exemplified by ordinary people.

In 1976, a Bang Rajan monument was erected. The monument consists of a water buffalo surrounded by eleven simply armed, life-size peasants. The erection of the monument coincided with the so-called democratic period under the leadership of Seni Pramoj (1973–76), the first non-military dominated government since the abolition of the absolute monarchy in 1932. The heroes of the democratic period were students and peasants, and consequently, there was ideological space for a patriotic 'grass-roots' monument.[42]

The story of Bang Rajan appeared as a novel at the beginning of the twentieth century, and it has since remained one of Thailand's most popular novels. From the beginning, the story has been recounted time and again in the form of stage plays, television dramas and as a movie, in 2000. In retrospect, *The Legend of the Village Warriors of Bang Rajan* was the first of an eventual series of films full of cinematic warfare with the Burmese. The film-makers wanted to make their work more convincing by taking the Bang Rajan monument as a point of departure to lend a greater 'credibility' to their rendering of history. The casting team's top priority had been 'a strong resemblance between the eleven statues at the [Bang Rajan] monument and the cast'. The team 'worked very hard to transform each of them [the actors] though various methods like gaining weight, losing weight, developing muscles and tanning'. The main actor, Jaran Ngamdee, 'was the casting team's pride thanks to his [close] resemblance to the statue of Nai Jan [the main hero] in Singburi in appearance like, for example, the typical Thai facial shape, high cheekbones and fierce eyes'. For Jaran: 'This film is very interesting in a sense that it is based on a true story of our brave ancestors. So everything is meant to be as real as possible'. According to the director, Tanit: 'Public familiarity with this famous "model" [the monument] would more easily convince the audiences. Believe me, the Nai Jan character is more or less an identical twin of the statue'.[43]

As a live scene, the monument appears in the movie itself. People who are familiar with the monument – that is, the fierce heroes caught in action in a circle around the water buffalo, ready to fight, ready to die – will recognise several movie scenes as re-enactments of the monument. In scenes of fights with the Burmese (a part of) the heroes' pose, with weapons in their hands, standing in a circle, protecting each other's backs, exactly mimics the form of the monument.[44] The case of Bang Rajan shows how the film director, in order to make a convincing movie, needed the reality of the monument as a point of departure in creating the ultimate sense of reality. There is no dividing line that demarcates where the monument gives way to the movie. For the Thai public, monuments determine to a significant degree what history looked like. They are used as techniques of authentication, comparable to the use in *Bupphesanniwat* of the engraving of Narai accepting the letter of the French envoy.

Veiled in traditional attire

Today, the Bang Rajan monument and village are a popular tourist destination with a dedicated temple, a museum and a traditional Thai food market (*talat thai boran yon yuk*). People can rent period (warrior) outfits to have themselves photographed with the statue or with monument lookalikes at the 'eighteenth-century' palisade fortress entrance. Likewise, although on a much larger scale, the ruins and monuments in Ayutthaya have become the setting for tourists dressed up as the elite inhabiting *Bupphesanniwat*.[45] Royalist, religious and nationalist motivations blend into trendy middle-class entertainment.

As with the earlier historiographic literature, dramas and films, the shared enthusiasm for *Bupphesanniwat* stretches beyond the general public. Thailand's prime minister, General Prayut Chan-o-cha, at the time head of the junta named National Council for Peace and Order, publicly praised the series for 'encouraging citizens to wear traditional costumes'. *Bupphesanniwat* connected very well with a nationalist government programme, a brainchild of the prime minister himself, aimed at promoting Thai culture and values.[46] Launched in February 2018, almost simultaneously with *Bupphesanniwat*, this 'Sustainable Thainess' (*thai niyom yangyuen*) programme builds upon earlier values and nationalism promotion programmes, the most important being the 'Twelve Official Thai Values', initiated by the junta upon the May 2014 coup. The Ministry of Culture added to both the *thai niyom* program and the *Bupphesanniwat* craze by offering everybody wearing traditional Siamese attire free admission to national museums and historical parks during the Historical Thai Heritage Conservation Week (1–8 April 2018) and organising special tours to Ayutthaya's *Bupphesanniwat*-related sites.[47] It goes without saying that Prayut also applauded *Bupphesanniwat* for augmenting the aims of King Vajiralongkorn's 'Love and Warmth at Winter's End' fair in 'educating Thai people about their history while at the same time perpetuating the beautiful culture of Thailand'.[48] Paradoxically, in spite of Thainess being an inherent Thai quality, Thai people need continuous (re)education in Thai history, culture and values, to guarantee that the country will remain independent and unified. On 9 December 2018, the king opened the second edition of the Winter Festival, fully dressed, as was his entire entourage, in the style of the reign of his illustrious great-grandfather, King Chulalongkorn.[49] As protocol requires, and 'as in the old times', the people – also in period outfits – kneeled in veneration when the king passed by. Veiled in the new attire of entertainment, the scene may be interpreted as a re-enactment of the absolute monarchy, veiling once again the colonial background of the modern absolutism of the period. This whole assembly of traditionalism wrapped up as entertainment precludes any critical distancing from history as well as from the current position of the monarchy, and thus from opening up a post-colonial perspective on the Thai nation and Thai kingship.

Acknowledgement

I am indebted to Jeroen Beets for his critical reading and editing of the text.

Notes

1. 'Final BuppeSanNivas episode smashes ratings record – at 18.6′, *The Nation*, 12 April 2018, www.nationmultimedia.com/detail/national/30343070 (accessed 28 March 2019). The series was broadcast by Channel 3, and could be followed via YouTube.
2. Ayutthaya was the capital of the Kingdom of Siam from 1350 until 1767.
3. 'PM in rare joyous mood as he plays host to lead characters of mega-hit drama series at the Government House', *Thai PBS*, 3 April 2018, https://lasvegasnews.media/thai/archives/4644 (accessed 11 November 2019).
4. 'TV drama leads Thais to don traditional dress', *Bangkok Post*, 3 April 2018, www.bangkokpost.com/news/general/1440031/tv-drama-leads-thais-to-don-traditional-dress (accessed 28 March 2019). Obviously, the popularity of traditional Thai dress does not include slave or peasant clothing.

5 Maevadi Rosenfeldt, 'Bangkok's Winter Festival "Love and Warmth at Winter's End"', *Modern Australian*, 9 February 2018, www.modernaustralian.com/holidays-travel/364-bangkok-s-winter-festival-love-and-warmth-at-winter-s-end (accessed 28 March 2019); 'Festival Un Ai Rak "Love and Warmth at the Winter's End" under the theme "The River of Rattanakosin" bustles', *MCOT News*, 15 December 2018, www.youtube.com/watch?v=hZhuEaF-Hgs (accessed 28 March 2019).
6 Tamara Loos, *Subject Siam: Family, Law and Colonial Modernity in Thailand* (Ithaca, NY and London: Cornell University Press, 2006), p. 13.
7 Thongchai Winichakul, 'Modern historiography in Southeast Asia: the case of Thailand's royal-nationalistic history', in Prasenjit Duara, Viren Murthy and Andrew Sartori (eds), *A Companion to Global Historical Thought* (Hoboken, NJ: Wiley Blackwell, 2014), pp. 257–68. In 2001, a first full translation of *Thai rop phama*, edited and introduced by Chris Baker, a compilation of earlier part translations, was published with the title *Our Wars with the Burmese, Thai–Burmese Conflict 1539–1767* (Chiang Mai: Silkworm Books).
8 Thongchai, *Modern Historiography*, p. 264; see also Baker, *Our Wars*, pp. xiv–xviii.
9 Thongchai, *Modern Historiography*.
10 *Ibid.*, p. 266.
11 For the definitive historical work on the reign of Narai and the life and role of Phaulkon, see Dirk van der Cruysse, *Siam and The West 1500–1700*, trans. Michael Smithies (Chiang Mai: Silkworm Books, 2002 [1991]).
12 Literally meaning 'land', *phaendin* is 'a deeply emotive term in official discourse that many Thais already believe to be important and valuable, and also to be related to royal power'. Pasoot Lasuka, 'The good individuals of the state: middle-class culture and politics in Thai biographical films after 2006', PhD dissertation, Australian National University, 2015, p. 43.
13 Patrick Jory, 'Bupphesanniwat fever: gendered nationalism and middle-class views of Thailand's political predicament', *Sojourn: Social Issues in Southeast Asia*, 33:2 (2018), 440–58. On the importance attributed to Thai drama series in terms of educating Thai values, beliefs and ideologies, see also the work of Kittiya Moonsarn, 'Combination of national identities and nation-building: historical drama and nationalism in Thailand', paper presented at the EUROSEAS Conference, 10–13 September 2019, Berlin.
14 The popularisation of this image began when it was published in *Magasin Pittoresque* (Paris) in 1840, after an engraving made in 1685.
15 I agree with Jory ('Bupphesanniwat fever') that some scenes depict Narai as weak, which does not comply with the general idealising of Thai kings. Yet, the series suggests an air of continuous commitment with the king and the kingdom.
16 Thongchai Winichakul, *Siam Mapped: A History of the Geo-body of a Nation* (Chiang Mai: Silkworm Books, 1994).
17 Thongchai, *Siam Mapped*, p. 145.
18 Benedict Anderson, 'Studies of the Thai state: the state of Thai studies', in Eliezer Ayal (ed.), *The State of Thai Studies: Analyses of Knowledge, Approaches, and Prospects in Anthropology, Art History, and Political Science* (Athens: Ohio University Centre for International Studies, 1978), pp. 193–247; Rachel V. Harrison and Peter A. Jackson (eds), *The Ambiguous Allure of the West: Traces of the Colonial in Thailand* (Hong Kong: Hong Kong University Press, 2010); Michael Herzfeld, 'The absence presence: discourses of crypto-colonialism', *The South Atlantic Quarterly*, 101:4 (2002), 899–926; Lysa Hong, 'Extraterritoriality in the reign of King Chulalongkorn 1868–1910: the cacophony of semi-colonial cosmopolitanism', *Intenerario: European Journal of Overseas History*, 27:2 (2003), 25–46; Peter A. Jackson, 'The performative state: semicoloniality and the tyranny of images in modern Thailand', *Sojourn: Social Issues in Southeast Asia*, 19:2 (2004), 40–74; Loos, *Subject Siam*; Thongchai, *Siam Mapped*.
19 See Irene Stengs, *Worshipping the Great Modernizer: King Chulalongkorn, Patron Saint of the Thai Middle Class* (Singapore: NUS Press, 2009).

20 See also Patrick Jory, 'Problems in contemporary Thai nationalist historiography', *Kyoto Review of Southeast Asia*, 3 (2003), https://kyotoreview.org/issue-3-nations-and-stories/problems-in-contemporary-thai-nationalist-historiography/ (accessed 28 March 2019).
21 In 2014, for instance, Sulak Sivaraksa, known as one of Thailand's prominent social critics, was accused of *lèse-majesté* because he questioned the historical accuracy of certain conventional depictions of the heroic deeds of Naresuan, in a Thammasat University seminar in October of that year. Because 'of a lack of evidence', the case against Sulak was dropped after more than three years of investigation, in January 2018. 'Lese majeste charges against social critic Sulak dropped in historical King Naresuan case', *The Nation*, 18 January 2018, www.nationmultimedia.com/detail/politics/30336519 (accessed 28 March 2019). For details on Naresuan's heroism, see further below.
22 Scot Barmé, 'Luang Wichit Wathakan: official nationalism and political legitimacy prior to World War II', MA dissertation, Australian National University, 1989, p. 30.
23 *Ibid.*, p. 27.
24 Wichit quoted in Barmé, 'Luang Wichit Wathakan', p. 47.
25 Quoted in Thongchai, *Siam Mapped*, p. 157.
26 Barmé, 'Luang Wichit Wathakan'.
27 Chaiyan Rajchagool, *The Rise and Fall of the Absolute Monarchy: Foundations of the Modern Thai State from Feudalism to Peripheral Capitalism* (Bangkok: White Lotus, 1994); Baas Terwiel, *Thailand's Political History, From the 13th Century to Recent Times* (Bangkok: River Books, 2005); David Wyatt, *Thailand: A Short History* (New Haven, CT and London: Yale University, 1984 [1982]).
28 Jory, 'Thai nationalist historiography'.
29 See Stengs, *Worshipping the Great Modernizer*.
30 Part I, *Hostage of Hongsawadi*, was released on 18 January 2007, Thai Army's Day; Part II, *The Reclamation of Sovereignty*, was released the same year, on 5 December, the birthday of the now late King Bhumibol (1927–2016) and Thailand's Father's Day.
31 Amporn Jirattikorn, 'Suriyothai: hybridizing Thai national identity through film', *Inter-Asia Cultural Studies*, 4:2 (2003), 296–308; Rachel V. Harrison, 'Amazing Thai film: the rise and rise of contemporary Thai cinema on the international screen', *Asian Affairs*, 33:3 (2005), 93–115; Rachel V. Harrison, 'Mind the gap: (en)countering the West and the making of Thai identities on film', in Rachel V. Harrison and Peter A. Jackson (eds), *The Ambiguous Allure of the West: Traces of the Colonial in Thailand* (Hong Kong: Hong Kong University Press, 2010), pp. 93–118; Adam Knee, 'Suriyothai becomes *legend*: national identity as global currency', in Leon Hunt and Leung Wing-Fai (eds), *East Asian Cinemas: Exploring Transnational Connections on Film* (London and New York: I. B. Tauris, 2008), pp. 123–37; Pasoot, 'The Good Individuals'.
32 Baker, *Our Wars*, p. 81.
33 *Ibid.*, p. 86.
34 *Ibid.*, p. 88.
35 *Ibid.*, p. 87.
36 *Ibid.*, p. 92.
37 Ka Wong, *Visions of a Nation: Public Monuments in Twentieth Century Thailand* (Chiang Mai: Silkworm Books, 2006), p. 91. Since 2007, Royal Thai Army Day has moved to 18 January.
38 Wong, *Visions of a Nation*, pp. 112–15.
39 Amporn, 'Suriyothai'.
40 Atiya quoted in Amporn, 'Suriyothai', p. 296.
41 The notion of the 'ideal wife' is rooted in Buddhist cosmology. An 'ideal wife' is regarded as one of the seven assets of 'Great Kings', Amporn, 'Suriyothai', pp. 303–4.
42 Wong, *Visions of a Nation*, p. 126.
43 Quotations taken from the (no longer available) Bang Rajan website: www.film bangkok.net/bangrajan.

44 In the movie, without the buffalo, although the buffalo performs regularly as a 'friend'.
45 'Book fair cashes in on BuppeSanNivas popularity', *ASEAN Breaking News*, 9 April 2018, www.aseanbreakingnews.com/2018/04/book-fair-cashes-in-on-buppesannivas-popularity/ (accessed 28 March 2019); 'Temple featured in Buppesannivas TV series open late until April 30', *ASEAN Breaking News*, 25 March 2019, www.aseanbreakingnews.com/2018/03/temple-featured-in-buppesannivas-tv-series-open-late-until-april-30/ (accessed 25 March 2019).
46 Paritta Wangkiat, 'Thainess: history doesn't repeat, but rhymes', *Bangkok Post*, 1 February 2018, www.bangkokpost.com/opinion/opinion/1405458/thainess-history-doesnt-repeat-but-rhymes (accessed 25 March 2019).
47 'Everyone's dressing in period costumes for Heritage Week', *The Nation*, 3 April 2018 www.nationmultimedia.com/detail/lifestyle/30342345 (accessed 28 March 2019).
48 'Un Ai Rak "Love and Warmth at the Winter's End", The Bangkok Winter Festival at the Royal Plaza', *Thai PBS World*, 13 December 2018, www.youtube.com/watch?v=JWAUmmWjLmA (accessed 28 March 2019).
49 King Vajiralongkorn opens 'Un Ai Rak "Love and Warmth at the Winter's End", *ProGress TH 789*, 9 December 2018, www.youtube.com/watch?v=EE0M6BEqcY0 (accessed 28 March 2019).

INDEX

Page numbers in **_bold italic_** print indicate illustrations.

abdications 6, 7–8, 10, 47, 56, 61, 71, 255–6
Abdul Aziz (Sultan of Perak) 104, 106, **_106_**
Abdul Rahman, Tunku 107, 145
abolition of monarchy
  Awadh 5
  Burma 5, 7, 82, 98
  Ceylon 5, 8
  Indian princes 48–50
  Indonesia 208
  Korea 5
  Laos 7, 17, 188–90
  Nepal 12, 17, 73, 74
  Sikh empire 5
  Sikkim 12, 17, 72, 74
Abu Bakar (Sultan of Johor) 103, 105
Aceh 203–4
Adams, Nel 84, 88
African monarchies 14–15
Ahmad (Sultan of Pahang) 103
Ahmad Tajuddin (Sultan of Brunei) 135, 136, 137
Ainuddin, Khan Bahadur 39
Air India 52–6, **_54_**
Aiyer, C.P. Ramaswamy 25, 32
Akali Dal 34
Akihito (Emperor of Japan) 253, 255–6
Akishino, Prince 256
All India Hindu Mahasabha 34, 38–9
All India Muslim League 34
Anderson, Benedict 2, 105, 214, 218
Anglo-Burmese Wars 82
Anti-Fascist People's Freedom League (AFPFL) 87–9
Asian kingship and monarchy
  Buddhist concepts 3, 66, 187
  conditions for survival 7–8, 13–14, 17, 75, 95–6, 105
  as 'galactic' concept 3
  Hindu concepts 3, 25, 66, 187
  Islamic law–rulership nexus 196, 199–201, 204
  kerajaan concept of 95, 99–102, 108
  Lao, concept of 3, 187
  scholarly studies 1–3
  see also religion and monarchy
Attlee, Clement 87, 89, 92
Auchinleck, Claude **70**
Aung San 87–90, 92
Auriol, Vincent 162, 182
Awadh 4, 5
Azahari, Shaik A. M. 142–6

Bahadur Shah Zafar (Mughal emperor) 5
Banerjee, Albion 29–30
Bang Rajan 261, 269, 277–8
Banganepalle, Nawab of 29
Bao Dai (Emperor of Annam) **155**
  abdication and self-exile 12, 16, 156, 171
  deposition 173
  failure to force decolonisation 172–3
  formative years in France 153–5
  as French colonial monarch 12, 155–6
Bhumibol Adulyadej [Rama IX] (King of Thailand) 274
Bhutan
  abdication rule 61
  British mission to (1907) 60–1, 63
  as British protectorate 63
  enthronement of Ugyen Wangchuk 60–1
  formation of unified kingdom 12
  modernisation and reform 62–3, 71
  relations with India 63
  survival of monarchy 74, 75
  Wangchuk dynasty 60, 63, 75
Bikaner, Maharaja of 36, 37
Birendra (King of Nepal) 73

INDEX

Bodawpaya (King of Burma) 81
Bolland, Edwin 230
Borneo *see* Brunei; North Borneo Federation; Sarawak
Boun Khong (Lao prince) 176
Boun Oum (Lao prince) 177, 179, 181, 183
BPUPKI *see* Investigating Committee for Preparatory Work on the Independence of Indonesia
Brett, Reginald (Viscount Esher) 119
British Empire
  end of imperial rule in Asia 9–10, 238–9
  protectorates 63, 64–5, 134
  Residency system 24, 27, 29, 45, 97–8, 102, 125, 134–5, 137–40
British Navy 113, 123
Brooke, Anthony (*Raja Muda* of Sarawak) 112, 117, 126, 128
Brooke, Bertram 124, 126
Brooke, Charles Antony (second Rajah of Sarawak) 115–17
Brooke, Charles Vyner (third Rajah of Sarawak) 117, 119, 123–6, 128
Brooke, James (first Rajah of Sarawak) 113–15
Brooke, Margaret 119
Brooke, Sylvia 117, 119, 121, 123, 125–6
Brooke dynasty
  centenary celebrations 119–23
  cult of personality 119, 127
  end of Brooke rule 11, 123–6
  inter-family feuding 112, 117
  Japanese occupation and 126
  legacies and memories 9, 127–8
  origins 113–14, 123
  relations with British government 116, 124
  self-presentation of Brooke rule 112–13, 121–3, 125–6
  see also names of Brooke family members
Brunei
  absolute monarchy 13–14, 148–9
  administrative ties with Sarawak 138, 140, 143
  as British protectorate 134

British Residential system 134–5, 137–9
  constitution and self-government (1959) 135, 140, 143–5
  independence 135
  Japanese occupation 136, 137–8, 142
  Malay nationalism 142–3
  national ideology 149
  refusal to join Malaysia 135, 145–7
  see also Omar Ali Saifuddin III (Sultan of Brunei)
Buddhism 61, 66, 74–5, 81, 175
Buganda 5
Buphessaniwat (TV series) 260, 262–5, 278–9
Burma (Myanmar)
  British conquest of 81–3
  Burma–Siam warfare 261, 270, 272
  deposition of King Thibaw 5, 82, 98
  end of Kon-baung monarchy 82
  independence and exit from the Commonwealth 89–90
  Japanese occupation 86
  military coup (1962) 90
  moves towards independence 86–90
  royal legacies 8–9, 92
  see also Shan princes; Shan states

Cambodia
  as member of French Union 159–63
  nationalist movement 159–61
  see also Sihanouk
Cannadine, David 118
ceremonial dress *see* regalia and ceremonial dress
Ceylon 5, 6, 8, 10, 16, 17
Chakri dynasty 13
Chamber of Princes 33, *33*, 45
Champassak dynasty 180–1
Charles, Eugène 153–4
China 3–4, 69, 77, 90, 100–1, 231
Chulalongkorn [Rama V] (King of Siam/Thailand) 5, 261, 265–6
Churchill, Winston 87
Cleveland, James 28
Commonwealth of Nations 10, 16, 90, 227

INDEX

communalism in India 34, 36–7, 38–9
Cooke, Hope 71–2, **72**
coronations, enthronements and installations
  Bhutan 60–1
  Brunei 148–9
  Cambodia 157
  Japan 8
  Laos 176
  Malaysia 8
  Morocco 164
  Sarawak 114, 119
  Thailand 8
Cousseau, Jean 153–4, 172
Curzon, Lord 82, 84

Dalai Lama
  Fourteenth 67, 69, 71, 74–5, 77
  Thirteenth 65, 67
Damrong Rajanuphab, Prince 261–2, 265, 269, 270, 272, 274, 277
darbars 24, 45, 61, 68, 84, **85**
Decoux, Jean 156–9
deposition of monarchs
  Bao Dai 173
  Dalai Lama 65, 69, 77
  Duy Tan 153
  Mohammed V 170–1
  Sisavang Vong 188–90
  Thanh Thai 153
  Thibaw 5, 82, 98
  Tribhuvan 69–70
dewans
  appointments and appointment processes 24, 28–30, 34
  backgrounds and abilities 25–6, 28–9
  British officials as 27, 30
  career patterns 30
  dewan-prince relations 27–30
  impact of communalism on 34, 36–7, 38–9
  Imperial recognition in New Delhi 34, **35**
  nomenclature 24–5, 27
  participation in international conferences 36–7
  roles and responsibilities 25, 31–2, 36–8

Diem, Bui 173
Diem, Ngo Dinh 156, 172–3
Dipendra (Crown Prince, Nepal) 73
Dirks, Nicholas 2
'doctrine of lapse' 22
Dumont, Louis 99
Dutch colonisation in Asia 4, 9, 16, 96, 108, 194, 196, 198, 203–4
Dutch East Indies *see* Indonesia
Duy Tan (Emperor of Annam) 153

Egypt 14
Elizabeth II (Queen of Great Britain) **235**
  as head of state of Commonwealth of Nations 227
  potential visit to Hong Kong (1968) 229–32
  royal visits to Hong Kong (1975, 1986) 232–8
enthronements *see* coronations, enthronements and installations
Ethiopia 15
exiled monarchs and royals
  Bao Dai 171
  Dalai Lama 69, 71
  Duy Tan 153
  Ham Nghi 153
  Indian princes 29
  Lao royals 7
  Mohammed V 170
  Mughal emperor 6
  Thanh Thai 153
  Thibaw 82
  Thutob 65
  Yukanthor 6

FACE (Frontier Areas Commission of Enquiry) 89
el-Fassi, Mohammed Allal 165–6, 167, 170
films 121, 123, 260, 262–3, 269, 275, 277
Free Aceh Movement 203–4
French Indochina *see* Cambodia; Laos; Vietnam
French Union 159–63, 168, 170, 171–2, 182
Frontier Areas Commission of Enquiry (FACE) 89

INDEX

'galactic' kingship 3
Gandhi, Indira 49–50, 51, 72
Gandhi, Karamchand Uttamchand 32
Gandhi, Mahatma 32, 38
Gauthier, Georges 158–9
Gayatri Devi (Maharani of Jaipur) 51
Geertz, Clifford 2
George VI (King of Great Britain) **10**, 227, 228
Glaoui, Thami El 168–9
Graeber, David 2
Guillaume, Augustin 169–70
Gulf states 15
Gurkha fighters 64
Gyanendra (King of Nepal) 70, 73, 74

Haile Selassie (Emperor of Ethiopia) 15
Haksar, Kailash Narain 25–6, 38
Ham Nghi (Emperor of Annam) 153
Hamengku Buwono IX (Sultan of Yogyakarta) **210**
  appointed governor for life 211
  cooperation with Pakualam VIII 212–13, 217–18, 221, 222
  inauguration 212
  Matara Canal project 213–14
  offers Yogyakarta as national capital 203, 211, 216, 220–1, 222
  secures Special Region status for Yogyakarta 211, 215–17, 220–1
  strengthens legitimacy during Japanese occupation 212–15
  supporter of fledgling republic 203, 209
Hamid, Abdul 36, 37, 39
Hassanal Bolkiah (Sultan of Brunei) 147, 148–9
Hatta, Mohammad 197, 201–2, 216, 220
Hilton, James 68
Himalayan kingdoms
  British intervention 60–1, 63–8, 75–6, 82
  demise of monarchies 17, 72–4
  religion and monarchy 61, 66, 74–5
  see also Bhutan; Nepal; Sikkim; Tibet
Hindu Mahasabha 34, 38–9
Hirohito (Emperor of Japan) **248**
  biographies of 2
  death and funeral 244–5
  meet-the-people tours 249–50
  renunciation of divinity 249
  role in ending the war 245–6
  as 'symbol emperor' 250–4
  war responsibility 246, 254
Hizh al-Istiqlal 168–9, 172
Ho Chi Minh 156, 167
homosexuality 128
Hong Kong
  as British crown colony 225–7
  decolonisation 226–7
  handover of British sovereignty 236, 238–9
  press coverage of royal visits 233–6, 237–8
  proposed royal visit (1968) 229–32
  riots (1967–68) 229, 230–2
  royal visits (1975, 1986) 232–8, **235**
  use of monarchy to cement British colonial legacy 236–8
  use of monarchy to legitimise British rule 228–32
Hydari, Akbar 38
Hyderabad 47–8

Idris (Sultan of Perak) 103–4
Illustrated London News 121, **122**
Imam, Ali 36–7
imperial tours *see* royal tours
India
  communalism 34, 36–7, 38–9
  darbars 24, 68, 84
  incorporates Sikkim as state 72–3
  see also dewans; Indian princely states; Indian princes
Indian National Congress 22–3, 30, 32, 46
Indian princely states
  under British administrative suzerainty 23–4, 45
  constituent assemblies 31
  discussions on an Indian federation 37–8
  integration into Independent India or Pakistan 23, 47–8
  numbers, size and power disparities 22, 24, 46–7, 57n7
Indian princes
  pre-independence
    Chamber of Princes 33, **33**, 45

INDEX

exile of 29
honorific titles 44, 48, 50
impact of communalism on 34, 36–7
Imperial recognition in New Delhi 32–4, **35**
pageantry and spectacle 24, 44–5
participation in international conferences 36–7
resistance to accession to India or Pakistan 23, 47–8
post-Independence
  as Air India symbol 52–6
  commercial ventures 52–3
  as Foreign Service diplomats 50–1
  loss of privy purses and privileges 48–50
  as parliamentary candidates 50–1
Indochinese Federation 159
Indonesia
  debates on form of independent state 192–4, 197–202, 215
  dissolution of sultanates and 'independent states' 203
  Free Aceh Movement 203–4
  Islamic law–rulership nexus 192–6, 199–201, 204
  Japanese sponsored independence 7, 196–201, 215
  massacres of sultans and families 7, 194
  multi-dynasties under Dutch rule 208–9, 212
  pre-colonial indigenous monarchies 194–6
  resumption of royal titles 204–5, **205**
  role of sultanates under Dutch colonialism 11
  royal legacies 204–5
  Surakarta sultanate 209, 210–11, 218–21
  Yogyakarta as temporary capital 209
  see also Yogyakarta sultanate
Investigating Committee for Preparatory Work on the Independence of Indonesia (BPUPKI) 197–202, 215
Iran 14

Iraq 14
Islam
  Brunei 149
  Indonesia 192–6, 199–201, 204
  Malaysia 98, 100, 104, 108, 135
  Morocco 164
Islamic State 92, 198–9, 204
Ismail, Mirza 23, 25, 32, 34, 38–9
Issara independence movement 6, 176–7, 179–80, 182–3
Istiqlal 168–9, 172

Jahfar, Ibrahim 138–40
Jang Bahadur Kumar 67
Japan
  from absolute monarch to 'symbol emperor' 13, 250–4
  acceptance of monarchy, post-1950 244
  colonial expansion 4
  debate over surrender 245–6
  'emperor phenomenon' 244
  imperial legacies 255–6
  loss of territory and colonies 243
  Reign Name Law (1979) 256
  renunciation of war 252
  Shinto—state relations 244
  see also Akihito; Hirohito; Japanese military occupation
Japanese military occupation
  Brunei 136, 137–8, 142
  Burma (Myanmar) 86
  Indonesia 7, 196–201, 211–15
  Laos 179
  Malaya 105
  Sarawak 126
  Southeast Asia 134
Jigme Khesar Wangchuk (King of Bhutan) 61
Jigme Singye Wangchuk (King of Bhutan) 61, 63, 71, 74
Juin, Alphonse 168–9
Junagadh 23, 47

Kandy, King of 8
Kashmir 22, 47–8, 76
Katay Don Sasorith 183
Kaul, Hari Kishen 28
Keng Tung, Prince of 84
kerajaan: as concept of monarchy 95, 99–102, 108

INDEX

Khai Dinh (Emperor of Annam) 153
Khamphoui Sisavady 188, **189**
Khan, Abdul Gaffar 38–9
Khan, Abdus Samad 29, 36
Khan, Liaquat Hyat 25
Khan, Masnad 29
kingship *see* Asian kingship and monarchy
Kishen Preshad (Maharaja of Hyderabad) 26
KNID–Yogyakarta 217–18
Kon-baung dynasty 82, 84
Kooka, Bobby 54–5
Korea 4, 5
Krishnamachari, V.T. 36, 39
Kutch, Maharao of 50

Labonne, Erik 167–8
Lacouture, Jean 169
Lao Renovation Movement 185
Lao Scout movement 184–6
Laos
  abolition of monarchy 7, 17, 188–90
  civics education in schools 186–7
  constitution (1947) 178, 179–80, 182–3
  Issara independence movement 6, 176–7, 179–80, 182–3
  Japanese occupation 179
  loyalist constitution (1947) 178
  loyalist movement (1945–57) 177–83
  mass youth movement 184–6
  member of French Union 182
  multiple royal lines 176–7
  national unification 180–1
  Second Indochina War and 176, 177–8, 185–6, 188
  unification of monarchy 178, 180–1
  see also Savang Vatthana; Sisavang Vong
League of Nations 36–7
legacies *see* royal legacies
Legend of Naresuan (film) 269
Legend of Queen Suriyothai (film) 275
Legend of the Village Warriors of Bang Rajan (film) 277
Lennox-Boyd, Alan 143

lèse-majesté restrictions 17, 252, 266
Lesotho 15
Libya 14
London Round Table Conferences 37–8, 45
Lost Horizons (Hilton) 68
loyalism (Laos) 177–83
Luang Wichit Wathakan *see* Wichit Wathakan

MacArthur, Douglas 247–8, **248**
MacDonald, Malcolm 136, 140–1
Maclehose, Murray 232–3, 236
Maha Vajiralongkorn [Rama X] (King of Thailand) 8, 260, 279
maharajas
  as Air India symbol 52–6, **54**
  see also Indian princes
Mahathir bin Mohammad 107
Mahendra (King of Nepal) 73
Malay Peninsular monarchies
  adaptation to Malay nationalism 105
  in the British period 96–9
  contemporary political role 107
  as custodians of Malay religion and custom 98, 100, 108, 135
  ethnic identification 101–2, 104–5
  under Japanese occupation 105
  kerajaan concept of monarchy 95, 99–102, 108
  opposition to Malayan Union proposal 105–6
  Perak–Pahang uprisings 97–8, 102, 108
  political and diplomatic skills 97, 101, 103–4
  resilience and survival 95–104, 108–9
  role in preparation of 1957 Constitution 107
Malayan Union 105–6, 142
Malaysia
  Brunei's refusal to join 145–7
  Independence Constitution 107
  as multi-monarchy 95
  survival of monarchy 95–6
  Yang di-Pertuan Agong (or king) 8, 17, 95, 147, 148
  see also Malay Peninsular monarchies

INDEX

massacres of royals 194
Matara Canal project 213–14
Matsushita, Keiichi 253
Mehta, Manubhai 25
Meiji (Emperor of Japan) 5, 249, 250
Menon, V.P. 46
Middle Eastern monarchies 14–15
Mindon (King of Burma) 82
Mocko, Anne T. 73–4
Mohammed V (Sultan of Morocco)
  coronation 164
  as crusader for Moroccan
    independence 168–70
  defender of Islamic faith 164
  deposition, exile and
    re-instatement 170–1
  as French colonial monarch 164–8
  and nationalist movement 164–8
  signs *dahir* of 1930 165
Mongkung Conference 87
Mongkut [Rama IV] (King of Siam/
  Thailand) 265
monuments *268*, 269–74, **271**, **272**,
  273, 277–8
Moon, Penderel 30
Morocco
  dahir (1930) 165
  as French protectorate 163, 167
  member of French Union 168, 170
  nationalist movement 164–8
  see also Mohammed V
Mountbatten, Lord 46–7
'mouse-deer' diplomacy 101, 103–4
muong system 80–1
Musée Chinois (Fontainebleau) 9
museums 9, 75, 120, 128
Myanmar *see* Burma (Myanmar)
Mysore 5, 22–5, 38

Nabha, Maharaja of 6
Narai (King of Ayutthaya) 262–5, **264**
Naresuan (King of Ayutthaya) 267,
  268, 270–4, **271**, **272**, **273**
Naruhito (Emperor of Japan) 8, 255–6
nationalism and nationalist
  movements
  Brunei 142–3
  Malay Peninsular 105
  Morocco 164–8
  and survival of monarchy 105
Ne Win 90

Nehru, Jawaharlal 23, 34, 69
Nepal
  abolition of monarchy 12, 17, 73,
    74
  dual system of government 67
  restoration of Shah dynasty 70, 73
  unravelling of the monarchy 73–4,
    76–7
New Delhi 32–4, **35**
Ngo Dinh Diem 156, 172–3
Nguyen dynasty 152–3
Nizam of Hyderabad 7
Noguès, Roger 166
North African monarchies 14
North Borneo Federation 135, 140–2

O'Brien, Gerard 117
Omar Ali Saifuddin II (Sultan of
  Brunei) 114
Omar Ali Saifuddin III (Sultan of
  Brunei) **139**
  competes with British Resident for
    power 138–40
  consolidation of sovereign powers
    143–5, 148–9
  early career 135–6
  manages constitutional change
    143–5
  as master strategist 135, 138–40,
    141, 143–5
  rejects amalgamation of British
    Borneo 140–2
  rejects merger with Malaysia
    145–7
  unwilling to accept democratic
    reforms 143, 147
Ornamentalism (Cannadine) 118
Osborne House 9

pageantry and spectacle 8, 44–5,
  60–1, 84, 118–20, 148–9
Pahang 98, 102, 103, 108
Pakistan 1, 6, 9, 10, 16, 17, 23, 47–8
Paku Buwono X (ruler of Surakarta)
  193
Pakualam VIII (ruler of Pakualaman
  Principality) 209, 211–12, 213,
  218, 220–1
Pakualaman Principality 209, 212,
  213
Palanpor, Nawab of 23

INDEX

Palden Namgyel (Chogyal of Sikkim) 71–2, **72**, 74
Panca Sila 200
Pangkor Engagement 96, 105
Panglong Agreement 87–9
Panikkar, K. M. 25, 38, 39
Parti Rakyat Brunei (PRB) 143, 145–6
Pasquier, Pierre 153–6, 171
Pataudi, Nawab 50–1
Patel, Sardar 23, 46, 49
Pathet Lao 176–7, 184, 185–6, 187–8
Patiala, Maharaja of 50
Pavie, Auguste 176
Perak 96, 97–8, 102, 103–5, 108
Perak, Sultan of **106**
Phaulkon, Constantine 262–3
Phetsarath Rattanavongsa (Lao prince) 6, 176
Philippines 4
Pignon, Léon 171–2
Portuguese expansion in Asia 4, 13
postage stamps 228, 233
Prayut Chan-o-cha 278
PRB *see* Parti Rakyat Brunei
Preshad, Kishen 26, 27
pretenders to thrones 6, 74
princely states *see* Indian princely states; Shan states
protectorates
  British 63, 64–5, 134
  French 5, 152–4, 156, 158–9, 160, 163, 165–6, 167, 172, 181
  Japanese 5, 243

Rampur, Nawab of 129
Rana dynasty (Nepal) 67, 69–70, 75
Rao, Umesh 54
rebellions and mutinies 5–6, 97–8
Rees-Williams, David 89
regalia and ceremonial dress
  British looting 82
  Delhi Darbars 84
  Indonesian 'weekend sultans' 204
  Japan 8, 255
  Sarawak 119
  Shan princes 81, 84, **85**
religion and monarchy 3, 9, 60–1, 66, 163–4, 171
  see also Buddhism; communalism in India; Islam; Islamic State; Shinto
Residency system
  British 24, 27, 29, 45, 97–8, 102, 125, 134–5, 137–40
  Dutch 209
  French 153
Rif Republic 164
Roosevelt, Franklin D. 166
royal legacies
  British Hong Kong 236–8
  Burma 8–9, 92
  Himalayan kingdoms 174–7
  Indonesia 204–5
  Japan 255–6
  Sarawak 127–8
royal rituals *see* coronations, enthronements and installations; pageantry and spectacle
royal tours and visits 63, 118, 155, 157, 165, 168, 229–38, 249–50
Royalist (ship) 114, 120, 121, 123, 127
Runciman, Steven 127

Sadiq, Mohammad 39
Sahlins, Marshall 2
Salafism 104
Salar Jung I 26
Sao Khun Yoong 90
Sao Nang Hearn Kham 85, 90, 91, 92
Sao Noan Oo *see* Adams, Nel
Sao Sein Nyunt 90
Sao Shwe Thaik (Prince of Yawngwhe) 87, 88, 90, 91
Sarawak
  administrative ties with Brunei 138, 140, 143
  before Brooke rule 114–18
  under Brooke rule 114–18, 128
  centenary of Brooke rule 119–23, **122**
  cession to Britain 126, 138
  Committee of Administration 125
  constitution (1941) 123–6
  end of Brooke rule 11, 123–6
  under Japanese military occupation 126
  see also Brooke dynasty
Sarawak Centenary (film) 121, 123
Sarila, Raja of 50
Sarraut, Albert 153–6

INDEX

Savang Vatthana (King of Laos) **189**
  creates mass youth movement 178, 184–6
  deposition, imprisonment and death 188–90
  partisan stance in Second Indochina War 178, 185, 187
  promotes civics in school curriculum 186–7
  supports French Union 182
  unification of Lao monarchy 178, 180–1
  use of loyalism 177–8
sawbwas see Shan princes
Scindia, Vijaya Raje (Rajimata of Gwalior) 51–2
Scout movement 12, 184–6
Second Indochina War 176, 177–8, 185, 187, 188
Second World War *see* Japanese military occupation
Shan princes *(sawbwas)* **85**
  British ties 84
  display and ceremonial dress 81, 84, **85**
  loss of power, property and privileges 7, 12–13, 17, 90–3, 91
Shan states
  armed Shan insurgent groups 92
  under British direct rule 83–5, 92–3
  under Burma's military regime 90–3
  dissatisfaction with Panglong Agreement 88–9, 90
  historical records 92
  impact of Second World War on 86
  number, location, ethnic groups 80–1
  traditional politics and culture 80–1
Shinto 8, 244, 256
Siam *see* Thailand/Siam
Sidkyong (Chogyal of Sikkim) 67–8
Sihamoni (King of Cambodia) 8
Sihanouk (King of Cambodia) **158**
  biographies of 1–2
  career summary 7–8
  as crusader for national independence 12, 161–3
  as French colonial monarch 157–61

  personality 157
  youth mobilisation 185
Sikkim
  abolition of monarchy 17, 72, 74
  British intervention 64–5, 67–8
  as British protectorate 64–5
  Indian annexation 12, 17, 72–3
  Namgyal archives 75
Singh, Bharat 29
Singh, Dalip (Maharaja of Punjab) 8
Singh, Ganga (Maharaja of Bikaner) 34
Singh, Hari 30
Singh, Hotu 28
Singh, Karni (Maharaja of Bikaner) 51
Sirikit, Queen of Thailand 275
Sisavang Vong (King of Laos) **189**
  dethroned and re-enthroned 179
  guides drafting of new constitution 178, 179–80, 182–3
Souphanouvong (Lao prince) 176–7, 188
South Africa 15
Souvanna Phouma (Lao prince) 176–7
Spanish colonisation in Asia 4
spectacle *see* pageantry and spectacle
Sri Lanka *see* Ceylon
Star Ferry Riots 229
statues *see* monuments
Stedman, Edward 83
Stevenson, H. N. C. 89
Sukarno 196, 197, 199–203, 216–17, 220
Surakarta sultanate 203, 209, 210–11, 218, 221
Suriyothai, Queen of Thailand/Siam 274–6, **276**
Swaziland 15
Swettenham, Frank 98

Taiwan 4
Tambiah, Stanley 2
Tashi Namgyal (Chogyal of Sikkim) 71
Thailand/Siam
  1932 *coup d'état* 13, 268, 277
  battles against the Burmese 261, 270, 272
  lèse-majesté legislation 266
  period films and TV series 260, 262–3, 269, 275, 277

Thailand/Siam (cont.)
  promotion of traditional culture and values 260, 276, 278–9
  royal monuments, statues and portraits 269–78
  royalist historiography 260–2, 265, 268–9, 270
  royalist/nationalist narratives in popular culture 262–6
  Thai identity and national independence 262, 265–9, 279
  veneration of monarchy 262, 266, 269, 279
Thanh Son Ngoc 159–61
Thanh Thai (Emperor of Annam) 153
Thibaw (King of Burma) 5, 82, 98
Thongchai Winichakul 261, 265, 268, 276
Thutob Namgyal (Chogyal of Sikkim) 65, 76
Tibet
  British intervention 12, 65
  Chinese invasions and neo-imperialism 69, 71, 74, 75, 77
  exile of Dalai Lama 67, 69, 71, 74–5
Tottenham, Alexander 30
Trench, David 229–31, 232
Tribhuvan (King of Nepal) 69–70, **70**
Tukoji Rao (Maharaja of Indore) 25
Tunisia 14

U Nu 90
U Saw 89
Uganda 15
Ugyen Wangchuk (King of Bhutan) 60–1, **62**, 66
Union Française *see* French Union

Vajiravudh [Rama VI] (King of Siam/Thailand) 266–7
Versailles Treaty 36
Vietnam
  'Bao Dai experiment' 153–6, 171–3
  French colonial rule 152–3
  Nguyen dynasty 2, 5–6, 152–3
  unification under ex-emperor 171–2
Vishweshwariya, M. 25
Vongsavang (Lao crown prince) 175

Wangchuck dynasty (Bhutan) 61, 63
'weekend sultans' in Indonesia 204
White, John Claude 60–1, 65, 76
White Rajahs *see* Brooke dynasty
Wichit Wathakan 267
Widodo, Joko **205**
Wylie, V.W. 30

Yang di-Pertuan Agong 8, 17, 95, 147, 148
Yawnghwe, Prince of *see* Sao Shwe Thaik
Yogyakarta: as temporary Indonesian capital 209, 216, 220, 222
Yogyakarta Sultanate
  'Special Region' status 211, 215–17, 220–1
  see also Hamengku Buwono IX
Youde, Edward 236–7
Younghusband, Francis 65
youth movements 178, 184–6, 216
Yukanthor, Prince 6

Zaidi, Bashir Hussain 28, 29
Zutschi, U.N. 30